EDITH WHARTON

———

THE UNCOLLECTED
CRITICAL
WRITINGS

Date Due	

EDITH WHARTON

THE UNCOLLECTED CRITICAL WRITINGS

EDITED,

WITH AN INTRODUCTION, BY

FREDERICK WEGENER

PRINCETON UNIVERSITY PRESS

PRINCETON, NEW JERSEY

Copyright © 1996 by Princeton University Press
Published by Princeton University Press, 41 William Street, Princeton, New Jersey 08540
In the United Kingdom: Princeton University Press, Chichester, West Sussex

All Rights Reserved

Second printing, and first paperback printing, 1999

Paperback ISBN 0-691-00269-X

The Library of Congress has cataloged the cloth edition of this book as follows

Wharton, Edith, 1862–1937.
[Selections]
The uncollected critical writings / edited, with an
introduction by Frederick Wegener.
p. cm.
Includes bibliographical references and index.
ISBN 0-691-04349-3 (alk. paper).
1. American literature—History and criticism—Theory, etc.
2. English literature—History and criticism—Theory, etc.
3. Literature—History and criticism—Theory, etc.
4. Aesthetics, American.
I. Wegener, Frederick, 1957– . II. Title.
PS121.W43   1997
810.9—dc20   96-8501

This book has been composed in Caledonia

The paper used in this publication meets the minimum requirements of
ANSI/NISO Z39.48-1992 (R1997) (*Permanence of Paper*)

http://pup.princeton.edu

Printed in the United States of America

3 5 7 9 10 8 6 4 2

CONTENTS

TRIBUTES AND EULOGIES

PREFACES, INTRODUCTIONS, FOREWORDS

SELF-RECONSIDERATIONS

ACKNOWLEDGMENTS

No one undertakes a project like this one without relying on the help of many people and the resources of many institutions. In the course of preparing this edition, I have been most fortunate in the scholars, archivists, colleagues, and friends to whom I have incurred so many debts.

There is no one to whom this collection owes more than R.W.B. Lewis, who took an early and ratifying interest in the project, strongly supported its development, and patiently addressed a long series of inquiries over several years. All Wharton scholars are in Professor Lewis's debt, and I have had no greater privilege in working on this project than the opportunity to consult his judgment and authority.

Joel Porte followed with keen and encouraging interest the development of a project that must have seemed at best tangential to the doctoral work that I pursued under his guidance at Harvard; his continuing support and commitment, in this as in so many endeavors of mine, have been sustaining throughout. Shortly after completing my degree, I started to work with Wharton's critical prose during a year at Boston University, and during the two following years that I spent at Brandeis University, where the Department of English generously assigned me a research assistant, provided funds that facilitated the initial tasks of preparing Wharton's critical texts, and otherwise enabled me to establish the groundwork of my edition. Few visiting or temporarily appointed junior-faculty members anywhere can have been welcomed as warmly and supportively as I was at BU and at Brandeis, and I am glad to have the chance to express my gratitude to the members of each department for helping to make my time there so enjoyable and productive.

At an early stage of my work, George Franklin, at Brandeis, placed me in touch with Kristin O. Lauer and Margaret Murray, who freely shared a wealth of material from their invaluable, then-forthcoming bibliographical index of Wharton criticism (along with their continuing enthusiastic interest in the project) and who referred me to Stephen Garrison, from whom, in turn, I quickly received copies of the many relevant portions of his work on the Wharton volume that soon appeared in the Pittsburgh Series of Bibliographies. Millicent Bell, Susan Goodman, Annette Zilversmit, and Elizabeth Ammons offered equally prompt and helpful responses to various inquiries. For timely information on James's correspondence, I am grateful to Michael

Anesko, Steven Jobe, and Philip Horne (who also provided me with a transcription of the fascinating letter to Katherine Fullerton quoted in my prefatory remarks on her cousin's Bryn Mawr lecture). On matters relating to Wharton's eulogy of Jean du Breuil de Saint-Germain, I received particularly informative replies from Professor Eugen Weber, Marion Mainwaring, and Alan Price, who thoughtfully placed at my disposal the manuscript of his definitive study of Wharton's life during the First World War. In an especially important service to this edition, Maud Ellmann, of King's College, Cambridge University, performed numerous urgent, time-consuming favors that made available to me, from overseas, those extensive portions of the Lapsley collection dealing with his unfinished work on Wharton's critical writings. From England also, Maggie Parham, of the Royal Society of Literature, sent me helpful information, while Ferdinand Mount, of the *Times Literary Supplement*, and Melanie Aspey and Damon Eyas, at the News International archive in London, responded at length to my inquiries regarding Wharton's contributions to the *TLS*. Through a representative of International Creative Management, the filmmaker Robert Benton, who had planned a documentary on Iris Origo, enabled me to contact her two daughters in Italy in search of Wharton's eulogy of their grandfather, Bayard Cutting, Jr.; I am grateful to both of them—particularly to Benedetta Origo—for providing me with a copy of the full text of Wharton's tribute (and of the chapbook in which it was published) and for granting me permission to include it here.

A portion of my introductory essay was presented, in somewhat different form, at the conference "Edith Wharton at Yale," held in April 1995 in honor of Professor Lewis; for an opportunity to rehearse some of my ideas about Wharton as a critical writer, and to benefit from the suggestions and criticisms of many other participants, I am obliged to the conference organizers, Claire Colquitt, Susan Goodman, and Candace Waid. Ludger Brinker kindly permitted me to serve as the respondent on a panel on Wharton's nonfiction at the 1995 convention of the Northeast Modern Language Association. Also helpful were the chances I had, at various times, to discuss Wharton's critical prose with Carol J. Singley, Elsa Nettels, Charlotte Goodman, Shari Benstock, Kathy Fedorko, Julie Olin-Ammentorp, and Nancy Bentley. Alfred Bendixen and Kenneth M. Price offered valuable advice and encouragement on what must have seemed to them fairly rudimentary textual and bibliographical matters. And I am indebted to my friend Louise Wills for her indispensable and thorough work on the translations of Wharton's tributes to Jean du Breuil and Paul Bourget.

As one might have expected from her voluminous early reading, Wharton's range of reference is extremely wide, diverse, and often esoteric, and no one scholar, pursuing the arduous task of annotating her critical texts, could have succeeded in tracking down or identifying all of her allusions and quotations unassisted. A few continue to elude me, and I might have missed a good many more without the knowledge and helpfulness of many scholars, colleagues, and friends in many different places: Rosemary Ashton, Joseph Bartolomeo, Germaine Brée, Alan Brinkley, Michael L. Brooks, Jean Bruneau, Jerome H. Buckley, Jonathan Bumas, Peter V. Conroy, Jr., Frank Coppa, James T. Engell, Barbara Hardy, John Hollander, Martha Hollander, Helen Killoran, Kenneth Langevin, Gregory Maertz, Jean Marsden, Diane Monticone, Robert Orledge, Joel Porte, Melvyn Richter, John D. Rosenberg, M. A. Screech, Anthony W. Shipps, N. G. Shrimpton, the late Francis Steegmuller, Gil Troy, Helen Vendler, David Venturo, Gail Weinberg, and Perry Willett. Those who were not able to identify the passage in question invariably referred me to someone who could or pointed me in a direction that quickly enabled me to do so on my own; the generosity of all who responded reaffirmed for me, at a time when I badly needed it, my sense of the spirit of community and collegiality among scholars.

For much additional help along these lines, I am grateful to Robert Scott and his staff at the Electronic Text Service, Butler Library, Columbia University, and to the efforts of my resourceful and tireless research assistants: Zuefei Xin, Doreen Eremita, Paul Reifenheiser, Kerry Hulsman, Tara Kudla, John McParland, and Constandina Minos. Early on Elizabeth Spiller expertly transcribed to disk the contents of most of Wharton's essays and reviews; for their transcription of subsequently included or discovered texts, and for many other good offices, I owe thanks to Mary Ran, Linda Reesman, Judy Crinion, and Kerry Hulsman.

Perhaps my happiest and most rewarding hours on this project were those devoted to the archival research underlying my approach to Wharton's critical prose. For their patient and courteous assistance with repeated inquiries (either by mail, over the phone, or in person), I am most grateful to Patricia Willis, curator of American Literature, and the staff of the Beinecke Rare Book and Manuscript Library, Yale University; Saundra Taylor, curator of manuscripts, and Heather Monroe, reference librarian, the Lilly Library, Indiana University; Margaret M. Sherry, reference librarian and archivist, Rare Books and Special Collections, Princeton University Library; Daria D'Arienzo, archivist of the college, and Deborah Pelletier, the Amherst College Library; Leslie A. Morris, curator of manuscripts, the Houghton

Library, Harvard University; Bertram Lippincott III, librarian, the Newport Historical Society, and David B. Offer, editor of the *Newport Daily News*; Sydney O. Williams, archivist, Newport School Department; Meredith Paine Sorozan, reference librarian, the Rhode Island Historical Society; Louis L. Tucker, director, and Jennifer Tolpa, reference librarian, the Massachusetts Historical Society; Lorna Condon, curator of library and archives, Society for the Preservation of New England Antiquities; and Nancy Johnson, archivist/librarian of the American Academy of Arts and Letters. Steven Peyser did me the essential service of transcribing or photocopying the bulk of Wharton's correspondence with William C. Brownell at Amherst College; at the University of Texas at Austin, Alice L. Batt examined on my behalf a number of Wharton's unpublished letters to Fullerton.

Every attempt has been made to determine the ownership of the rights to those few critical writings of Wharton that are not in the public domain. "A Little Girl's New York," Copyright © 1938 by *Harper's Magazine* (All rights reserved), is reproduced from the March issue by special permission; "Tendencies in Modern Fiction," "Permanent Values in Fiction," and "A Reconsideration of Proust" are all reprinted by permission of The Saturday Review © 1934, S.R. Publications, Ltd. "William C. Brownell," "The Writing of *Ethan Frome*," and the introductions to the 1922 edition of *Ethan Frome*, to *Ghosts*, and to *Eternal Passion in English Poetry* are reprinted with the gracious permission of Watkins/Loomis Agency and the Estate of Edith Wharton. "Fiction and Criticism" and the letter eulogizing Sir Louis Mallet are published also with their permission and with the permission of the Yale Collection of American Literature, Beinecke Rare Book and Manuscript Library, Yale University. Excerpts from other manuscripts and from Wharton's unpublished correspondence are quoted with the permission of the Watkins/Loomis Agency, the Estate of Edith Wharton, and the following institutions where parenthetically cited in the text: the Yale Collection of American Literature, Beinecke Rare Book and Manuscript Library; Rare Books and Special Collections, Princeton University Libraries; Lilly Library, Indiana University; Amherst College Library; the Massachusetts Historical Society; and the Houghton Library, Harvard University. Henry James's letter to Katherine Fullerton is quoted with the additional permission of Bay James; unpublished letters of Charles Scribner and William C. Brownell at Princeton are quoted also with the permission of Simon & Schuster. H. S. Milford's letters to Wharton are quoted also by permission of Oxford University Press. Documents in the Gaillard Lapsley Collection are quoted by permission of the Master and Fellows, Trinity College, Cambridge University. Material at Yale belongs to the Edith Wharton Collection (YCal 42); material at Princeton is drawn from the Scribner Archives (Author Files I, boxes 167–68, and the Brownell Letterbooks, vols. 8–10), except for James's letter to Katherine Fullerton (General Manuscripts [Misc], box JA–JE); at Amherst Wharton's letters are among the William Crary Brownell Papers, box II, folder 3, Amherst College Archives, and her letters to Bessy Lodge are among the George Cabot Lodge Papers at the Massachusetts Historical Society.

Finally, I am especially grateful to my editors at Princeton: to Robert E. Brown, who initially sponsored the project, and more recently to Mary Murrell and Deborah Malmud, who patiently and indulgently awaited a host of much delayed revisions and who shepherded the manuscript through each stage of preparation. The exemplary carefulness and forbearance of my assiduous copy editor, Victoria Wilson-Schwartz, rescued the manuscript from many errors and infelicities.

This edition was completed under professionally difficult circumstances that would have been all the more dispiriting without the supportiveness and interest of many friends, both within and outside academe. It is a pleasure to mention Jonathan Bumas and Martha Hollander, William and Zita Kreindler, Michael Billig and Nina Shapiro, David and Jacqueline Gorman, Michael Marx and Catherine Golden, Ruth Moskowitz, Andrew Hrycyna and Alice Flaherty, Laura Rosen and Jonathan Zerkowski, Robert Gabbay and Teresa Swenson, Pico Iyer, Chandos Brown, Benjamin Kaplan, Greg Maertz, Maud Ellmann, and Irene Kacandes. For their warm hospitality during more than one research visit, I have other good friends to thank: in New Haven, Alison Hickey and Claudine Kahan, and at Princeton, Deborah and Philip Nord. As for the small portion of this book that consists of my words rather than Wharton's, I would like to dedicate it, with love and gratitude, to my mother, to my brother, and to the two nephews born in the time since I began my work on the project.

This edition assembles all of Edith Wharton's miscellaneous uncollected critical writings, including reviews, essays, literary eulogies, introductions and prefaces to her own work or the work of others, and items of related interest: an unreprinted parody, letters to the editor, an unreprinted auto-biographical essay, a newspaper transcription of an early lecture, and a sample of her unpublished critical prose. Four of the previously published pieces ("Newport's Old Houses," "Impoverishing the Language," her review of *The Architecture of Humanism*, and the complete text of her tribute to Bayard Cutting, Jr.) have eluded all bibliographies of Wharton's work, encouraging the suspicion that others, hitherto undetected, might also resurface in the future. Excluded from this volume are the five essays that Wharton republished in book form herself as *The Writing of Fiction* (1925): "In General," "Telling a Short Story," "Constructing a Novel," "Character and Situation in the Novel," and "Marcel Proust." Her essay "Confessions of a Novelist," published in *Atlantic Monthly* in April 1933, reappeared the following year as "The Secret Garden," the ninth chapter of *A Backward Glance*, and is therefore omitted here. Also omitted are Wharton's various articles on the First World War or on her experiences in the war-relief effort ("My Work among the Women Workers of Paris," "How Paris Welcomed the King," "Christmas Tinsel," and "L'Amérique en Guerre"), which are more appropriately classified with her many other wartime writings. Another essay of that period, "Jean du Breuil de Saint-Germain," eulogizing a young friend killed in battle in 1915, holds considerable additional interest, however, and is published here in English translation for the first time. While there is much to be said for a strictly chronological arrangement of texts, Wharton's critical writings readily lend themselves to the sort of grouping employed here, even at the risk of some apparent arbitrariness. (For example, "The Sonnets of Eugene Lee-Hamilton" was occasioned by the death of its subject no less immediately than, say, "George Cabot Lodge" or "William C. Brownell," each of which quotes just as extensively from the works of its subject; yet the former is more briefly eulogistic than the tributes to Lodge or Brownell—to whom Wharton was far closer, in any event, than to Lee-Hamilton—and focuses on a single work rather than providing an overview, as in the other texts, of its subject's career.)

During Wharton's lifetime, four of her miscellaneous essays ("The Great American Novel," "William C. Brownell," "Tendencies in Modern Fiction," and "The Writing of *Ethan Frome*") were republished in collections of writings by various hands; each reprinting simply follows the original periodical version. These and all of the other texts included here thus exist in essentially one published form and, as a result, present few particular editorial problems. On the other hand, Wharton's critical writings were published by a number of English and American journals and presses with widely differing house styles, each of them not always consistently applied in every case. While typographical errors have been corrected, and the format of block quotations has been standardized for the sake of clarity and the reader's convenience, Wharton's texts are otherwise presented without alteration. Adeline Tintner's unannotated translation of "Souvenirs du Bourget d'Outremer," published in the spring 1991 issue of the *Edith Wharton Review*, appeared after a translation had already been completed for this volume; her rendering, while an important contribution to the Wharton bibliography, is occasionally unidiomatic or inaccurate, omits one paragraph, and elsewhere alters the original paragraphing of Wharton's article, and I have therefore retained the alternative translation. "The Art of Henry James," published under W. Morton Fullerton's name, but revised and completed with Wharton's help during their lengthy affair, is included in an appendix as a collaborative effort.

As specified in the concluding bibliography, a number of the texts reprinted here, particularly from Wharton's later years, exist in manuscript or typescript (or, occasionally, both). In keeping with the work habits that she had established before the 1920s (composing as she did by hand, before turning the manuscript over to a secretary to be typed), the typescript (often corrected in turn) would obviously represent the more finished version. In the case of a text like "George Cabot Lodge" (the earliest of Wharton's articles to survive in manuscript), the manuscript is virtually identical to the version that appeared in *Scribner's Magazine*. In other cases (the tribute to Brownell, for example, or "A Further Glance," which became "A Little Girl's New York"), collation of the manuscript with the published version discloses numerous differences in phrasing and other stylistic or organizational discrepancies. Rather than compile an inventory of variants, however, I have tried to keep any textual apparatus to an unobtrusive minimum, taking as my chief purpose the task of making readily available, in convenient and easily readable form, an important body of critical work, hitherto dispersed and neglected, by an otherwise preeminent figure in American letters.

ABBREVIATIONS

WORKS

AI	*The Age of Innocence*, rpt. (New York: Scribner's, 1968)
BG	*A Backward Glance* (New York: Appleton-Century, 1934)
CC	*The Custom of the Country* (New York: Scribner's, 1913)
CS	*The Collected Short Stories of Edith Wharton*, ed. R.W.B. Lewis, 2 vols. (New York: Scribner's, 1968)
DH	*The Decoration of Houses*, rpt. (New York: Norton, 1978)
GA	*The Gods Arrive*, rpt. (New York: Scribner's, 1969)
GM	*Glimpses of the Moon* (New York: Appleton-Century, 1922)
HRB	*Hudson River Bracketed*, rpt. (New York: Scribner's, 1969)
IB	*Italian Backgrounds* (New York: Scribner's, 1905)
IVG	*Italian Villas and Their Gardens* (New York: Scribner's, 1904)
L	*The Letters of Edith Wharton*, ed. R.W.B. Lewis and Nancy Lewis (New York: Macmillan, 1988)
MF	*A Motor-Flight Through France* (New York: Scribner's, 1908)
N	*Novellas and Other Writings* (New York: Library of America, 1990)
SF	*A Son at the Front* (New York: Scribner's, 1923)
TS	*Twilight Sleep* (New York: Appleton-Century, 1927)
WF	*The Writing of Fiction* (New York: Scribner's, 1925)

Bell	Millicent Bell, *Edith Wharton and Henry James: The Story of Their Friendship* (New York: Braziller, 1965)
Benstock	Shari Benstock, *No Gifts from Chance: A Biography of Edith Wharton* (New York: Scribner's, 1994)
Lewis	R.W.B. Lewis, *Edith Wharton: A Biography* (New York: Harper & Row, 1975)
Powers	Lyall H. Powers, ed., *Henry James and Edith Wharton: Letters, 1900–1915* (New York: Scribner's, 1990)

ARCHIVES

Amherst	Amherst College Library
Harvard	Houghton Library, Harvard University
Indiana	Lilly Library, Indiana University
MHS	Massachusetts Historical Society
Princeton	Rare Books and Special Collections, Princeton University Libraries
Yale	Yale Collection of American Literature, Beinecke Rare Book and Manuscript Library

EDITH WHARTON

———————

THE UNCOLLECTED
CRITICAL
WRITINGS

"ENTHUSIASM GUIDED BY ACUMEN":
EDITH WHARTON AS A
CRITICAL WRITER

I

Writing in October 1924 to her old friend and mentor William Crary Brownell, Edith Wharton found herself in the midst of one of the busiest periods of her career, "with a novel overdue & howling to be finished; & 'Fiction' II & III only half done, & more terrifying to me than any novel I ever undertook—& a rashly promised article on Proust (for the Yale Review) dogging me like Banquo whenever I attempt to take wine with you." By "'Fiction' II & III," Wharton is referring to the second and third in a series of essays that were soon to appear in *Scribner's Magazine* and would be collected a year later, along with the Proust article, as *The Writing of Fiction*—hardly, one would have thought, the sort of task to intimidate a seasoned writer at the height of her prosperity and accomplishment, and more confident than ever in her own powers as a novelist. That she should have expressed herself in such hyperbolically fearful terms about a work not of fiction but of literary criticism points to a remarkable, and still largely unknown, aspect of Wharton's struggles as a writer. Her letter to Brownell goes on to offer a moving reason why an ostensibly routine commitment had somehow aroused such feelings of anxiety and dismay: "The truth is, my irrepressible desire to write critical articles is equalled only by my cowardice & incapacity when I sit down to the task. Each time I swear, Never Again!"[1]

It was an admonition that Wharton nonetheless frequently ignored, producing as she did an extensive body of critical work that includes nearly a dozen reviews and around three times as many essays, public letters, introductions, and prefaces. Substantial as they are in the aggregate, however, her critical writings are scattered unevenly throughout a long and productive career, while it is striking that a writer so articulate about the intricacies of her craft should have remained only sporadically active as a critic. Unlike many other aesthetically informed and sophisticated novelists, Wharton served no apprenticeship in critical or journalistic writing (publishing her first review in her fortieth year, a full decade after her first short story and with two volumes of tales, a novella, a couple of travel essays, and numerous poems already to her credit) and seems never to have looked upon the writing of criticism as an ongoing and continuous accompaniment to her imaginative work. Several items—her eulogies of various friends, the essay on Eugene Lee-Hamilton, her reviews of Henry James's letters and of works by Howard Sturgis and Geoffrey Scott—were undertaken primarily out of personal devotion to her subject, while many others were commissioned by editors or publishers; few were unsolicited, or written on Wharton's initiative. As for the first book that she reviewed, one of its authors (Edwin H. Blashfield) had favorably discussed *The Decoration of Houses* a few years earlier, while the other (his wife, Evangeline) was a cousin of Brownell, through whom Wharton had already become acquainted with the couple. It seems doubtful that she would have bothered to write a review of a work like Maurice Hewlett's *The Fool Errant* if she had not recently published a historical novel of her own with a similar eighteenth-century Italian setting, or produced such a long and searching essay to introduce an English version of Gottfried Keller's *A Village Romeo and Juliet* if the translator had not been her old tutor, Anna Bahlmann. As she indicated in another letter to Brownell, it was his essay on Matthew Arnold, "which I re-read with increasing enjoyment," that impelled Wharton to declare, "I almost think I'll have to have a 'crack' at Mr. [Herbert] Paul on the poetry side," referring to the Arnold study that she reviewed in 1903.[2] Even an important essay like "The Criticism of Fiction" (1914), leading an issue of the *Times Literary Supplement*, begins as a response to a much lengthier preceding article by James. Her correspondence, moreover, is full of laments—sometimes rather melodramatically expressed—about the difficulties and deferrals that beset Wharton's work on one or another critical piece. It took her nearly two years to deliver the "rashly promised" essay on Proust, while Henry S. Canby of the *Saturday Review of Literature* initially approached Wharton a full decade before finally receiving an article from her; the composition of *The Writing of Fiction*, which began as a pair of articles in 1920 and evolved fitfully into a four-part series that took her five years to complete, serves all by itself as a fascinating object lesson in avoidance and delay.[3] Clearly, there persisted throughout Wharton's career a severe, unrelieved tension between her "irrepressible desire to write critical articles" and the sense of "cowardice & incapacity" that she described to Brownell.

What explains such conflicting impulses on the part of an otherwise prolific and rarely impeded writer? To be sure, as Wharton herself reminded Canby, "I am not a professional critic," while she was also understandably reluctant to divert her attention from more pressing tasks, warning the *Yale*

Review at one point that "the date of delivery of my critical articles is conditioned by my novel writing" and instructing her secretary to decline repeated petitions from the *Forum* on the grounds that "her time is almost wholly given to the writing of fiction, such critical articles as she publishes having been promised too long beforehand for her to undertake any additional work at present."[4] Moreover, as R.W.B. Lewis astutely observes, Wharton throughout her career seems to have "found it hard to believe herself worthy to discourse, from a personal standpoint, upon larger questions of the art of fiction and the creative experience" (Lewis 297). In documents like many of her unpublished letters to Brownell, one senses, however, that she was afflicted by a rather more pervasive and profoundly inhibiting sense of unworthiness along these lines, as in her own comments, for example, on the introduction to *A Village Romeo and Juliet*:

> The Keller scribble hasn't much shape or continuity, & you can't expect any one who reads *you* not to know it; but you saw what I was driving at, & pulled it out & disengaged it from its lump of clay—& deep down to my roots that does me good! . . . There are certain things I always carry to you, & that you shed a wireless ray on across all the distances; & it's that very ray that illuminates for me the fumbling inadequacy of such attempts as the Keller scrap. But then it's the very breath of my life to commune with the people who make me feel my shortcomings![5]

In no other aspect of her work did these shortcomings seem as apparent to Wharton as in her efforts at criticism, and to no one was she more candid about such shortcomings than to Brownell, whose example she found at once inspirational and humbling. "When I read such a piece of work as this," she declared in 1905, after receiving a copy of his essay on James, "I feel like *trying all over again* to do something good myself," only to produce no more than two or three critical pieces over the next five years. In a letter of December 1924, with "still the last half of my third fiction article hanging over me" and the series about to begin its run in *Scribner's*, Wharton quotes several phrases from Brownell's latest study and finds that "dozens, hundreds of such felicities taunt me with my own incapacity & fill me with a deep satisfaction in the thing perfectly done." As for the first installment, Wharton had already concluded an earlier letter by confessing to Brownell, "I shall . . . tremble like an aspen when *you* read 'Fiction I.'"[6]

Few of her admirers will be unaffected by so many remarks like these, which disclose an Edith Wharton startlingly different from the indomitable and self-assured novelist, traveler, correspondent, literary businesswoman, and cultural observer about whom so much has been written in recent years. This sort of timorousness, uncharacteristic as it seems, may be traced, however, to a source that Wharton herself evoked, perhaps inadvertently, with regard to one of her own earliest essays, proposing "The Three Francescas" (1902) to William Dean Howells in terms that sound a good deal less facetious than one might wish: "I had thought of offering the article to the North American [Review], but . . . I do not know Mr. [George] Harvey, & am not sure if he condescends to such frivolities as a dramatic criticism by a woman" (*L*, 62). Fiction writing might be one thing, or the writing of poems, travelogues, or books about interior decoration or landscape gardening, but critical writing, for Wharton, appears to have been quite another; and the assumption that criticism, "dramatic" or otherwise, could not be taken seriously if written by a woman, or that the prospect of an essay by a woman was somehow inherently frivolous, helps illuminate Wharton's painful and lingering doubts about her own abilities in that mode. It is an assumption that would have had much to do, of course, with the peculiarities of her own upbringing and acculturation. Miscellaneously self-educated as she was in the "gentleman's library" of her indulgent father, Wharton received meager encouragement from an uncomprehending mother, whose famously inapt response to her daughter's "first attempt" at a novel (*BG*, 73) would have epitomized, for the young Wharton, the operation of the critical faculty in a member of her own sex. Evidently it did not take her long to absorb the implications of these early experiences. As she would recall it in "Life and I," Wharton's recently published autobiographical fragment, "Never shall I forget the long-drawn weariness of the hours passed with 'nice' little girls, brought in to 'spend the day,' & unable to converse with me about Tennyson, Macaulay, or anything that 'really mattered.'" Her discovery (on a brother's bookshelf) of such esoteric volumes as "Coppée's Elements of Logic" and "Sir William Hamilton's History of Philosophy" had a similar effect: "Now I was going to know all about life! Now I should never be that helpless blundering thing, a mere 'little girl,' again!" Second in importance only to "Chambers's Encyclopaedia of English Literature," and further reinforcing such distinctions in her mind, a work like "Coleridge's 'Friend' . . . answered to some hidden need to order my thoughts, & get things into some kind of logical relation to each other: a need which developed in me almost as early as the desire to be kissed & thought pretty!" (*N*, 1076, 1086, 1084.)

The conventional behavior and yearnings of a "'nice'" or "a mere 'little girl,'" on the one hand, and on the other, logic, knowledge, conversa-

tions about literary subjects or any of the other things "that 'really mattered'"—thus did the analytic, critical intellect become situated, quite early
on, in what Gloria Erlich has called Wharton's "sexual education." It is only
fitting, therefore, that she should have confided such misgivings about her
aptitude as a critic to someone like Brownell, one of the more powerful in
a series of male figures (including Longfellow, Howells, James, Bourget,
Charles Eliot Norton, and Egerton Winthrop) whose critical and cultural
authority had guided Wharton at various stages of her own emergence and
development. Important later friendships with, say, Bernard Berenson or
Louis Gillet and with younger, critically gifted men like Geoffrey Scott,
Percy Lubbock, Charles Du Bos, and Kenneth Clark (not to mention the
prevailing "maleness" of her own "inner circle," incisively explored in Susan
Goodman's recent study) would have helped to make criticism seem all the
more, in Wharton's eyes, a province of the opposite sex. (As for another
younger friend, John Hugh Smith, "Wharton thought that his talents would
be better served writing literary criticism rather than directing the Hambros
Bank" or serving in any of his other financial capacities.)[7] Striking as it is
to be reminded that Wharton's first and final books (*The Decoration of
Houses* and the posthumously published anthology *Eternal Passion in English Poetry*) were both critical works of a sort, rather than works of fiction,
it seems even more telling that she should have produced the first with one
male collaborator (Ogden Codman, Jr.) and the last with another (Robert
Norton), or that each volume should have benefited from the additional help
of a second man (Walter Berry in one case and in the other Gaillard Lapsley,
to whom she dedicated *The Writing of Fiction*) on whose critical judgment
Wharton relied for most of her writing life. On certain projects, Wharton
either anonymously assisted or deferred altogether to one or another critical
male presence, patiently working with her lover W. Morton Fullerton in
revising and polishing his extensive review of the New York Edition of
James's works, and even helping to find a publisher for it, before she began
drafting, only to abandon, an essay of her own on the same subject.[8] (Similarly, she informed Fullerton, a couple of years later, "The ed. of the Yale
Review wrote & asked me if I wd give them an article on Moreau de St.
Méry," whose journal of a trip to postrevolutionary America had just appeared in a new edition, "& I suggested that you might" [*L*, 324], as if he
were somehow obviously more qualified than she to discuss such a work,
while after Berry's death Wharton "recommended . . . that Morton Fullerton
undertake a biography, offering to make available to him her letters from

Walter," and even "volunteered to help him write the book" [Benstock 405].)
Later declining an invitation from Oxford University Press to launch a series
of American literary biographies with a volume on Henry James, Wharton
nominated Lubbock for the task instead, much as she had vigorously cam-
paigned to have Lubbock edit the 1920 selection of James's letters.[9] Note,
also, the terms in which she appears to have welcomed Brownell's magis-
terial essay on James, years earlier, as a pretext for dispensing with any
commentary of her own: "Every line so exactly expresses my own feeling
about him, to the last shade of a shade, that I feel as if I had had the article
celestially written for me—like which saint[?]—while I slept!" (qtd. in Bell
222).[10] Even more revealing, the excellence of his essay on Hawthorne
makes Wharton reconsider what seems to have been her own dearest aspira-
tion as a critic: "How I wish you'd do a book on [the] art of fiction. I often
dream of it, & then, when I read one of your essays, I see that my insight
ends where yours begins, & that I had much better entrust the task to you."[11]
Clearly, Wharton could have found little in her background, or in the intellectual world around her, to make her at all comfortable with the role of
critic. It seems no coincidence that her one model of a critically accomplished writer among members of her own sex should have been the sexually
ambiguous Violet Paget, better known by the famous male pseudonym
("Vernon Lee") under which she published so many works on literature,
culture, and the arts.

For many, this peculiar tendency on Wharton's part will take its place in
what one scholar has called "a long historical process of feminine ambivalence toward the role of the critic/observer" (toward "the masculinized
power implicit in critical observation"), although it may also be affirmed, just
as plausibly, that "[t]he decidedly male direction of her philosophical and
literary education allowed her," as Katherine Joslin puts it, "to link herself
. . . to the dominant culture, the intellectual and public world of the powerful white male."[12] Yet it seems hard not to conclude, at the same time, that
the "cowardice & incapacity" with which she reproached herself in her own
attempts at all such tasks ultimately rested for Wharton on a withering skep-
ticism of the critical capacities of women generally or an uneasiness with
the notion of women as literary or cultural critics. While she was prepared
to sponsor works by women on already conventionally available subjects
(gardening in the case of Mrs. Philip Martineau, animal life in that of Vivienne de Watteville), works of criticism, even by a writer whom she greatly
esteemed, were another matter. Regarding her *Studies of the Eighteenth
Century in Italy*, for example, Wharton once told Vernon Lee, "It will be

a real pleasure to write an article on your delightful—if I were not torn with contending sympathies, I should say most delightful of books" and "the one specially dear to me as opening my eyes to that dear despised foolish and brilliant 18th century in Italy, which no one saw till you told us to look."[13] Yet she never got around to writing an article on Lee, mentioning her work only briefly in *A Backward Glance* and in a couple of essays, although she had already found time to publish an appreciation of her brother's negligible, now forgotten sonnets. Moreover, few of the women among Wharton's predecessors in criticism are substantially mentioned in her own critical writing, and none is discussed or acknowledged specifically as a critic. Addressing the complaint that George Eliot "was too 'scientific,' that she sterilised her imagination and deformed her style by the study of biology and metaphysics," and comparing her on that basis with other scientifically informed writers like Milton, Goethe, and Tennyson, Wharton surely has her own similar interests in mind as she asks, in an early review of the Leslie Stephen biography, "Is it because these were men, while George Eliot was a woman, that she is reproved for venturing on ground they did not fear to tread?" Yet she nonetheless proceeds to applaud the role of Herbert Spencer and George Henry Lewes in facilitating Eliot's development, while referring to none of her many, often recondite essays and reviews. Another such illustrious predecessor, and one who had a pioneering critical interest in the work and legacy of literary women, is invoked once, and then only parenthetically, in her memoirs, as Wharton introduces "the Comte d'Haussonville (Madame de Staël's grandson and biographer)" among the members of Rosa de Fitz-James's Parisian salon. Later, de Staël is further implicitly discounted in Wharton's account of one of the few women among the members of the salon, the Italian writer Matilde Serao, whose "training as a journalist . . . had given her a rough-and-ready knowledge of life, and an experience of public affairs, totally lacking in the drawing-room Corinnes whom she outrivalled in wit and eloquence" (*BG*, 269, 276). Mentioning at the same time, however, that she had been "described by Bourget as 'Dr. Johnson in a ball-dress,'" Wharton thus promptly accommodates even the exceptional Serao to the same dominant, belittling pattern in her own critical thinking. And their hostess, even as she assembles such an impressive roster of guests, seems almost comically bereft of anything resembling a critical faculty; in Wharton's portrayal, "Madame de Fitz-James was a book-collector, not a reader," whose "books were an ornament and an investment. . . . If one of her guests was raised to Academic honours she bought his last work and tried to read it—usually with negative results; and her intimates were all familiar with the confidential question: 'I've just read So-and-So's new book. *Tell me, my dear: is it good?*'" (*BG*, 266–67; EW's emphasis).

Finding in her salon a sign, even so, that in Paris "the ineradicable passion for good talk, and for seeing the same people every day, was as strong at the opening of the twentieth century as when the *Précieuses* met at the Hôtel de Rambouillet" (*BG*, 262), Wharton appears to be honoring the notion of such a celebrated community of critical women or of an intellectual center presided over largely by members of her own sex. Yet one remembers, of course, that the ideal salon, in her eyes, nonetheless consisted of women whose listening attentiveness forms a backdrop for the superior conversation among its male participants. Elsewhere, in an astonishing passage, even a prominent figure like George Sand is imagined as having performed just such a self-diminishing service for certain critically assertive guests at Nohant: "Here, one likes especially to fancy, Maurice Sand exercised his chisel on the famous marionettes for the little theatre, while his mother, fitting their costumes with skilful fingers, listened, silent *comme une bête*, to the dissertations of Gautier, Flaubert, or Dumas" (*MF*, 81). Mentioning to a friend "the wonderful letters" of Flaubert, Wharton does refer with admiration to "G. Sand's equally wonderful answers"; yet she quickly adds that they are "equal not, of course, in 'brilliancy'" (*L*, 173), while she quotes none of Sand's letters (or any of her critical writings, for that matter) in her own critical prose, and more than a couple of Flaubert's.[14] Other women among her critical predecessors suffer from similar implicitly disparaging comparisons. Among the works of "[a]rt history and criticism" that she had read in her youth, "Mrs. [Anna] Jameson's amiable volumes" are mentioned alongside far more reverently described works of Ruskin, Hamerton, and others, while the very leader of the *Précieuses*, and the only woman whose writings Wharton recalled "[a]mong French prose classics" in her father's library is referred to as "Sévigné the divinely loitering," by contrast to "Sainte-Beuve's 'Lundis,' bracing fare for a young mind" (*BG*, 71, 66–67). (Interestingly, Wharton's brief vignette of Madame de Sévigné in *A Motor-Flight Through France*, poignant as it is, focuses on her later life in Provence, self-exiled from the intellectually sustaining world of Paris and her salon.) When she remarks that the Blashfields' *Italian Cities* "doubtless owes something of its artistic balance to the technical competence of one of the authors," it is clear which of the two, husband or wife, Wharton has in mind. An admirer of Lytton Strachey, Desmond MacCarthy, and Arthur Waley, among critical writers associated with Bloomsbury, Wharton predictably bristled at Virginia Woolf's comments in an essay on American fiction, while later recalling her friendship with Alice Meynell, "whose poems I admired far more than her delicate but too self-conscious essays" (*BG*, 222).[15] Finally, as her favorite illustrations of weak or shortsighted critical judgment, Wharton refers more than once in her own critical prose to a pair of apocryphal remarks by women regarding the imaginative works of certain male writers: Madame de Sévigné's contention that Racine, like coffee, would someday go out of fashion and Anna Letitia Barbauld's famous complaint about "The Ancient Mariner" (that the poem was "improbable"). It is surely calculated that Wharton, in "The Vice of Reading" (1903), should cite as examples of poor or inept readers "the case of the lady who could not approve of Balzac's novels, but was of course willing to admit that 'they were written in the most beautiful French,'" and that of "a lady" who, "on being suddenly asked what she thought of '*Quo Vadis*,' replied that she had no fault to find with the book except that 'nothing happened in it.'"

Equipped though she was with a highly refined and penetrating critical intelligence, this is a woman who obviously found it difficult to take women seriously as writers of criticism.[16] And Wharton's fiction is rather dismally consistent, in this regard, with her other works, offering as a typical image of the woman as critic a figure, for example, like Margot Crash in *The Gods Arrive* (1932), "a slender young lady with a face adorned by movie-star teeth and eyelashes," who "represented in London the literary page of the Des Moines 'Daily Ubiquity'" (*GA*, 275) and who plagues Vance Weston with a series of inane questions about his work. In *The Age of Innocence* (1920), the magazine for which Newland Archer's bohemian friend Ned Winsett ends up desultorily working, "after publishing one volume of brief and exquisite literary appreciations," is, significantly, "a women's weekly, where fashion-plates and paper patterns alternated with New England love-stories and advertisements of temperance drinks" (*AI*, 124–25). One thinks, moreover, of the way in which those outlets of critical or interpretive activity popularly open to women around the turn of the century (public lectures, reading clubs, and the like) are routinely and brutally satirized in Wharton's fiction. Even those women who are more seriously, if misguidedly, inclined along these lines tend to be eclipsed by the arrival of a usurping male presence. Mary Anerton in "The Muse's Tragedy" (1899), for example, or Paulina Anson in "The Angel at the Grave" (1901) each gives way, as caretakers of a beloved literary celebrity's legacy, to a younger male critic or scholar who is presented as more thoroughly informed and qualified on the same subject. After editing Vincent Rendle's "juvenilia," Mrs. Anerton herself authorizes "[a] complete interpretation" of the poet, "a summing up of his style, his purpose, his theory of life and art," from the young Danyers, who has already "written, at college, the prize essay on Rendle's poetry" and "brought out his first slim volume, in which the remodeled college essay on Rendle figured among a dozen somewhat overstudied 'appreciations'" (CS, 1: 73, 67, 70). Paulina Anson—having earnestly, laboriously compiled an unpublishable *Life* of her once venerated transcendentalist grandfather—ends up assisting George Corby in preparing an article on the one obscure and utterly overlooked achievement that will restore his reputation. Halo Spear, whose husband "appropriate[s] her opinions" in forming his own critical judgments after taking over the editorship of a literary journal in *Hudson River Bracketed* (1929), acts as Vance Weston's most trusted critic and literary confidante until she finds herself unceremoniously supplanted, in *The Gods Arrive*, by "Derek Fane, of the 'Amplifier,'" and by Savignac, one of the "scholarly, analytical, intellectually curious" "young men" whom the couple has befriended in Paris (*HRB*, 225; *GA*, 98, 77–78). True, the "suddenly acquired technical standard" by which Claudia Keniston, wandering through a Parisian gallery, discovers in "The Recovery" (1901) the low quality of her husband's naively overrated paintings "seemed as though it were a standard outside of herself, as though some unheeded inner sense were gradually making her aware of the presence, in that empty room, of a critical intelligence that was giving out a subtle effluence of disapproval" (*CS*, 1: 271). Yet her awareness of such a force does not result in any critical expression on her own part, merely enabling her to support Keniston when he undergoes the same realization. It seems no wonder, then, that the one indisputably superior critical intellect among Wharton's imaginary women, Fulvia Vivaldi in *The Valley of Decision* (1902), is abruptly murdered as soon as she finishes delivering her triumphant doctoral oration.

However they happen to be portrayed, such women, in any event, remain exceptions in the world of Wharton's novels and tales. Throughout this critically literate and erudite woman's fiction, the figure of the critic, reviewer, or scholar—from Maurice Birkton in "That Good May Come" (1894), an indigent poet who "resign[ed] his clerkship in a wholesale warehouse in order to give more leisure to the writing of the literary criticisms with which he supplied the *Symbolic Weekly Review*," to Vincent Craig in "Permanent Wave" (1935), who "sat up late writing learned articles for historical reviews and philosophical quarterlies"—is predominantly and conspicuously male (*CS*, 1: 25, 2: 791). In "The Legend" (1910), for example, Arthur Bernald, "the dramatic critic of a daily paper," competes with a vulgar popularizer to produce the definitive study of a mysteriously vanished writer's work, while in "Afterward" (1910) Ned Boyne, an engineer like the narrator whom Wharton impersonates in *Ethan Frome*, "dreamed of the production of his long-planned book on the 'Economic Basis of Culture'" and decamps with his wife to England in search of a more conducive environment (*CS*, 2: 93, 154). Although "they lacked the freshness and audacity of his youthful work," the narrator of "The Long Run" (1916) still decides that his friend Halston Merrick's "essays were judicious, polished and cultivated" (*CS*, 2: 306). Early in *Glimpses of the Moon* (1922), Nick Lansing is "doing a dreary job on a popular encyclopedia" after "his essay on 'Chinese Influences in Greek Art' had created a passing stir" (*GM*, 8, 16); in her notes for "Love Among the Ruins," Wharton's unwritten sequel, Nick "does articles, reviews, odds & ends" after he and Susy return to New York.[17] Even in the case of the one woman among Wharton's reputable fictitious novelists, the life and work of Margaret Aubyn becomes the interpretive property of a "Professor Joslin," the male biographer who places the announcement to which Stephen Glennard responds in *The Touchstone* (1900). And it is also to male protagonists that Wharton entrusts even those subjects in which she herself was especially interested. Although Darwin remained one of her heroes, and although she read widely in the literature on evolution, it is the eccentric Galen Dredge who authors, in "The Debt" (1909), the revolutionary *Arrival of the Fittest*. Similarly, Wharton compiled extensive notes toward a Whitman study, but it is Ralph Marvell, in *The Custom of the Country* (1913), who plans an "essay on 'The Rhythmical Structures of Walt Whitman,'" while also evidently manifesting one of her own inner conflicts in his desire to "write some good verse if possible; if not, then critical prose. A dramatic poem lay among the stuff at his elbow; but the prose critic was at his elbow too, and not to be satisfied about the poem; and poet and critic passed the nights in hot if unproductive debate. On the whole, it seemed likely that the critic would win the day" (*CC*, 77). Invariably male, as well, are the critics and editors who gather at the "Cocoanut Tree" with Vance Weston, the protagonist of Wharton's only *Kunstlerroman*, while Vance himself composes "a monthly article on current literary events" (*HRB*, 244) to support himself while writing fiction.[18]

   Even more striking than her choice of a male alter ego in *Hudson River Bracketed*, that clumsy but illuminating *summa* of its author's literary views and values, is the fact that it should be yet another male critic who serves not only as Vance's reluctant mentor but as Wharton's own mouthpiece, and in many ways as the most intriguing character in the novel. Introduced to

Vance as "our great critic," and by Halo herself as "[t]he man who can talk to you better than anybody else about English poetry," George Frenside, "the literary critic of *The Hour*" (a "high-brow review") becomes Wharton's fullest and most complex representation of the literary critic and is in many ways advanced as a model of what a critic should be, dismissing as "nonsense" the notion of "his acting as literary adviser to anybody" on the grounds that "his honest advice would almost always be: 'To the wastepaper basket'" (*HRB*, 112, 102, 121, 180). A critic who "had written, a good many years earlier, a brief volume of essays called *Dry Points*, which had had a considerable success in the limited circle of the cultivated," and who has since "lingered on the outskirts of success, contributing fierce dissections of political and literary ideas to various newspapers and reviews," Frenside embodies throughout the novel an oddly paradoxical force, expert but ineffectual, potent yet only intermittently or fitfully focused, severe but at the same time diffuse, "elderly, poor, unsuccessful, and yet more masterful, more stimulating" in Halo's eyes "than any one else she had ever known" (*HRB*, 73, 72). Confronted by "Frenside's decomposing irony," his "congenital lack of generosity," and "his unencouraging stare," it is no wonder that Halo at one point finds herself agreeing with others "when they said Frenside's way of encouraging you was like a doctor's saying: 'Nothing will make any difference now'" (*HRB*, 431, 177, 162, 176).

Explaining to Halo that "the critical faculty outweighed all others in him" (*HRB*, 72), Frenside seems close in Wharton's imagination to Walter Berry, who "was born . . . with a critical sense so far outweighing his creative gift that he had early renounced the idea of writing" (*BG*, 108). Yet "Dry Points," curiously enough, had been one of the working titles of her second collection of stories nearly thirty years earlier, and although Frenside's "life of unsettled aspirations and inconsecutive work" (*HRB*, 224) bears little resemblance to hers, one gradually suspects that Wharton has invested a good deal of herself, and more than a few of her own most recognizable attributes, in her fictitious critic's brittle, refractory temperament.[19] First shown a few of Vance's poems, "Frenside adjusted his eye-glasses . . . as if he were fitting his eyes to an exceptionally powerful microscope," only one in a series of rather forbiddingly clinical images through which he presents the literary critic as "a walking radiograph," someone who "saw . . . the skeletons of things and people" and "would rather not have had a decomposing mind," who was moved only by "beauty of man's making, something wrung by human genius out of the stubborn elements" and who was prone to "parcel[ling] it out into its component parts with those cool classifying eyes."

Preserving among her earlier memories Frenside's "short stocky figure, his brooding Socratic head, his cigar and eyeglasses," and as a friend who "knew him so well, knew also the communicative glow he could give out," Halo "wondered if one could say of those small deep-sunk eyes, forever watchful behind their old-fashioned pince-nez, that anything they rested on escaped them" (*HRB*, 164, 71–73). Evidently fulfilling the Jamesian injunction to be "one of the people on whom nothing is lost," Frenside serves not only as the literary conscience of the novel but also as the character through whom Wharton principally expresses her own critical convictions and ventilates (none too subtly at times) her apprehensions about the changes besetting the world of letters in modern America. As Frenside describes the demands of the writing life and fulminates against publishers and reviewers, the new literary careerism, the latest intellectual fashions, or the modernist nuisance, one easily hears in his remarks the contemptuous, pontifical voice of Wharton's later essays. "A fire that warms everything but itself" is the way in which Halo "had once defined him"; and Wharton, had she described her own exercises in criticism, might well have "snapped back," with Frenside himself, "I don't warm, I singe" (*HRB*, 72).

Evidently, the woman who liked to think of herself as "a self-made man," who preferred the company of men, and who "had envisioned her creative self," in the words of one recent scholar, "as masculine" (Erlich 149) thought of her "critical" self in much the same way, deciding that it was through a male voice, at least in her fiction, that she could speak most authoritatively as a critic. And, if she seems to have been incapable, at nearly every point in her long career, of imagining women as critics or portraying any woman in such a role, Wharton evidently thought very little of her own efforts in critical writing as well. Although she saw fit to collect in book form nearly all of her travel essays, her gardening and architectural writings, her literary contributions to the war effort, and even two volumes' worth of her verse, Wharton passed over the bulk of her critical prose. Allowing no more than four of her essays to be reprinted by others,[20] she herself agreed to prepare for republication (and then only at Charles Scribner's suggestion) only those that compose *The Writing of Fiction*, a volume itself somewhat cobbled together with the last-minute addition of the *Yale Review* article on Proust. Ultimately, no aspect of her own work mattered less to Wharton, it appears, than her criticism; and even her most admiring critics and scholars seem content to follow Wharton's cue along these lines, continuing for the most part to overlook her essays and reviews while focusing ever more intently on her work in virtually every other mode. Judging from its reception, Wharton herself might have found it ironically appropriate that the woman who regarded the critical art as a male domain has barely survived, nearly sixty years after her death, as a literary critic.

II

Wharton's chronic uncertainties in this respect are nonetheless surprising, given the variety of subjects addressed in her critical writing and the fact that works of criticism, along with discursive writing of other kinds, played such a notable role in her formative early reading. Of the hundreds of volumes in "the kingdom of my father's library" (*BG*, 43), Wharton later recalled, "Those I devoured first were the poets and the few literary critics, foremost of course Sainte-Beuve," as well as Coleridge and Ruskin, but also including "Augustin Thierry and Philarète Chasles," Carlyle and Froude, and Schliemann and Kugler, along with essayists like Addison, Lamb, and Macaulay, among others (*BG*, 71, 67). The woman whose European childhood had introduced her to French, German, and Italian, who "ranged through four literatures" (*N*, 1085) with an older friend by the time she was thirteen, and who spent her adolescence studying Middle High German, Old Norse, and Anglo-Saxon (before turning to comparative philology, no less) could not have helped but develop a critical intelligence almost preternaturally acute.[21] Its adroitness is already discernible in what Viola Hopkins Winner describes as Wharton's three "sprightly mock reviews" of her own satirical novella, *Fast and Loose*; in them she reveals "an unusual sophistication and detachment" and adopts a "world-weary, waspish tone" that "amusingly parodies the style of American and English reviewers of the day."[22] A rather more earnest approach to criticism dates from around the same time: "When I was about fifteen or sixteen I tried to write an essay on English verse rhythms. I never got beyond the opening paragraph, but that came straight out of my secret wood. It ran: 'No one who cannot feel the enchantment of "Yet once more, O ye laurels, and once more," without knowing even the next line, or having any idea whatever of the context of the poem, has begun to understand the beauty of English poetry'" (*BG*, 70). Just the sort of effusive pronouncement that "Lycidas," or any one of a number of other English poems, might have drawn from a precociously literate fifteen-year-old of an earlier era,[23] it is unlikely to have been her only other attempt at critical writing among the countless poems, stories, sermons, and blank-verse dramas that Wharton remembered composing throughout her bookish youth.

Its topic, moreover, would continue to excite her critical attention, for poetry, "my chiefest passion and my greatest joy" (*BG*, 170) and "to me so august a thing that I always feel as if I should be struck by lightning when I sidle up to the shrine,"[24] became also the form to which Wharton often responded most strongly as a critic. Her correspondence, otherwise seldom critically revealing, shows how expansive and impassioned she could be in this regard, as in these comments from 1914 on a friend's second book of poems:

> Their great sincerity & directness are as striking as in the earlier volume, but it seems to me you have not quite avoided a certain monotony of rhythm in the longer ones, & especially that in blank verse. . . . The cultivation of the rhythmical sense is all the more important because there develops with it, undoubtedly, an acuter sense for the right word, right in sound, significance, colour—& also in expressiveness. The whole thing—all the complex process—is really one, & once one begins to wait attentively on the mysteries of sound in verse, the need of the more expressive word, the more imaginative image, develops also, & one asks more of one's self, one seeks to extract more from each sensation & emotion, & to distil that "more" into fewer & intenser syllables.

Betraying little of the hesitation that she would later express to Brownell, Wharton goes on to remark, "Please forgive my slipping into a treatise—but all these things 'me passionnent' so much (& more & more) that I can't help it!" (*L*, 314). And it is a sign of how enthralling she found such matters that most of her earlier essays and reviews are addressed, interestingly enough, to works not of fiction but of lyric or dramatic verse, while the last piece of her critical writing to be published turned out to be a preface to the anthology of English verse that she compiled with Robert Norton. Having received at sixteen a copy of "that stimulating work, Quackenbos's rhetoric, & . . . learned from it the difference between the forms of English (or rather Latin) verse" (*N*, 1092), Wharton remained, in Lewis's words, "a close student of poetic technique" (Lewis 237), and these early reviews display an ostentatiously (if, at times, rather pedantically) sound command of metrical conventions and complexities, as Wharton scolds the once popular dramatist Stephen Phillips for having "chosen to make his gods speak in rhymed pentameter, a doubtful vehicle for majestic speech," makes short work of Herbert Paul's qualifications as a critic of verse, and aligns herself with "[t]hose who refuse to test English verse by the rules of Latin prosody" in debating

the virtues of accentual as opposed to syllabic measurement. Already a devoted Whitmanite by this time, Wharton seems far more adventurous and
receptive in her thinking about verse than, say, in her later essays on the
novel, noting for example "that the average English critic is still afraid of
vers libre, still in bondage to the superstition of the Latin foot," or that "critics are still frightened when poetry ventures out of sight of rhyme, and even
rhymed irregular verse is looked upon as a hazardous experiment." The
writer for whom "the gift of precision in ecstasy" would later elegantly constitute "the best definition I can find for the highest poetry" (*BG*, 170) exhibits in her remarks on verse the same casual authority that she brings to the
discussion of fiction.

  After 1910, however, Wharton rarely again focused, as a critic, on poetry
or drama, and while the range and distribution of her interests at the time
are striking, the early reviews that are most informative, for us, are obviously
those in which she discusses novels or novelists. From the start, Wharton
numbered herself among those who have not only "attempted the art of
fiction" but "even considered it critically" ("Visibility in Fiction"). As she
would later put it in recalling her own literary emergence, "I had never
consciously formulated the principles of my craft, but during my years of
experimenting I had pondered on them deeply" (*BG*, 114), and perhaps
because she came to the medium relatively late, Wharton's criticism of fiction may be said to have begun with a set of convictions and axioms already
firmly established, along with a vocabulary that would remain essentially,
even dogmatically, intact throughout her career. Many passages in, say, *The
Writing of Fiction* or the later essays are essentially reformulations of, or
elaborations upon, various critical statements first enunciated two decades
earlier. The declaration, "All forms of art are based on the principle of selection," in "The Vice of Reading," or her remark, in the Hewlett review, that
"art is limited, is a compromise, a perpetual process of rejection and elision,"
initiates a persistent theme of Wharton's critical prose, while her observation that writers "could not now revert to the psychological novel of the
eighteenth century, with its action suspended in the void," because "[f]iction
has been enlarged by making the background a part of the action," antici-
pates one of the arguments with which *The Writing of Fiction* begins. Other
basic formal and historical distinctions around which her later essays revolve
are already at work in the most significant of Wharton's early critical works.
In reviewing Stephen's life of Eliot, for example, she wittily claims that its
subject "began to write at a time when the psychological novel, which . . .
preceded in England, as well as in France, the novel of incident, was disap-

pearing before the story with a 'plot'—the type of fiction wherein the adventure grows, not out of the development of character and the conflict of moral forces, but out of the recovery of a missing will or the concealment of somebody's parentage." Observing that Eliot's "plots are as easily detachable from her books as dead branches from a living tree," Wharton neatly encapsulates her later contention that "[t]he plots of Scott, Thackeray, Dickens, George Eliot and their successors are almost detachable at will, so arbitrarily are they imposed on the novel of character which was slowly but steadily developing within their lax support" (*WF*, 132).

Here, and throughout her essays and reviews, Wharton tacitly contrasts herself to the sort of critic who is "still much concerned with plot, that complicated and arbitrary combination of incidents which, in the English novel of the nineteenth century, replaced the absent logic of life," as she puts it in "The Criticism of Fiction," and which "[t]he critic of this school appears to regard . . . as something extraneous which may be fastened on to the author's subject like false hair, false teeth or any other artificial aid to loveliness." Having warned in "The Vice of Reading" that "the mechanical plot-extractor is fast superseding the critic" in the evaluation of fiction, Wharton later contests the definition of form "in either of the oddly limited senses in which the word is generally used by English-speaking critics; that is, either as an antithesis to subject or as something that subject puts on like an outer garment." Maintaining that "it is only by viewing the novel as an organic whole, by considering its form and function as one, that the critic can properly estimate its details of style and construction," an essay like "The Criticism of Fiction" would have played an estimable role in the promotion of an aesthetically serious and exacting approach to the novel, arguing not only that "design is inevitable" but that "the best art must be that in which it is most organic, most inherent in the soul of the subject." As Wharton declares in reviewing James's letters, "The rule of composition is, in short, never to be applied from the outside, but to be found in germ in each subject, as every vital principle of art must be," a postulate that recurs in "A Cycle of Reviewing," which maintains that "the only rules to be considered in art evolve from the inside, and are not to be applied ready-made from without." Again and again, Wharton insists upon this autotelic, self-generating nature of the literary work of art, from her remark in the 1922 preface to *Ethan Frome* that "every subject (in the novelist's sense of the term) implicitly *contains its own form and dimensions*" (EW's emphasis) to the familiar, and even more conclusive, stipulation in her memoirs: "Every short story, . . . like every other work of art, contains within itself the germ of its own particular form and dimensions, and *ab ovo* is the artist's only rule" (*BG*, 114). Such a rule ordains that "the first page of a novel ought to contain the germ of the whole" (*WF*, 51), just as "the conclusion of the tale should be contained in germ in its first page" ("The Criticism of Fiction"); indeed, "no conclusion can be right which is not latent in the first page," for "as every subject contains its own dimensions, so is its conclusion *ab ovo*" (*WF*, 108, 51). It is a formula that Wharton likes to find exemplified in her own work: "My last page is always latent in my first" (*BG*, 208). Under such a rule, moreover, "It is always a necessity to me that the note of inevitableness should be sounded at the very opening of my tale" (*BG*, 204), not unlike the "quality of dramatic inevitableness" that she cited early on when reviewing plays, or what she once described as one of the more striking attributes of a particular Italian garden: "There is a quality of inevitableness about it—one feels of it, as of certain great verse, that it could not have been otherwise" (*IVG*, 132). The basic rule formulated in Wharton's criticism also embraces other aspects of narrative—say, its tone or language. "As every tale contains its own dimension," she again maintains, "so it implies its own manner, the particular shade of style most fitted to convey its full meaning" (*WF*, 114), a synthesis that corresponds, as Wharton puts it in reviewing Herbert Paul's study of Arnold, to "that which makes the peculiar structural beauty of a sonnet—the simultaneous rise and break of the wave of thought and rhythm."

The pervasive organicism clearly shaping Wharton's temperament as a critic thus informs her understanding not only of fiction but of verse and drama as well, and also of the plastic arts, as the various critical remarks embedded here and there in her better-known works on travel, architecture, and landscape gardening share the language, along with the aesthetic princi- ples, of her literary criticism. One could say that Wharton's discursive prose, whatever the mode, itself constitutes a unified whole, and that works like *The Decoration of Houses* or *Italian Backgrounds* borrow a good deal of light, and indeed cannot be fully understood apart, from the organicism of her critical writings. "There is hardly a way of controverting the axiom," as Wharton puts it elsewhere, "that thought and its formulation are indivisible" (*MF*, 177–78), while she finds in considering the poems of her friend George Cabot Lodge that, "as with his blank verse, so in the metric of his sonnets, the beauty of form grew with the growing richness of content." With such a firm grasp of these essential interrelationships, Wharton can argue, in "The Vice of Reading," that "to speak as though the analysis of a book were one kind of criticism and the cataloguing of its contents another," in the manner of so many reviewers, "is a manifest absurdity," while she can later deplore, even more sternly than arbitrary contrivances like plot, "the purely artificial necessity of the double plot . . . in which two separate groups of people were concerned, sometimes with hardly a link between the two, and always without any *deep organic connection*" (*WF*, 81; my emphasis). To establish just such a link, in other respects, was in fact the primary challenge that Wharton herself later remembers confronting in an early work like *The House of Mirth*, where "my trouble was that the story kept drawing into its web *so many subordinate themes* that *to show their organic connection with the main issue*, yet keep them from crowding to the front, was a heavy task for a beginner" (*BG*, 207; my emphasis). Nor is this sort of organically generated cohesiveness required only of fiction. Just as the distant setting of a historical novel like *The Fool Errant* "makes it necessary that every stroke should be subordinated to the effect of the mass" in which "individual characters become . . . parts of the general composition," so "every subordinate character is a necessary link in the chain of action" in Shakespeare's "dramas of passion" (according to "The Three Francescas"), and so any "fanciful element" in architectural design is "always strictly subordinated to some general scheme of composition" (*DH*, 168). Despite its attempt "to weave a number of episodes from the Odyssey into a dramatic form," one of the Stephen Phillips plays reviewed by Wharton "remains rather a series of more or less dramatic incidents than a dramatic whole," just as "there is no satisfying whole" for Wharton in most of Arnold's sonnets, while "the scattered graces" of Lodge's earlier verse "were more often knit into a homogeneous whole" in his last poems.

The overriding value that she obviously attached to this sort of organic wholeness throughout her critical prose, and in her discussion of her own work, doubtless reflects the profound impact on Wharton's sensibility of certain nineteenth-century critical traditions represented in much of her early reading. More immediately, however, her stress on such a value arises out of another revealing gender-based distinction that permeates Wharton's thinking on various formal matters, a distinction that she employed in 1907 in a now familiar letter to her friend Robert Grant, who had commented favorably on *The Fruit of the Tree*: "The fact is that I am beginning to see exactly where my weakest point is.—I conceive my subjects like a man—that is, rather more architectonically & dramatically than most women—& then execute them like a woman; or rather, I sacrifice, to my desire for construction & breadth, the small incidental effects that women have always excelled in, the episodical characterisation, I mean. . . . I am very glad, though, that you *do* feel a structural unity in the thing" (*L*, 124). It is surely no accident that Wharton, in assuming the role of critic, should have espoused such a division of imaginative labor, focusing on those formal properties that she associated, just as closely as the writing of criticism itself, with the opposite sex. Both as a critic and as a practicing novelist, Wharton is far more attracted to the "architectonically" than to the "episodically" conceived and constructed work, whether she is discussing in her tribute to Lodge "the balanced architecture of the sonnet" and "[i]ts structural severity," or admiring "those [poets] most distinguished for the mastery of the recalcitrant form," as she puts it in the essay on Eugene Lee-Hamilton, or analyzing the merits of her own first novel: "'The Valley of Decision' was not, in my sense of the term, a novel at all, but only a romantic chronicle, unrolling its episodes like the frescoed legends on the palace-walls which formed its background; my idea of a novel was something very different, something far more compact and centripetal, and I doubted whether I should ever have enough constructive power to achieve anything beyond isolated character studies, or the stringing together of picturesque episodes" (*BG*, 205). One derives a powerful sense of the urgency that she brought to such critical and aesthetic questions from a letter in which she declares to Brownell, who had complimented her on *The House of Mirth*, "the whole thing strikes me as so loosely built, with so many dangling threads, & cul-de-sacs, & long dusty stretches, that . . . your seeing a certain amount of architecture in it rejoices me above everything—*my theory of what the novel ought to be is so exorbitant*, that I am always reminded of Daudet's 'Je rêve d'un aigle, j'accouche d'un colibri [I dream of an eagle, I give birth to a hummingbird]'" (*L*, 94–95; my emphasis). Whether or not her work falls quite so badly short of her own aspirations, few earlier American writers would have spoken in such an exalted way of the possibilities and potential of the form or associated the "exorbitance" of such a theory with its emphasis on "constructive power," "structural unity," and "architecture" as basic desiderata in the writing of novels.

III

That she entertained such a theory, or reflected theoretically on the novel to any great extent, is hardly a commonplace of Wharton scholarship, which has remained for the most part psychologically or biographically oriented, or inclined to approach her thinking on the novel more by way of, say, her travel books or writings on architecture and interior design. Yet Wharton's critical prose makes even clearer something that should go without saying, and indeed is more often left unsaid, in the study of her work: that Wharton came both to the writing and to the criticism of fiction, to what she called "the newest, most fluid and least formulated of the arts" (*WF*, 3), with an inveterate, highly developed formal awareness still relatively rare among American and English critics at the time she began her career. As she declares in "The Criticism of Fiction," it is "the possession of the sense of technique . . . of the necessity of form" that marks not only "[t]he fundamental difference between the amateur and the artist" but also a corresponding difference between the untrained and the trained critic, of whom Wharton adds that, "above all, he must have a sense of form; form in fiction and form in his criticism of it." Nor, again, is this demand restricted to the literary critic, or this distinction to the practice of literary criticism; indeed, her earliest review finds in the Blashfields' *Italian Cities* "an admirably drawn contrast between the critical standpoint of artist and amateur," much to the advantage of the former, that "might well be written up in every critic's laboratory." The artist's is certainly the "critical standpoint" adopted by Wharton, and its subscription to "the sense of technique" and of "the necessity of form" remained an essential piece of equipment in her own "laboratory" as a critic. As she put it in responding to a friend's book of poems, "You know I think criticisms of technique are the only useful ones" (*L*, 314), and in an attempt to overcome "[t]he distrust of technique" that she later detected in the work of her younger contemporaries and to dispel certain misplaced assumptions about the putative dangers of technical proficiency, Wharton asserts, "In the case of most novelists, such thought as they spare to the art, its range and limitations, far from sterilizing their talent will stimulate it by giving them a surer command of their means. . . . If no art can be quite pent-up in the rules deduced from it, neither can it fully realize itself unless those who practise it attempt to take its measure and reason out its processes" (*WF*, 118–19). As late as 1928, in "A Cycle of Reviewing," she remains "persuaded that all artists should be interested in the processes of their art, if not articulately, as the French are, yet at least inwardly, cogitatively, with the desire that some one who *is* articulate should try to divine and formulate the principles stirring in them."

For Wharton, as she had put it a couple of years earlier in *The Writing of Fiction*, "Henry James was of this small minority" of writers critically "articulate" enough to carry out such a task, and indeed "almost the only novelist who has formulated his ideas about his art" (*WF*, 117, 44–45). Part of the great value of her critical prose lies in the way that it freshly illuminates the still vexing question of the literary relationship between Wharton and James, while allowing us to follow—through her extended, complex engagement with his authority—the evolutions of Wharton's own thinking on many of the formal issues with which he had already become associated. "On the subject of technique," she would later recall, "I have found only two novelists explicitly and deeply interested: Henry James and Paul Bourget," each of them favorably contrasted on that basis to someone like Hardy, who "seemed to take little interest in the literary movements of the day, or in fact in any critical discussion of his craft" (*BG*, 199, 216). Not surprisingly, her review of the Lubbock selection of his letters—in which "Henry James continually stated and re-stated his theory of composition" and in which readers "will find a clearer and more accessible, if less deeply reasoned, compendium of his theory" than in the prefaces to the New York Edition—is her longest and most substantial such exercise on a single writer. While many passages from the first and largely anecdotal section of her review ("The Friend"), as later incorporated in *A Backward Glance*, are among the most famous of Wharton's remarks on James, the other, less familiar section ("The Man of Letters") consists of an unusually judicious and penetrating appraisal of the novelist's aesthetic. Distinguishing James from his Anglo-American predecessors and contemporaries, Wharton initially advances the sort of exaggerated claim that typified the early cult of the "Master." For Wharton, as for a disciple like Lubbock, "The writing of fiction was still, when his career began, an unformulated art in English-speaking countries," and where "the great question of form" is concerned, "it had not yet dawned upon English-speaking novelists that a novel might be anything other than a string of successive episodes," as opposed to the sort of "organic whole" promoted so often in her own critical work. "Only in France, and among men but slightly his elders," her version of this by-now-familiar critical narrative continues, "had an attempt been made to define the story-teller's main purpose and guiding principles, to enlarge and to define his field"; regarding James's leadership of this Copernican revolution in criticism of the novel, Wharton maintains, "It was one of his profound originalities to feel, and to illustrate in his own books, the three-dimensional qualities of that rich art which had hitherto . . . been practised in the flat." In Wharton's elegant reformulation, "two things were essential" to what she calls "the application of the new method" in fiction, "the choice of a central situation, and of what might be called centripetal incidents." In other words, "the tale must be treated as a stellar system, with all its episodes revolving . . . round a central *Reason Why*" (EW's emphasis). For James, "The way of attaining this centralised vision is . . . to select, among the characters of a projected novel, a reflecting consciousness." Here Wharton invokes the famous Jamesian principle of "point of view," through which he manages to avoid what she will later call, in expatiating on his methods, "the slovenly habit of some novelists of tumbling in and out of their characters' minds, and then suddenly drawing back to scrutinize them from the outside as the avowed Showman holding his puppets' strings" (WF, 89).

Unlike James, those novelists who indulge in such a "slovenly habit" are incapable of cultivating "the objective faculty," as Wharton elsewhere calls what remained for her the supreme virtue of a work of fiction, one "which sets apart the born novelist from the authors of self-confessions in novelform. . . . The subjective writer lacks the power of getting far enough away from his story to view it as a whole and relate it to its setting" (WF, 78). Indeed, on such terms, "the autobiographical tale is not strictly a novel," according to Wharton, "since no objectively creative effort has gone to its making" (WF, 78), while a large part of what makes the Anglo-Russian writer William Gerhardie's first novel so successful, and one of the reasons she was eager to sponsor it, is that "he has . . . enough of the true novelist's 'objectivity' to focus the two so utterly alien races to which he belongs . . . to sympathize with both, and to depict them for us *as they see each other*, with the play of their mutual reactions illuminating and animating them all." A particular strength of one of Lodge's poems, along these lines, is the fact that its protagonist "is a version of the poet's own personality, but a new version, and one rendered *from the outside*," in the kind of salutary self-objectification that benefits any imaginative work: "This power of dissociation, and the ability to project one['s] self far enough for the other to focus it, is the very mainspring of the dramatizing faculty; for to draw one's neighbour is a much easier business than to draw *one's self as seen by one's neighbour*" (EW's emphasis throughout). In no form, however, was such a faculty so valuable (because, traditionally, so rare) as the one in which Wharton herself most often worked. As she declared to Grant, in praising his novel *Unleavened Bread*, "I am so great a believer in the objective attitude that I have specially enjoyed the successful use you have made of it; your consistent abstinence from comment, explanation & partisanship, & your confidence in the reader's ability to draw his own conclusions" (L, 40).

It is on this "objective faculty," and on the accompanying technical strategies through which such a faculty manifests itself, that the artistry of the novel rests for Wharton. In honoring those writers, like James, for whom "the novel was always by definition a work of art, and therefore worthy of the creator's utmost effort" (WF, 89), and in explicating James's aesthetic by way of so many passages from his letters, Wharton seeks to combat what she calls "an inveterate tendency on the part of the Anglo-Saxon reader to regard 'feeling' and 'art' as antithetical." On such grounds, she argues, "[a] higher sensibility is supposed . . . to inhere in artless effort," while "every creative writer preoccupied with the technique of his trade—from grammar to syntax to construction—is assumed to be indifferent to 'subject,'" or "is nowadays accused," as Wharton later added, "of being absorbed in technique to the exclusion of the supposedly contrary element of 'human interest'" (WF, 9). In what she had once called the "critic's laboratory," such an attitude toward "the sense of technique" and "of the necessity of form" belonged to the "untrained critic" and thus to the amateur in both art and criticism, as opposed to an artistically and technically trained critic and novelist like James.

Eventually, however, James himself becomes the writer whom Wharton charges, more than anyone else, with precisely this sort of "absorption" in technique. By the time she reviewed his letters, Wharton had already grown uncertain about the Jamesian method itself, suggesting, for example, that "Henry James, as his years advanced, and his technical ability became more brilliant, fell increasingly under the spell of his formula," which "became an inexorable convention" instead of an enabling formal discovery. As if to hold at arm's length the accomplishment of a writer with whom she had seen her own work habitually compared, Wharton places James in a demystifying (if inevitably diminishing) perspective, later including him among those writers who "consciously lay down rules, and in the search for new forms and more complex effects may even become the slaves of their too-fascinating theories," and who thus remain "the true pioneers, who are never destined to see their own work fulfilled, but build intellectual houses for the next generation to live in" (WF, 117). A member of that generation, and an occupant of one of those houses, Wharton delicately positions herself with respect to James by writing as a grateful yet not uncritical successor and beneficiary, while her carefully pondered assessment of his innovations and eccentricities reflects both a debt and a firm resistance to James's dominating example.

Paradoxically, the very grounds on which she set him apart in 1920 from other English and American novelists had already provided the basis of Wharton's strongest objections, as expressed fifteen years earlier in her review of Belchamber, the novel by their friend Howard Sturgis. "Form is much—so much that, to the plodder through the amorphous masses of Anglo-American fiction, it seems sometimes all in all," as it did to a formally conscious novelist like James, and often to Wharton herself; "but when it is the mere lifeless reproduction of another's design," she adds, ". . . it is of no more artistic value than any other clever reproduction." Here Wharton appears to reconsider, or at least to modify drastically, her own emphasis on form and technique, perhaps reflecting "a defensiveness," as Millicent Bell suggests, "that surely had grown out of the personally-felt challenge of James's ordered art" (243), but also challenging in turn what she came to think of as the devitalized orderliness of Jamesian narrative. Detecting "faults of construction and perspective, such as the hack writer would easily have avoided," Wharton seems to elevate a very different and even less tangible element, as she argues that *Belchamber* "has, above all, . . . *something of the desultoriness, the irregularity, of life caught in the act*, and pressed still throbbing between the leaves of the book," by implicit contrast to the work of James, about whom she would later eloquently observe that, "though I greatly admired some of the principles he had formulated, such as that of always letting the tale, as it unfolded, be seen through the mind most capable of reaching to its periphery, I thought it was paying too dear even for such a principle to subordinate to it *the irregular and irrelevant movements of life*" (*BG*, 190; my emphasis throughout).

The similarity of the language in these two passages, written thirty years apart, is no accident, for Wharton seems to have composed her review partly in an effort to answer, and to dispute, James's own response to *Belchamber* as well as the assumptions underlying his response. After "Henry James . . . pointed out with some truth that Howard had failed to utilize what should have been his central effect, and privately pronounced the book old-fashioned and feebly Thackerayan," Sturgis "was unduly distressed," as Wharton later recalled the episode, "and it was in vain that I pointed out how foolish it was to be discouraged by the opinion of a novelist who could no longer judge impartially any novel not built according to his own theories" and who "was himself so engrossed in questions of technique and construction . . . that very few 'fictions' (as he called them) but his own were of interest to him" (*BG*, 234–35, 180). His comments, as recorded in letters to Sturgis, are in fact a good deal milder than one would guess from either her account or their friend's reaction, but they appear to have verified for Wharton a distinction that gathers increasing force in her assessments of James's formal preoccupations and in her critical writing as a whole. As a result of her gradually deepening ambivalence toward the Jamesian aesthetic, Wharton reverses the priorities under which she celebrated James in her 1920 review, ultimately restoring the "element of 'human interest'" to which

"technique" is "supposedly contrary" in the eyes of untrained, amateurish
readers or critics. "I was naturally much interested in James's technical theories and experiments," Wharton later claimed, "though I thought, and still
think, that he tended to sacrifice to them *that spontaneity which is the life of
fiction*" (*BG*, 190)—a familiar mystification of the imaginative process in
which she had already managed to implicate James himself, remarking in
her review of the letters that, "however much Henry James, toward the end
of his life, formalised his observance and disciplined his impulses ... he
continued, to the end, to take the freest, eagerest interest in *whatever was
living and spontaneous* in the work of his contemporaries" (my emphasis
throughout). It seems difficult to reconcile "spontaneity," conventionally
defined as a primary sign of "life" and "liveliness" in fiction, with any of those
other properties ("selection," the "sense of form," the "subordination" of
individual elements to the "design" of a "general composition") elsewhere
required of novelists and critics alike in Wharton's own critical writing.
"Technique" and "human interest," "art" and "feeling," "design" and "spontaneity" do indeed remain contrarieties for Wharton, who seems to have
softened, when confronted with its results in the work of a writer like James,
her own most cherished formal preference as a novelist: "As he became
more and more preoccupied with *the architecture of the novel* he unconsciously *subordinated all else to his ever-fresh complexities of design*, so that
his last books are magnificent projects for future masterpieces rather than
living creations" (*WF*, 117; my emphasis throughout). As if to dilute her own
earlier contention that "design is inevitable," Wharton in her memoirs rec-
ommends discarding "the incubus of an artificially pre-designed plan," declaring that, in works of James's so-called major phase, "Everything ... had
to be fitted into a predestined design, and design, in his strict geometrical
sense, is to me one of the least important things in fiction" (*BG*, 115, 190).

Having maintained that "all artists should be interested in the processes
of their art" and "should try to divine and formulate the principles" of their
craft, Wharton thus succumbs, nearly as often, to the assumptions of "inartistic" readers, falling on the other side of the divide artificially separating
"technique," or theoretical reflection on such matters, from "human interest" and the "higher sensibility" supposedly "inher[ing] in artless effort."[25]
According to *The Writing of Fiction*, "General rules in art ... are necessary
for the sake of the guidance they give, but it is a mistake, once they are
formulated, to be too much in awe of them" (*WF*, 42), as James ultimately
was, in Wharton's eyes. The critic and novelist who once claimed to espouse
so "exorbitant" a "theory of what the novel should be" nonetheless con-

cluded, in reviewing James's letters, that "no reader who takes the theories of a great artist too literally is ever likely to surprise his secret." The artist's "secret," like the image of "the secret garden" that Wharton associated with the source of her creative life, is not to be confused with "the theories," no matter how "exorbitant" they might be, of any writer. On the basis of the various gender-oriented distinctions that appear to have governed her thinking on these matters, Wharton in the "male" role of critic eventually exchanged the "architectonic" and the "technical," also defined as "male," for a more mystical realm culturally identified with her own sex. With this conflicting emphasis on "secrecy" and the ineffable, it may well be said that Wharton "retreats into oracular utterances," if not quite "in all her discussions of technique," as one scholar has argued,[26] certainly in the passage in which she later distinguishes the prefaces to the New York Edition, as a novelist's account of his imaginative life, from her own very different attempt:

> Not a few painters have painted themselves at their easels, but I can think of nothing corresponding to these self-confessions in the world of letters, or at any rate of fiction, except the prefaces of Henry James. These, however, are mainly analyses of the way in which he focussed a given subject, and of the technical procedure employed, his angle of vision once determined. . . . What I mean to try for is the observation of that strange moment when the vaguely adumbrated characters whose adventures one is preparing to record are suddenly *there*, themselves, in the flesh, in possession of one, and in command of one's voice and hand. It is there that the central mystery lies, and perhaps it is as impossible to fix in words as that other mystery of what happens in the brain at the precise moment when one falls over the edge of consciousness into sleep. (*BG*, 198)

At the heart of the creative process, Wharton thus places a liminal, indefinable experience radically at odds, to say the least, with the ideal of conscious, wide-awake, deliberate craftsmanship generally promoted in her critical work. In an uneasy effort to harmonize such an ideal with her stress on this mysteriously self-animating power of a novelist's characters, Wharton confesses, "I do not think I can get any nearer than this to the sources of my story-telling," while nonetheless assuring us, "I can only say that the process, though it takes place in some secret region on the sheer edge of consciousness, is always illuminated by the full light of my critical attention" (*BG*, 204–5).

The "attention" of the "trained critic," unlike that of the "untrained" "amateur," is able to illuminate the creative process, as one recalls from some of her earlier statements, thanks to its "possession of the sense of technique" and "of the necessity of form"; in its cryptic hiddenness, however, the process evidently requires an additional source of light with which the "critical attention" awkwardly coexists in Wharton's understanding. According to one of her few categorical observations, "The analysis of the story-telling process may be divided into two parts: that which concerns the technique of fiction (in the widest sense), and that which tries to look into what, for want of a simpler term, one must call by the old bardic name of inspiration" (*BG*, 199). For Wharton, earlier maintaining that the "central difficulties" of form and structure could not be dismissed as "'purely technical' . . . even were it possible to draw a definite line between the technique of a work of art and its informing spirit" (*WF*, 86), these two engines of critical "analysis," and of creative action, are bound as indissolubly as "form" and "function" or "subject" and "manner." Elsewhere, however, it becomes clear which of the two ultimately commands her allegiances, occluding the light of critical analysis in which "the gist of the matter always escapes," as Wharton puts it in a famous phrase, "since it nests, the elusive bright-winged thing, in that mysterious fourth-dimensional world which is the artist's inmost sanctuary and on the threshold of which enquiry perforce must halt" (*WF*, 119). This sort of devotional, sacrosanct image of artistic essence obviously retained a considerable appeal for Wharton, competing with—and often displacing in value—the elements of technique and form without which the artwork, and any criticism of it, is otherwise inconceivable in her critical writing. As she applies rigorous, hard-nosed technical schema at one moment, while ethereally renewing the ancient mystique of "inspiration" at others, one senses Wharton hovering indecisively between these two candidates in trying to settle upon a primary originating agent of both imaginative and critical labor.

IV

"Form" and "function," technique and inspiration, "art" and "feeling"—the poles between which Wharton continually oscillated as a critic throughout her career could not be more familiar, or even commonplace, to the historian of criticism. In thus revolving around a set of perennial antitheses, her critical prose—if somewhat limited in its reach and not intellectually as adventurous as that of some of her contemporaries—nonetheless registers Wharton's tenacious, lucid observance of certain firmly held aesthetic principles.

If she resolved few of the many tensions in her own critical thinking, and if, in the words of one scholar, "she fails to formulate clearly a theory of the technique of fiction that balances her account of inspiration" (Vita-Finzi 27), those tensions remain fruitfully unresolved, reflecting not so much a confusion or impoverishment on Wharton's part as a conscientious, worrying inclination to revisit (if only, most often, to reassert) the premises on which she built her aesthetic.

Indeed, it seems in many respects an undeniable strength of Wharton's critical writing, when considered in toto, that it stubbornly defies classification, refusing to accommodate or to bind itself to any of the various reigning critical orthodoxies of her day. Its recurring paradoxes and often contradictory tensions also make Wharton difficult to place, however, as a critic in her own time. In the course of thirty years, she published reviews and essays in a wide variety of journals, both mandarin and popular, that more or less cover the spectrum of cultural opinion and taste during that period, from the venerable *North American Review* and *Quarterly Review* to mass-circulation newcomers like the *Saturday Review of Literature*, from established turn-of-the-century literary magazines like *Bookman* and *Scribner's* to the refurbished and liberalized *Yale Review* under Wilbur Cross. Nor is it easy, despite her obvious and reiterated admirations, to trace Wharton's credo to a single chief authorizing source. The autobiographer who would recall first coming upon "the few literary critics, foremost of course Sainte-Beuve" (*BG*, 71), in her father's library also referred in more than one essay to "Sainte[-]Beuve, probably the most acute literary critic who ever lived," and to "that master of all critics, Sainte-Beuve." Yet apart from an occasional reliance on vibrant biographical profiles or from the intriguing speculations that conclude Wharton's piece on George Eliot, there is little evidence that Sainte-Beuve's critical approach had any very lasting effect on her own. Once declaring to a friend, "Taine was one of the formative influences of my youth—the greatest after Darwin, Spencer & Lecky" (*L*, 136), and finding it "still broadly true that *la morale est purement géographique*," as she puts it in an early essay, Wharton nonetheless remarks early on to Brownell, in applauding one of his essays, "I specially enjoyed . . . your emphasizing that it is the temperament & *not* the environment that makes the artist,"[27] and her criticism generally bears little resemblance, on the whole, to Taine's famous deterministic method. While sharing its loftiness and urbanity, Wharton's critical work is happily free of the ponderous mannerisms that make so much of Brownell's prose no longer very readable today; in any event, her outlook—although close to his in tone and conviction—remained distant from the moralistically inclined New Humanist ideology with which Brownell was often associated. From the early essay in which she includes herself among "those who regard literature as a criticism of life" to later statements like her tribute to Brownell, Arnoldian cadences and formulas echo throughout her critical prose, significantly qualifying the aestheticism otherwise at the root of her outlook. At the same time, the work of a critic who would remember reading *Studies in the History of the Renaissance* "with such zest" (*BG*, 141) and who languidly alluded to it before the age of twenty in a youthful Swinburnian poem (Lewis 43), could not help acquiring a distinctly Paterian flavor, as in Wharton's emphasis on the importance of what she calls "the *illuminating incident*" (*WF*, 109) in fiction, or in the remarkably frank declaration with which she eulogized her friend Bayard Cutting, Jr., "Nothing so clarifies the moral sense as a drop of aesthetic sensibility," or in her stipulation that "the art of rendering life in fiction can never, in the last analysis, be anything, or need to be anything, but the disengaging of crucial moments from the welter of existence" (*WF*, 14). Much of the considerable interest of Wharton's hitherto unpublished "Fiction and Criticism" lies in its illustration of her resourcefulness and ingenuity in attempting, however inconclusively, to square the Arnoldian and Paterian ingredients of her critical thinking and to negotiate the conflict between the "moral" and "aesthetic" as categories of critical value.

Although prepared to handle the Jamesian method skeptically, as we have seen, Wharton's criticism also tacitly sustained his example, even as the anti-Jamesian reaction of the 1920s began to take hold in Anglo-American letters, by devoutly espousing a strict adherence, on the part of novelist and critic alike, to the canons and demands of form and technique. In its more doctrinaire form, however, this adherence prevented Wharton from entertaining, and perhaps even from comprehending, the formal experimentation of her younger contemporaries, as in the misleading connection that she draws between "stream of consciousness" and the naturalistic "slice-of-life," or in her even stranger characterization of fiction like Woolf's and Joyce's as a descendent of "that unhappy hybrid, the novel with a purpose," or in equally disparaging remarks on other writers as different as Lawrence and Katherine Mansfield. The displacement of "innovation" by "renovation," in a later essay like "Permanent Values in Fiction," as the phenomenon that "critics of any of the arts should surely remember" has the effect of neutralizing or disarming unfamiliar, threatening new departures in artistic expression; while her emphasis on "selection" as a formal necessity leads Wharton, around the same time, to conclude that "the novelists most in view reject

form not only in the structure of their tales but in the drawing of character,"
thus mistaking as formless the various new artistic forms, or the mutations
of inherited forms, emerging under the pressure of enormous widespread
cultural change. At the same time, however, Wharton was one of the first
writers in English to understand Proust's unique importance, and her pair
of essays—well received at the time—remains a highlight of early Anglo-
American response to his work. As Wharton herself acknowledged in more
than one essay toward the end of her career, "even great critics go notoriously wrong in judging contemporary art and letters," while even "Sainte[-]
Beuve . . . went hopelessly and almost invariably astray in trying to estimate
the work of his contemporaries." And, in any event, a writer capable of ap-
preciating Colette and Rilke, Yeats and *Spoon River Anthology*, Gide and
Huxley, Cocteau and *Vile Bodies* and *The Great Gatsby*, seems far from
wholly or indiscriminately unresponsive to the work of newer poets and
novelists of the time. Even so, one wishes that she had left more of a record,
in her obstreperous and intemperate later essays, of the diversity of her
tastes during the closing years of her career. Certainly, her impatience with
what she called "Freudianism & all its jargon" (*L*, 451) and her observation
in "The Great American Novel" (1927) that "the modern American novelist
is told that the social and educated being is an unreality unworthy of his
attention, and that only the man with the dinner-pail is human, and hence
available for his purpose," offer some sense of how unyielding Wharton
could be as a critic, while completely disengaging her work from two of the
most prominent and influential emerging critical developments of the age.

Several years later, Wharton would repeat this animadversion on "the
demand . . . that only the man with the dinner pail shall be deemed worthy
of attention" (*BG*, 206), while also regrettably complaining (in "Tendencies
in Modern Fiction") that "the younger novelists" in America "naturally incline to situate their tales among the least developed classes." Such remarks,
and others scattered throughout her later essays, remind us of how lightly
this American novelist regarded the writers of the literary tradition to which
she belonged. That she had immersed herself in that tradition is apparent
from an essay like "The Great American Novel" or from her contention,
regarding Brownell's *American Prose Masters* (1909), that "[t]he firmness
with which he situates his authors, withour fear or favour, exactly where
each belongs, makes the book unique in American criticism." As a contribution to the criticism of American literature, Wharton's own critical
prose, however, has decidedly little to offer, despite some tastes that would
have been unusually prescient at the time. It is striking, for example, to find

"Melville's 'Moby-Dick'" included among her current reading in a letter to Fullerton in 1911 (some years before its celebrated rediscovery), but dispiriting that Wharton should proceed to ask him, "Do you share my taste for Melville? I like him almost as well, & in the same way, as Borrow" (*L*, 238), or that Melville should later be made to represent "[t]he writer who sees life in terms of South-Sea cannibals" or *Moby-Dick* classed with *Rob Roy* and *Lord Jim* as examples of "'good yarns,' in the old sense of the tale of adventure."[28] To be sure, Melville is also leagued in "The Great American Novel" with Poe and Hawthorne, by contrast to their successors among American writers of fiction, for "instinctively choosing those scenes and situations which offered the freest range to their invention," while earlier Wharton had summed up her appraisal of her own literary heritage by declaring to Brownell that Poe and Whitman, "with Emerson, are the best we have—in fact, the all we have." Yet she rarely otherwise mentions any of those figures in print and had many censorious things to say about Hawthorne elsewhere in her correspondence with Brownell (qtd. in Lewis 236–37). The language in which she describes to Brownell her re-encounter with Emerson's works around 1909—astutely intuiting their impact on Nietzsche and finding herself "amazed at his facilities, and his clear cold amenity, flushing now and then like some beautiful bit of pink crystal"—offers a particularly enticing glimpse of the essay Wharton might have composed on such a figure (qtd. in Lewis 236).

One cannot help but notice also that the only American novelists on whom she spends an entire essay or review (Howard Sturgis and Henry James) both happened to be reassuringly Europeanized friends and that the only "American" work of fiction that she chose to review (*Belchamber*) is a novel of manners set in aristocratic England. Her sardonic reference, in "The Great American Novel," to what she calls "the tottering stage-fictions of a lavender-scented New England" dismisses out of hand the local-color school of the late nineteenth century, looking ahead to Wharton's more famous, and no less imperceptive, remark that she strove to depict in *Ethan Frome* a New England "utterly unlike that seen through the rose-coloured spectacles of my predecessors, Mary Wilkins and Sarah Orne Jewett" (*BG*, 293). Few today would mention *Unleavened Bread* and David Graham Phillips's *Susan Lenox* with *McTeague* as the "great American novels" at the turn of the century, however keen her additional remark that "their bitter taste frightened a public long nurtured on ice-cream soda and marshmallows." Indeed, those writers, like Dreiser and Sinclair Lewis, who extended the naturalistic strain that she admired in such works are the only prominent

American novelists of the next generation whom Wharton praises in her later essays. As she looked askance at Faulkner and T. S. Eliot, while publicly declaring that *Gentlemen Prefer Blondes* "is *the* great American novel" (qtd. in Lewis 468), Wharton's critical judgment on writers among her own compatriots, if often shrewd and irreverent, can be erratic, even whimsical, while her distance and increasing alienation from the United States had an even more deleterious effect on the critical prose than on the fiction (such as *Twilight Sleep* or the Vance Weston novels) of Wharton's last decade. Despite their titles, essays like "The Great American Novel" and "Tendencies in Modern Fiction" capture little of the variety and liveliness of American writing in the 1920s and 1930s. And, apart from a negligible reference to Van Wyck Brooks, her later criticism registers virtually no awareness of the extraordinary reclamation of a national literary tradition under way at the time, offering little more than alarmist caricatures of postwar critical dogma in the United States.

Part of the reason her views hardened and grew so inhospitable to the work of her younger contemporaries is that Wharton's sensibility underwent relatively little development in the course of her long career. One is startled to find many observations in her initial reviews and essays reappearing, almost verbatim, in critical statements of her later phase. Her remark, for example, about George Eliot in a 1936 interview ("If she hadn't gone to live with George Henry Lewes, and felt obliged in consequence to defend conventional morality, she might have been one of the greatest of English novelists") repeats in essence the assessment that Wharton first advanced over thirty years earlier in reviewing Leslie Stephen's biography.[29] Many of the same deviations from standard English usage attacked in a 1901 letter to the *New York Tribune* are cited again in both "The Great American Novel" and *A Backward Glance*. One of James's remarks on the French realists is paraphrased in 1905, in the Hewlett review, and then again in 1934 in "Tendencies in Modern Fiction," while *The Writing of Fiction* recycles (if slightly blunting) Wharton's dry quip, in "The Criticism of Fiction," about *The Way of All Flesh*, "which Samuel Butler had to keep unpublished for twenty years because it dealt with causes as well as effects." From her earliest set of reviews to her last few essays, Wharton's critical prose keeps drawing on the same limited fund of allusions and illustrative references—not only Madame de Sévigné on Racine and coffee or Mrs. Barbauld on "The Ancient Mariner" but the same favorite phrases from *Faust* and Balzac's review of *La Chartreuse de Parme*, the same few lines from Keats and Kipling and *Cymbeline*. Rather than reflecting a paucity of thought or insight, however, these recurring quotations emerge for Wharton as durable touchstones, culled from a vast breadth of erudition that ranges throughout her critical prose (particularly in the highly allusive earlier essays and reviews) from Montesquieu to Nietzsche, natural science to art history, Dante to Schopenhauer, the Elizabethan tragedians to the nineteenth-century Russian novelists, Thomas Nashe to Leopardi to Leconte de Lisle. Finally, as in her remark that "the scale of detail" in *A Village Romeo and Juliet* "is exactly commensurate with the beauty of subject and the tale has the careless completeness of a cloud or a flower" or that Keller's "style could expand to a fresco-like sweep or contract to the minute enamelling of tiny surfaces," or as in so many of the formulations in "The Criticism of Fiction" or the review of James's letters, the images through which she frequently conveys her judgments invariably reflect the elegance and incisiveness that typify Wharton's critical writing at its strongest.

To that extent, her exercises in criticism often carry an authority or weight that belie the tentativeness and conviction of inadequacy so often expressed in Wharton's letters to Brownell. And, whatever doubts and inhibitions might have surrounded her efforts to write as a critic, Wharton is rarely ambiguous or hesitant in addressing the nature and purpose of criticism itself. As "The Vice of Reading" flatly declares, anyone who "cares for any criticism . . . wants the only kind worthy of the name—an analysis of subject and manner," further asserting that whenever "the principle of selection . . . is held of no account in the sum total of any intellectual production, there can be no genuine criticism." The writer who once claimed, "[I]t is hard at this date to be patient with any form of artistic absolutism, with any critical criteria not based on that sense of the comparative which is the nineteenth century's most important contribution to the function of criticism" (*IB*, 182), had started out with an unequivocal notion of the capacities required of every critic. Recalling one of the pieces of advice that she had received early on from Walter Berry ("It is easy to see superficial resemblances between things. It takes a first-rate mind to perceive the differences underneath"), Wharton remarked toward the end of her life, "Nothing has ever sharpened my own critical sense as much as that" (*BG*, 117). And she found the sharpest sort of critical sense in a figure like Brownell, whom she regarded as "in all ways formed to compare and to choose, and above all to exercise that subtlest critical function of detecting differences where most observers see only a resemblance." A contemporary scholar, shaped by the very different pressures of an ever-more-minutely specialized intellectual culture, might find it chastening to come upon Wharton's assertion that "no great critic has ever been able to do with less" than what she places at "the beginning of William Brownell's art," the "sense of perspective, this power to comprehend and relate to each other different traditions and alien ideals." It was a power that Wharton had in mind when, many years earlier, she compared his essays on Ruskin and Arnold and observed, "To 'do' such different types equally well is to illustrate Arnold's own conception of the critic's qualifications."[30] No-where does Wharton pronounce her own ideal along these lines more clearly than in her remark that Brownell, as a critic, "achieved the difficult feat of setting up a standard which was classical without being academic," through which "the eagerest open-mindedness was combined with an un-wavering perception of final values." And she might have been defining the single primary attribute to which she herself aspired as a writer of criticism when she concludes her tribute by declaring, in a memorable phrase, that "[i]n all his writings" Brownell "showed his essential quality: enthusiasm guided by acumen. He could not have been so great a critic had he not had so generous a nature."

This sort of generosity, it must be said, is not necessarily the most conspic-uous trait of Wharton's own critical "nature," especially in the acerbic and truculent essays of her later phase. While an agility in moving among so many cultures and languages certainly gives her work that "sense of per-spective" and of "the comparative" that she found in Brownell's, Wharton the critic often seems more acute than enthusiastic, as likely to censure as to celebrate. Even when less than ingratiating, however, her criticism is nearly always a model of restraint and balance and does each of its subjects the justice of applying the sort of analytically precise and penetrating attention that seemed on the verge, in her eyes, of disappearing from Anglo-American letters. For all its serenity and Olympian detachment, Wharton demon-strates throughout her critical prose an abiding, even anguished concern with the state of criticism, both of literature and of the other arts. "Such catholicity of judgment," she asserted with an air of authority, for example, in reviewing *Italian Cities*, "has not always marked the English or American art critic." In 1902, the response to her first novel led her to declare that "American & English reviewers of fiction are . . . disinclined to recognize that novels may be written from a dozen different standpoints, & that the 'heart-interest' need not always predominate" (*L*, 59), while what she called in "The Vice of Reading," a year later, "the mechanical reader, by . . . his inability to distinguish between the means and the end" in the composition of a novel, "has misdirected the tendencies of criticism," according to Whar-ton, "or rather, has produced a creature in his own image—the mechanical critic." In a more prescriptive mode, Wharton could claim to Brownell, with regard to the opening of the Sudermann play that she had translated, "The reviews of Es Lebe certainly showed the lack of what Arnold called a public force of correct literary opinion,"[31] later maintaining in "The Criticism of Fiction" that "familiar axioms as to the necessary subjectiveness of criticism do not alter the fact that any criticism whatever implies references to a collective standard." By 1925, she was conscious of writing as a critic at a time of increasingly chaotic debate about the role both of fiction and of criticism, observing that "the conception of the art of fiction . . . has been unsettled by a series of experiments, each one too promptly heralded as the final and only way of novel-writing" (WF, 153), a remark on which she later elaborates in "A Cycle of Reviewing": "Certainly it would appear that in the last quarter of a century there have been more frequent changes of opinion, more contradictory attempts to set up new principles of fiction writing (and reviewing) than in the previous corresponding interval." Here, and in an essay like "The Criticism of Fiction," Wharton issues a plea for stability, order, and consensus amidst such turbulent fluctuations in taste and value. Complaining that "the criticism of fiction is practically non-existent in England and America," and vividly observing that "English-speaking criticism is in the ascidian stage, and throws out or retracts its blind feelers with the same indiscrimination of movement" as the "rudimentary contractions" of an insect, some of her most trenchant critical writings offer a sustained diagnosis of its shortcomings, which "all proceed from one fundamental deficiency: the absence of any clear notion as to how, and on what grounds, a work of fiction should be judged." As she offers some ways of establishing such grounds and advocates a scrupulous return to first principles, Wharton's criticism undertakes nothing less than a mission to reform, and to renovate, common critical practice in her own culture—not a role in which one often finds her cast in the biographical and scholarly record on her career.

Most striking of all, perhaps, is the degree of intellectual refinement and preparation that Wharton demands of criticism. In opposing not only everyday hack reviewing but also the dilettantish impressionism of Anglo-American belletristic writing, Wharton asks "when, in the short history of the art of fiction, has criticism of it, except in France, attained the point of being a regular and organized process of appraisal? When, in short, has it dealt with its subject with anything like the average consecutiveness and competence that the criticism of history, of language, or of any of the exact sciences is expected to display?" From the cosmopolitan perspective that she shared with James and Brownell, Wharton finds in France "a society where every sort of artistic creation has always been accorded the seriousness of attention that sport, politics, and finance monopolize in other countries," and where "some kind of critical criterion is in any case bound to form itself." Ever since she "first came to know . . . the French historians and literary critics of the day" (*BG*, 94), early in her married life, under the tutelage of Egerton Winthrop, Wharton remained intimately acquainted with the critical tradition in France. Recalling "the days when the *Revue de Paris* . . . rivalled (if it did not out-rival) the *Revue des Deux Mondes* in interest and importance," she later revealed, "I was lucky enough to be made welcome in the editorial groups of both reviews, and to be much invited out in those agreeable circles" (*BG*, 287).[32] Accordingly, for Wharton, "The principal difference" between criticism in the Anglo-Saxon world and in France "is that, in the latter country, the reviewer of fiction is expected to have as disciplined an acquaintance with his subject, its forms, its limitations and its history, as the critic, say, of history or of paleontology." Thanks not only to the example of Sainte-Beuve but to successors like Anatole France and Jules Lemaître, "French literary criticism" exhibits, in Wharton's eyes, "so rich a deposit and so high a standard" as to constitute, all by itself, "a sufficient plea for the cultivation of an art of criticism." The very fact that she can ask such questions and employ such language suggests a fairly elevated assumption, on Wharton's part, of what criticism should be and do, and her essays have much to say about what she calls "the critic's office, and his peculiar honour," about the value of "a systematically and intelligently exercised criticism," and about "the tradition that a work of art is something worthy of the attention of a trained intelligence."

Part of the reason she felt such an intelligence should be trained, or that a trained intelligence should be required of the critic, is that its attention is potentially so important and valuable to the work of art itself. Referring in 1928 to "the conviction of reviewers that they can enlighten novelists," Wharton agrees that "the reviewer should be as helpful to the author as to the reader"; earlier, in extending her entomological image of Anglo-American criticism, she claimed in "The Criticism of Fiction" that "[t]he chief reason" why criticism, "since it inevitably does throw its feelers out, . . . should be helped to develop them into finer instruments of precision" is the fact that "it will help the novelists themselves." Once again, Wharton borrows an instructive counterexample from across the channel, where "French literature is conscious of criticism, and has been modified by it, to a degree that no thoughtful French writer could seriously deny." Like that of "form" and "subject," or "technique" and "inspiration," another traditional dichotomy is hereby reexamined by Wharton, as in this compelling passage from "The Criticism of Fiction":

> It ought to be unnecessary to combat the strange dogma that criticism is of no service to the creative arts. Whether it is or not, however, is relatively unimportant, since, wherever creative artists exercise their art, and have an audience to react to them, criticism will function as instinctively as any other normal appetite. To discuss its usefulness is therefore as idle as it is perverse to regard it as a practice confined to a few salaried enemies of art. Criticism is as all-pervading as radium, and if every professional critic were exterminated to-morrow the process would still be active wherever any attempt to interpret life offered itself to any human attention.

The process would remain active simply because all serious creative artists—at every stage of their endeavor, and as a fundamental part of the process in which they are engaged—serve as their own most vigilant critics, for "the possession of the sense of technique" and of "a sense of form," the very attribute that fundamentally distinguishes "amateur" from "artist" in Wharton's critical lexicon, also "implies an ever-active faculty of self-criticism, and therefore a recognition of the need, and indeed of the inevitability, of criticism."

In what should be a truism of aesthetics but is more often denied in a critical tradition given over to the fetishizing of the creative imagination, Wharton thus reminds us of the ways in which the imaginative act is itself intrinsically and necessarily critical in function; or, put another way, it is ultimately the critical faculty that is primary and not the creative, which presupposes, and is indeed constituted by, that of criticism. Looking back on the reception of her own work, Wharton later points to this fundamental symbiosis when she maintains that "the novelist's best safeguard is to put out of his mind the quality of the praise or blame bestowed on him by reviewers and readers, and to write only for that dispassionate and ironic critic who dwells within the breast" (*BG*, 212). In a presumably deliberate echo of the line that she had quoted from *Faust*, years earlier, to describe George Eliot's divided sensibility ("Two souls, alas, do dwell within my breast!"), such an admonishment reflects the inevitable coexistence of creator and critic, and even the dependence of one upon the other, in the writer's imaginative life. For Wharton, criticism, inherent in any act of aesthetic expression, is itself also an aesthetically expressive form. And, perhaps more than anything else, her belief that the critical process is not only far from secondary but in fact essential to the creative process—along with her extension of its domain to other phenomena as well—should strike an unusually responsive chord among informed readers today. In a passage eventually deleted from her tribute to Brownell, Wharton notably elaborates on a remark about the ways in which one of Brownell's works enables the reader "to understand why the art of criticism has been called creative": "It is called so because, by selecting, comparing, & isolating the elements of the stuff on which it works, it re-creates the society, the book or the picture, pouring them into a new mould of thought and enriching them in the process. The critic who leaves a book or a social group exactly as he found it lacks the quality without which criticism can have no vital influence."[33] At a time when the preeminence and prestige of criticism remain major themes of contemporary intellectual discourse, the extraordinary cultural salience and power that she assigns the critical faculty, along with such an ardent faith in its transformative energies, should command for Wharton's critical prose more of the audience that her other works have enjoyed for so long.

V

Invited in 1921 by the *Literary Review* of the *New York Evening Post* "to write something for our columns," Wharton replied, "I welcome any attempt to establish a standard of serious literary criticism in America."[34] Evidently, however, she did not welcome the attempt strongly enough to participate in it, for nothing of Wharton's ever appeared in the journal, while she seems on many occasions to have felt, without acting upon, the urge to serve more frequently as a critic. At one point, in fact, she briefly considered serving as a critic on a regular basis: from Italy in 1903, having produced five reviews and essays in the space of eighteen months, she complimented Brownell on one of Scribner's new journals and asked, "[W]ould you like me to write a kind of monthly article for it, about books and general impressions? I have always thought I should like to try it for a few months." Although Brownell claimed to be "pleased at the offer," Wharton soon reconsidered it, explaining that she had "made that suggestion . . . in the large leisure of European days," as the press of resuming business at home—and perhaps a recurrence of the anxieties that she would later begin to share with Brownell—prevented her from developing this intriguing idea.[35] On the other hand, in addition to "act[ing] as an outpost of the *Yale Review*," as its editor recalled, "by sending in the names of men among her wide acquaintance in France who might be willing to write on current public questions," Wharton did contribute three articles from 1925 to 1929 and contemplated his suggestion of others on "the modern European novel" and on "modern French fiction."[36] Moreover, her abortive essays on Whitman and on the New York Edition were not the only attempts that Wharton either discarded or left unfinished,[37] while she also planned or pledged various critical works that never materialized. A year after publishing *The Age of Innocence*, for example, Wharton decided, as she put it in a letter to her sister-in-law, "I should write a preface for the next edition . . . stating my theory as to the writing of 'historical' novels, & the small importance of anachronisms" (*L*, 440); and her brief remarks on the subject in other letters, in her unfinished critical writings, in her review of *The Fool Errant*, and in *Italian Backgrounds* make one regret that Wharton never wrote such an essay. Enthusiastically rereading Trollope in 1930, she declared to Lapsley, "I want to write an article called 'Jane & Anthony'" (*L*, 527), while four years later she answered an invitation to present a paper to the Royal Society of Literature by proposing either Trollope or "Fiction and Pathology" as her subject, later deciding to combine them, rather improbably, into a talk entitled "Anthony Trollope, or Pathology and Fiction"; but nothing ever came of these or various other possibilities.[38] In 1935, withholding permission to reprint "Permanent Values in Fiction," Wharton declared through her secretary that "she is planning a book on fiction herself, where this article will be included."[39] No such book appeared, of course, for *The Writing of Fiction* would remain Wharton's only full-length work of literary criticism. Examining the manuscript of her devoted sister-in-law's unfinished memoirs, Wharton "even offered to contribute an introduction" but managed to write only a few sentences before her death.[40]

Not long afterward, Lapsley began to assemble, as her literary executor, a volume that he called "The Service of Letters: A Collection of Edith Wharton's Literary, Critical and Biographical Studies," deriving his title not only, as Goodman observes, from Wharton's description of herself as "a faithful servant of English letters" (in the introduction to the Davis & Davis adaptation of *Ethan Frome*) but also from the statement that her sister-in-law recited in accepting on her behalf the Gold Medal for Literature of the National Institute of Arts and Letters: "You say it is given in recognition of my services to Letters. I have tried to serve Letters all my life, and it is because I believe that the word service best expresses the true, the necessary, relation of the artist to his Art—with all that the word implies of faithfulness, application, reverence and devotion—that I am particularly happy in having my work designated in these terms."[41] Aiming for "a collection . . . which shows Mrs. Wharton indirectly as engaged in her own higher education and directly as training herself in the art of criticism by analysis and appraisal of current literature and later by discussion of the nature and theory of the art itself,"[42] Lapsley planned to include most of the miscellaneous uncollected essays and reviews that were available or known to him at the time. By 1943, he had arranged for its publication with Appleton-Century (Scribner's successor as Wharton's firm of choice during the second half of her writing life), secured the necessary permissions, and accumulated a mass of notes toward what might have proven to be a comprehensive but somewhat querulous introduction in which he claims, for example, that Wharton "disliked & disbelieved in metaphysics & deliberately I think left the fundamentals of her system of criticism unformulated."[43]

Lapsley's work, however, was far from complete by the time he died six years later, and with her reputation already in eclipse, Appleton-Century evidently chose to cancel the project, leaving unretrieved ever since one of the most rewarding and extensive portions of Wharton's achievement as a writer. Seldom anthologized or reprinted in any form since her death,[44] and typically omitted from the standard histories of twentieth-century criticism or of criticism of the novel, her scattered critical writings have been mentioned only in passing, with few exceptions, in the scholarship on her work, bypassed even by the remarkable recent, ongoing revival of interest in her career.[45] The powerful critical narrative that has more or less dominated Wharton studies since the reemergence of her work—casting her as a heroic figure mightily resisting the constraints of a stifling background and triumphantly forcing her way into expressiveness—has strangely neglected the very area in which Wharton's struggles as a writer are especially pronounced and poignant. While new editions of *The Decoration of Houses*, *Italian Villas and Their Gardens*, her travel books, and all of the novels of her long-forgotten later period have appeared at one time or another over the past fifteen years (along with juvenilia like *Fast and Loose*, an ample selection of her correspondence, and even the recently rediscovered journal of an early cruise), Wharton's critical prose continues to meet with an indifference and inattentiveness surprising in scholars otherwise so devoted to her work.[46] Indeed, it would be difficult to name an equally substantial body of critical work by another writer of her stature that has gone so conspicuously unnoticed for so long.

In any event, it is hard to predict or gauge the sort of response that her critical writings are likely to attract in the landscape of contemporary literary scholarship and opinion. To be sure, even those long familiar with her career will find a number of surprises in this material, which should present some welcome, if occasionally embarrassing, challenges to Wharton's enthusiasts of all ideological postures. Balzac, Austen, Stendhal, Thackeray, Meredith, Tolstoy, Proust—if, as she herself suggests in an early review, "[i]t is always more instructive to study a critic in his preferences than in his dislikes," then the roster of novelists to whom Wharton keeps reverting in her criticism is firmly, unexceptionably traditional or "canonical," and perhaps too routinely so for many academic scholars today. Those of us schooled to look upon figures in a novel as effects or constructions of language (ink-marks on a page awaiting vivification in the reader's mind) are likely to quarrel with Wharton's emphasis, in an essay like "Visibility in Fiction," on "the mysterious element which seems to possess, above all others, the antiseptic quality of keeping a novel alive" or her later emphasis on "the creating of characters which so possess us with the sense of their reality that we talk of [them] as of real people whom we have known and lived with," and to be disarmed by the quaintness of a critical mind capable of declaring, "The only novels that live are those whose characters the reader calls by name." Many of the least agreeable features of her later period—the deepening intolerance, the reactionary hauteur, the abrasive antimodernism—surface even more virulently in her critical work, while making immitigably explicit the regressive and rather unappetizing social preconceptions on which so much of Wharton's aesthetic judgment ultimately rests. Those Americanists still bravely endeavoring to restore a native line of homegrown critical thinking will justly recoil from the illiberal sentiments of her later work, having already received little encouragement from Wharton's abhorrence of progressive education, her flippant references to "William o' the wisp James" or to "all the psychological-pietistical juggling of which . . . W. James is the source & chief distributor" (*L*, 205, 101–2), and her approval of the opposing, anti-Emersonian strain of American thought represented by John Jay Chapman, Santayana, and others. Her description of Lewis's *Main Street* as "that pioneering work which . . . hacked away the sentimental vegetation from the American small town" or of an early George Eliot work as "appeal[ing] to the facile sentimentalism of the early Victorian public" should have a strange ring at a time when the sentimental tradition in the English and American novel continues to receive unprecedentedly serious critical attention.

These and many other remarks will create various additional difficulties for the effort (already awkwardly complicated by some recent disclosures)[47] to locate a genuinely feminist sensibility in Wharton's work. Of the novelists whom Wharton regularly cites as models or major figures, only two or three

(Madame de La Fayette, Austen, Eliot) are members of her own sex; in her review of the Stephen biography, Eliot's qualities are clearly preferred to "the spontaneity of Charlotte Brontë," whose novels, as Wharton remarks elsewhere, "now seem in some respects so romantically unreal" (*WF*, 63). In "Permanent Values in Fiction," she suggests that Emily Brontë, although "a woman of genius, . . . might have made, out of the daily stuff of life at Haworth, a greater and more deeply moving book than by picturing a houseful of madmen," while the same essay dismissively places Stowe and "Mrs. Gaskell" among "the pleaders of special causes." Should it come as a surprise, then, that the one earlier woman novelist to whom Wharton devotes an entire review essay (George Eliot) famously shared her own impatience with "silly novels" by "lady novelists" (and thus with another notable line of women's writing)? Long before she mourned, in her memoirs, "that ancient curriculum of house-keeping which, at least in Anglo-Saxon countries, was so soon to be swept aside by the 'monstrous regiment' of the emancipated: young women taught by their elders . . . to substitute the acquiring of University degrees for the more complex art of civilized living" (*BG*, 60), Wharton had begun an early essay by derisively attributing "the production of a new vice—the vice of reading" to "[t]he 'diffusion of knowledge' commonly classed with steam-heat and universal suffrage in the category of modern improvements"—not the only occasion on which she made public some of her privately expressed views on such divisive issues of her time. By the same token, however, her neoconservative apologists, eager to rescue Wharton from a putative ideologically motivated abduction on the part of certain contemporary scholars, are sure to be just as nonplussed by the astonishing retractions and concessions, in her previously untranslated tribute to Jean du Breuil, regarding the women's movement in Europe.

What should emerge, in other words, from this material, finally assembled in one place, is an Edith Wharton even more complex and mercurial than the figure with whom we have become so familiar in the past generation of scholarship on her work. Many of her most closely reasoned statements on writing and on the arts occur, as we have seen, in reviews and essays that have remained largely inaccessible to scholars. If it is true that a writer's accomplishment can be fully appreciated only in its totality, then we cannot say we know Wharton until this last remaining forgotten corner of her output is adequately presented and absorbed. And its availability should serve a larger additional purpose as well; however strongly she might have denied or disliked the idea, Wharton's work in literary and cultural criticism belongs to a sudden and rapidly increasing proliferation of discursive writing by women (not only Woolf or Vernon Lee, say, but also Rebecca West, Willa Cather, Elisabeth Luther Cary, and Ellen Glasgow, among others) in the first half of the twentieth century and thus claims an honorable position in what Susan Lanser and Evelyn Beck described, some years ago, as "the female critical tradition buried and obscured" by conventional Western literary histories.[48] And if the neglect of Wharton's critical prose, or indeed her own attitudes on this score, would appear to exemplify "the erasing of women from the 'official' versions of literary history" (Lanser and Beck 85), then it is one of the curious paradoxes of the Wharton revival that the remarkable feminist rehabilitation of her work, by persistently contributing to this neglect, should have the ironic effect of tacitly endorsing the preconceptions to which Wharton herself evidently assented regarding women as critics. Even in their ground-breaking essay, Lanser and Beck do not mention Wharton, although her critical work, as a whole, seems worthier than that of many women whom they do, and surely ranks among the most sophisticated and polished critical achievements by a woman up to her own time. Its reappearance should help foster what they call "an accurate picture of women's contributions to the study of literature" and redress "the omission of women's critical perspectives" from the history of criticism (Lanser and Beck 80, 81), while also recovering an important chapter in the rather disheveled history of American critical thought. It is not an exaggeration to say that, of her predecessors among leading American writers of fiction, only Poe or James or Howells produced a more voluminous body of distinguished critical work, or one of more lasting value, than Wharton. Persuaded that the critical art had no room for writers of her own sex, and yet struggling so often and so doggedly to express herself as a critic, Wharton occupies a considerable, if problematic and ambiguous, place in a tradition to which so many other previously muted voices have lately been restored.

NOTES

[1] EW to William Crary Brownell, 18 October 1924 (Amherst).

[2] EW to Brownell, 26 October [1902] (Amherst).

[3] For an account of this little-known episode in her career, see my "Edith Wharton and the Difficult Writing of *The Writing of Fiction*," *Modern Language Studies* 25 (Spring 1995): 60–79.

[4] EW to Henry S. Canby, 15 March 1934; to Wilbur Cross, 7 January 1929; and to H.G. Leach, 30 October 1928 (Yale).

[5] EW to Brownell, 2 November 1913 (Amherst).

[6] EW to Brownell, Monday night [1905] (her emphasis), 14 December 1924, and 18 October 1924 (Amherst). Brownell, for his part, could not have been more encouraging, if at times in unnecessarily colorful terms, as when he remarked, after reading Wharton's tribute to George

Cabot Lodge, "Is there any kind of composition, now, whose scalp is not at your belt—to speak of it unfeelingly as a mere piece of writing." As for "the Keller scrap," which she spoke of in such disparaging terms in apparently more than one letter, Brownell asked, "What was that deprecation of yours about awkwardness in tackling this sort of thing? How reconcile it with immediately 'going' and showing not only how it is, but how it ought to be, done?" (Brownell to EW, 28 December 1909 and 22 October 1913 [Yale]).

[7] Susan Goodman, *Edith Wharton's Inner Circle* (Austin: University of Texas Press, 1994), 22.

[8] "I have begun my article on Henry," she announced to Fullerton in May 1911, a year after his review had appeared, "but I have a very tired head & the inhalations are stupefying. So no great results" (*L*, 238).

[9] EW to G. F. J. Cumberlege, 4 June 1935 (Yale). Her recommendation is particularly striking, since she and Lubbock had been estranged for many years by that point.

[10] Indeed, a distinct evasiveness marks her initial approach to James, for Wharton's abandoned essay on the New York Edition was not the only occasion on which she might have discussed his work in print before reviewing his letters. Invited in 1902 to review *The Wings of the Dove* for the *Book Buyer*, Wharton "declined on the excuse of overwork," although she found time to publish other reviews that year; she added, "'I have always made it a rule not to review novels'" (qtd. in Benstock 142), although she would do so twice in 1905. Later, she averted what might have proved a far more intriguing possibility by declining Ezra Pound's request for a contribution to the August 1918 Henry James memorial issue of the *Little Review* (EW to Ezra Pound, 26 March 1918 [Yale]). When she finally brought herself to write about James publicly, it was the editor of the *Quarterly Review*, George Prothero, and not Wharton herself, characteristically, who suggested that she review Lubbock's edition of the letters.

[11] EW to Brownell, 17 October [1907] (Amherst).

[12] Kristina Straub, "Women, Gender, and Criticism," in *Literary Criticism and Theory: The Greeks to the Present*, ed. Robert Con Davis and Laurie Finke (New York: Longman, 1989), 857; Katherine Joslin, *Edith Wharton* (New York: St. Martin's, 1991), 43. On her general ambivalence with regard to writing and "the conditions of female identity," see, for example, Candace Waid, *Edith Wharton's Letters from the Underworld: Fictions of Women and Writing* (Chapel Hill: University of North Carolina Press, 1991), 3–14.

[13] EW to Violet Paget, 5 October [1907], in Hilda M. Fife, "Letters from Edith Wharton to Vernon Lee," *Colby Library Quarterly*, ser. 3 (February 1953): 143–44.

[14] According to one biographer, Wharton transcribed in her commonplace book Georges Faquet's description of Sand as "a distinguished woman who would have had the instincts of a thinker without the force to be one" (exhibiting "a love of ideas without the capacity to fully understand them") and wrote alongside it the comment, "applicable to any 'intellectual' woman" (qtd. in Benstock 163).

[15] What she called, in a letter to Berenson, "A really striking, brilliant yet impartial book on Mme de Maintenon [mistress of Louis XIV], by my friend . . . Mme St René Taillandier," was a doubly safe exception: its subject a woman famous for privately influencing a supremely powerful male figure and its author the niece of Hippolyte Taine, whom Wharton so admired, and the sister of André Chevrillon, "who is certainly now the first literary critic in France," as she had once characterized him to a friend. For obvious filial reasons, it would have been safe also, following the death of Charles Eliot Norton, to persuade Sara Norton, "I still think you should publish your father's letters, with an introduction, & a slight thread of narrative to string them on. . . ." (*L*, 434, 136, 166).

[16] Perhaps forgivably making allowances, however, for those whose reviews of her own work she found perceptive; in response, for example, to Catherine Gilbertson's 1929 article, which she recommended for publication, Wharton wrote to the editor of the magazine in which it appeared that "the author has sound principles of criticism & a real desire to get at the inner

significance of the works she is reviewing" (EW to *Century*, 25 November 1929 [Yale]). Fullerton's cousin, Katherine Fullerton Gerould, published around 1922 a brief overview of her fiction that Wharton considered "'an admirable piece of literary criticism,'" suggesting that its
author "include it in a volume of essays"; even here, though, Wharton could be grudging, as in
her remarks on Gerould's earlier review of *Glimpses of the Moon* in the *New York Times*: "'it
was I who sent her first ms. to Mr. Scribner, and called his attention to the literary promise
which she already gave. So you see I deserve a good word from her'" (qtd. in Lewis 445).

[17] Edith Wharton, Synopsis of "Love among the Ruins," MS (Yale), 2.

[18] Many other examples come to mind. Note how, in "The Descent of Man" (1904), Professor
Linyard's foray into popular-science writing, *The Vital Thing*, "had been given to the *Inves-
tigator*'s 'best man'" for review, after which "the other journals followed, finding it easier to let
their critical man-of-all-work play a variation on the first reviewer's theme" (*CS*, 1: 357). Professor Clyde, in "The House of the Dead Hand" (1904), commissions his friend Wyant to bring
from Siena a description of a privately owned Leonardo, saying, "I want badly to use it in my
monograph on the Windsor drawings" (*CS*, 1: 507). In search of "certain details necessary for
the completion of his book: 'The Art of Horace Fingall,'" Willis French visits the painter's
widow in "The Temperate Zone" (1926), only to find her remarried to Donald Paul, "a not
especially rising young barrister, who occupied his briefless leisure by occasionally writing
things for the reviews," who "had written an article about Mrs. [Emily] Morland" and who,
"when, soon afterward, he happened to meet her, . . . had suddenly realized that he hadn't
understood her poetry in the least, and had told her so and written another article—under her
guidance, the malicious whispered" (*CS*, 2: 450, 456). As in the Vance Weston novels, criticism
and romantic intimacy are frequently intertwined in this way, while the male critic is not always
necessarily placed in a positive light. By arriving at a belated realization of her husband's mediocrity as a painter, even Claudia Keniston in "The Recovery" (1901), for example, is favorably
contrasted to a "Professor Wildmarsh," who "was the first critic to publish a detailed analysis of
the master's methods and purpose," and whose article, which ironically deepens Claudia's initial interest in Keniston, "was illustrated by engravings which . . . were declared by Professor
Wildmarsh to give but an imperfect suggestion of the esoteric significance of the originals" (*CS*,
1: 260). In "Writing a War Story" (1919), Ivy Spang, author of a volume of sentimental poems,
"was honored by an article by the editor of *Zigzag*, the new 'Weekly Journal of Defiance,' in
which that gentleman hinted . . . that their esoteric significance showed that she was a *vers-
librist* in thought as well as in technique" (*CS*, 2: 359). The narrator of "The Verdict" (1908), a
friend of the painter Jack Gisburn, mentions "little Claude Nutley, who, in all good faith,
brought out in the Burlington a very handsome 'obituary' on Jack—one of those showy articles
stocked with random technicalities" (*CS*, 1: 655). More dilettantish yet are figures like Paul
Dastrey in *A Son at the Front* (1923), "whose utmost adventure had been an occasional article
in an art review" (*SF*, 10), or Stanley Heuston in *Twilight Sleep* (1927), who "dabbled in literary
reviewing" (*TS*, 210). Most sinister of all is Culwin, the aimless undisciplined aesthete in "The
Eyes" (1909), who recalls that he once "decided to write a great book—I forget about what," and
that he later "settled in Rome—where I was planning . . . to write another great book—a definitive work on Etruscan influences in Italian art" (*CS*, 2: 118, 123).

[19] The passages about Frenside and Berry are juxtaposed by Janet Goodwyn, in a discussion
of Wharton's abandoned earlier novel "Literature," in *Edith Wharton: Traveller in the Land of
Letters* (New York: St. Martin's, 1990), 113, while Gloria Erlich finds Berry "touchingly portrayed as the faithful witness of Halo Tarrant's life, Frenside" (*The Sexual Education of Edith
Wharton* [Berkeley: University of California Press, 1992], 151); at the same time, Frenside's role
in the growth of Vance Weston is just as pronounced, while his views and attitudes seem
obviously close to Wharton's.

[20] "The Great American Novel" reappeared a year after its initial publication, in *Mirrors of
the Year: A National Revue of the Outstanding Figures, Trends and Events of 1927–8*, ed. Horace

Winston Stokes (New York: Stokes, 1928), 159–70. Wharton's eulogy of Brownell later led off a privately distributed collection, *W. C. Brownell: Tributes and Appreciations* (New York: Scribner's, 1929), 3–15. The editors of the *Saturday Review of Literature* promptly included "Tendencies in Modern Fiction" in *Designed for Reading: An Anthology* (New York: Macmillan, 1934), 37–42. Finally, "The Writing of *Ethan Frome*," already partly incorporated into *A Backward Glance*, was reprinted in *Breaking into Print*, ed. Elmer Adler (New York: Simon & Schuster, 1937), 189–91. "The Sonnets of Eugene Lee-Hamilton" was briefly excerpted in *The Mosher Books* (Portland, Maine: Thomas B. Mosher, 1908), 19.

[21] Remarking upon "that critical discernment so early developed in her nature," Wharton's friend Sara Norton noted, in a 1906 record of some of their conversations, "She once said to me, 'Oh! you know I was born with critical spectacles on my nose'" ("Notes about E.W.'s Early Life: Things She Has Told Me" [Yale]).

[22] Viola Hopkins Winner, introduction to *Fast and Loose*, by Edith Wharton (Charlottesville: University Press of Virginia, 1977), xv. The ghostwritten reviews, "supposedly from the *Saturday Review*, the *Pall Mall Budget*, and the *Nation*," appear on 117–21.

[23] Wharton might have been recalling this youthful effort when she asserted, years later, in an unpublished essay, that in order "to produce the thrill" of fine poetry "there must be the rhythmic magic of 'Yet once more, O ye laurels, & once more—'" ("Olifant," MS [Yale], 2).

[24] EW to Brownell, 22 October [1908?] (Amherst).

[25] See also, among her remarks on other art forms, Wharton's similar use of corresponding distinctions between "two recognized ways of judging a picture—by its technique and by its expression" (*IB*, 112) and between "two ways of feeling those arts . . . which appeal first to the eye: the technical, and what must perhaps be called the sentimental way" (*MF*, 177), or her later distinction between "the trained scholar" and "the cultured amateur" in "art-criticism" (*BG*, 140–41).

[26] Penelope Vita-Finzi, *Edith Wharton and the Art of Fiction* (New York: St. Martin's, 1990), 42.

[27] EW to Brownell, 17 October [1907] (Amherst).

[28] As Lewis notes, Melville keeps even stranger company in *The Writing of Fiction*, which refers to "the novel of adventure" and mentions "the joyous clatter of Dumas the elder, Herman Melville, Captain Marryat and Stevenson" (*WF*, 68), and in which American writers otherwise scarcely figure at all.

[29] Quoted in Loren Carroll, "Edith Wharton in Profile," *New York Herald Tribune*, Paris edition, 16 November 1936, 6.

[30] EW to Brownell, 30 June [1902?] (Amherst).

[31] EW to Brownell, 26 October [1902] (Amherst).

[32] In a sign of how conversant she became with the latest critical developments in France, the postscript of a letter to Fullerton declares, "I want you to read the very remarkable article on Lemaître and Chateaubriand by one [Albert] Thibaudet, in the N. Revue Française of last month. . . . It's worth a 100 of Maurras paradoxes. More like Gourmont at his best" (qtd. in Alan Gribben, ed., "'The Heart *Is* Insatiable': A Selection from Edith Wharton's Letters to Morton Fullerton," *Library Chronicle of the University of Texas* 31 [1985]: 67).

[33] Edith Wharton, "William C. Brownell," holograph MS (Yale), 2.

[34] EW to *Literary Review*, 21 October 1921 (Yale).

[35] EW to Brownell, 29 April 1903; Brownell to EW, 27 May 1903; EW to Brownell, 5 June 1903 (Princeton).

[36] Wilbur C. Cross, *Connecticut Yankee: An Autobiography* (New Haven: Yale University Press, 1943), 195; EW to Wilbur Cross, 26 October 1927 and 6 March 1928 (Yale). Clearly admiring Wharton as a critic, Cross goes on to describe one of her *Yale Review* essays as "a very fine analysis of Proust's literary art; I have never read a better," and he later enthusiastically reviewed *The Writing of Fiction* in his own journal.

[37] In 1907, for example, she informed Brownell, "I have bâclé [i.e., "knocked off"] a little article" in French comparing the verse of her friend Anna de Noailles to Whitman's, shared with him an apparently complete draft of the article, and said she planned to "hurl it at the head of one of the Revues" (EW to Brownell, 6 November 1907 [Amherst]); but Wharton never published such an essay, and no draft survives among the various manuscripts of fragmentary essays in the Wharton collections at Yale and Indiana (as discussed in appendix B).

[38] EW to Royal Society of Literature, 1 October 1934 (Yale). Lewis reports that after "her brother Lytton Strachey declined to write a preface" to "a little study of Conrad which Dorothy Bussy was translating" into English, André Gide "asked Mrs. Wharton if she might be induced to do it" (400); but this seems to have involved the possibility of a preface to the English translation of *La porte étroite*, for which Gide and Bussy considered approaching Wharton (*Selected Letters of André Gide and Dorothy Bussy*, ed. Richard Tedeschi [Oxford: Oxford University Press, 1983], 33–34). Despite her admiration for Conrad, however, Wharton did pass up at least two invitations (from Alfred Knopf, his American publisher, and from Booth Tarkington, both in 1914) to write about his work.

[39] EW to A. Starbuck, 13 August 1935 (Yale).

[40] As Wharton's niece, Beatrix Farrand, and her husband note in their own preface, "A preliminary pencilled note is all that was found: 'My sister-in-law has always written slowly. She seems to lay her ear to each sentence sounding it to catch its beat. She would not consider this a merit or the reverse; it is simply her way of working. She has such a love of our English speech, such a sense of its rhythmic beauty, that she is forever trying to keep step with it as she goes on; and the attempt is not a labour, but an enchantment'" (qtd. in Mary Cadwalader Jones, *Lantern Slides* [Boston: Merrymount Press, 1937], viii).

[41] Speech delivered on accepting a medal from the National Institute of Arts and Letters, TS (Yale). On Lapsley and his "collection of Wharton's fugitive pieces," see Goodman (37). I owe my awareness of the Lapsley project to Professor Goodman's study, published in time to be of great help at an already advanced stage of my own similar edition; hers is the only study of Wharton to make any use of the Lapsley collection at Trinity College, Cambridge University, which turned up, among other items of interest, Wharton's early letters to the *Newport Daily News* and the *New York Tribune*.

[42] Gaillard Lapsley to John L.B. Williams, 17 January 1943 (Gaillard Lapsley Collection, Trinity College, Cambridge University).

[43] "General Notes on Work of Edith Wharton," Gaillard Lapsley Collection, Trinity College, Cambridge University, box A, 128.

[44] "Permanent Values in Fiction" reappeared, in badly truncated form, in *Writing for Love or Money: Thirty-Five Essays Reprinted from the Saturday Review of Literature*, ed. Norman Cousins (New York: Longmans, 1949), 52–57; "The Writing of *Ethan Frome*" was again reprinted in *Readers for Writers*, ed. William Targ (New York: Hermitage, 1951), 145–47; Richard Ruland included "The Great American Novel" in his valuable collection *A Storied Land: Theories of American Literature, Vol. 2* (New York: Dutton, 1976), 410–17. The second part of "Henry James in His Letters" figures in *Henry James: A Collection of Critical Essays*, ed. Leon Edel (Englewood Cliffs, N.J.: Prentice-Hall, 1963), 31–36; but the review has never before been reprinted intact. Wharton's preface to *Ghosts* has been reprinted twice (CS, 2: 875–78, and in *The Ghost Stories of Edith Wharton* [New York: Scribner's, 1973], 1–4). Recent reissues of *Futility* and *Speak to the Earth* have retained Wharton's prefaces.

[45] A rare early, if brief, consideration of "Mrs. Wharton's theory of the novel" can be found in Olga Avendaño de Valdivia, "Edith Wharton: Chapter II," *Andean Quarterly* (Summer 1943–44): 39–40. In the first substantial full-length survey of her career, Blake Nevius briefly observes that, "As *The Writing of Fiction* (not to speak of her miscellaneous essays) shows, Edith Wharton was well read in the history of the novel, in the novel literature of the continent, and was self-consciously traditional in her technical approach"; see *Edith Wharton: A Study of Her*

Fiction (Berkeley: University of California Press, 1953), 159. Marilyn Jones Lyde draws upon some of Wharton's critical prose in resolving, perhaps too neatly, the paradoxes and antinomies of her sensibility in *Edith Wharton: Convention and Morality in the Work of a Novelist* (Norman: University of Oklahoma Press, 1959). In a sign of how unsettled any appraisal of her critical writing remains, one standard introduction to Wharton's career mentions the "numerous critical articles" of her "late years" but refers to none of the earlier pieces; another, remarking that Wharton "was never a journalist," observes that "we have very few prewar reviews or articles," while describing "Visibility in Fiction" as "on the whole a rather inconclusive article"; by contrast, yet a third scholar, noting that Wharton "published a score of critical essays in leading journals during the period 1902–1936," presents her as "a serious, articulate, impressively well-informed critic." See Margaret B. McDowell, *Edith Wharton*, rev. ed. (Boston: Twayne, 1991), 93; Geoffrey Walton, *Edith Wharton: A Critical Interpretation* (Rutherford, N.J.: Fairleigh Dickinson University Press, 1970), 161, 163; and Richard H. Lawson, *Edith Wharton* (New York: Ungar, 1977), 91. Even Lawson, however, implicitly follows the traditional consensus on this material by relegating his discussion of it to the next-to-last chapter, "Critical and Other Writings." As an English scholar, and thus freer of that consensus, Walton can observe, with the Wharton revival barely under way in the United States, "She was in fact an intelligent critic" and "belongs with the distinguished company who during the last fifty years have worked toward precision in critical terminology and standards of critical evaluation"; yet he says of Wharton's "first more general essay, 'The Criticism of Fiction,'" only that it "foreshadows Virginia Woolf's comments on the immaturity of English 19th-century fiction and goes on to stress the organic quality of great novels in a manner clearly indebted to James" (163, 161). Like Millicent Bell, Walton finds the *Belchamber* review "of considerable interest in that her remarks on Edwardian Society are closely related to what she had just written about American Society in *The House of Mirth*." Although he also claims that "[h]er review of Leslie Stephen's *George Eliot* is, despite her admiration for the subject, insignificant" (161), the piece has in fact become the most frequently cited of the earlier critical writings, primarily as an illustration of Wharton's developing sense of herself as a novelist (Lewis 108–9; Benstock 127–128). Bell devotes some useful pages to "The Criticism of Fiction," but always contrasts it to James's work and concludes that Wharton's "own contribution to the theory of fiction is slight," that "she made occasional statements about literary theory, and . . . attempted a summary of her aesthetic creed," and that "she had little to add to doctrines already expressed in James's prefaces and essays" (289). Any full exploration of her literary criticism makes it difficult to agree, in any case, with the notion that Wharton "was far more interested in the aesthetics of the visual (architecture and landscape) than in literary theory" (Benstock 282); and it is unfortunate that the one reasonably thorough overview of Wharton's critical prose concludes by remarking, "the observer of life that is seen in her autobiography and fiction is a better writer than the critic and authority, who is often either shrill and didactic or unsubstantial" (Vita-Finzi 39). Other recent studies drawing significantly upon her critical writings (both published and unpublished) are Janet Goodwyn, *Edith Wharton: Traveller in the Land of Letters* (New York: St. Martin's, 1990), and Carol J. Singley, *Edith Wharton: Matters of Mind and Spirit* (Cambridge: Cambridge University Press, 1995). Relevant unpublished scholarship includes Nancy R. Leach, "Edith Wharton: Critic of American Life and Literature," diss., University of Pennsylvania, 1952, and Melvin W. Askew, "Edith Wharton's Literary Theory," diss., University of Oklahoma, 1957. For a fuller sampling of secondary works in which Wharton's critical prose is addressed, see my concluding bibliography.

[46] For example, her famous 1922 preface regularly accompanies reprints of *Ethan Frome*, but Wharton's later essay on the work, along with her fascinating brief introduction to a stage adaptation, remains consistently overlooked. Interestingly, a critic no less distinguished than Edmund Wilson once complained to Blake Nevius, in acknowledging a copy of his 1953 study of Wharton, "Why do you omit from your bibliography the prefaces to the later editions of

Ethan Frome and *The House of Mirth?* Since the latter appears only in the English World's Classics edition, not many people here know about it" (*Letters on Literature and Politics, 1912–1972*, ed. Elena Wilson [New York: Farrar Straus & Giroux, 1977], 546). Not many more will know about it today, for over forty years after Wilson's remark, Wharton's absorbing introduction to the 1936 Oxford reprint of *The House of Mirth* remains unavailable, omitted not only from scholarly editions of the novel, where one might have expected to find it, but even from Oxford's recent paperback reissue of its own original edition. (Elsewhere, though, even the great Wilson nodded, citing at length the portrayal of George Cabot Lodge in *A Backward Glance* in prefacing his reprint of Henry Adams's life of the poet but ignoring Wharton's earlier tribute to Lodge, from which Adams himself quotes with considerable admiration; see *The Shock of Recognition, Vol. 2: The Twentieth Century* [New York: Grosset & Dunlap, 1955], 744–45, 779, 819–21, 827). To take another example, one of the Wharton volumes in the Library of America follows *A Backward Glance* with the first publication of "Life and I," but inexplicably omits "A Little Girl's New York," the posthumously published sequel to Wharton's memoirs.

[47] For example, Wharton's recent biographer reports that she "was opposed to educating women for the professions" and that when "she endowed a $500 scholarship for a student at the Paris division of the newly organized New York School of Design" in 1923, she "specified that the recipient be a male." Moreover, "When asked to contribute to a fund for travel scholarships for women," Wharton claimed to be "'not much interested in travelling scholarships for women,'" remarking that "'they'd much better stay at home and mind the baby'" (Benstock 387).

[48] Susan Sniader Lanser and Evelyn Torton Beck, "[Why] Are There No Great Women Critics? And What Difference Does It Make?" in *The Prism of Sex: Essays in the Sociology of Knowledge*, ed. Julia A. Sherman and Evelyn Torton Beck (Madison: University of Wisconsin Press, 1979), 81.

REVIEWS, ESSAYS,
AND OTHER WRITINGS,
1896–1914

Newport's Old Houses

To the Editor of the Daily News:

Sir: May I beg the space to draw a few conclusions from the article on Newport's old houses which appeared in your issue of yesterday?[1] The writer justly remarks that Newport is rich in houses built during the Colonial period; and it is to be regretted that their example has hitherto exercised no influence upon our later local architecture. When the Georgian houses of the United States were named "Colonial" the word took so strong a hold upon popular fancy that it was to be hoped that the style so designated would receive some study. We hear continually of "Colonial" houses and "Colonial" furniture; the name (in itself a misnomer) is daily before us, in the newspapers, in advertisements of furniture dealers and house decorators, and in popular magazine articles; but in spite of this general interest in the subject, eighteenth-century architecture has had no real effect upon the development of taste in America.[2]

The reason is not far to seek. It is easier to talk of a style than to study it, and vaguely to admire than intelligently to reproduce. Then, too, the so-called imitators of our Colonial architecture, through a profound misapprehension of its true meaning, have devoted themselves to reproducing its ornamental details rather than that admirable distribution of parts which is the secret of its charm. The modern "Colonial house" is simply our old Queen Anne friend, with a few gables suppressed, a substitution of eighteenth-century for seventeenth-century ornament, and painted yellow and white instead of mud color.

Now, the Palladian style, of which the Georgian is of course a development, depends for its beauty entirely upon an obedience to the laws of proportion, which our architects scorn even to consider. Remove from a Georgian house its fluted angle-pilasters, its roof balustrade and columned porch; the dignified outline which remains, the relation of the openings to the wall spaces, and of the attic to the height of the lower stories, will be seen to be the essential features upon which its excellence is based. But the modern architect does not even intelligently reproduce the ornamentation of the period. To be original at any cost is apparently the first quality demanded of the modern architect; and the popular interpretation of originality in architecture is the application of structural forms or ornamental detail to uses for which they were not intended. Thus, the decoration of modern "Colonial" houses is mainly borrowed from the interior decoration of eighteenth-century houses. The ornate exterior frieze, with garlands and bow-knots, which seems an essential feature of the style as now practiced, is taken from the frieze of eighteenth-century mantel-pieces. In fact, the "Colonial" house of today looks more like an Adam room[3] turned inside out than like any actual house of the Colonial period. Now there is no crime in adapting any decorative detail to a use other than that for which it was intended, provided it is equally suitable to its new purpose. But the Georgian architects were remarkable for common sense and a keen feeling for architectural fitness; and a little reflection will show that, by applying to the outside of their houses the delicate and elaborate detail which they reserved for interior use, we are doing away with the essential characteristics of the style, which were simplicity, sobriety and beauty of proportion. Originality which consists in a misapplication of the materials at its command is never to be commended. The desire to do differently for the sake of doing differently is puerile. Certain things are done in a certain way because the common consent of mankind has pronounced that way the best; and a man who went out with his shoes on his head, simply to distinguish himself from his hat-wearing fellow-citizens, would be called not original but idiotic.

It is very true, as Fergusson says, that archaeology is not architecture.[4] The benefit we derive from the study of past styles lies in extracting from them their abiding qualities of propriety and usefulness. Now the abiding qualities of the Georgian style, the qualities which commend it to our use in the present day, are precisely those which our architects overlook. The true Georgian house is rectangular, thus providing more accommodation in a given space than any of the gabled and pinnacled structures which at present adorn our streets. Relying for its effect upon the proper adjustment of its parts, it requires far less outward ornament than the wilfully irregular house, which can only be saved from looking like an aggregation of woodsheds around a central cow-barn by a liberal display of expensive ornamentation. The Georgian house is above all sincere. It does not affect to be a castle, a fortress, or a farmhouse. It does not pretend to have been added to by successive generations with different wants. It is direct, simple and obvious in its response to ordinary domestic requirements. Affectations in architecture are almost always expensive; none more so than the affectation of simplicity and quaintness. Therefore the Georgian house, in addition to its other merits, possesses the important one of affording more space, light and comfort for a given price than any other structure with the slightest architectural pretensions.

The writer of the article in yesterday's Daily News speaks of the admiration which we Newporters feel for our old houses. It is to be hoped that we do; but if so, why have so many been demolished, and so many ruthlessly mutilated? Of those which have been altered, it may safely be said that not one has been intelligently treated; and as long as we lie under the threat of losing (and losing through the vandalism of our rulers!) the beautiful old Sheffield house,[5] the less we say about our appreciation of our old houses the better.

Newport Daily News, 8 January 1896

[1] The article, "Colonial Houses" (signed, "N"), appeared in the *Newport Daily News* on 7 January 1896.

[2] As Wharton would similarly maintain, the following year, in a passage from her first book, "The application of the word 'Colonial' to pre-Revolutionary architecture and decoration has created a vague impression that there existed at that time an American architectural style. As a matter of fact, 'Colonial' architecture is simply a modest copy of Georgian models" (*DH*, 81–82).

[3] After the style of architecture and decoration introduced, late in the eighteenth century, by the English firm of Robert and James Adam.

[4] James Fergusson (1808–86), whose three-volume *A History of Architecture in All Countries From the Earliest Times to the Present Day* (1862–67), the first encyclopedic history of its subject, exerted a pivotal influence on Wharton during her early married years in Newport: "Another book . . . figured among my more recent Awakeners; and that was James Fergusson's 'History of Architecture,' at that time one of the most stimulating books that could fall into a young student's hands. A generation nourished on learned monographs, monumental histories, and works of reference covering every period of art from Babylonian prehistory to the present day, would find it hard to believe how few books of the sort, especially on architecture and sculpture, were available in my youth. Fergusson's 'History of Architecture' was an amazing innovation in its day. It shed on my misty haunting sense of the beauty of old buildings the light of historical and technical precision, and cleared and extended my horizon as Hamilton's 'History of Philosophy,' and my little old handbook of logic, had done in another way" (*BG*, 91).

[5] The Levi Gale House, also known as the Sheffield house, built around 1834, is now the Jewish Community Center on Touro Street, where it was moved in 1915 to make room for the Newport City Court House.

Schoolroom Decoration

I want your help in completing the decoration of the Newport schools;[1] not your contributions but your personal cooperation in making your pupils and their parents understand the purpose of our undertaking: in making the people feel that to put some beauty into the bare rooms of Newport is not only a good thing but a necessary thing, and necessary not only on artistic grounds but on moral grounds as well. Our object in decorating the schoolrooms is not to turn all the school children into painters and sculptors or to teach them history, but to surround them with such representations of beauty as in older civilizations the streets, the monuments and galleries of almost every city provide. In our country the conditions are unfavorable to the development of taste. We must teach our children to care for beauty before great monuments and noble buildings arise. There are signs of improvement; the desire for beauty is increasing and people are beginning to understand the immense educational value of good architecture and art. Our object is to advance this development of taste by surrounding our school children with an atmosphere of beauty, by putting in the rooms representations of the best works of art. If with your aid we can prove to the fathers and mothers that in surrounding the children with beauty we are also protecting them from ugliness—the ugliness of indifference, the ugliness of disorder, the ugliness of evil; having done this our cause is gained.

Beautiful pictures and statues may influence conduct as well as taste. To keep children out of mischief they must be kept busy. Every one knows the ceaseless irrepressible activity of children's hands and tongues. The hands are always investigating, the tongue is always asking questions, and the more thoughtful parent realizes that the child's eyes are equally busy; and to supply fitting objects for its investigation is one of the most important duties of parents and teachers. In decorating the schoolrooms we strive to provide answers for the questions which the child's eye is always asking. No child will sit with his eyes perpetually glued to his lesson-book. Now and then his glance will wander, and his thoughts with it. These distractions will not be met by a bare expanse of dreary, white-washed wall, but rather by some object which will instantly present to the child's mind an image of beauty, heroism, wisdom or virtue. We have learned to make the schoolbook interesting, and the next step forward in the science of education is to make the schoolroom interesting too.

Education is the discipline of learning, the train of thought aroused by what is learned, the formation of a child's character. The fact that schooling is a means, not an end—the means of making efficient, enlightened and useful citizens—has almost become a truism. The tendency of modern education is rather towards the harmonious development of the whole character than to the acquisition of any set of facts. The value of object lessons is more generally recognized. The underlying principle of the kindergarten system is applied to the higher branches of education. Everywhere the exaction of the eye is considered—that is, everywhere except on the school room walls. But even these, happily, are no longer always bare. In several cities a change has been made.

In time perhaps the need for which we are pleading will be recognized by the municipalities. But first the citizen must educate the city; we must prove our readiness to be taxed for beautiful as well as for useful things, or rather we must prove that beauty is useful. Thrift, order, refinement, ambition and the countless daily pleasures of the observant eye are qualities which are kept alive by the miraculous influence of beauty. Every woman knows how hard it is to take pride in a house that hasn't a single pretty thing in it, and many a man, who may never have thought about the matter, and may appear quite insensible to such things, is unconsciously influenced by the beauty and refinement of his home. We all know how children, so unmerciful to torn carpets and shabby furniture, can be taught to respect what is fresh and pretty and to take a pride in helping to keep it so.

And this is the way in which beauty fosters the civic virtues. Who can long be rough and slatternly and indifferent in a pretty, well-kept house? If a little of the prettiness and order is allowed to overflow into each room, each member of the family will come to regard himself as holding a share in the capital of beauty, and as vitally interested in preserving and increasing that capital. Every woman who knows the truth of what I have been saying, takes pains to surround her children with beautiful things. They teach them to love and reverence beauty, as they love and reverence goodness. The child who is shut out from beauty during a great part of each day, in the schoolroom with its bare walls, will soon lose his feeling for it, and become indifferent to the graces and refinements of his home.

The importance of beautiful surroundings in making study interesting and teaching easy is another point worth considering. How it helps a teacher, who is talking of art, or history, or literature, to point to some noble bas-relief or picture, to some portrait of the poet or hero in question. And how easily the child remembers the lesson so aptly illustrated. Some of you have anticipated the work of this association by hanging photographs, prints and various decorations of your own making. Every attempt of this kind made by a teacher is direct evidence of the need, the vital need, of the work we have undertaken. To those who have been the pioneers in this work I wish to point out the fact that beauty, as a means of education, performs a double office. True beauty teaches not only love of itself but hatred of ugliness; and not only of positive ugliness but of the negative kind which is less perceptible to the untrained eye, but really just as harmful and deteriorating.

In art, as in literature and in conduct, the child must be taught to care only for the best. It is as easy to buy a plaster cast or a photograph of some really great work of art as a foolish pink and white chromo. It pays to buy the best. Care only for the best, and be content to go without art rather than tolerate its inferior forms. Don't indulge your pupils in a diet of trashy prettiness.

Such a diet is as harmful as a perpetual nibbling of sugar plums. It destroys
the healthy appetite for beauty, as eating sweets between meals destroys the
appetite for wholesome food. Beauty is not a sugar plum; it is sterner fare.
Feeding on this trashy beauty may be compared to the perpetual reading of
trash. Every teacher knows how soon such reading destroys a taste for the
best literature. Better bare walls in a schoolroom than bad art. But nowadays
there is no excuse for either. The best reproductions in plaster or in photographs can be obtained for a small amount of money. The best is within
reach; let us for ourselves and our children refuse anything less than the
best.

[In conclusion Mrs. Wharton said:] Ladies and Gentlemen: You now see
what it is we ask of you. We want you to join us in giving a series of object-
lessons in beauty, not only to the school children of Newport but to the
public and to the municipality. We want to teach this lesson of beauty so
clearly and so forcibly that, when Newport builds her next school, a special
appropriation for decorating it with works of art will be regarded as a matter
of course; and meanwhile we want you to help our association in carrying on
the work that has been begun.

I have only to add that the rooms which we have decorated were selected
entirely with reference to their size, their lighting or some such practical
conditions. Our object was to decorate first the rooms most likely to produce
a good effect, and the choice was left entirely to us by the school committee
and the superintendent. Next year we hope that all the rooms will be done,
and that all will give satisfaction to both teachers and pupils.

Newport Daily News, 8 October 1897

[1] During the late 1890s, in one of the more intriguing and least-known activities of her
married life in Rhode Island, Wharton "did volunteer work for the Newport schools, choosing
several plaster busts of classical and mythic figures for school-rooms" (Benstock 84) and making
other gestures on behalf of students. At the end of the 1896–97 academic year, having "already
manifested her interest . . . by giving prizes in several grades for excellence in English composition upon the subject of cruelty to animals" and by contributing "twelve pictures which . . . she
carefully selected for the express purpose of adorning our school rooms," Wharton wrote to
inform the superintendent that she was "anxious to form an association for the purpose of
embellishing the Newport schools and placing before the children such reproductions of works
of art, portraits of great men, etc., as may develop their sense of beauty and form a series of
permanent illustrations of their successive studies" (*Annual Report of the School Committee of
the City of Newport, R.I.* [1897], 87, 88–89). That fall, the *Newport Daily News* reported on a
meeting "in the large west room in the Clarke street schoolhouse," where "the teachers of the
public schools almost without exception gathered," along with members of the Newport school
committee and others, "[i]n response to an invitation to listen to a paper by Mrs. Edward R.
Wharton on 'Schoolroom Decoration.'. . . The room is one that has been decorated by the
association of which Mrs. Wharton is the head, and the photographs and plaster casts were

much admired by all present." The article proceeds to offer a transcription of the lecture in which "Mrs. Wharton . . . addressing herself to the teachers spoke substantially as follows." It is striking that Wharton, ordinarily so reluctant to speak in public or to participate in cooperative endeavors of any kind, should not only have led such an association but consented to make such an appearance. Although she obviously did not prepare the text for publication, and while it is impossible to determine the accuracy of the reporter's account, the address as represented in the *Daily News* article is unmistakably hers in flavor and tone, and very close in purpose to Wharton's recent work on *The Decoration of Houses*, echoing many passages from the chapter "The School-Room and Nurseries," in which she warns that "the aspect of the school-room too often aggravates instead of mitigating the weariness of lesson-learning" and bravely contends, "If art is really a factor in civilization, it seems obvious that the feeling for beauty needs as careful cultivation as the other civic virtues" (*DH*, 174).

Impoverishing the Language

To the Editor of The Tribune.

Sir: It is a pleasure—and not an every day one—to find an American newspaper coming to the defence of good English, as The Tribune recently did in explaining to a puzzled correspondent why "an historian" is a preferable form to "a historian."[1] That a reader capable of observing such niceties should yet be unacquainted with one of the most familiar rules of English euphony speaks volumes for the way in which English is taught in this country, but will surprise no one familiar with the grammatical standards of the average American writer on syntax and composition.

Such shades of speech are, however, mainly literary, and much as the language must suffer in losing them it is in far greater danger from the impoverishment of our spoken vocabulary. The American language is, in fact, rapidly differentiating itself from the English, and not always to the profit of the younger branch. Thus we have practically lost the subjunctive, "may" and "can" are regarded as synonymous, the interchangeable use of "shall" and "will" has passed from Irish-English speech to our own, and is finding its way into newspapers and books, and past participles manufactured out of nouns are weakening the few inflected verbs we have left.

It is inevitable that time and altered surroundings should modify the language, and such changes as enrich it are welcome, whatever their source. Unfortunately, however, the tendency of American speech (and not only that of the uneducated) is to impoverish rather than to enrich the mother tongue. We are continually replacing some good word with a definite and familiar meaning by another of quite different significance, and in no way better adapted to the service into which it is suddenly impressed. In this way hundreds of useful distinctions have been lost—not the pedantic shades of meaning with which speech has no time to reckon, but the kind of distinction that helps the average man to express his meaning more quickly and precisely.

Such losses, it is true, originate among the uneducated, but owing to our lax habits of speech and imitative tendencies they spread rapidly from the street to the newspaper and from the newspaper to the book. It is not only in the street that one hears "back of" used for behind, "cunning" for "pretty" or "engaging," to "fix" for to "set right" or to "arrange." The two latter words have, in fact, been so successfully wrenched from their true meaning that those who would not think of using them in their perverted sense instinctively avoid them in speaking, so that it has become almost pedantic to talk of a man's cunning or of fixing a tablet to a wall.

In other cases the word may be studied in various degrees of deterioration. Thus "team" has come to mean one horse to the man in the street, while it apparently stands in newspaper parlance for a pair, and preserves only in cultivated speech and in the vocabulary of the sport (where the need of definiteness is felt) its specific sense of four. A curious instance of the perversion of this word is to be seen on several roads near Lenox, where the public is warned that "loaded teams are forbidden," etc. "Loaded" for "laden" is a good example of the loss of a fine inflection, and it is distressing to learn that many of the works of art in the Metropolitan Museum are "loaned" instead of being "lent" to that institution.

Oddly enough, it is in the domestic branches that our spoken language has suffered some of its most needless perversions. Is this because women are less sensitive than men to shades of meaning and less accustomed to the necessity of expressing themselves with precision? There is no reason why such distinctive words as "mercer" and "haberdasher," for instance, should have been lost in the general term "dry goods," or why "shop" should have been sacrificed to "store," which wears on its very face its inappropriateness to such a purpose. Why, again, should so good a word as "bodice" be in danger of extermination through the senseless and vulgar "waist," which, in its most ridiculous form, "shirt waist," has already passed into the language? "Petticoat" (perhaps through some prudish euphuism) is being rapidly discarded for "skirt," another instance of one word being forced to serve two distinct purposes, since no substitute has yet been provided for "skirt." The use of the word "laundry," to signify washing or the wash, has not yet reached polite speech, but is on its way thither via the advertisement and the newspaper, and such a euphuism is sure to appeal to the order of mind which prefers "elevator" to "lift" and "mucilage" to "gum."

Such changes as I have cited are to be deplored, since they weaken and blur the language, and they are taking place among us with such rapidity that the vocabulary of the average American is now distinctly poorer than it was a generation ago.

New York Tribune, 23 April 1901

[1] Addressing the inquiry of a reader who objected to "an eccentric use of 'an' for 'a,' that is, when the following word does not begin with a vowel sound,"as in "an historian," the *Tribune* maintained, "The rule is that 'an' is to be used instead of 'a' before a word beginning with a vowel or with an unaccented or silent 'h,' in which latter case the word practically begins with a vowel sound. Thus . . . we say 'an historian' because the accent falls, not on the first, but on the second, syllable, and the 'h,' being unaccented, is strongly sounded" ("Grammar and Pictures," *New York Tribune*, 13 April 1901, 7). The subhead run by the *Tribune* in printing Wharton's response ten days later ("A Popular Writer's Protest against Slipshod Habits of Speech among Educated Americans") affords some sense of the reputation that she had already achieved by 1901, even before publishing her first novel.

The Blashfields' *Italian Cities*

Italian Cities. By Edwin H. and Evangeline W. Blashfield. 2 vols.
New York: Charles Scribner's Sons, 1901.

The only possible plea on which the average writer can speak of Italy is that of having lit on some unnoticed place, some unrecorded phase of art, some detail insignificant enough to have dropped out of the ever-growing catalogue of her treasures. For the privilege of adding one more foot-note to those glowing pages, the lover of Italy will wade patiently through much vague theorising and feeble rhetoric; but the author who comes forward with a book on the great land-marks—who boldly heads his chapters with immortal names—must expect to be measured by another standard. He who has anything to say about Rome, Florence or Siena must justify himself by saying it extraordinarily well.

This condition Mr. and Mrs. Blashfield have admirably fulfilled in their two volumes on *Italian Cities*.[1] They have brought to their task, in addition to exact technical knowledge, that imaginative sensibility not often combined with it; and these qualities have been merged and mellowed, as it were, in a long familiarity with Italian life and speech. In these days of "superficial omniscience" few writers can show such an equipment, and

those who have it do not always know how to use it. The command of a vivid
and flexible prose has enabled the authors of *Italian Cities* to present their
results in the most interesting book of Italian impressions that has appeared
in English since Symonds's volumes.[2] To the most superficial reader Mr.
and Mrs. Blashfield's pages must be full of charm; and to one familiar with
the aspect of Italy, and knowing something of its artistic and political past,
they possess the varied suggestion which characterises the country itself.
Perhaps, indeed, the most remarkable quality of the book is the skill with
which various tastes are taken into account, with which the claims of erudition and emotion, of historic exactness and poetic fancy, are fused into a
homogeneous "sensation" of Italy. To compare, for instance, the analogy
drawn between Saint Francis and Epictetus, in the chapter on Assisi, with
the charming little *genre* picture of a visit to the nuns of Cortona gives some
idea of the flexibility of view that has enabled the authors to survey so many
aspects of their subject. Equally striking in its way is the sombre record of
the great siege of Siena, extracted with masterly conciseness from the pages
of Brantôme and Monluc,[3] while the curiously graphic picture of the Perugia
of to-day is like some raised topographical map in its vivid and minute precision. It was to be expected that in their study of Italy the main interest of the
authors should centre in her art. The impartiality with which they have
traced the successive manifestations of this art may be observed from the
opening pages on the Byzantine craftsmen to those in which Correggio, the
painter's painter, is discussed with the same discriminating sympathy as
the unknown artists who lined the tomb of Galla Placidia with mosaics "blue
as the heart of a sapphire." Such catholicity of judgment has not always
marked the English or American art-critic, and the present work doubtless
owes something of its artistic balance to the technical competence of one of
the authors. Some of the happiest of the reflections with which it abounds
are drawn from this professional experience. The analysis of the early
Sienese school of painting contains, for example, an admirably drawn contrast between the critical standpoint of artist and amateur. "The inarticulate
work of art," the authors say, "appeals to the critic: he 'discovers' it, pleads
for it, reveals it. Indeed, he soon ceases to see it objectively, and it often
appeals to him only through the medium which his own fancy has created.
Why has so much been written about Botticelli, so little about Donatello?
Why is Simone Martini more stimulating to eloquence than Veronese? Because . . . the master-craftsmen need no apologists and offer no handle to
facile criticism. . . . Finally, to analyse or define the enduring charm of a
world-famous picture is a form of mental exercise; to rhapsodise over a Sano

di Pietro or a Matteo Giovanni . . . an inexpensive form of mental dissipation." Words of gold, which, omitting the specific reference to painting,
might well be written up in every critic's laboratory.

Felicity in summing up a series of deductions or impressions is in fact
characteristic of Mr. and Mrs. Blashfield's book. What, for instance, could be
a better way of defining Mantegna's talent than to say that he resolved the
almost impossible proposition of *achieving grandeur without simplicity?* Another telling phrase defines one of the least-understood exigencies of decorative painting: "When he [the decorative artist] can draw and paint every
detail of his subject, then, and not till then, can he suppress judiciously; for
a man may leave out intelligently only what he has entirely possessed."
Equally effective, but with the quite different quality of metaphorical apt-
ness, is the definition of the axioms of Epictetus as possessing "the noble
nudity of antique marbles;" or the description of the mosaics of the Lower
Empire, when the imagery of paganism was being remodelled for Christian
use, and "as in these same mosaics the Magi bring gifts to the Mother of God,
so each dethroned goddess pays tribute to the new Queen of Heaven."

To those who love the mere visible Italy, irrespective of her latent appeals
to the imagination, the descriptive touches scattered through the book will
have a special charm. None who know Mantua can fail to appreciate the
delicately-pencilled vignette with which the chapter on that city opens; and
how vividly is Siena called to sight in the passage beginning: "We have seen
the city in many phases: under black clouds, with hailstones shining in
stormy, struggling sunshine against the sculptures of the Fonte Gaia . . . and
set like a town in a missal-border against a still, flat, blue background of sky"!
The sureness of touch with which the writers have differentiated the outer
aspect of the cities they depict, so that each stands forth in individual outline
and colour, must convince even readers unacquainted with Italy that their
descriptions are the result of personal impressions, and not of any precon-
ceived literary or artistic ideal. The whole book, in fact, has this quality of
spontaneous observation and reflection, of having, in the French phrase,
been *felt* rather than filtered through other sensibilities.

"Here in Italy," our authors cry, "where the civilisations overlie one another, and where history is piled strata upon strata, we are perforce obliged
to limit our impressions;" and so with an estimate of their book: it is impossible to trace the innumerable threads of suggestion branching off from every
subject on which they touch. To have placed these threads in their readers'
hands, to have started them afresh on the endless quest of knowledge and
beauty, is to have fulfilled in a noble sense Montesquieu's definition of a

great thought: "C'est lorsqu' on dit une chose qui en fait voir un grand nombre d'autres."[4] As faithful lovers of Italy, this is doubtless the end the authors would most wish to have attained.

Bookman, August 1901

[1] Edwin H. Blashfield (1848–1936), mural painter, also co-authored with his wife several magazine articles on medieval and Renaissance art. A leader in the world of American art, his many commissions included the central dome of the Library of Congress.

[2] John Addington Symonds (1840–93), English art historian and critic, author principally of *The Renaissance in Italy*, 7 vols. (1875–86).

[3] Pierre de Bourdeille, seigneur and abbé de Brantôme (c.1540–1614), author of the *Vies des dames galantes* (published posthumously in 1665–66); Blaise de Lasseran-Massencôme, seigneur de Monluc (1502–77), whose *Commentaires* (1592), a volume of historical memoirs, is famous in France.

[4] "Ce quit fait ordinairement une grande pensée, c'est lorsque l'on dit une chose qui en fait voir un grand nombres d'autres [What ordinarily makes a great thought is when it expresses one thing that opens to our view a great many other things]," from *Essai sur le goût dans les choses de la nature et de l'art* (1757), of Charles de Secondat, baron de Montesquieu (1689–1755), political philosopher.

Stephen Phillips's *Ulysses*

Ulysses: A Drama. By Stephen Phillips. New York:
The Macmillan Company, 1902.

Mr. Phillips has endeavoured to weave a number of episodes from the *Odyssey* into a dramatic form.[1] How far the result may justify the undertaking only the acted play can prove: the most theatrically-minded critic must, in reading, set aside theatrical limitations and use the term *dramatic* in that wider sense permissible when the reader's mind is the stage. Even from this larger standpoint it is doubtful if Mr. Phillips has justified his choice of a subject; since the story of Ulysses, as handled by him, remains rather a series of more or less dramatic incidents than a dramatic whole. The temperament of Ulysses makes this inevitable: it would be hard to imagine a more centrifugal hero. He was an adventurer in the fine old sense, taking good and evil "with a frolic welcome,"[2] animated by no definite purpose, making for no fixed goal, but living life for life's sake with the thoroughness though without the self-consciousness of the modern Cyrenaic. Such a character might, by its action on others of different mould, produce situations full of dramatic possibilities, as, for instance, the hero's parting from Calypso or his return to Ithaca. Each of these situations contains the germ of a drama; but when they are used episodically their dramatic value is lost, and they become merely heterogeneous fragments of experience. Mr. Phillips might reply that this was what he intended them to be, and that the episodical nature of his hero's adventures was typical of such a temperament—that to centralise the diffused emotions of the "fluid" Ulysses into a single dramatic crisis would have been to recast the hero of the *Odyssey*. To say this, however, is to admit the dramatic unfitness of the subject; and this Mr. Phillips is far from admitting. He declares, indeed, that the story of Ulysses seems to him to "afford matter for telling dramatic presentment," and adds that he has tried to weave his hero's adventures "into the fabric of a properly-knit play;" but he would doubtless not quarrel with the critic who should prefer to extol his work as a poetic narrative rather than to condemn it as a drama.

Viewed in the former light, it is seen to be full of detached beauties, even of detached dramatic effects, though there are intervals of weakness and inadequacy, where the dramatic and the poetic inspiration seem to fail simultaneously. It will doubtless generally be admitted that the two scenes in which Mr. Phillips has been least successful are those on Olympus and in Hades. His muse, Antaeus-like, draws fresh strength from contact with the earth, and it is to be regretted that he did not discard the whole Olympian machinery and deal with the purely human side of the story. The poem might have lost in picturesqueness, in a masque-like effect of quaintness, but would have gained, one feels, a deeper beauty and significance. At all events, Mr. Phillips has not justified his attempt to walk with the immortals. The prologue on Olympus is the weakest part of the play. The author has chosen to make his gods speak in rhymed pentameter, a doubtful vehicle for majestic speech, but one probably selected to give what the Germans call a "humoresque" touch to the scene. Mr. Phillips, perhaps mistrusting his ability to report "that large utterance of the early gods,"[3] has preferred to present his divinities in a serio-comic aspect; a permissible alternative, had it been successfully carried out. Unhappily, Mr. Phillips is deficient in both humour and irony, and that "smile of the universe,"[4] which was evidently intended to play over the scene, somehow fails to make itself visible: like a recalcitrant stage-moon refusing to rise at the right moment. Here and there, indeed, the prologue rises to poetry; but this is when Mr. Phillips drops the ironic masque and lapses into the elegiac or the introspective key. Such a line as

Mocked by the green of some receding shore

is among the gifts for which one must ever be grateful to Mr. Phillips; but, placed as it is, it produces the effect of having been drawn from its original context to eke out Athene's rhymes. Lines of this quality are, moreover, infrequent, and the verse of the prologue moves chiefly on the level of:

> Who hath so suffered, or so far hath sailed,
> So much encountered, and so little quailed?

or (in Zeus's address to Poseidon):

> In thy moist province none can interfere—

or (worse yet) in the description of Calypso:

> All his wisdom swoons beneath the charm
> Of her deep bosom and her glimmering arm.

These examples will probably suffice to show that the rhymed pentameter, always difficult to use in dialogue, is not Mr. Phillips's native element.

The first act opens with a page or two of decidedly prosy prose; but with the appearance of Athene, the words fall into the stately beat of Mr. Phillips's blank verse. Mr. Phillips has been criticised for writing lines which resist all attempts at scansion; but when the pedants give up trying to scan English verse by Latin feet, and measure it instead by accentual stress, his lines will be found to present few difficulties. Athene's opening speech is a good example of his more complex rhythms, and one may conceive that the Latin measuring-rod must fly into splinters in contact with such uncoercible lines as:

> When he leapt among them, when he flashed, when he cried,
> When he flew on them, when he struck, when he stamped them dead.

Those who refuse to test English verse by the rules of Latin prosody may maintain that in such measures Mr. Phillips is at his best, and that his courage and originality in the use of rhythm are his surest safeguard against a certain effeminacy—a leaning to the Tennyson of the Idylls rather than of the Ulysses.[5]

The first scene of the first act undoubtedly contains some of the best verse in the play, and not only its finest line, but, perhaps, on the whole, the finest line the author has ever written: when Athene, striving to turn Telemachus against the suitors, replies to his whining

> Goddess, I am but one and they are many—

with the godlike cry:

> Thou art innumerable as thy wrongs!

The scene shifts to the sea-cave of Calypso, where the blandishments of the enchantress are interspersed with lyrics unfortunately reminiscent of an opera libretto: as when the nymphs declare in chorus:

Alas! we have seen the sailor asleep
Where the anchor rusts on the ooze of the deep,
But never, never before
Have we seen a mortal dance on the long seashore.

One hastens on to escape the pursuing remembrance of Ariel's song.

There are high imaginative touches in the leave-taking between Ulysses and Calypso, and here again Mr. Phillips is at his best in Calypso's cry:

And now I do recall
Even in your wildest kiss a kiss withheld.

Indeed, the whole scene is effective in verse and movement, and provokingly suggests how well it might have served as the nucleus of a drama.

Mr. Phillips, however, hurries us on to Hades; and here, it must be owned, one is inclined to address to him the warning which Charon gives Ulysses:

Back to the earth or fear some monstrous doom!

Mr. Phillips's doom is that of inadequacy; a fact the more to be regretted as there is one profoundly imaginative touch in the scene—where Ulysses, as he passes in turn "the woes" of the mighty doomed, recognises his own sufferings in each, and cries out:

There is no torment here that is not mine.

In the second part of *Faust*, where Mephistopheles tells Faust that, to evoke the phantom of Helen, he must descend to the *Mothers*, the hero shudders at the mysterious word, and the reader feels the recoil of the shudder.[6] This is the effect which Mr. Phillips has failed to produce: he does not transmit his *frisson*. *Facile est* can no longer be said of the literary descent into Avernus: two great seers have been there, and we carry the reflection of their vision in our eyes. Compared with that dark, unbottomed infinite abyss, Mr. Phillips's Hades seems chiefly the product of stage-mechanism and lime-lights, and one is glad, for a different reason, to emerge and rebehold the stars.

The third act opens on the seashore of Ithaca. Athene reappears with a fresh stock of rhymed couplets; but her rhymes happily giving out, she murmurs some beautiful lines over the sleeping Ulysses. There follows an episodical scene of no great merit in the swine-herd's hut, and the action is then transferred to the banqueting-hall of the palace of Ulysses. It is the day on which Penelope is finally to choose between the suitors, and these in turn press their claims, while Ulysses, an unheeded beggar, crouches in the ashes by the hearth. This scene is dramatically the finest in the play; but precisely for this reason one most resents the intervention of Athene, whose promise to tell Ulysses when he is to arise and smite reduces the climax to a purely mechanical effect. There remains, however, much to praise, especially in Penelope's answers to the suitors; and the whole scene moves at a stirring pace, with a fine accord between rhythm and action.

Mr. Phillips's explanatory note seems, by its very tone of self-defence, to admit the dramatic inferiority of his subject, and it is almost superfluous to say that as a play *Ulysses* will not bear comparison with *Herod*. Unfortunately, the same must be said of it as a poem. There are still those who question whether Mr. Phillips has ever crossed the line dividing rhetoric from poetry. If, as Flaubert says, continuity constitutes style as constancy makes virtue,[7] then Mr. Phillips has not, perhaps, established his claim to take rank among the poets; but assuredly he has written poetry. There are lines in *Ulysses* that prove it, though they are less frequent than in *Herod*. There are fewer passages where imaginative passion has moulded speech to its own glowing shape, where the mystical fusion of word and meaning has taken place; but the existence of one such line suggests the possibility of others, and encourages the optimistic reader to hope that Mr. Phillips may yet be capable of sustaining life permanently on Parnassus.

Bookman, April 1902

[1] Stephen Phillips (1864–1915), English poet and playwright; his other verse dramas included *Paolo and Francesca* (1897), discussed the following year by Wharton in "The Three Francescas," and *Herod* (1900).

[2] From Tennyson's monologue "Ulysses" (l. 47).

[3] From Keats's *Hyperion: A Fragment* (1820), part 1, l. 51.

[4] Dante, *Paradiso*, canto 27, ll. 4–5.

[5] Referring, of course, to Tennyson's *Idylls of the King* (1859–72; 1885).

[6] A favorite passage of Wharton's from part 2 of Goethe's *Faust*, ll. 6212–16, later providing a central reference point for the protagonist of her novels *Hudson River Bracketed* and *The Gods Arrive*.

[7] "La continuité constitue le style, comme la Constance fait la Vertu" (Flaubert to Louise Colet, 18 December 1853).

George Eliot

George Eliot. By Leslie Stephen. New York:
The Macmillan Company, 1902.

Mr. Leslie Stephen has performed an invaluable service, not so much to the genius of George Eliot, which may well trust its case to posterity, as to those among her admirers who resent the momentary neglect into which she has fallen. Such "interlunar" phases are the lot of all great writers. It is not long since Macaulay was rescued from the contempt of the very schoolboy in whose omniscience he placed such flattering faith; and Racine, according to Madame de Sévigné, was destined *passer comme le café*.[1] This, as it turns out, is precisely what he did; and some such fate doubtless awaits other reputations rashly condemned to a like evanescence.

Meanwhile, it is encouraging to see a critic of Mr. Stephen's authority set himself resolutely against that belittling process by which each generation thinks to mark its advance over its predecessors. No such conscious motive, of course, underlies the inevitable reactions of taste, and their very inevitableness makes them, self-evidently, a subject rather for analysis than for criticism; but it is well that the popular judgment should now and then be called on to account for itself, to reckon up losses and gains, and see whither its tidal impulses are carrying it.

In the case of George Eliot, the influences determining the change are somewhat difficult to trace. The principal charge against her seems to be that she was too "scientific," that she sterilised her imagination and deformed her style by the study of biology and metaphysics. The belief that scientific studies have this effect on the literary faculty has received what is regarded as striking confirmation in Darwin's well-known statement that, as he grew more engrossed in his physiological investigations, he lost his taste for poetry, so that at last he became incapable of finding any pleasure in the great writers who had once delighted him.[2] This statement seems convincing till examined more closely; then it will be remembered that there is more than one way of studying the phenomena of life, and that the fixity of purpose and limited range of investigation to which the scientific specialist is committed differ totally from the cultivated reader's bird's-eye view of the field of scientific speculation. George Eliot was simply the cultivated reader, and her biological acquirements probably differed in degree, rather than in kind, from those, for instance, of Tennyson, who is acknowledged to have enlarged the range of poetic imagery by his use of metaphors and analogies drawn from the discoveries of modern science. Certainly, no one can deny the poetic value of the evolutionary conception. Guyau has finely said: *L'hypothèse c'est le poème du savant*;[3] and almost all the famous scientific hypotheses have an imaginative boldness and beauty which justify the metaphor. The great investigators have never wearied of repeating that all the forward steps in science have been made by an imaginative effort, by the deductive rather than the inductive method. Goethe the poet was nourished, not stunted, by the scientific inductions of Goethe the morphologist; and Milton's allusion to Galileo's "optic glass"[4] shows how early the poetic mind was ready to seize on any illustration furnished by the investigations of science. Is it because these were men, while George Eliot was a woman, that she is reproved for venturing on ground they did not fear to tread? Dr. Johnson is known to have pronounced portrait-painting "indelicate in a female";[5] and indications are not wanting that the woman who ventures on scientific studies still does so at the risk of such an epithet.

Aside from such prejudices, it will probably be agreed that the use any writer makes of his or her knowledge is the sole test of its specific value. If it be found that George Eliot's studies had the effect generally ascribed to them, it may at once be conceded that, in her case, they were misdirected. If it can be shown that she was originally a buoyant poetic creature, with a bright play of fancy and a light flexible style—that the spontaneity of Charlotte Brontë or the precision and limpidity of Jane Austen were among her inherent gifts—then it must be owned that the chance which threw her into the society of George Lewes and Mr. Herbert Spencer was one to be deplored by her readers. It remains to be seen whether any such case can be made out against destiny. George Eliot passed from the narrowest evangelicalism of an English provincial town to the freest intellectual atmosphere of a great city. In her youth she gave no signs of any natural welling-up of the poetic faculty. Her preoccupations were mainly theological. Her discussions with her friends suggest the lucubrations of Milton's archangels. When she ceased to be a dogmatic Christian, she did not rest in agnosticism, but took refuge in the fold of Comte.[6] She was predestined to a "chapel" of one kind or another. Not only did she write no poetry at this period, but she showed not the slightest leaning toward creative work. Her imagination was dormant. Her style, as shown in her letters, was prolix, ponderous and pedantic. Not a metaphor gives promise of the wealth of imagery so characteristic of her later work, not an epigrammatic phrase foreshadows the coiner of proverbs and aphorisms, not a gleam of humour suggests the creator of Mrs. Poyser, the Dodsons and Mr. Brooke. Such indications of future development as the letters give are all in the line of uneasy heart-searchings combined with great intellectual curiosity. What was so likely to free such a spirit from the bonds of ethical pedantry as the contact with that vast speculative movement which was just then opening countless new avenues into the mind of man and the phenomena of the universe?

Mr. Stephen appears at first to make some concession to the popular superstition, as when he says that "Mr. Herbert Spencer's philosophy may be admirable in its own sphere, but is not of itself likely to stimulate an interest in purely imaginative work;" but his subsequent summing-up of George Eliot's achievement proves once again how impossible it is to say what influences are likely to quicken the creative faculty. Mr. Stephen himself admits that "it almost seems as if George Eliot would never have written a novel at all had it not been for the quick perception of Lewes." Is not this an admission that she had at last found the *milieu* she needed?

In other respects Mr. Stephen's estimate is at once judicious and appreciative; and he touches in a happy phrase on one point of special significance when he says, in speaking of the *Scenes of Clerical Life*, that "it is the constant, though not obtrusive, suggestion of the depths below the surface of trivial life which gives an impressive dignity to the work; and, in any case, marks one of the most distinctive characteristics of George Eliot's genius."

Perhaps he does not do quite as full justice to the Shakespearean quality of her humour, that humour which is of the very texture of life, and which has its source in those "depths below" to which only the divining-rod of genius penetrates. But George Eliot might have said of herself as an author what Faust said of himself as a man:

Zwei Seelen wohnen, ach, in meine Brust![7]

The philosophic observer of life's ironies—the humourist who records with such zest the sayings of Mr. Brooke, Mrs. Poyser, the Pullets, and Gwendolen's family group in *Daniel Deronda*—this genial spectator of the human comedy is too often thrust aside by the preacher who feels called upon to draw a somewhat obvious moral from the spectacle which his collaborator would have left to speak for itself. Her style shows the same curious quality. Rapid and varied in dialogue, it lacks both these qualities in narrative; yet in character-drawing it is far less heavy and diffuse than in passages of "reflection." In other words, the observer of life is a better writer than the moralist.

The critics who accuse Lewes of having thwarted his wife's development include in their accusation the specific charge that he injured her style; but a fair-minded comparison of her earlier with her later works will prove the injustice of the assertion. George Eliot started in life with the worst style—or with the greatest lack of style—that ever hampered a writer of genius. The fact that the *Scenes of Clerical Life* and *Adam Bede* have the naturalness and spontaneity of manner characteristic of early successes has led to the assumption that they are better *written* than the later books. That this is not the case a hasty comparison will show. The *Scenes of Clerical Life* are related with a wearisome diffuseness, and the description of Milly's death-bed, though it appealed to the facile sentimentalism of the early Victorian public, is a poor performance compared with the death of Tom and Maggie Tulliver, or with the far more tragic episode of Lydgate's survival. George Eliot, in fact, as she advanced in the study of life, came to seek her pathos deeper, and to render it with more restraint, with less appeal to the superficial emotions but a far more poignant sense of the *lachrymae rerum*.

In the matter of style, she showed an almost continuous development in the true direction of her talent; that is, in dialogue and characterisation. Compare the laboured and ineffective attempt to describe a fat man in the person of Mr. Casson (the innkeeper in *Adam Bede*) with the brief and masterly strokes which put before us such figures as Mr. Brooke, Dorothea, Sir James Chettam, Grandcourt and Mr. Gascoigne! *Middlemarch* abounds in vivid portraits drawn in half-a-dozen lines. Take that of Mr. Cadwallader, "a large man . . . very plain and rough in his exterior, but with that solid imperturbable ease and good-humour which is infectious, and, *like great grassy hills in the sunshine*, quiets even an irritated egotism" . . . or the briefer but even more vivid summary of Mr. Brooke: "Mr. Brooke's conclusions were as difficult to predict as the weather: it was only safe to say that he would act with benevolent intentions, and that he would spend as little money as possible in carrying them out."

Such phrases bring one face to face with the man; and as George Eliot grew in the power of sketching in her characters, of placing them before her readers, so she advanced in the ability to hold them there, to maintain the definiteness of the outline she had once indicated. Do we see any of the characters in *Adam Bede* as distinctly as Maggie Tulliver, Casaubon, Dorothea, Lydgate, Grandcourt or Gwendolen? Even Mr. Stephen admits that Mrs. Poyser is painted with "a little more of Goldsmith's beautifying touch than of Crabbe's uncompromising realism;" and spite of her aphoristic fireworks she is, in fact, less real, less *immediate* a presence than her successors, Mrs. Gleg and Mrs. Pullet or (in another sphere) Lady Chettam and Mrs. Cadwallader. When George Eliot wrote *Adam Bede* the veil of literature still hung between her eyes and life, her principal figures were the familiar marionettes of fiction, and only in the subordinate characters (where stock types were less available) did she show the direct grasp of reality that was to be a distinguishing mark of her matured talent.

Perhaps the gravest defect of George Eliot's novels is their cumbersome construction. This fault is less chargeable to the author than to the taste of her day. The greatest writers have made concessions (if unconsciously, yet inevitably) to the requirements of their public; and George Eliot was no exception to the rule. Unfortunately for the normal development of her art, she began to write at a time when the psychological novel, which (it should be remembered) preceded in England, as well as in France, the novel of incident, was disappearing before the story with a "plot"—the type of fiction wherein the adventure grows, not out of the development of character and the conflict of moral forces, but out of the recovery of a missing will or the concealment of somebody's parentage. The "story with a plot" is a perfectly legitimate branch of fiction. Life is sometimes governed by just such extraneous incidents; and though their record is intrinsically less interesting than the drama of character and circumstances, no one needs to be reminded of the brilliant use to which such material has been put by novelists like Dumas, Defoe and Stevenson. The explanation of their success is that the incidental, external side of life was the side they naturally saw; and that, beholding life as a succession of outward accidents and mechanical complications, they rendered it with the truth of direct vision. George Eliot did not see life thus. To her it was a drama of the soul, a battle of spiritual forces; and the endeavour to reconcile this study of moral crises with the popular demand for a plot, resulted as grotesquely as might the attempt of a portrait-painter to reproduce the inner economy as well as the physical exterior of his sitters. The world of incidents and the world of emotions do, indeed, overlap and react on each other; but only to some myriad-minded seer is it given to behold and report life "in the round," as it were: the greatest among the less great can seize but one angle of the complex vision.

In George Eliot's case the fusion of the external and the emotional was peculiarly unsuccessful: her plots are as easily detachable from her books as dead branches from a living tree. It is, therefore, perplexing to note that, as she advanced in insight and mastery, these plots became more complicate and obstructive. The evolution of *Adam Bede, Silas Marner* and *The Mill on the Floss* is simple and natural, compared with that of *Middlemarch, Felix Holt* or *Daniel Deronda*; and this fact partially justifies the critics who maintain the superiority of her early work. It was, in truth, more homogeneous; but what her later books lost in structural unity they gained in penetration, irony and poignancy of emotion: an exchange almost purely advantageous in the case of an author whose psychological insight so far surpassed her constructive talent.

It remains to be asked why, as her powers developed, her weaknesses increased; why she sacrificed more to convention in her later than in her earlier books; why the novels of her maturity are her worst as well as her greatest. The answer must probably be sought in her personal situation. From her letters, and from the few published records of her life, one gathers that she was above all else a moralist. Her ethical sensibilities were peculiarly acute: she vibrated to *nuances* of conduct as an artist vibrates to subtleties of line and colour. She was, moreover, what might be called a conservative in ethics. She felt no call to found a new school of morals. A deep reverence for the family ties, for the sanctities of tradition, the claims of slowly acquired convictions and slowly formed precedents, is revealed in every page of her books. In *The Mill on the Floss*, when Maggie parts from Stephen, the burden of her cry is, "I cannot take a good for myself that has been wrung out of their misery . . . it would rend me away from all that my past life has made dear and holy to me" . . . and her first instinct is, not to fly from the scene of her grief and humiliation, but to return to it, and reknit again, at whatever cost of personal anguish, the ties which a moment of passion had so nearly severed. This faithfulness to inherited or accepted duty is, in fact, the keynote of George Eliot's teaching. The stern daughter of the voice of God stands ever at the side of Romola and Dorothea, of Lydgate and Maggie, and lifts even Mr. Farebrother and poor Gwendolen to heights of momentary heroism.

All George Eliot's noblest characters shrink with a peculiar dread from any personal happiness acquired at the cost of the social organism; yet her own happiness was acquired at such cost. That she felt herself justified by special circumstances her letters assert, and those who knew her best have repeatedly affirmed. She wrote, in a moment of profound insight, that "the great problem of the shifting relation between passion and duty is clear to no man who is capable of apprehending it;"[8] but she never ceased to revere the law she had transgressed, and her later books proclaim with a passionate reiterance the truth of Goethe's words:

> *Ein guter Mensch in seinem dunkeln Drange*
> *Ist sich des rechten Weges wohl bewusst.*[9]

This reiterance may help to explain the course of her literary evolution. If her life in London was at first a moral and intellectual liberation, a setting-free of unsuspected activities of heart and brain, it came to be, from the nature of circumstances, as narrowing, as restricting as her early existence in Coventry. She may have been satisfied that her own course was defensible; but, to all appearances, it was an open contradiction of her teachings, and the seeming inconsistency must have tortured her as social disapproval would have tortured an inferior nature. Pride, and the inability to justify herself to the world, drove her into seclusion, and, unconsciously, perhaps, she began to use her books as a vehicle of rehabilitation, a means, not of defending her own course, but of proclaiming, with increasing urgency and emphasis, her allegiance to the law she appeared to have violated. Some such unconscious attempt at readjustment seems at least to explain the strange deflection of her talent; and it is, perhaps, not a paradox to say that if George Eliot had been what the parish calls "respectable," her books would have been a less continuous hymn to respectability.

Their increasing seriousness, the greater prominence of the moral issue, may have suggested the need of propitiating her readers by a correspond-ing development of plot; and from this need the complicated machinery of *Middlemarch* and *Daniel Deronda* may have originated. Certainly, from one cause or another, her novels, as they gained in psychological truth, in depth of sympathy, in power of characterisation, lost in breadth of vision, narrow-ing as they grew deeper. This, again, seems explicable when the artificial conditions of her life are considered. Her growing preoccupation with moral problems coincided with an almost complete withdrawal from ordinary con-tact with life. She retired from the world a sensitive, passionate, receptive, responsive woman; she returned to it a literary celebrity; and in the interval ossification had set in. Her normal relations with the world ceased when she left England with Lewes. All that one reads of her carefully sheltered exis-tence after she had become famous shows how completely she had cut her-self off from her natural sources of inspiration. It is idle to lay down any general rule as to the necessary relation between the creative imagination and its surroundings; but it may at least be said that the novelist of manners needs a clear eye and a normal range of vision to keep his picture in per-spective; and the loss of perspective is the central defect of George Eliot's later books.

Bookman, May 1902

[1] "Every schoolboy knows who imprisoned Montezuma, and who strangled Atahualpa," fa-miliar line from "Lord Clive" (1840) of Thomas Babington Macaulay (1800–59), English his-torian and essayist; "La mode d'aimer Racine passera comme la mode du café," remark as originally ascribed to Marie de Rabutin Chantal, marquise de Sévigné (1626–96), by Voltaire in the preface to *Irene* (1778) and later compressed into more epigrammatic form by Jean-François

de La Harpe (1739–1803), literary critic and disciple of Voltaire, in his *Lycée; ou, Cours de littérature ancienne et moderne* (1799–1805). The statement occurs nowhere in the remarkable letters for which Madame de Sévigné is best known.

[2] Darwin's remark occurs in his posthumously published *Autobiography* (1887).

[3] "L'hypothèse est une sorte de roman sublime, c'est le poème du savant," from *Les problèmes de l'esthétique contemporaine* (1884), by Jean-Marie Guyau (1854–98), French philosopher.

[4] *Paradise Lost*, book 1, l. 288.

[5] As quoted in Boswell's *Life of Johnson* (1766–76), Tuesday, 18 April 1775.

[6] Auguste Comte (1798–1857), influential nineteenth-century social philosopher, founder of positivism, much admired by John Stuart Mill and others in Eliot's London circle.

[7] "Two souls dwell, alas, within my breast," from Goethe's *Faust*, part 1, l. 1112 ("meine" should read "meiner"); a favorite line of Wharton's, quoted again, for example, a few months afterward in a letter to Sara Norton (*L*, 72–73).

[8] From Eliot's novel, *The Mill on the Floss* (1860), Book 7, chap. 2.

[9] "A good man harried in his dark distress / Is well aware of the right path," from Goethe's *Faust*, part 1, ll. 328–29.

The Theatres

Mrs. Fiske last night opened a supplementary season at the Manhattan Theatre with a brilliant presentation of *Tess of the D'Urbervilles*.[1] The Anglo-Saxon stage has its accepted code of signals—its hieroglyphs of speech and gesture. According to these, a person who in real life would be likely to sit quietly and speak in restrained tones, is required to pace the stage like a panther and bellow out his sentiments or pronounce them in a slow, chanting drawl. To any one objecting that this tissue of unrealities does not suggest a rendering of real life, managers and critics reply with unanimous contempt that the stage perspective must be preserved, and that natural acting will not "carry."

To this argument there could be no more complete and destructive answer than Mrs. Fiske's acting of "Tess." Mrs. Fiske has not, it is true, disregarded the perspective of the stage; no actress with a grain of dramatic feeling could do that. She has simply had the courage to sweep aside a mass of superannuated conventions, to trust a little to the intelligence of her audience, and to give them, in the most direct and simple terms of which dramatic interpretation is capable, a superbly living presentment of Hardy's heroine.

To a theatregoer seeing Mrs. Fiske for the first time, and insensibly prepared for a more or less skilful use of familiar methods, the performance must come with almost startling effect. Is it possible, such a spectator might exclaim, that the American stage has at last produced an actress who, without losing for a moment the sense of theatrical limitations, and without obtaining her effects by the use of a cheap colloquialism, has managed to express a simple character in simple terms, without resorting to a single recognizable stage device? This is in fact what Mrs. Fiske has done, and in celebrating the feat one is tempted to rate her courage almost as high as her talent.

The story of Tess is too familiar to need recapitulation here. Mr. Stoddard's dramatization has robbed the tale of much of its poetic value and human significance, and Mrs. Fiske deserves the higher praise for keeping her representation on a level with the novelist's original creation. All through her acting one feels that sense of fatality so characteristic of Mr. Hardy's conception. Strong, courageous and loyal as Tess is, she is nevertheless the sport of the gods. In the play her misfortunes are piled up with crude prodigality, and at one or two points it requires all Mrs. Fiske's talent to save the tragedy from toppling over into burlesque. With so sensitive an actress the sense of unreality cannot but make itself felt; and once or twice, when disaster cumulates, Mrs. Fiske drops into conventionality. But it is only for a moment. At the first chance she regains possession of the real Tess, and brings her before the audience with all the force of a profound artistic conviction.

Where there is so much to praise it is difficult to select, but perhaps Mrs. Fiske's chief distinction lies in her remarkable sobriety of method, in her marvellous skill in producing effects with the smallest expenditure of voice and gesture. In a part like that of Tess such a capacity for silence and immovability is invaluable. All through the play Mrs. Fiske is the passionate, inarticulate peasant, and not the clever actress in a peasant makeup. Her extraordinary realism deserves special commendation, because it never once oversteps the bounds of stage illusion, because in every detail it is the product, not of haphazard divination, but of a keen sense of stage requirements—the art that conceals art. But no less noteworthy is the skill with which Mrs. Fiske, without sentimentalizing her part, has managed to preserve its poetry. Her Tess is a crude, rudimentary creature, but never a vulgar or a brutal one. Mrs. Fiske has heroically eschewed the temptation to take her audience by the two "effects" most certain of success—sentimentality and coarseness. And the result, last night, was a triumph for that much underrated faculty, the intelligence of the theatrical public. The audience vibrated to every one of Mrs. Fiske's touches. A breath of fresh air, an unwonted thrill of reality, permeated the stale atmosphere of the theatre.

Every gesture, every intonation of Mrs. Fiske reached its mark. When, after the murder, she stood mechanically brushing her hair—when Angel Clare loosened the brush from her rigid fingers and said "Come"—one felt through the whole packed and breathless house the sweep of that mighty force which "purges the emotions by pity and terror." The actress had every heart-string in her grip.

Such talent, united to such art, cannot be too highly commended in these days of theatrical clap-trap and triviality. Let Mrs. Fiske give New York a few more such impersonations—if possible, in plays more worthy of her powers—and she will do more than all the managers and all the dramatic critics to raise the theatrical ideals of the public and restore the dignity of the drama.

New York Commercial Advertiser, 7 May 1902

[1] [Mrs.] Minnie Maddern Fiske, born Marie Augusta Davey (1864–1932), prominent American actress who appeared with great success in a revival of a dramatization of Thomas Hardy's novel that she had commissioned from Lorimer Stoddard (1864–1901), an American playwright, a few years earlier. According to her biographer, who quotes at length from Wharton's review, "the critic of the New York *Commercial Advertiser* relinquished his column for a day to one of the elite of the four hundred," among whom the production was particularly triumphant (Archie Binns, *Mrs. Fiske and the American Theatre* [New York: Crown, 1955], 126–27); however, the circumstances under which Wharton undertook this one-time assignment are unclear. A few days later her review was reprinted, minus one paragraph, with the title "Mrs. Fiske in the Special Production of *Tess of the D'Urbervilles*," in the *New York Herald,* 11 May 1902, 7. On the same day her review appeared, she remarked to Howells, "I wish *you* would write something about Mrs. Fiske, who seems to me, from what I saw last night, worthy of being singled out by some one whose good opinion counts with our poor muddled 'doped' theatrical public" (*L,* 62). Her "eulogistic piece" was much appreciated, as "Mrs. Fiske's gratitude took the form of a free box for the rest of the season" (Lewis 108). Wharton also admired the actress's reprise, shortly after *Tess,* of her role as Nora in *A Doll's House,* in which her initial performances, eight years earlier, had been instrumental in adding prestige and acceptability to Ibsen's work in America. For the text of Stoddard's adaptation, see *"Tess" in the Theatre,* ed. Marguerite Roberts (Toronto: University of Toronto Press, 1950), 73–129; Wharton's notice is cited in the highly informative introduction (xliii).

The Three Francescas

The almost simultaneous production of three plays on the subject of Francesca da Rimini, by play-wrights of three different nationalities, illustrates in an interesting manner that impulse of the creative fancy which so often leads one imaginative writer to take up a theme already dealt with by another.[1] The greatest geniuses have been swayed by such currents of suggestion:

there are moments when certain subjects are in the air and present themselves irresistibly to imaginations of the most different order. This is perhaps especially the case when the situation or the story dealt with is one already familiar to the world, when it has grown to be an integral part of human culture, as in the case of the tragedy of Rimini. The Elizabethan dramatists repeatedly exemplified this tendency of the creative mind to re-mint the currency of fiction, to individualize stock types in its own image. An inexhaustible suggestiveness is the property of certain great stories dealing with universal passions and instincts, and there will probably never come a time when Romeo and Juliet, Lear and Othello do not furnish material for re-embodiment.

Where—as in the plays just cited—a dramatic situation has taken definitive form in the hands of genius, the later comer is of course debarred from deliberate use of the fable; but what is *"Le Père Goriot"* but another telling of "Lear," and in how many later tales of thwarted love or death-dealing jealousy are the germs of "Romeo and Juliet" and of "Othello" wholly absent? With the story of Francesca the case is different. Here the episode was simply hinted at by Dante, and perhaps even those to whom his lines are familiar will be surprised, on turning to them again, to see how little of the story he tells: so closely has it come to be associated, in every incident, with his evocation of the two who go forever on the accursèd air. Dante gave but the central fact of the great love against which the gates of hell could not prevail; but his contemporaries knew how to fill up this outline with the familiar details of a tragedy still recent when he wrote.

Of the authors now under consideration, Mr. Phillips was earliest attracted by the dramatic possibilities of the tale. His play was written some four years ago; and in a discussion of the three dramas it should therefore come first. Before examining the plays separately, however, it is necessary to find some basis of comparison; since they are too different to be compared at all points. In form, for instance, Mr. Phillips has chosen blank verse, Signor d'Annunzio *vers libres*, rhymed and unrhymed, and Mr. Crawford (for special reasons) a prose simple to the verge of baldness. These vehicles of expression cannot be profitably compared, and one must seek elsewhere for an attribute common to the three versions. This is found in the fact that all three were written for the stage; and from this stand-point they must be considered.

In dealing with so well-known a theme, the dramatist's task is complicated by the fact that he must discount the suspense of his audience. From the first line they are in the secret with him: every spectator knows that Francesca and Paolo love each other, and that in the end their love will be found out and punished. The author, therefore, cannot play on the conjectures of his audience; and suspense being avowedly one of the most important factors in dramatic presentment, he must make up for this deficiency by keeping his characters in the dark and letting his audience become absorbed in their gropings through the labyrinth of fate. From the outset, the spectator knows the doom suspended over the house of Malatesta; and the chief interest in the play must lie in watching "the gods creep on with feet of wool"[2] upon their unsuspecting victims. How, then, has Mr. Phillips fulfilled this condition?

The recorded facts of Francesca's story need amplification to fit them for dramatic purposes, and Mr. Phillips has broken with tradition in making a jealous woman sow the first seeds of suspicion in Malatesta's mind. His cousin Lucrezia, a childless widow who for years has been deep in his counsels, is embittered by his marriage to the young and beautiful Francesca, and seizes the first chance to hint at the likelihood of his having a rival in his brother. Lucrezia is the most life-like and forcible character in the drama— the only man in it, one might say—but her intervention so early in the play removes the important element of suspense, and makes of the remaining acts a merely episodical progress toward an anticipated catastrophe. Herein lies the weakness of the play. From the middle of the second act the audience knows that Giovanni is aware of his brother's love for Francesca. He is still ignorant, indeed, if that love be returned, or, if returned, how far feeling has been curbed by duty; but these minor considerations, though used with ingenuity, fail to arrest the interest of the spectator, who feels that, since *he* knows, and Giovanni knows, and Lucrezia knows, it is idle to keep up the mystery.

If Mr. Phillips has thus sacrificed one element of dramatic effectiveness, he has missed another by his neglect of local color, both in the atmosphere and in the psychology of the play. Local color of the external sort is, on the whole, an overrated pigment; but there is a subtle way of suggesting the atmosphere of a period and country, of indicating, allusively, the racial point of view and the natural environment; and this Mr. Phillips has failed to do. In a general—a very general—sense, it may be said that such primary passions as love and jealousy are the same in all races and ages; but this generalization will not stand the test of specific application. If the exponents of these passions are to have any more individuality than the vices and virtues of an old Morality, they must be given a local habitation. It is still broadly true that *la morale est purement géographique*, and that, in an Italian and an

Anglo-Saxon temperament, love and jealousy do not operate in the same way or with the same results. More especially is this the case when the Italian is a thirteenth-century tyrant, the Anglo-Saxon his modern interpreter. It is safe to say that Giovanni Malatesta (quaintly described in the *Ottimo Commento*[3] as "an open-hearted man, warlike and cruel") would not have behaved like a gentlemanly Englishman with a tendency to introspection and melancholia. He certainly would not have made such a to-do about killing his wife and brother. It was thus that such matters were settled in mediaeval Italy. To a lord of the *haute justice* it was as natural, as obligatory, one might say, to kill an unfaithful wife with his own hands, as it would be for a modern Englishman to apply for a divorce.

The moral susceptibilities of the other characters are equally tender. Francesca's innocence verges on *niaiserie*, and Paolo is a Werther with a dash of University Settlement.[4] From the first he shuns Francesca's perilous nearness, and when love prevails, and he finds himself powerless to flee, he buys poison and resolves to die at her feet. Giovanni, overhearing the avowal of his love (an avowal which Paolo forces somewhat needlessly on the reluctant apothecary who sells him the drug), is so moved by his brother's suicidal intentions that he exclaims: "I cannot have thee die, my Paolo!" In thirteenth-century Rimini, the chances are that, before Paolo had time to swallow the potion, he would have had his brother's knife in his back; but Mr. Phillips's characters have read "The Data of Ethics"[5] and cultivated the other-regarding virtues. Even the virago Lucrezia, who, at the outset, seems disposed to take somewhat illogical revenge on the world in general for the fact of her childlessness, melts suddenly at an affectionate word of Francesca's, and tries to check the machinery of murder that she has set in motion. If, as Mr. Phillips obscurely hints, Lucrezia's hatred of Francesca is based on a not always unreciprocated passion for Giovanni, it seems unlikely that the young wife's advances should have such a softening effect, especially as Francesca's appeal reveals her love for Paolo; but Mr. Phillips, who refuses to let any of his characters *savourer* their vengeance in good Italian fashion, appears to believe in "changes of heart" as rapid and complete as revivalist conversions.

Lucrezia, then, having been asked by Francesca to "think of her as a little child," is so touched by this request that she dashes out in pursuit of Giovanni, to whom she had previously suggested the classic expedient of a feigned departure, in order that he should return and surprise the lovers. Her repentance naturally comes too late. Paolo and Francesca have to be killed, and the audience knows that, while Lucrezia rushes out by one door,

Giovanni will come in by another. In a moment he does come in. He has found and killed the lovers, and he says to Francesca's frightened waiting-woman:

> Is it not time you dressed her all in white,
> And combed out her long hair as for a sleep?

Dramatically, this scene is the finest in the play. Malatesta for a moment ceases to be a modern altruist, and becomes a mediaeval Italian drunk with revenge. "And now," he exclaims,

> And now their love that was so secret close
> Shall be proclaimed. Tullio, Carlo, Biagi!
> They shall be married before all men. Nita!
> Rouse up the house and bring in lights, lights, lights!
> There shall be music, feasting and dancing.
> Wine shall be drunk. Candles, I say! More lights!
> More marriage lights! Where tarry they the while,
> The nuptial tapers? Rouse up all the house!

This is not only fine poetry but good psychology. For the first time since the opening of the play one feels one's self in Italy—at least in the Elizabethan Italy of "The White Devil" and "The Duchess of Malfy"; for, as Vernon Lee has pointed out in "Euphorion," the real meridional went about his bloody business in much more prosaic and instinctive fashion than his northern interpreter could even then conceive possible.[6] Still, such minor differences do not spoil the illusion, for the Elizabethan Italy has long since become a recognized fief of the imagination. But the key soon changes. Malatesta begins to talk of the curse of Cain, and the scene closes, nobly indeed, as regards poetry, but on a note of sentimental fatalism unworthy of the opening. Since we have it on Dante's authority that Paolo and Francesca did not repent in hell, why should Malatesta repine on earth?

If Mr. Phillips has been chary in the use of local color, Signor d'Annunzio has laid it on with a lavish hand. It was of course easier for him, as an Italian, to enter into the psychology of his characters, to brush in their background by those allusive touches which are so much more suggestive than explicit statement. But the element of dilettanteism in his talent has led him to attempt a minute "reconstitution" of the period, so that the thread of his drama is almost lost in a labyrinth of archaeological and etymological details. The mere reading of Signor d'Annunzio's list of characters shows how large a part he allots to the episodical portrayal of life in a mediaeval Italian city. In a

chronicle-play there would have been room for his supernumeraries; but in
a psychological drama, of which the direct action is limited to three persons,
this swarming of musicians, soldiers, torch-bearers, cross-bowmen and so
on, affects one as though the figures in the tapestry hangings of the castle
had come down and thrust themselves between the living actors. To keep
such a crowded background in perspective requires the large scenic brush
of a master-dramatist; and even Shakespeare did not pack his middle distance in the plays where he wished the principal action to stand out in high
relief. Moreover, in his dramas of passion, every subordinate character is a
necessary link in the chain of action, as in the case of Oswald, the Fool and
the rival men-at-arms in "Lear." Signor d'Annunzio lacks the skill to utilize
his accessory figures in this way: they are merely put in to "look pretty," as
a collector arranges his bric-à-brac.

The result, it must be owned, is distinctly effective. The play unrolls a
series of vivid pictures, all suffused with the atmosphere of the old chronicles and the *novelle*. This is the real Italy of the Middle Ages—not the "academy of manslaughter, the sporting-place of murder" of the terrified English
imagination, but the bright fierce inconscient Italy of Mattarazzo and Boccaccio.[7] The pasteboard "flies" are replaced by the actual walls of the Malatesta keep, war-dinted, blood-stained walls, frowning over a fortified town
of trembling burghers and a land tilled by serfs and ravaged by the merce-
naries of rival tyrants. We are in Dante's Rimini.

Signor d'Annunzio has composed a fable in keeping with this background.
He reverts to the traditional story of Francesca's marriage—a story of fraud
and violence, for the real Francesca was no Patient Grizzel, but a damsel so
high of spirit—*d'altiero animo*—that, to trick her into marriage with the
deformed Giovanni Malatesta, it was necessary to make her think that his
brother Paolo—himself a married man, and sent to wed her by proxy—was
to be her real husband. This at once secures the spectator's sympathy for
Francesca. She has been basely used, and her husband is a party to the
fraud. In the first act, Signor d'Annunzio shows Francesca at her father's
court in Ravenna, surrounded by her attendant damsels and her brawling
scheming brothers. One of these, Ostasio, who for political reasons is set
on the Malatesta alliance, but who wavers at the thought of sacrificing the
girl, thus describes her to the notary who is urging the expediency of the
marriage:

> Ah, she were worth a crown! How beautiful!
> No blade is straighter than the gaze she plants
> Straight in the eyes of whoso speaks with her.

> But yesterday she said: "What man is this
> To whom you give me, brother?" When she goes,
> Her great hair all about her to the knees . . .
> She gladdens me like ensigns in the wind
> Over a conquered city . . . then it seems
> The eagle of our House sits on her wrist
> Like a jessed falcon straining for high prey.
> But yesterday she said: "What man is this
> You give me to?" *Ah, who shall see her end?*

Eight centuries and the Alps lie between this Francesca and Mr. Phillips's.

Expediency overrules Ostasio's scruples. He imprisons a wandering *jongleur* whom he suspects of having come to Ravenna in Paolo's train, and of knowing that this brilliant cavalier is but a vicarious wooer; and the act closes with the picture of Francesca handing a rose to her supposed husband through the courtyard gates.

The second act shows the interior of the castle of Rimini. The fortress is besieged by Ghibelline forces, and Francesca has mounted to the upper story of the keep. Here she is joined by Paolo, newly come from besieging Cesena with Guido de Montfort. This Paolo is not the carpet-knight of tradition, "more given to the arts than to warfare." A year has passed since the marriage of Francesca, and since then

> Peace and the soul of Paolo Malatesta
> Forevermore are foes in life and death.
> For all about me turned to enmity
> The day thine unreturning foot was set
> Within this fatal house, and mine withdrawn.
> Bloody deeds
> That night did medicine my wounded soul.
> Tindaro Omodei I slew, and left
> His roof in ruins, flinging him as prey
> To the insatiate furies at my heels.

Francesca listens, trembling and invoking the saints; but in that moment of violence and terror their love for each other flames up like the Greek fire blazing about them. This scene, where the air hums with flying missiles and the sky is lit by the flare of blazing roofs, is one of the finest in the play. The lovers are swept into each other's arms by the heightened passion of the moment. Suddenly Giovanni appears. The day is nearly won, and he comes to tell his brother that the Florentine envoys have brought the good news of his election as Captain of the People. Francesca tells her Cypriote slave to bring a draught of wine to the thirsty warriors. Giovanni drinks first, and then bids her hand the cup to his brother; and she offers it with the words

> O brother of my lord, drink the cup
> Thy brother drinks of—

a phrase on which the act should have closed.

The scene of the third act is the bedchamber of Francesca, "panelled with pictures of the story of Tristan." Francesca is reading aloud to her damsels the tale of Guinevere and Lancelot. Presently Paolo arrives from Florence, and the latter half of the act is a prolonged love-scene, closing upon the fatal kiss. It is impossible, without going into detail, to render the incidental charm of this act, especially in its earlier portion, where Francesca talks with the merchant who has ridden in Paolo's train from Florence. Signor d'Annunzio has drawn with singular felicity on the legends, the poetry and the superstitions of the period, and the *gaia brigata* of Francesca's court live before us like the knights and ladies in the prologue of the Decameron. Dramatically, the effect is less successful, since the situation remains what it was at the close of the previous act.

Signor d'Annunzio, like Mr. Phillips, has had to devise a means of exciting Giovanni's suspicions. To this end, he has given Malatesta a younger brother, the terrible one-eyed Malatestino, a stripling who might have been drawn from Mattarrazzo's Grifonetto Baglione. This young bird of prey loves Francesca, and when she indignantly rejects his love, hints to her that he knows her secret and holds her fate and Paolo's in his hands. She drives him from her, and Malatestino, going to Giovanni, offers to give him proof of his wife's guilt. One episode in this scene, though quite unrelated to the action of the play, is too characteristic to be overlooked. Messer Montagna dei Parcitadi, one of the leaders of the Ghibellines whom Giovanni has success-fully repulsed, has been taken prisoner and cast into the dungeon of the keep. All through the lugubrious scene between Francesca and Malatestino, the captive Ghibelline's cries are heard. They unnerve and madden Francesca, and at length Malatestino declares that he will go down and silence the prisoner. Fascinated but helpless, she watches him go, and in a few moments the boy returns, dragging Montagna's head behind him in a linen cloth. "How heavy it is!" is his comment, as he drops his dripping burden.

Meanwhile Giovanni, at Malatestino's suggestion, has planned the usual feigned departure, and Paolo and Francesca forget their peril in the prospect of being for once alone together. The fifth act shows Francesca's bedchamber at midnight. She lies in an uneasy sleep, from which her maidens will not rouse her, because it is dangerous to waken a dreamer—*un cuor che vede*. They talk in undertones by the bedside. One says that Francesca always has her dreams interpreted by the Cypriote slave, Smaragdi; another whispers that she has seen Giovanni and Malatestino ride away under the starlight toward Pesaro, the younger brother carrying Parcitadi's bloody head at his saddle-bow; and a third sighs out that one can breathe freely again, now that the hunch-back and the one-eyed are gone. The whole scene is full of mystery, of fantastic sounds and shadows. Suddenly Francesca wakes. She calls for Smaragdi, the watchful slave, who is always at her side, who never fails to warn her of impending danger. But Smaragdi has vanished. She was last seen washing up the bloodstains on the court-yard pavement, where Malatestino had tied Parcitadi's head to his saddle-bow. The maidens seek her, calling softly down the dark stone corridors; but no answer comes. Smaragdi has been spirited away, and the air is full of doom.

Francesca dismisses her attendants. Suddenly she hears a low knocking on the door; she calls out "Smaragdi," but it is Paolo who enters. The scene moves rapidly to its end. Another knocking, this time loud and furious, tears the lovers from each other's arms. Giovanni bursts in and the brothers draw their daggers on each other; but Francesca flings herself between and receives Giovanni's blade in her breast.

It would have been impossible to do justice to Signor d'Annunzio's drama without dwelling at some length on the exquisite incidental touches which create its peculiar charm; yet it must be owned that these touches impede the action, and that the drama, when stripped of them, shows a complete arrest of movement in the third act. Far different is the construction of Mr. Crawford's "Francesca." Though in the French version (which includes a prologue) the action covers a space of fourteen years, it moves with a rapidity beside which Mr. Phillips's action drags and Signor d'Annunzio's seems to remain stationary. Yet this impetus is not acquired by mere stage ingenuity; indeed, it is to Mr. Crawford's credit that his skill in the construction of mechanical plots has not led him to turn a tragedy into a melodrama. He has preserved the simple outline which such a theme demands, and his dramatic instinct has saved him from clogging it with unessential detail.

His play was written for Madame Sarah Bernhardt, with the view of its being translated into French;[8] and these peculiar conditions restricted Mr.

Crawford to the use of the simplest prose. The English version necessarily suffers from this restriction. In a language which, like the English and the Italian, possesses a special poetic vocabulary, it is hard to render lofty situations in prose without running into colloquialism or bathos. Mr. Crawford has at least refrained from making his personages talk "prose poetry." They use the plainest and most direct English, and the play seems almost like the skeleton of a drama in blank verse.

This nudity makes the structure of the tragedy more salient. To turn from the crowded scene of Signor d'Annunzio's "Francesca" to the open spaces of Mr. Crawford's, is like passing from a modern English play with an elaborate stage-setting to the bare *mise-en-scène* of a classic drama at the Théâtre Français, where, if there is a glass of water on the stage, the spectator knows it has its special relevancy. Mr. Crawford, alone of the three authors, has turned to history for the chronology of his drama. According to the old chronicles, Paolo and Francesca loved each other for fourteen years before Giovanni discovered their secret; and, in the original version of Mr. Crawford's play, his heroine is the mother of a girl of thirteen when the action begins. A brief prologue, setting forth the fraud of Francesca's marriage, has been added to the French translation; but the addition, though cleverly made, detracts from the unity and simplicity of the original, and ought not to be included in its consideration.

Mr. Crawford, put to it, like his fellow-dramatists, to invent an effective way of exciting Giovanni's suspicions, has made the daughter, Concordia, the innocent means of her mother's betrayal. In the opening act, Francesca and Paolo are shown in the security of their long-established relation—a relation which Francesca believes to be completely justified by the abominable deception of her marriage. But a woman's voice is heard in the castle court, shrieking out maledictions on Paolo; and the latter, looking from the window, recognizes his wife Beatrice in the disguise of a peasant. Francesca's jealousy is immediately roused. She couples this mysterious incident with the fact that Paolo has suddenly and inexplicably accepted the post of Captain of the People, proffered by the Florentine government; the woman cries out again, "Paolo Malatesta! Coward! Betrayer!" Paolo, losing his self-command, dashes down to the court-yard, and Francesca, left alone, murmurs to herself: "A woman crying out his name—a woman leading a child—and on this very day he talks of leaving me!"

The next act opens, effectively, with the holding of a court of justice. Malatesta, as lord of the *haute et basse justice*, is to pass sentence on the various offenders who come under his jurisdiction. While the men-at-arms are preparing for the trial, Giovanni chats with his little daughter, and Concordia asks him what has become of the strange madwoman who had so frightened her mother and her uncle Paolo. Little by little, from the child's talk, Giovanni pieces out a fragmentary hint of the truth—enough to rouse a vague suspicion, without directing or defining it. One simply feels that henceforth he will be on the alert. Beatrice, meanwhile, has been seized and imprisoned and Paolo knows that she will be brought before his brother for trial. This must be prevented, and Paolo bribes the gaoler to let her escape; but Francesca, mad with jealousy, is equally determined that the prisoner shall not be shuffled out of sight. She appears, and insists on Giovanni's summoning the mysterious woman first. Paolo, at bay, makes a sign to the gaoler, and in a moment the latter returns with the announcement that the stranger has strangled herself. Giovanni bids the bearers bring in the body, and himself uncovers the dead woman's face. There is a pause full of dreadful significance, as each in turn recognizes Beatrice; then Malatesta, looking at his brother, says in a tone of solemn command: "Paolo Malatesta, bury your wife."

Francesca's jealousy has been lulled, but Giovanni's is awakened; and on Paolo's soul lies the weight of his wife's death. This psychological situation, brought about with masterly simplicity, serves to maintain the interest of the two remaining acts. Properly speaking, indeed, these form but one act in two scenes, which together compose the climax of the tragedy.

The scene opens in the walled garden under Francesca's window. Giovanni has set his spies in motion, and learns that Paolo has left Florence clandestinely. Without doubt he has come to Rimini, is perhaps even now in hiding in Francesca's chamber. As Giovanni talks with his wife he hears the casement stir overhead. The day is sultry, and he suggests to her that they should go indoors; but she declares that her room is stifling and that she has come into the garden for air. Every word and gesture confirms his suspicions. Now begins the most masterly scene in the play. Giovanni, the openhearted and cruel, has transformed himself into a smooth and subtle hypocrite, in order the more surely to compass his revenge. He tells his wife that Paolo has betrayed him, conspiring with the exiled Ghibellines to get possession of Rimini as a base of operation against the Florentine republic. This is no vague rumor—Giovanni has the facts from the Florentine government. Paolo has left Florence suddenly, without warning, and the question is—whither has he fled? "If he is innocent of treason he will either come here to escape from his enemies, or he will go back to Florence and face them. Which do you think he will do?"

Francesca falters: "I—I think he may come here"; and Giovanni answers quietly: "Yes, I think it is likely that you will see him here to-day."

She extracts a promise from Giovanni that he will not move against his brother till he has seen Paolo and heard his defence; but when her husband asks: "Will you give me nothing for this, Francesca?" she shrinks back with uncontrollable abhorrence, and Giovanni, clasping her with sombre passion, cries out: "I love you! I love you! *I shall love you still when you are dead.*"

The scene shifts to Francesca's room. Paolo, concealed there, has heard the conversation between husband and wife, but the two lovers, in each other's presence, are once more forgetful of impending danger. Francesca, indeed, suggests that they should take counsel together for Paolo's safety, but he answers, "Not yet!" and their talk strays back to the days of their early love, and to the book which had betrayed them. "Where is the book?" Paolo asks, and Francesca gives it to him. He begins to read and then hands it to her. She takes up the tale: "And when Launcelot saw Guinevere's lips—," but suddenly she exclaims: "It grows so dark that I can hardly see." The darkness is caused by a shadow falling across the book; the shadow of Giovanni who, his dagger between his teeth, noiselessly enters by the window before which the lovers sit. He reaches them unperceived, but as his arm is raised, Francesca sees him and flings herself across her lover. Up to this point the scene moves with a sombre rapidity; but its close is marred by a "death-bed speech" from the dying Francesca, which one suspects of having been composed at the request of Madame Bernhardt. Certainly, its effect is to let the play down suddenly from tragedy to melodrama; a fact the more to be regretted, as this is Mr. Crawford's only obvious concession to stage— or rather "stagy"—conventions. Signor d'Annunzio's Francesca makes a nobler end.

Whatever the merits of the two other plays—and they are many—Mr. Crawford has undoubtedly been most successful from the dramatic point of view. He has written the best "acting" play. His action is more rapid and simpler than that of the other dramatists, and has a higher quality of dramatic inevitableness. He has been clever in letting the surprise of the lovers take place without the time-honored device of the feigned departure. The psychology of his principal characters is firmly drawn, and though his play is as bare of metaphor as a tragedy of Alfieri's,[9] it does not lack high imaginative touches, as where Francesca exclaims on the sudden darkening of the light behind her: a touch which suggests, though on a lower plane, such lightning-flashes of significance as Keats's

> So the two brothers and their murder'd man
> Rode past fair Florence,[10]

and Imogen's exclamation on the road to Milford Haven:

> Why, one that rode to's execution, man,
> Could never go so slow.[11]

It is curious to note that the French critics, who have written much and favorably of Mr. Crawford's play, take exception at the two most characteristic *racial* traits in the drama: the long attachment of the lovers, and Malatesta's change from a violent and outspoken man to a stealthy smiling assassin. It is at these two points that Mr. Crawford has shown his insight into Italian character and his courage in departing from stage conventions. He has had the audacity to draw his characters as Italians of the Middle Ages, and not as scrupulous and sentimental modern altruists. Italian fidelity in love was for centuries the theme of wondering comment to French travellers, who saw only a *vieux collage* in the long devotion of a lover growing gray in his lady's service. According to the curious code of sexual morality in Italy, the tie between the lover and his mistress was as sacred as marriage, or was rather in fact what that abeyant bond was in theory; and Mrs. Piozzi, in her travels, gives a quaint picture of an old Milanese lady of noble birth, whose old *cicisbeo*, attended by his old servant, presents himself every evening at the same hour.[12] To those who understand this tradition, the long affection between Paolo and Francesca gives an added dignity and pathos to their situation, though it may prove a stumbling-block to English and American theatrical managers, whose recipe for historical drama consists in dressing up modern characters in the costumes of the period, and permitting the playwright the lavish use of "What ho!" and "Marry come up!" as a satisfying substitute for historic truth and racial psychology.

North American Review, July 1902

[1] Early in May 1902, Wharton wrote to Howells, "I should like to write an article on the three Francescas now before the public—Mr. Phillips's, Mr. Crawford's & d'Annunzio's—of which the two latter, at least, seem to me worth discussing," asking him "to transmit my suggestion" to the *North American Review* "if you think such an article would be acceptable." The plays she had in mind, all of them based on the famous canto 5 of Dante's *Inferno*, were *Paolo and Francesca* (1897), by Stephen Phillips (1864–1915), English playwright and poet; *Francesca da Rimini* (1902), by Gabriele d'Annunzio (1863–1938), Italian novelist and poet; and *Francesca*

da Rimini, by F. Marion Crawford (1854–1909), prolific American writer better known for his novels. Already giving a sign of the low priority that she would typically accord her own critical writing, Wharton added to Howells, "My reason for making the proposition in advance is that I have to economize my strength, & that the article is not likely to get itself written unless it is likely to be taken by the North American" (*L*, 61–62), where it in fact appeared in July. Another letter to Howells, a few days afterward, refers to a pair of earlier adaptations, *Francesca da Rimini* (1829), by Silvio Pellico (1788–1854), and *Francesca da Rimini* (1855), the best-known work of American playwright George Henry Boker (1823–90): "It had not occurred to me to speak of Pellico's & Boker's versions, as I supposed they were well known to the general reader ... & I feared my article might be too long if I included them in a critical survey" (EW to William Dean Howells, 12 May 1902 [Harvard]). Her fears were understandable, for the article would remain one of her fullest and most substantial. A week later, Wharton explained its genesis at length to Margaret Terry Chanler: "By the way, Mr. Crawford sent me about ten days ago the French version of his Francesca, & I am so emballée about it that I am writing for the North American an article on the three Francescas. It seems to me a very strong & simple play, & quite different in quality from anything he has ever written." Mentioning "d'Annunzio's Francesca" as well, Wharton adds, "I am not an admirer of the great man's, but in his case too, the theme seems to have inspired him, & though the play is absurd *as* a play, it is full of beauty as a romantic poem, & as mediaeval as a gothic tapestry" (*L*, 63). As for her third example, Wharton subsequently remarked to Brownell, "Certainly, I prefer Mr. Phillips plaintive to Mr. Phillips heroic. . . . But d'Annunzio can give him points this time! I hate to admit it, for I hate d'Annunzio, but his Francesca is very fine" (EW to William Crary Brownell, 23 May 1902 [Princeton]).

[2] "Thus, as the gods creep on with feet of wool / Long ere with iron hands they punish men / So shall our sleeping vengeance now arise / And smite with death thy hated enterprise"; lines of the Pope to Bruno in Christopher Marlowe's *Doctor Faustus*, act 3, sc. 1, ll. 100–104.

[3] Anonymously written fourteenth-century commentary on the *Divine Comedy*.

[4] As in "settlement houses," social-service establishments that began to be founded in urban neighborhoods, typically by educated professionals, toward the end of the nineteenth century in England and in the United States. Like her later observation that "Mr. Phillips's characters have ... cultivated the other-regarding virtues," the remark reflects the scornfulness with which Wharton regarded forms of organized benevolence.

[5] Published in 1879, and serving as volume 1, part 1, of *The Principles of Ethics* (1879–93), one of the chief works of Herbert Spencer (1820–1903), popular English evolutionary philosopher and scientific writer.

[6] *The White Devil* (1612) and *The Duchess of Malfi* (1612–13), plays of John Webster (1580?-1625?), English dramatist; "Vernon Lee," pseudonym of Violet Paget (1856–1935), English critic and aesthetician, author of *Euphorion: Being Studies of the Antique and the Mediaeval in the Renaissance* (1884) and many other works much admired by Wharton, who had first met her around a decade earlier.

[7] "O Italie, the Academie of man-slaughter, the sporting place of murther, the Apothecary-shop of poyson for all Nations," a passage from *Pierce Pennilesse his Supplication to the Devil* (1592) of Thomas Nashe (1567–1601); Francesco Matarazzo (c. 1443–1518), author of *Chronicles of the City of Perugia, 1492–1503*; Giovanni Boccaccio (1313–75), famous as the author of *The Decameron*.

[8] The French version of Crawford's play, with the celebrated actress in the title role, had opened in Paris on 22 April 1902.

[9] Vittorio Alfieri (1749–1803), leading Italian poet and dramatist of the eighteenth century.

[10] From Keats's *Isabella; or, The Pot of Basil* (1820), st. 27, ll. 219–20; elsewhere describing some of her own objectives as a writer, Wharton claims to have found it "always a necessity . . .

that the note of inevitableness should be sounded at the very opening of my tale, and that my characters should go forward to their ineluctable doom like the 'murdered man' in 'The Pot of Basil'" (*BG*, 204).

[11] From Shakespeare's *Cymbeline*, act 3, sc. 2, ll. 71–72. Nearly two decades later, the same passage exemplified for Wharton one of the "many ways of conveying [the] sense of the footfall of Destiny" so common in novels as well, illustrating her contention that "nothing shows the quality of the novelist's imagination more clearly than the incidents he singles out to illuminate the course of events and the inner workings of his people's souls" (*WF*, 161).

[12] Hester Lynch Thrale Piozzi (1741–1821), Englishwoman best remembered as the author of *Anecdotes of the Late Samuel Johnson* (1786). Wharton refers here to a passage from her *Observations and Reflections Made in the Course of a Journey through France, Italy, and Germany* (1789).

Mr. Paul on the Poetry of Matthew Arnold

Matthew Arnold. By Herbert W. Paul. London:
The Macmillan Company, 1902.

Biography makes strange bedfellows, and none stranger than some to be found in the English Men of Letters series. Since Trollope produced that astounding volume on Thackeray from which an hour's innocent mirth may still be extracted,[1] the appearance of the little volumes has continued to reveal a succession of surprising propinquities; indeed, some of the couples thus literally bound together suggest the grim hazard of a noyade rather than a deliberate selection of affinities.

Never, perhaps, has this system of grouping more curiously exemplified itself than in the choice of Mr. Herbert Paul as the biographer and critic of Matthew Arnold.[2] One is assailed by Landseerian images of dignity and impudence at the mere collocation of such names. To have chosen as the critic of the great critic one who, whatever irrelevant gifts he may possess, is, so to speak, aggressively destitute of those in which Arnold declared the critical equipment to consist—to have made such a choice seems almost a slight upon one of our purest glories.

The public has felt it as such, and there has been a general murmur of resentment, an audible clamour for revenge. Matthew Arnold needs no avenging: he can no more be patronized than he can be snubbed. But his readers feel the distinct need of some balm to their feelings; and their opportunity, their revenge, has been provided for them by Mr. Paul himself. For, however much his axiomatic flippancies about Arnold's prose may confuse the judgment of susceptible readers, the most inexperienced critic feels safe when Mr. Paul touches the subject of poetry. Here he rises from exasperating cleverness to a consoling density; here he has provided his readers with an arsenal of arms against himself.

The most accomplished critic may not be able to write with equal discrimination of prose and poetry, of critical, historical, and imaginative work; but Mr. Paul attacks his author's verse with the same cheerful dogmatism as his prose. Mr. Paul, however, is at heart a kindly ogre, and before proceeding to cut up his victim he announces that every poem in the latter's first volume "now forms a permanent part of English literature." This statement leads the thoughtful to speculate upon Mr. Paul's powers of divination, or upon his definition of permanency; but perhaps it was merely intended to show that Mr. Paul is a new Prometheus, who is not afraid of defying the immortals. Mr. Paul next proceeds to an analysis of the different poems; and here we have him at his best. It is, indeed, hard to say whether he is more felicitous in the framing of general rules or in their special application. "The Strayed Reveller," we learn, "opens well," but, alas, "full many a sovran morning have I seen," etc. For it appears that the author almost immediately falls into cacophany; and he is duly advised by his monitor that "poets, from the least to the greatest, have to reckon with the necessity of external forms." This striking admonition calls attention to the fact that the average English critic is still afraid of *vers libre*, still in bondage to the superstition of the Latin foot. In blank verse even any marked departure from the iambic pentameter is viewed with apprehension. The richness of Mr. Stephen Phillips's rhythms fills his admirers with a touching alarm, and Mr. Clement Scott, in a memorable page, went so far as to show him by actual example how some of his most Elizabethan measures might be rewritten in pentameters as smooth as those of Lord Derby's Iliad.[3] But it is not only the Mr. Clement Scotts who are afraid of accentual complexities. Mr. Paul, who believes that he regards English rhythms as accentual, really judges them as quantitative; or rather, he has substituted for the tyranny of the Latin scansion a convention equally alien to the spirit of English verse: the law of the regular accentual beat. This is to create a "foot" as definite as the Latin, though measured by stress and not by quantity. It rules out the noblest rhythms of Shakespeare and all the later Elizabethans, and makes many of Milton's lines tremble on the verge of cacophany. It would be interesting to see Mr. Paul apply his foot-rule to the spondees of Lycidas! It is curious, in this connection, to note how little Sidney Lanier's "Science of English Verse"—the most illuminating book ever written on the subject—has enlightened current criticism of metres.[4] In England especially, in spite of some admirable pages on metre in the second volume of Mr. Robertson's "Essays Toward a Critical Method,"[5] the critics are still frightened when poetry ventures out of sight of rhyme, and even rhymed irregular verse is looked upon as a hazardous experiment.

Mr. Paul next raises the question of where Arnold's sonnets should rank, and immediately settles it by saying, "No one, I suppose, would class them with Keats's or Wordsworth's. They might fairly be put on a level with Rossetti's." This pronouncement is perhaps the most original in the book. Mr. Paul selects with apparent deliberation the worst writer of sonnets among the great English poets, and after declaring his productions to be superior to Arnold's, adds that the latter's sonnets may, however, be put on a level with those of the one English poet of the second flight who surpasses all others in the use of this particular form of verse. Keats wrote one great sonnet, and one great line in a poor sonnet. With these exceptions it would be difficult to find among his sonnets one which, in idea or execution, rises above the keepsake level. To classify Arnold's sonnets in this way is like saying that his blank verse is profoundly inferior to Byron's, but may fairly be ranked with Milton's. As a matter of fact, lovers of Arnold's poetry do not lay great stress on his sonnets. They all abound in fine ideas, and here and there a fine line occurs; but, excepting "Immortality" and "Written in Butler's Sermons," there is no satisfying whole, and even these two, in that which makes the peculiar structural beauty of a sonnet—the simultaneous rise and break of the wave of thought and rhythm—are far below Rossetti's best. But Mr. Paul's most interesting comment is that which he makes on the last line of the sonnet "Written in Emerson's Essays":

> Dumb judges, answer, truth or mockery?

The line is bad enough, certainly; that Arnold had no natural gift for sonnet-writing is shown by the fact that almost all his last lines are inadequate. But it is not of this that Mr. Paul complains. "What is the use," he inquires, "of asking dumb judges to answer?" A few pages farther on he speaks of "a forgotten poet, remembered, if at all, as Wordsworth's son-in-law." How, as Mr. Paul would say, can he be remembered if he is forgotten? Mr. Paul's meaning is intelligible enough; but so, surely, is Arnold's, to readers aware that, in poetry at least, dumbness does not always mean a congenital atrophy of the vocal cords.

It will not surprise the discerning reader to find that in his judgment of the earlier poems, Mr. Paul's chief praise is given to "Mycerinus." It is always more instructive to study a critic in his preferences than in his dislikes. "Mycerinus" is exactly to Mr. Paul's taste and he has an excellent reason for it. "Wordsworth," he says, "could hardly have done better." Certainly he could hardly have done more like himself; but when a poet is past his first volume it is not for his resemblances that one cherishes him.

Most readers of Arnold will probably agree that, although all his later poetry has an individual note, his unrhymed *vers libres* are his most original contribution to English verse. But it is these that Mr. Paul especially deplores, and no wonder, since in his opinion some of the unrhymed lyrics "lead one to ask whether he (Arnold) had any ear at all." May not some readers turn this interrogation upon the critic? They will certainly be tempted to do so when he adds that, though "The Future" has "one beautiful line . . . it is not by these metrical or unmetrical experiments that Matthew Arnold lives." This being Mr. Paul's feeling, it is not surprising to find that he avoids all mention of "Growing Old" and "Philomela," rushes by "Rugby Chapel" as it were with averted head, and shudderingly alludes to "Heine's Grave" as containing "some grotesque instances of metrical eccentricity." So mistrustful of *vers libres* (even rhymed) is Mr. Paul, that in praising certain passages of "Empedocles" he omits all mention of the exquisite lyric by virtue of which it survives in the minds of most readers—the song of Cadmus and Harmonia.

Judging from these instances one might have supposed that Mr. Paul's taste would have found complete satisfaction in the severely heroic couplets of "The Church at Brou," but, alas, this otherwise commendable poem sins against the canons of accuracy—"the church," Mr. Paul assures us, "is not in the mountains, but in the treeless, waterless Burgundian plains." One is reminded of the fact that Mrs. Barbauld "pronounced the Ancient Mariner improbable."[6] Mr. Paul finds some compensation in the jingling lyrics of "Tristram and Iseult" ("Raise the light, my page, that I may see her"), though here again he feels it his duty to point out that, in the first edition, Arnold made another topographical error—he thought Tyntagel was a dactyl! No such blemishes, however, disturb Mr. Paul's enjoyment of "the pretty lines,"

> Eyes too expressive to be blue,
> Too lovely to be grey.[7]

Why, he seems to ask, should a poet with such evident aptitude for the valentine waste himself on less congenial themes?

But Mr. Paul, in his analysis of the successive volumes of poetry, goes from felicity to felicity. Perhaps he culminates in his remarks on "Thyrsis" and "The Scholar-Gipsy." This at least is the point at which all lovers of poetry are sure to await him, and here he will not disappoint them. "Fine as they are," he says, "the last two stanzas of 'The Scholar-Gipsy' are a little out of place." This is Mr. Paul's verdict on the analogy of the Tyrian trader— Arnold's most sustained imaginative flight, clothed in some of his loftiest and most musical verse! The comments on "Thyrsis" are equally instructive. Mr. Paul admires "Thyrsis;" and to justify his admiration he cites the first stanza, which, he thinks, "is unsurpassed in the whole poem." There are some lovers of Arnold's verse who would willingly strike out the whole first stanza of "Thyrsis" in order to eliminate the fatal second line—"In the two Hinkseys nothing keeps the same." And indeed the sacrifice would not be great: the stanza is insignificant in itself, and doubly so when compared with the splendours which follow it—with the "tempestuous morn in early June," and "When Dorian shepherds sang to Proserpine." Indeed in this comment Mr. Paul has given his final measure, has summed up with singular completeness all that his readers would like to say about his capacity for judging poetry. After this, they are content to watch the boomerang speed home.

Lamp, February 1903

[1] *Thackeray* (1879), by the English novelist Anthony Trollope (1815–82), is not usually considered objectionable in the way that Wharton describes.

[2] Herbert W. Paul (1853–1935), English Liberal parliamentarian, historian, and essayist, biographer of Gladstone and J. A. Froude, and author also of a five-volume *History of Modern England*. According to one spirited recent profile of Paul, the volume reviewed by Wharton "mainly serves to show up his limitations—the limitations of a solid but anachronistic country-house culture, and of long years spent being drilled in hexameters and 'longs and shorts' "; see John Gross, *The Rise and Fall of the Man of Letters: Aspects of English Literary Life since 1800* (London: Weidenfeld & Nicolson, 1969), 123–24.

[3] Stephen Phillips (1864–1915), English verse dramatist, whose works *Ulysses* and *Paolo and Francesca* were each reviewed by Wharton within the previous year; Clement Scott (1841– 1904), famously conservative English drama critic; Edward George Geoffrey Smith Stanley, fourteenth earl of Derby (1799–1869), whose translation of the *Iliad* appeared in 1864. Among "the 'poetical works' " in her father's library, Wharton later recalled "those of Homer (in Pope's and Lord Derby's versions)" (*BG*, 66).

[4] *The Science of English Verse* (1880), the major critical work of American poet Sidney Lanier (1842–81).

[5] *New Essays towards a Critical Method* (1897) followed *Essays towards a Critical Method* (1889), by John MacKinnon Robertson (1856–1933), English historian and critic.

[6] Statement attributed to Anna Letitia Barbauld (1743–1825), English poet and critic, by Coleridge, as recorded in the 31 May 1830 entry of *Table Talk* (1835), a report of conversations with the poet posthumously assembled by his nephew: "Mrs. Barbauld once told me that she admired *The Ancient Mariner* very much, but that there were two faults in it—it was improbable, and had no moral."

[7] From Arnold's poem "On the Rhine" (1852), ll. 19–20.

The Vice of Reading

That "diffusion of knowledge" commonly classed with steam-heat and universal suffrage in the category of modern improvements, has incidentally brought about the production of a new vice—the vice of reading.

No vices are so hard to eradicate as those which are popularly regarded as virtues. Among these the vice of reading is foremost. That reading trash is a vice is generally conceded; but reading *per se*—the habit of reading—new as it is, already ranks with such seasoned virtues as thrift, sobriety, early rising and regular exercise. There is, indeed, something peculiarly aggressive in the virtuousness of the sense-of-duty reader. By those who have kept to the humble paths of precept he is revered as following a counsel of perfection. "I wish I had kept up my reading as you have," the unlettered novice declares to this adept in the supererogatory; and the reader, accustomed to the incense of uncritical applause, not unnaturally looks on his occupation as a noteworthy intellectual achievement.

Reading deliberately undertaken—what may be called volitional reading—is no more reading than erudition is culture. Real reading is reflex action; the born reader reads as unconsciously as he breathes; and, to carry the analogy a degree farther, reading is no more a virtue than breathing. Just in proportion as it is considered meritorious does it become unprofitable. What is reading, in the last analysis, but an interchange of thought between writer and reader? If the book enters the reader's mind just as it left the writer's—without any of the additions and modifications inevitably produced by contact with a new body of thought—it has been read to no purpose. In such cases, of course, the reader is not always to blame. There are books that are always the same—incapable of modifying or of being modified—but these do not count as factors in literature. The value of books is proportionate to what may be called their plasticity—their quality of being all things to all men, of being diversely moulded by the impact of fresh forms of thought. Where, from one cause or the other, this reciprocal adaptability is lacking, there can be no real intercourse between book and reader. In this sense it may be said that there is no abstract standard of values in literature: the greatest books ever written are worth to each reader only what he can get out of them. The best books are those from which the best readers have been able to extract the greatest amount of thought of the highest quality; but it is generally from these books that the poor reader gets least.

To be a poor reader may therefore be considered a misfortune; but it is certainly not a fault. Why should we all be readers? We are not all expected to be musicians; but read we must; and so those that cannot read creatively read mechanically—as though a man who had no aptitude for the violin were to regard the grinding of a barrel-organ as an equivalent accomplishment! It must be understood at the outset that, in the matter of reading, the real offenders are not those who restrict themselves to recognized trash. There is little harm in the self-confessed devourer of foolish fiction. He who feasts upon "the novel of the day" does not seriously impede the development of literature. The cast of mind which discerns in the natural divisions of the melon an indication that it is meant to be eaten *en famille*, might even look upon certain works—the penny-in-the-slot or touch-the-button books, which require no effort beyond turning the pages and using one's eyes—as especially designed for the consumption of the mechanical reader. Providence turns out an unfailing supply of authors whose obvious mission it is thus to protect literature from the ravages of the unintelligent; and it is only when he strays from his predestined pastures that the mechanical reader becomes a danger to the body of letters. The idea that reading is a moral quality has unhappily led many conscientious persons to renounce their innocuous dalliance with light literature for more strenuous intercourse. These are the persons who "make it a rule to read." The "platform" of the more ambitious actually includes the large resolve to keep up with all that is being written! The desire to keep up is apparently the strongest incentive to this class of readers: they seem to regard literature as a cable-car that can be "boarded" only by running; while many a born reader may be found unblushingly loitering in the tea-cup times of stage-coach and posting-chaise, without so much as being aware of new means of locomotion.

It is when the mechanical reader, armed with this high conception of his duty, invades the domain of letters—discusses, criticises, condemns, or, worse still, praises—that the vice of reading becomes a menace to literature. Even so, it might seem in questionable taste to resent an intrusion prompted by motives so respectable, were it not that the incorrigible self-sufficiency of the mechanical reader makes him a fair object of attack. The man who grinds the barrel-organ does not challenge comparison with Paderewski, but the mechanical reader never doubts his intellectual competency. As grace gives faith, so zeal for self-improvement is supposed to confer brains.

To read is not a virtue; but to read well is an art, and an art that only the born reader can acquire. The gift of reading is no exception to the rule that all natural gifts need to be cultivated by practice and discipline; but unless the innate aptitude exist the training will be wasted. It is the delusion of the mechanical reader to think that intentions may take the place of aptitude.

So far is this from being the case that there are certain generic signs by which the born reader detects his manufactured copy under whatever guise the latter may assume. One of these idiosyncrasies is the habit of regarding reading objectively. The mechanical reader, as he always reads consciously, knows exactly how much he reads, and will tell you so with the pride of the careful housekeeper who has calculated to within half an ounce the daily consumption of food in her household. As the housekeeper is apt to go to market every day at a certain hour, so the mechanical reader has often a fixed time for laying in his intellectual stores; and not infrequently he reads for just so many hours a day. The statement in one of Hamerton's youthful diaries—"I shall now commence a course of poetical reading, beginning with 50 hours of Chaucer, and as I gave him 1½ last night it leaves me exactly 48½"—is a good example of this kind of reading.[1] It follows that he who reads by time often "has no time to read"; a plight unknown to the born reader, whose reading forms a continuous undercurrent to all his other occupations.

The mechanical reader is the slave of his book-mark: if he lose his place he is under the irksome necessity of beginning again at the beginning; and a story is told of one such reader whom a flippant relative kept for a year at "Fire and Sword in the Soudan"[2] by the unfeeling stratagem of shifting the marker every night. The born reader is his own book-mark. He instinctively remembers at what stage in the argument he laid his book down, and the pages open of themselves at the point for which he is looking. It is due to the mechanical reader to say that he is uniformly scrupulous in the performance of his task: it is one of his rules *never to skip a word*, and he can always meet with a triumphant affirmative Dr. Johnson's immortal "Do *you* read books *through?*"[3] This inexorable principle is doubtless based on the fact that the mechanical reader is incapable of discerning intuitively whether a book is worth reading or not. In fact, until he has read the last line of a book he is unable to form any opinion of it; nor can he give any adequate reasons for his opinion when formed. Viewing all books from the outside, and having no point of contact with the author's mind, he makes no allowances for temperament or environment; for that process of transposition and selection that makes the most impersonal book the product of unique conditions.

It is obvious that the mechanical reader, taking each book separately as an entity suspended in the inane, must miss all the by-paths and cross-cuts of his subject. He is like a tourist who drives from one "sight" to another without looking at anything that is not set down in Baedeker. Of the delights of intellectual vagrancy, of the improvised chase after a fleeting allusion, suggested sometimes by the turn of a phrase or by the mere complexion of a word, he is serenely unaware. With him the book's the thing: the idea of using it as the keynote of unpremeditated harmonies, as the gateway into some *paysage choisi* of the spirit, is beyond his ken.

The mechanical reader considers it his duty to read every book that is talked about; a duty rendered less onerous by the fact that he can judge beforehand, from the material dimensions of each book, how much space it will take up in his head: there is no need to allow for expansion. To the mechanical reader, books once read are not like growing things that strike root and intertwine branches, but like fossils ticketed and put away in the drawers of a geologist's cabinet; or rather, like prisoners condemned to life-long solitary confinement. In such a mind the books never talk to each other.

The course of the mechanical reader is guided by the *vox populi*. He makes straight for the book that is being talked about, and his sense of its importance is in proportion to the number of editions exhausted before publication, since he has no means of distinguishing between the different classes of books talked about, nor between the voices that do the talking.

It is a part of the whole duty of the mechanical reader to pronounce an opinion on every book he reads, and he is sometimes driven to strange shifts in the conscientious performance of this task. It is his nature to mistrust and dislike every book he does not understand. "I cannot read and therefore wish all books burned." In his heart of hearts the mechanical reader may sometimes echo this wish of Envy in Doctor Faustus;[4] but, it being also a part of his duty to be "fond of reading," he is obliged to repress his biblio-cidal impulse, and go through the form of trying the case, when lynching would have been so much simpler.

It is only natural that the reader who looks on reading as a moral obliga-tion should confound moral and intellectual judgments. Here is a book that every one is talking about; the number of its editions is an almost unanswer-able proof of its merit; but to the mechanical reader it is cryptic, and he takes refuge in disapproval. He admits the cleverness, of course; but one of the characters is "not nice"; *ergo*, the book is not nice; he is surprised that you should have cared to read it. The mechanical reader, after a few such exper-iments, learns the potency of disapproval as a critical weapon, and it soon becomes his chief defence against the irritating demand to admire what he cannot understand. Sometimes his disapprobation is tempered by philo-sophic concessions to human laxity: as in the case of the lady who could not approve of Balzac's novels, but was of course willing to admit that "they were written in the most beautiful French." A fine instance of this temperate disapproval is furnished by Mrs. Barbauld's verdict upon The Ancient Mariner: she "pronounced it improbable."[5]

The obligation of expressing an opinion on every book which is being talked about has led to the reprehensible but natural habit of borrowing opinions. Any one who frequents a group of mechanical readers soon becomes accustomed to their socialistic use of certain formulas, and to the rapid process of erosion and distortion undergone by much-borrowed opinions. There have been known persons heartless enough to find pleasure in taking the mechanical reader unawares with the demand for an opinion; and it must be owned that the result sometimes justifies the theory that no sports are so diverting as those which are seasoned with cruelty. In such extremities, the expedients resorted to by mechanical readers often do justice to their inventiveness; as when a lady, on being suddenly asked what she thought of *"Quo Vadis,"*[6] replied that she had no fault to find with the book except that "nothing happened in it."

Thus far the subject has dealt only with what may be called the average mechanical reader: a designation embracing the immense majority of book-consumers. There is, however, another and more striking type of mechanical reader—he who, wearying of the Philistine diversion of "understanding the obvious," boldly threads his way "amid the bitterness of things occult."[7] Transcendentalism owes much of its perennial popularity to a reverence for the unintelligible, and its disciples are largely recruited from the class of readers who consider it as great an intellectual feat to read a book as to understand it. But these votaries of the esoteric are too few in number to be harmful. It is the average mechanical reader who really endangers the integrity of letters; this may seem a curious charge to bring against that voracious majority. How can those who create the demand for the hundredth thousand be accused of malice toward letters?

In that acute character-study, "Manoeuvring," Miss Edgeworth says of one of her characters: "Her mind had never been overwhelmed by a torrent of wasteful learning. That the stream of literature had passed over it was apparent only from its fertility."[8] There could hardly be a happier description of those who read intuitively; and its antithesis as fitly portrays the mechanical reader. His mind is devastated by that torrent of wasteful learning which his demands have helped to swell. It is probable that if no one read but those who know how to read, none would produce books but those who know how to write; but it is the least offence of the mechanical reader to have encouraged the mechanical author. The two were made for each other and may prey on one another with impunity.

The harmfulness of the mechanical reader is fourfold. In the first place, by bringing about the demand for mediocre writing, he facilitates the career of the mediocre author. The crime of luring creative talent into the ranks of mechanical production is in fact the gravest offence of the mechanical reader.

Secondly, by his passion for "popular" renderings of abstruse and difficult subjects, by confounding the hastiest *réchauffé* of scientific truisms with the slowly-matured conceptions of the original thinker, he retards true culture and lessens the possible amount of really abiding work.

The habit of confusing moral and intellectual judgments is the third cause of his harmfulness to literature. The inadequacy of "art for art's sake" as a literary creed has long been conceded. It is not by requiring that the imaginative writer shall be touched "to fine issues"[9] that the mechanical reader interferes with the production of masterpieces, but by his own inability to discern the "fine issues" of any book, however great, which presents some incidental stumbling-block to his vision. To those who regard literature as a criticism of life, nothing is more puzzling than this incapacity to distinguish between the general tendency of a book—its technical and imaginative value as a whole—and its merely episodical features. That the mechanical reader should confound the unmoral with the immoral is perhaps natural; he may be pardoned for an erroneous classification of such books as *"La Chartreuse de Parme"* or the "Life of Benvenuto Cellini"; his harmfulness to literature lies in his persistent ignorance of the fact that any serious portrayal of life must be judged not by the incidents it presents but by the author's sense of their significance. The harmful book is the trivial book: it depends on the writer, and not on the subject, whether the contemplation of life results in Faust or Faublas.[10] To gauge the absence of this perception in the average reader, one must turn to the ordinary "improper" book of current English and American fiction. In these works, enjoyed under protest, with the plea that they are "unpleasant, but so powerful," one sees the reflection of the image which the great portrayals of life leave on the minds of the mechanical reader and his novelist. There is the collocation of "painful" incidents; but the rest, being unperceived, is left out.

Finally, the mechanical reader, by his demand for peptonized literature, and his inability to distinguish between the means and the end, has misdirected the tendencies of criticism, or rather, has produced a creature in his own image—the mechanical critic. The London correspondent of a New York paper recently quoted "a well-known English reviewer" as saying that people no longer had time to read critical analyses of books—that what they wanted was a *résumé* of the contents. It is of course an open question (and one hardly within the scope of this argument) how much literature is benefited by criticism; but to speak as though the analysis of a book were one kind of criticism and the cataloguing of its contents another, is a manifest absurdity. The born reader may or may not wish to hear what the critics have to say of a book; but if he cares for any criticism he wants the only kind worthy of the name—an analysis of subject and manner. He who has no time for such criticism will certainly spare none to the summing-up of the contents of a book: an inventory of its incidents, ending up with the conventional "But we will not spoil the reader's enjoyment by revealing, etc." It is the mechanical reader who demands such inventories and calls them criticisms; and it is because the mechanical reader is in the majority that the mechanical plot-extractor is fast superseding the critic. Whether real criticism be of service to literature or not, it is clear that this pseudo-reviewing is harmful, since it places books of very different qualities on the same dead level of mediocrity, by ignoring their true purport and significance. It is impossible to give an idea of the value of any book, except perhaps a detective-story, by the recapitulation of its contents; and even those qualities which differentiate the good from the bad detective-story lie not so much in the collocation of incidents as in the handling of the subject and the choice of means used for producing a given effect. All forms of art are based on the principle of selection, and where that principle is held of no account in the sum-total of any intellectual production, there can be no genuine criticism.

It is thus that the mechanical reader systematically works against the best in literature. Obviously, it is to the writer that he is most harmful. The broad way that leads to his approval is so easy to tread and so thronged with prosperous fellow-travellers that many a young pilgrim has been drawn into it by the mere craving for companionship; and perhaps it is not until the journey's end, when he reaches the Palace of Platitudes and sits down to a feast of indiscriminate praise, with the scribblers he has most despised helping themselves unreproved out of the very dish prepared in his honor, that his thoughts turn longingly to that other way—the strait path leading "To The Happy Few."

North American Review, October 1903

[1] Reported by Philip Gilbert Hamerton (1834–94), English artist and art critic, in his posthumously published *An Autobiography: 1834–1858* (1896), 125.

[2] Translation of the popular personal narrative by Rudolf C. Slatin (1857–1932).

[3] Quoted in Boswell's *Life of Johnson* (1787), Monday, 19 April 1773.

[4] Christopher Marlowe, *Doctor Faustus*, act 2, sc. 2, ll. 133–34.

[5] See n. 6 to "Mr. Paul on the Poetry of Matthew Arnold."

[6] An English translation of Henryk Sienkiewicz's popular historical novel *Quo Vadis?* had appeared in 1896.

[7] "Thy name, O Lord, each spirit's voice extols, / Whose peace abides in the dark avenue / Amid the bitterness of things occult"; concluding lines of "For 'Our Lady of the Rocks'" by Leonardo Da Vinci," by Dante Gabriel Rossetti (1828–82), English Victorian poet.

[8] Description of Miss Walsingham in "Manoeuvring," from *Tales of Fashionable Life* (1809), by Maria Edgeworth (1767–1849), Irish novelist.

[9] "Spirits are not finely touch'd / But to fine issues"; lines of the Duke in Shakespeare's *Measure for Measure*, act 1, sc. 1, ll. 37–38.

[10] *Vie et amours du Chevalier de Faublas* (1789–90), light, frivolous novel by Jean Baptiste Louvet de Couvray (1760–97).

Mr. Sturgis's *Belchamber*

Belchamber. By Howard Sturgis. New York: G. P. Putnam's Sons, 1905.

Mr. Howard Sturgis has been known for several years to lovers of delicate workmanship and directness of insight as the author of a simple and charming tale called *All that was Possible*.[1]

His resources and versatility are shown by the remarkable degree in which his new novel differs from this earlier story. *All that was Possible*, a tragedy in miniature, has the pearl-grey tints of a sunless day; *Belchamber* is overhung by storm-clouds and shot through with baleful lightnings. The former book presented three persons, who were studied only in their relation to one another; while *Belchamber* shows a large group of people depicted in their relation to society. The two tales have, however, one quality in common; and that is the directness of observation that marks them both.

In a day when almost every one writes too much, Mr. Sturgis has the rare fault of writing too little, and *Belchamber* in some respects suffers from the fact that its author's hand has been inactive since the production of the shorter tale; but the redeeming merit of this inactivity is found in the preservation of that freshness of view so often sacrificed to technical facility. Mr. Sturgis has not seen his story through other novels, his own or those of others; if his first pages are reminiscent of Thackeray, that is merely a literary echo, the *tâtonnement* of the infrequent writer not quite in possession of his formula. As the story develops, Mr. Sturgis instinctively throws off this method, and tells his tale in his own way: in a confidential, desultory, but not prolix manner, as though he were sitting over the fire with his reader, and giving the facts as they had come under his observation.

Belchamber, in short, has at once the faults and the freshness of the novelist who has told little but observed much: faults of construction and perspective, such as the hack writer would easily have avoided, and freshness of sensation and perception such as he could never have achieved. It has, above all, the quality of the "thing in itself," with something of the desultoriness, the irregularity, of life caught in the act, and pressed still throbbing between the leaves of the book.

Form is much—so much that, to the plodder through the amorphous masses of Anglo-American fiction, it seems sometimes all in all—but when it is the mere lifeless reproduction of another's design, the dreary "drawing from a plaster-cast," twice removed from reality, it is of no more artistic value than any other clever reproduction; whereas the *chose vue*, the thing personally felt and directly rendered, asserts itself through all accidental difficulties of expression.

Mr. Sturgis's choice of a theme may be thought to mark his relative inexperience as a novelist. Some may say that, in his desire to present life as it is, he has chosen what Balzac called "a situation true in life, but not in art:"[2] that is, unfitted to the restrictions and conventions of the novelist's craft. But the sincere critic's first business is to accept the author's postulate, and if Mr. Sturgis has chosen to hamper himself with a "difficult" subject, the question in point is to find out how he has dealt with it.

The difficulty lies in the character of his hero, the Lord Belchamber who gives the book its name. Mr. Sturgis has evidently said to himself: "I am tired of the so-called manly hero, the brawny and beautiful being who has pervaded English fiction for the last fifty years, always brilliant, victorious and irresistible. I will show that, in real life, this showy person often produces his effects at the cost of a great deal of suffering and shame inflicted on the adoring group about him; and by way of contrast I will present as my protagonist a man at odds with life, at odds with his situation, a man crushed under his rank and wealth, and miserably, ironically conscious of his inability to play the part which the other would fill with such consummate grace. I will show how this man, ridiculed, misunderstood and exploited by those about him, gives his life to repairing the evil wrought by the brawny and beautiful being who, according to the conventions of fiction, ought to be the hero of my book."

Lord Belchamber is heir to a great name and great estates; but he is lame, sickly, shy, and tormented by a morbid disbelief in the august institutions which he represents. The circumstances of his life have all tended to increase his self-distrust, his consciousness of being a square peg in a round hole. His mother, an energetic and ambitious woman, who has laboured through his minority to restore the fallen fortunes of the house, turns instinctively to the showy and brilliant younger son, who has the normal tastes of his class for war, woman and sport. The clever Cambridge Don, from whom Belchamber has imbibed some of his discontent with existing institutions, instead of responding to the young lord's desire to give up his title and devote himself to Settlement work in the East End,[3] takes refuge in platitudes about the duty of remaining in the station to which one has been called; and all the persons nearest to Belchamber turn a deaf ear to his aspirations, and make him feel that, inadequate and out of place as he is, there is no escape from his situation.

Belchamber has never thought of marrying; his brother Arthur is tacitly regarded as his heir; but when Arthur ends a long course of extravagance and dissipation by giving his name to a vulgar-souled variety actress, Belchamber is confronted by the fact that, unless he takes a wife, this irresponsible spendthrift couple will succeed to the estate so carefully nursed by his mother, and to the public duties and responsibilities connected with it. Sceptical as Belchamber is about the usefulness of the class to which he belongs, he has all its inherited devotion to the ancestral acres, and to the accumulated duties of the great landowner; and he allows his mother to push him gently toward marriage. A marriage of convention would be impossible to him; and the way in which he is captured by Cissy Eccleston and her mother is one of the cleverest and saddest chapters in the book. It is a profound touch of nature to make this self-critical, self-depreciatory man the victim of the first bold huntress who sets her cap at him; the vain man would have been warier, and even Cissy is surprised at the promptness with which she lands her prey.

The subsequent chapters of the book deal with the tragic results of this tragic marriage; and Cissy herself, the feminine counterpart of Arthur, is perhaps the most brilliant study in the book. She is not the caressing hypocrite dear to the novelist of fifty years ago. Whatever blushing and sentimentalising has to be done, she leaves to her mother, who, in deference to the traditions of a past generation, contrives to throw a glamour of romance over the crudity of the situation. Cissy scorns such pretences; her frankness would be a redeeming trait, were it not so obviously the expression of a callous nature. During the engagement she allows her mother to represent her as the lovesick maiden, rendered mute by the intensity of her feelings;

but once married she pours out her disdain upon her dupe with savage indifference to his anguish. Mr. Sturgis has been criticised for his heroine's reckless indifference to consequences in these sudden revelations of her real character; but as an extreme expression of a selfish nature's unwillingness to pay for what it has got, her rash outbreaks are surely logical enough.

Indeed, it is the most noteworthy thing about *Belchamber* that all its characters appear to do, not what the author has planned for them, but what is true to their natures. They are full of human inconsistencies and inconsequences, with the result that they are all alive, that one can walk all around them and see them on every side. This is as true of the subordinate characters as it is of the principal figures. Gerald Newby, the young Cambridge Don, whose "splendid opinions on all sorts of subjects" are so suddenly and surprisingly modified by his introduction to the aristocratic party assembled at Belchamber for his pupil's coming of age; the terrible old Duchess of Sunborough, with her wig, her sachets, her "spurious freshness," her shoulders "displaying to the world with the indifference of long habit their great expanse of lustreless pallour;" Claude Morland, the charming, tactful, adaptable young cousin, who ruins Arthur, corrupts Cissy, and thrives and grows more charming on the misery he spreads about him; Belchamber's mother, the earnest, downright, narrow-minded woman, who works so hard for her son's material welfare while she remains so blind to his spiritual needs; all these diverse figures are drawn with energetic strokes, and once set on their feet, remain there, instead of collapsing, as the most promising novel-characters have a way of doing after they have stood erect for a few moments. It is this effect of sustained life-likeness which distinguishes *Belchamber* from the mass of smartly written books made out of the stock accessories of fiction. Mr. Sturgis's little world is full of sound and movement: one learns to know how his people look, one would recognise the tone of their voices.

The tale in which they figure belongs to the class which is sometimes described as "unpleasant" by readers who do not pause to distinguish between a writer's purpose and his theme. Books dealing with the adventures of idle and fashionable people do not generally make for edification, for the reason with which Dr. Watts has furnished us.[4] But there is a noble way of viewing ignoble facts; and that is the view which Mr. Sturgis has taken of the world he depicts. He has shown us, in firm, clear strokes, the tragedy of the trivial: has shown us how the susceptibilities of a tender and serious spirit, hampered by physical infirmity, may be crushed and trampled under foot in the mad social race for luxury and amusement. A handful of vulgar people, bent only on spending and enjoying, may seem a negligible factor in the social development of the race; but they become an engine of destruction through the illusions they kill and the generous ardors they turn to despair.

Bookman, May 1905

[1] Howard Overing Sturgis (1855–1920), son of the prominent Boston banker Russell Sturgis, host at Qu'Acre (Queen's Acre), the family home in Windsor, to Wharton, Henry James, Percy Lubbock, and other members of her "inner circle." Wharton had unsuccessfully persuaded Brownell to have Scribner's arrange an American edition of *Belchamber*, published in England in 1904:

> Mr. Sturgis has only written two books before—a boys' book called "Tim" which had a great success in England, & a year or two later . . . , a short novel called "All That Was Possible," full of delicate qualities which were never fully appreciated in England, & was refused by American publishers on the ground that the heroine was a lady with a past!— Since then, he has done nothing till this new book, "Belchamber," a novel of English "hig lif" which seems to me so remarkable in donnée & character-drawing that, as soon as I read it, I asked if he had already found a publisher in America. . . . Mr. James, whom I saw in London before I read "Belchamber," thinks the situation very strong & original—but I am sure it will need neither his commendation nor mine to interest you & Mr. Scribner & I am writing to you quite spontaneously, simply because, when there is a good thing going, I want you to have it. (*L*, 87–88)

Neither Brownell nor Scribner became sufficiently interested, and *Belchamber* was eventually published in the United States by G.P. Putnam's Sons a year after its appearance in England. For Wharton's later, somewhat different account of Sturgis's *Belchamber*, and James's response, see *A Backward Glance*, 234–35.

[2] The phrase "un sujet vrai dans la nature qui ne l'est pas dans l'art" occurs in Balzac's famous review of *La chartreuse de Parme* (1839) in the *Revue Parisienne* (25 September 1840), with reference to Stendhal's handling of the Battle of Waterloo.

[3] Hideously impoverished quarter of London and the site of Toynbee Hall, established in 1884 as the first "settlement house"; see also n. 4 to "The Three Francescas."

[4] Isaac Watts (1674–1748), celebrated English divine, hymnist, and educator.

Maurice Hewlett's *The Fool Errant*

The Fool Errant. By Maurice Hewlett. New York:
The Macmillan Company, 1905.

Mr. Hewlett, deserting his chosen field of mediaeval adventure,[1] has laid the scene of his last book in eighteenth-century Italy; and though the period is evidently less familiar to him, and in some ways less adapted as a background to his figure-painting, the novel shows, on the whole, an advance over its predecessors.

This advance is displayed in a greater distinctness of characterisation. The absurdly chivalrous, credulous, charming young Englishman, whose autobiography Mr. Hewlett affects to set down, manages to keep his personality before the reader through the whole succession of serio-comic adventures in which he is involved. The heroine, too, while on the whole less vivid, and certainly less interesting, detaches herself with a semblance of reality from the impersonal phalanx of Mr. Hewlett's earlier leading ladies, of whose carnal charms one has been told in so many more or less similar pages that even these much-emphasised attributes are blurred into a kind of composite portrait, while their moral idiosyncrasies fail to leave any impression at all. Virginia Strozzi, young Francis Strelley's handmaiden and worshipper, rescued by him from the gutter, and exalted to be a sharer in all the incidents of his chequered career, stands before the reader with a certain definiteness of outline, marred only by an occasional reversion to type. She starts out, for instance, thin to emaciation, and pale to the point of evanescence; but as the novelist warms to his subject (and Mr. Hewlett is nothing if not warm) she grows into the "high-bosomed beauty" with whom his pen habitually consorts, and surprises the reader by an unexplained accession of embonpoint and complexion. As she and her companion are subjected to almost continuous hardships, physical and mental, and for a great part of the time are engaged in hard manual labour on an insufficient diet, one can only assume that Mr. Hewlett, bored by the company of a thin girl with no colour, has let his imagination momentarily stray to more congenial society.

This is not a serious charge; but it leads up to one which may be made with more emphasis. It is, precisely, that Mr. Hewlett's own tendency to emphasise makes him bear somewhat too heavily on the brittle surface of eighteenth-century manners. Much commerce with the noisy middle ages has given him a stentorian voice and an earth-shaking tread. He has forgotten that it was characteristic of the *sette-cento* to roar as gently as any sucking-dove. And this observation leads up to the real defect—as it has appeared to one reader—in his drawing of Virginia Strozzi. He has desired to depict her as a creature with undeveloped powers of expression, consumed by an inner intensity of emotion that occasionally flames out through her impassive exterior. So far, so good; the type is picturesque, and Goethe has set up an enduring model of it in Mignon. But it has betrayed Mr. Hewlett into greater indulgence of his besetting foible. If Virginia must be quiet and reserved for, say, a dozen pages, then, by the god of noise, she shall make up for it on the thirteenth. And make up for it she does. Mr. Hewlett is there to see that she gets her opportunity. Some of the passages in which she gives way to her feelings read like a realistic description of an attack of hydrophobia: one longs to hurry off poor Strelley to the nearest Pasteur Institute.

Well, it may be argued, if Mr. Hewlett had such a character in mind, why should he be criticised for daring to give it full expression? Only for the old familiar reason—that art is limited, is a compromise, a perpetual process of rejection and elision. In the case of the novelist who lays his scene in a bygone century, this fact is the more insistently present because he is obliged to give his readers a picture of the times as well as of the characters of his story. This widens his canvas, and makes it necessary that every stroke should be subordinated to the effect of the mass. The individual characters become, in this connection, parts of the general composition: each must do duty as a mere line in the general portrait.[2] And it is in conveying this synthesised image of the middle ages that Mr. Hewlett's talent has served him so well. His ranting, roaring personalities have served to build up a general impression of tumult and disorder, which is precisely the effect left on the modern mind by any reading of mediaeval history.

The eighteenth century, on the other hand, was all in *nuances*. Colours had paled, voices been lowered, convictions subdued; in Italy especially, if one may trust the social records of the day, people lived *au jour le jour*, taking pain and pleasure lightly, and without much sense of the moral issue. Virginia Strozzi might have followed her hero as faithfully, but she would not have stormed at him so loudly. Above all, it may be doubted if she would have sacrificed herself to the extent of going through a mock marriage (which he took for a real one), in order not to be a burden on him when he came into his fortune and estate. Such far-sighted altruism savours of the romantic northern races: beneath a hot sun there is less weighing of remote contingencies.

So also with Mr. Hewlett's villainous Capuchin friar, one of the most effectively drawn figures in the book. Fra Palamone is admirably truculent; but does he not even antedate Boccaccio? The Cavaliere Aquamorta certainly roars and threatens louder than his infamous prototype: the biggest bullies of the eighteenth century made their way by adroitness rather than by bluster. Still, Fra Palamone might well stand as a probable exception, if the learned Doctor Lanfranchi's voice were not pitched to the same bellow, and his table-manners of the same carnivorous order. When two persons so divergent speak in the same tone, one suspects that the voice is Mr. Hewlett's. Let the reader, for justification of this criticism, turn to any of the delightful memoirs in which the daily life of the Italy of that period has been so variously depicted. Let him search through the amiable Goldoni, the pungent de Brosses, the peppery Carlo Gozzi, the unqualifiable Casanova, for any signs of extreme vehemence and primitive intensity of feeling.[3] Let him—if he can!—follow the desultory trail of Venetian love-adventures in Lorenzo da Ponte's *introuvable* recollections; let him study the family life of the day in Ippolito Nievo's remarkable "Confessioni," or observe the eighteenth century on stilts in the pompous pages of Alfieri's memoirs: the total impression remains one of vivacity, elegance, good-humour, rather than of deep passion and gloomy violence.[4]

Not that Mr. Hewlett's book is gloomy. He is too conscientious an artist not to have "reconstituted" his background with all possible care, and to have got the utmost attainable effect from the familiar properties of the period—strolling players, rhyming abbés, ruffling gallants, village fairs and carouses, the pleasures of the casino and the *ridotto*. (Even here—out of pure pedantry—one might open a parenthesis to ask if, at that period, the Paterini were still heard of, if the art-loving traveller, as he approached Florence, thought first of seeing Brunelleschi's dome and Giotto's tower, and if the *cognoscenti* discussed the technique of Fra Angelico and Mantegna?)

It is only when Mr. Hewlett sets his characters in motion that they clash with their frivolous background, and seem to have come out of Cellini[5] rather than out of Gozzi or Goldoni. One feels as if there would not have been a bit of Venice glass or of Bologna pottery left whole, after Lanfranchi and Palamone had butted and slashed their way through the land. And this impression is, in the last analysis, a tribute to Mr. Hewlett's powers of realism. Mr. Henry James once said that the French novelists of the realistic school could render with inimitable vividness any impression received through the so-called "five senses"—anything that could be heard, seen, smelt, touched or tasted.[6] The same may be said of Mr. Hewlett; and it is no light praise. One could not now revert to the psychological novel of the eighteenth century, with its action suspended in the void. Fiction has been enlarged by making the background a part of the action, and it is only when the stage-setting fails to merge with the drama that its details become importunate. This is by no means the case with Mr. Hewlett: he gets admirable effects out of his sensuous impressionability—the chapter called "The Tower of the Flies," in *Richard Yea-and-Nay*, is there to prove what he can achieve in this direction. It is on the other side that he pays the penalty: by tending to make his characters too purely physiological, reducing them to mere bundles of sensation. Civilisation has produced differentiation: human nature is still a bundle of sensations, but of a more complex order. And for this reason one reverts, in the end, to Mr. Hewlett's hero. Young Strelley, with his Quixotism, his gullibility, his courage, gaiety and comic resignation to ill-luck, is certainly the most successful figure in the book; and the series of mischance into which he is plunged show how readily Mr. Hewlett is able, when he chooses, to depart from the somewhat rudimentary psychology of his earlier volumes. Strelley is interesting, in the first place, because the incidents which befall him—and very entertaining some of them are— spring from his own character, and his puzzled contact with another race; and secondly, because, sentimentalist as he is, he sees something in life beyond the love-adventure on which Mr. Hewlett's other heroes have always been persistently bent. He has general ideas, conceptions of conduct, a fine, gallant view of the world; and the inconsistencies tempering his high theories give the requisite touch of charm to his character.

Mr. Hewlett, in short, not satisfied, like most novelists of incident, to set a group of marionettes in lively motion, has tried to draw real people, whose good and bad fortunes spring from their character and their attitude toward life; and has proved, by the charm and animation of his tale, that imagination and a sense of style need not, under favourable circumstances, seriously interfere with the writing of a good novel.

Bookman, September 1905

[1] Maurice Hewlett (1861–1923), popular English novelist, whose earlier historical romances included *The Forest Lovers* (1898), *The Life and Death of Richard Yea-and-Nay* (1900), and *The Queen's Quair* (1904).

[2] Discussing the work of a novelist who "has succeeded . . . in reproducing the atmosphere of eighteenth-century Venice," Wharton had argued a few months earlier that "the patient accumulation of detail," as she put it, "[t]hough not the most important feature in the construction of a good historical novel, . . . is an essential part of the process," which combines "artistic sensibility and . . . its accompanying faculty, the historic imagination" (*IB*, 211–12). Such issues had been much on her mind since completing *The Valley of Decision* (1902), which shares the setting of Hewlett's novel.

[3] Carlo Goldoni (1707–93), pioneering Italian comic dramatist who composed his *Mémoires* in French; Charles de Brosses (1709–77), French magistrate of Burgundy and scholar, remembered chiefly for his *Lettres familières écrites d'Italie en 1739 et 1740*; Carlo Gozzi (1720–1806), Venetian aristocrat and dramatist, author of *Memorie inutili* (1797); Giacomo Casanova (1725–98), Italian adventurer renowned for his posthumously published *Mémoires*.

[4] The *Memorie* (1823–27) of Lorenzo da Ponte (1749–1838), celebrated Italian poet and librettist; *Le confessioni di un Ottuagenario* (1867), by Ippolito Nievo (1831–61), Italian novelist and patriot, a work Wharton celebrated elsewhere, around the same time, as "that delightful book, half romance, half autobiography, which, after many years of incredible neglect, has just been republished in Italy" and as "a volume which, for desultory charm and simple rendering of domestic incidents, is not unworthy to take rank with 'Dichtung und Wahrheit'" (*IB*, 209); *Vita scritta da esso*, completed shortly before his death by the Italian poet and dramatist Vittorio Alfieri (1749–1803). Her work on *The Valley of Decision* had drawn on many of the volumes cited in her review, including those of Gozzi, Nievo, and "the Chevalier de Brosses," along with

"the original (French) version of Goldoni's memoirs, and the memoirs of Lorenzo da Ponte, published in Boston (of all places!) about 1824" (*BG*, 128–29).

⁵ Benvenuto Cellini (1500–1571), sculptor and goldsmith whose *Vita* is a panoramic document of social life in sixteenth-century Italy.

⁶ Wharton appears to have in mind the following remark from James's essay "Emile Zola" (1903), later reprinted in *Notes on Novelists* (1914): "If we imagine him asking himself what he knew of the 'social' life of the second Empire to start with, we imagine him also answering in all honesty: 'I have my eyes and my ears—I have all my senses: I have what I've seen and heard, what I've smelled and tasted and touched.'" A similar formulation occurs in an earlier essay, "Pierre Loti" (1888), reprinted in *Essays in London and Elsewhere* (1893), in which James cites the "profuse development of the external perceptions—those of the appearance, the sound, the taste, the material presence and pressure of things" as "the master-sign of the novel in France as the first among the younger talents show it to us to-day. They carry into the whole business of looking, seeing, hearing, smelling, into all kinds of tactile sensibility and into noting, analyzing, and expressing the results of these acts, a seriousness much greater than that of any other people."

The Sonnets of Eugene Lee-Hamilton

Eugene Lee-Hamilton, who died last month in Florence, made his poetic testament in a volume of sonnets published by Elliot Stock in 1894, and far less known than they should be to readers of verse in America.¹

> Seek not to find me, [he says]
> Where angel trumpets hail a brighter sun
>
> . . . .
>
> But in some book of sonnets, when day's done.
> There in the long June twilight, as you read,
> You will encounter my immortal parts,
> If any such I have, from earth's clay freed.

Lovers of English poetry, and especially of that subtle form in which Mr. Lee-Hamilton delighted to exercise his skill, will not think that he prophesied too rashly, or that the qualifying clause was necessary. A re-reading of his best-known volume, *Sonnets of the Wingless Hours*, confirms and even strengthens the impression received from its first perusal: that it contains some twenty sonnets of exceptional beauty, and four or five which rank not far after the greatest in the language.

This seems no small praise if one reckons up the number of satisfying sonnets in the "literary baggage" of any one of the English poets, excluding only the master-sonneteers, Shakespeare and Rossetti. Even those most distinguished for the mastery of the recalcitrant form—Wordsworth himself not excepted—can hardly show more than five or six sonnets of sustained perfection. The halting sonnet with one or two immortal lines is familiar enough in the work of the greatest poets; but the rounded whole, even in the case of the greatest, is astonishingly rare. If Mr. Lee-Hamilton's best falls below the supreme instances his average, in both form and thought, is markedly above the lesser sonnets of the great poets. He is indeed distinguished not only for sustained dignity of thought and felicity of image, but for a verbal flexibility which almost always enables him to control the exigencies of the sonnet, instead of being controlled by them.

In spite of their intrinsic beauty Mr. Lee-Hamilton's poems are of the kind best appreciated in the light of the writer's circumstances and environment; and before analysing his work it is necessary to speak of the exceptional conditions under which it was produced. The author of the *Sonnets of the Wingless Hours* drew the name of his volume from his own cruel experience. Beginning life brilliantly in the English diplomatic service, he was seized at the age of twenty-eight by a mysterious illness, presumably of nervous origin, which put an end to all hopes of an active career, and kept him for over twenty years stretched on the low-wheeled couch—"hybrid of rack and of Procrustes' bed"—which several of his sonnets mournfully or ironically apostrophise.

It was thus that, in the Florentine villa of his sister, Miss Paget ("Vernon Lee"), I first saw him, some fifteen years ago, stretched flat and immovable on the "dire bed" where, year after year, he lay gazing with "hungry eyes . . . derided by uneatable gold all round."[2] Completer imprisonment it would be hard to conceive. Mental exertion was almost as difficult as physical movement; and it is proof of the indefatigable vivacity of the poet's fancy that he was able to find so many ways of picturing a state of such unbroken monotony. During those wingless hours, when all use of his eyes was impossible, and his weakness so great that he could not bear to have more than a single line of verse read to him at a time, Mr. Lee-Hamilton still contrived to maintain high commerce with the greatest in art and letters. How he kept his "immortal parts" alive on such meagre fare—how he kept the black flood of the sea of misery from submerging his little "green isles" of intellectual life—those only will understand who know how intensely the flame of thought burns in his poems, and to what high and airy realms his imagination had access.

The *Sonnets of the Wingless Hours* picture the successive phases of despair, submission and triumphant courage through which their author passed in the course of his long illness. The first division of the book, "A

Wheeled Bed," paints with the aid of every dark analogy the early period of unrelieved gloom. Yet even then the writer was aware that, among the evil fairies about his cradle, there was a single pitiful one who "In every little tankard full of gall" let fall a drop of the golden wine of poetry; and it is noteworthy how the range and beauty of his poetic expression develops as this magic gift begins to sweeten the bitter draught of life, and to reveal to him that

> Through the bars of shadow and their chinks
> A face can look, *and twilight's few great stars*.

In the second division the horizon has widened, and the high fixed stars of art and poetry are pouring their rays between the bars of shadow. To this group of sonnets—"Brush and Chisel"—belongs one of the noblest in the volume, "On Raphael's Archangel Michael": a poem that must be cited in full, not only because of its beauty of conception and excellence of form, but because it is so representative of the writer's final attitude toward life.

> From out the depths of crocus-coloured morn,
> With rush of wings, the young Archangel came,
> And diamond spear; and leapt, as leaps a flame,
> On Satan, where the light was scarcely born;
> And rolled the sunless Rebel, bruised and torn,
> Upon the earth's bare plain, in dust and shame,
> Holding awhile his spear's suspended aim
> Above the rayless head in radiant scorn.
> So leaps within the soul on Wrong or Lust
> The Warrior Angel whom we deem not near,
> And rolls the rebel impulse in the dust,
> Scathing its neck with his triumphal tread,
> And holding high his bright coercing spear
> Above its inexterminable head.

Mr. Lee-Hamilton did not always face his fate with this bright equanimity. He suffered too much, and was too keenly sensitive to all the joy and beauty denied him, not to have his moods of dark relapse; but his verse proves that, as the years passed, he found increasing strength to bear his pain, and increasing consolation, in that very sensitiveness to imaginative reactions that had once been the cause of his intensest misery.

The world of beauty that had so tormented him became more and more his solace and his refuge. He sent his mind down the long vistas of art and history and human thought, and it came back stored with high images and fortifying memories. Such sonnets as "The Waifs of Time," "The Horses of Saint Mark," and "The So-called Venus of Milo" bear witness to this increasing mental detachment, and fitly lead up to the third division of the book, in which the poet meditates on the problems of life and fate.

His thought has come full circle; but he has found himself again as a part of the world-all, a sharer in the general lot of man. If the note of sadness still sounds through these sonnets it is wrung from him by the "tears of things" and is not the utterance of an isolated grief. He formulates his creed in two of the finest sonnets of this division, "The Ring of Faustus" and "Caesar's Ghost." Faust's ring, which keeps him magically young and fair, is "Faith-in-good"—

> Remove it not, lest straightway you behold
> Life's cheek fall in, and every earthly thing
> Grow all at once unutterably old.

And Caesar's ghost, which "with a sword of shadow" turned the tide of battle, is "The ghost of some high impulse or great plan" which, in a moment of moral crisis, may appear to the man who has murdered it, and turn the tide of his struggle against evil.

Mr. Lee-Hamilton never lost his robust faith in each man's power to mend the world a little.

> Just because we have no life but this,
> Turn it to use; be noble while you can;
> Search, help, create; then pass into the night.

This is the keynote of the division entitled "The After-Life." Professor Le Dantec has brilliantly said: *"La mort c'est le triomphe de l'athée"*;[3] and substituting agnostic for atheist, and illness for death, the phrase may well be applied to Mr. Lee-Hamilton. His attitude toward suffering and privation is the noblest vindication of his creed, and has inspired some of the most serene and beautiful of his poems. "Sea-Shell Murmurs," perhaps the finest sonnet in the volume, is one of these, and another of almost equal imaginative quality is "Idle Charon."

One may have been tempted, in reading Mr. Lee-Hamilton's earlier pages, to see the same analogy between his *Weltanschauung* and that of Leopardi as between their physical infirmities.[4] To both poets "The gates of pearl are crumbling fast. . . . And earth is the reality"[5]—but Mr. Lee-Hamilton, in a sonnet written, appropriately enough, "On the fly-leaf of Leopardi's poems," has shown the fundamental difference of the conclusion he draws from this premiss.

> There was a hunch-back in a slavish day,
> Crushed out of shape by Heaven's iron weight,

who poured scorn on the God imprisoning him, "And called the world the mud in which he lay." And mud it is—but a tillable and fruitful mud; and even to those imprisoned in the most cruel moral or physical anguish, its bare tracts

> Conceal, perchance, some buried urn all filled
> *With golden Darics stamped with a winged shape.*

Mr. Lee-Hamilton's book testifies to the truth of his faith. Perhaps because of that latent power of renewal which, some ten or twelve years since, miraculously drew him to his feet, and gave him a Saint Martin's summer of health and happiness; or simply, perhaps, because the angle of his moral vision was different, his rage against the "miscreated world" was the expression of a passing mood and not the essential basis of his philosophy. From the bare tract of his twenty years' bondage he delved out painfully the golden Darics of his verse; and it is not only, or chiefly, because of the precious substance in which they are wrought, but most of all because of the winged shape stamped upon them, that the best of them seem likely—in a phrase he has applied to other works of art—to "stand before us as immortals stand."

Bookman, November 1907

¹ Wharton refers to *Sonnets of the Wingless Hours*, principal work of Eugene Lee-Hamilton (1845–1907), English poet whose service in the British Embassy in Paris during the Franco-Prussian War left him an invalid for many years afterward.

² According to her later accounts, it was with "a letter from Paul Bourget" that Wharton first met Vernon Lee and her brother, of whom she could still remark, as late as 1934, "His long years of suffering and helplessness had made Eugene Lee-Hamilton . . . into a poet, and I have never understood why the poignant verse written during his illness, and published in a volume called 'Sonnets of the Wingless Hours,' is not more widely known" (*BG*, 130–131).

³ Quoted from *L'athéisme* (1906), one of the philosophical works of Félix Alexandre le Dantec (1869–1917), French biologist; "c'est" should read "est."

⁴ Giacomo Leopardi (1798–1837), leading Italian lyric poet, similarly afflicted by a series of chronic ailments.

⁵ Wharton refers to "The Wreak of Heaven: II" (ll. 1, 9), from Lee-Hamilton's earlier collection, *Apollo and Marsyas, and Other Poems* (1884).

The Criticism of Fiction

Mr. James opens the first of his two recent articles on the younger generation of English novelists by saying that (in English-speaking countries) there
is no such thing as literary criticism; and with this assertion, in the technical
sense in which Mr. James intends it to be taken, probably no novelist would
disagree.[1]

Mr. James, in his first phrases, seems to suggest that, at some more privileged stage in the growth of this last-born of the arts, English fiction did
actually receive critical consideration, and that its own alarming and ever-
increasing bulk is, partly at least, the cause of a corresponding shrinkage of
the out-numbered forces of criticism. The notion is a pleasing one, and likely
to receive corroboration from the "weary reviewer" (surely a close relation of
Mr. Wells's Weary Giant)[2] who occasionally describes himself as "refreshed
by picking up" Miss Somebody-or-other's wholesome and pleasing love-
story. But is it not rather a play of fancy than a statement of fact? And when,
in the short history of the art of fiction, has criticism of it, except in France,
attained the point of being a regular and organized process of appraisal?
When, in short, has it dealt with its subject with anything like the average
consecutiveness and competence that the criticism of history, of language, or
of any of the exact sciences is expected to display?

The novelist may here intervene to say that, if it never has, the loss is not
great, or the difference appreciable. Nor is it only among English-writing
authors that this conviction prevails. The contempt of critics is general
among creative writers of all tongues and all traditions. But though the
French novelist may, and often does, speak as slightingly of his analyst as the
Anglo-Saxon, yet French literature is conscious of criticism, and has been
modified by it, to a degree that no thoughtful French writer could seriously
deny. The French intelligence, moreover, perpetually exercises itself in conversation upon questions of literary interest, thus creating an atmosphere of
critical sensibility into which the novelist is born. France is given to lament-
ing the extinction of the great literary critic and the fact that there is seemingly no demand for his resuscitation; but France should know more about
the average of so-called literary criticism in other countries before she de-
preciates her own. The generation of Sainte-Beuve is gone, that of M.M.
Anatole France, Jules Lemaître and Emile Faguet is going;[3] but two such
generations leave in the minds succeeding them so rich a deposit and so
high a standard that French literary criticism, at one of its least original moments, is still a valuable contribution to literature. And this ought, in itself,

to be a sufficient plea for the cultivation of an art of criticism. In a society where every sort of artistic creation has always been accorded the seriousness of attention that sport, politics, and finance monopolize in other countries, some kind of critical criterion is in any case bound to form itself, whatever the indifference of authors or the relative inadequacy of critics. There is not a hack reviewer on a daily paper in France who does not, as it were, know by which handle to pick up his subject. He may have no commentary of value to make on it, but at least he does not forget to mention what it is, or place it before his bewildered readers upside down. He possesses a few elementary principles of exposition, knows in what order to apply them, and, if he fails to illumine his subject, at least does not leave it darker.

It ought to be unnecessary to combat the strange dogma that criticism is of no service to the creative arts. Whether it is or not, however, is relatively unimportant, since, wherever creative artists exercise their art, and have an audience to react to them, criticism will function as instinctively as any other normal appetite. To discuss its usefulness is therefore as idle as it is perverse to regard it as a practice confined to a few salaried enemies of art. Criticism is as all-pervading as radium, and if every professional critic were exterminated to-morrow the process would still be active wherever any attempt to interpret life offered itself to any human attention. There is no way of reacting to any phenomenon but by criticizing it; and to differentiate and complicate one's reactions is an amusement that the human intelligence will probably never renounce.

I

It is, nevertheless, true that, in Mr. James's sense of the word, the criticism of fiction is practically non-existent in England and America. The ascidian "criticizes" the irritation to which it reacts, but its rudimentary contractions are not varied by the nature of the irritating agent. And it is hardly too much to say that English-speaking criticism is in the ascidian stage, and throws out or retracts its blind feelers with the same indiscrimination of movement. This, however, is not an argument for suppressing criticism, but only for finding reasons why, since it inevitably does throw its feelers out, it should be helped to develop them into finer instruments of precision.

The chief reason is that it will help the novelists themselves. This assertion must be made, and if possible established, in spite of the outcry of the interested parties. And perhaps the simplest way of silencing their outcry is to remind the novelists that they have lately taken to addressing the most vehement appeals to be understood to the very tribunal in whose non-existence they profess to see no disadvantage. They have been—in England mainly—explaining and commenting themselves with an almost pathetic implication of belief in the existence of a listening and understanding ear. "Si le ciel est vide—" but they can hardly think it so, for far from contenting themselves with a few untechnical generalizations, or appeals to the common stock of human sympathies, they specifically address an intelligence capable, if not of discriminating between methods, at least of understanding that a novelist has to have one, and that it is worth discussing. And to whom can such a demand be addressed but to the professional critic? Probably few novelists could affirm that they have not, at some time or other, either from spoken word or written comment, obtained new views of their own work and of the general conditions of their art. The fundamental difference between the amateur and the artist is the possession of the sense of technique: that is, in its broadest meaning, of the necessity of form. This sense implies an ever-active faculty of self-criticism, and therefore a recognition of the need, and indeed of the inevitability, of criticism; and it is curious, in face of this, to find the modern novelist, while he courts comment, and scatters manifestos broadcast, somewhat impatiently discriminating against what is called "professional criticism"—as Mr. Wells, for instance, does in the chapter on the Contemporary Novel in his latest book.[4] Criticism is good or bad according to the critic's capacity, and not because he does or does not exercise that capacity professionally; though it would seem that, other things being equal, the disciplined exercise of any faculty ought to be as advantageous in one profession as another.

It is, at any rate, the novelist who may at present be heard calling in the wilderness for the absent critic to approach, and listen, and understand; and to do the latter, in even the mild measure they require, is certainly beyond the competence of the majority of writers at present aimlessly exercising their syntax in the void of the Book Review columns. What the novelist's attitude virtually proclaims is not that he scorns all criticism, but that he scorns the kind he knows he is going to get; and on this point the fraternity is no doubt unanimous.

II

If this much be taken for granted the next step will be to inquire why criticism is what it is, or why, as Mr. James more tersely says, it simply isn't. The usual answer is that, economically speaking, criticism does not pay, and that, therefore, first-rate ability looks elsewhere for expression. This is true; but it is probably as true in France as in England. In neither country, moreover, does the literary critic depend wholly on reviewing for his support; and even in France the critic is not always, or often, of first-rate ability. The principal difference is that, in the latter country, the reviewer of fiction is expected to have as disciplined an acquaintance with his subject, its forms, its limitations and its history, as the critic, say, of history or of palaeontology. He must have some range of reference, and consequently some kind of perspective. And above all, he must have a sense of form; form in fiction and form in his criticism of it.

These are elementary requirements, yet the English-writing critic seems almost unconscious of their meaning. And the fact that he is so has surely always been reflected in the English novel. It is a commonplace to say that no amount of criticism, of whatever quality, will call forth a great novel. The assertion is outside of discussion, since it can neither be proved nor disproved; but any comparison between French and English fiction seems to show that a systematically and intelligently exercised criticism has at least a negative and repressive value. It not only results in the mediocre book's being less bad—itself not an unmixed benefit—but it leads directly and unmistakably to the good book's being better. Criticism is, of course, much more than the tracing out of mere "form," at least in either of the oddly limited senses in which the word is generally used by English-speaking critics; that is, either as an antithesis to subject or as something that subject puts on like an outer garment. Criticism is concerned with every detail of creation, and hence, and above all, with the point of view of the creator. And it is in this connexion that the strongest argument for trained criticism may be sought from the whole body of French fiction. All intelligent criticism of any art presupposes an intelligent criticism of life in general, and the value of such a commentary is visible in the freedom with which French fiction has always been allowed to deal with life.

Mr. Wells complains that Thackeray's attitude to life was "sham thoughtful" and "sham man-of-the-world."[5] If he had said "sham" alone it would have sufficed, and the epithet would then have covered Dickens, as well as Trollope and their other lesser contemporaries. Both Thackeray and Dickens were dazzlingly real in their presentation of the surface of human relations, its endlessly varied external pattern of incident and humour. But it is impossible to analyse any English novel of their period, save in some degree those of George Eliot (and the somewhat later "Way of All Flesh," which Samuel Butler had to keep unpublished for twenty years because it dealt with causes as well as effects)—it is impossible to examine any of this great group of novels, in so many of which, as Mr. James puts it, "the miracle of genius" is manifest, without perceiving that again and again the whole immense machinery of the passions is put in motion for causes that a modern school-girl would smile at. In the greatest of the group the inexhaustible play of mirth and irony, the vividness of characterization, the poetry, the eloquence, the abundance, what rhetoricians call the "number," are so overwhelming and enchanting that the rapt reader half forgets the futility of the springs of action and the infantile unreality of the moral conflict. It is as if grown people with faces worn by passion and experience were acting a play written in the nursery. It is enough to glance at what the novelist of equal parts was doing, at the same moment, beyond the Channel—to set Balzac and Stendhal beside Thackeray and Dickens, Flaubert and Tolstoy beside Charlotte Brontë and Meredith—to see how even the most soaring genius needs to keep touch with the solid earth of reality.

Mr. Wells will perhaps say that such comparisons are out of order, since the English novelist has taken the matter into his own hands, and is now dealing with "life" as frankly as his French predecessors—and models. Yes; but not critically, or in its right perspective; and that is where the argument for criticism comes in. The modern English novelist is playing with his new blocks in much the same artless spirit with which he built up the old ones on the nursery floor. He is so enchanted with the new pictures on them that he has not yet concerned himself much with the significance or the stability of the shapes he piles them in; and he is so eager to use them all at once that his architecture is more likely to take the shape of a long flat wall than of a more complicated and concentric structure. It is at this very moment, when the stuff of life is at last in the hands of the modeller, that the modeller needs to be taught how to model.

It may well be that some new theory of form, as adequate to its new purpose as those preceding it, will be evolved from the present welter of experiment; but to imagine that form can ever be dispensed with is like saying that wine can be drunk without something to drink it from. The boundless gush of "life," to be tasted and savoured, must be caught in some outstretched vessel of perception; and to perceive is to limit and to choose. The novelist may plead as much as he pleases for the formless novel, the unemphasized notation of a certain stretch of a certain runnel of the stream of things; but why has he chosen that particular stretch of that particular runnel? Obviously, because it reflected, or carried on its current, more things he thought worth studying and recording. *Recording*—the act is a key to the method; for the instant one has set down certain things one has created a reason for setting down certain others, and the pattern begins to show. The novelist who proclaims himself beyond and above selection and composition, and considers it his business merely to reproduce with all possible veracity any casual "cross-section" of life, regardless of its aesthetic significance, on the plea that "wo Ihr's packt, da ist es interessant,"[6] is very much like a man who goes into the garden to pick a peach—any peach. No matter how good he thinks all peaches, the chances are that he will take the trouble to choose the best in sight; the rosiest, velvetiest, completest, the one combining more of the attributes of peachiness than any of its neighbours. The novelist most averse to composition will instinctively exercise the same selection in choosing a subject, and once selection is exercised, why limit its uses, why not push it to the last point of its exquisite powers of pattern-making, and let it extract from raw life the last drop of figurative beauty?

If, then, design is inevitable, the best art must be that in which it is most organic, most inherent in the soul of the subject. This has been the case with the greatest French fiction, and the sense that it was so, necessarily and inevitably, has been the foundation of the best French criticism. The recognition of the fact has enabled French criticism to formulate a certain number of guiding principles, within which the critic's personality has all the individual scope it needs. The familiar axioms as to the necessary subjectiveness of criticism do not alter the fact that any criticism whatever implies references to a collective standard. The greater the critic, the fewer these references need be; the more they are, the safer is the critic who is not great. It is hardly disputable that intelligent criticism is a help to every degree of ability short of genius; and even genius may be helped by criticism intelligent enough to recognize it.

III

What, then, has criticism to say to the modern novelist? First, it has to find out what to ask of him. Mr. Wells makes a brilliant plea for the greatest possible laxity in the interpretation of the term "novel"; and certainly nothing could be stupider than to apply hard and fast measures to so wonderfully elastic a form. A sonnet is a sonnet, but a novel may be almost anything.[7] Let the critic, then, first seek to find out what particular thing each particular novel is trying to be. This would not seem an exorbitant demand on the part of the novelist, yet it is the one the average critic least considers. As a rule he is too busy either recording the number of pages (an item hardly ever omitted), or saying what subject he would have found more interesting than the one chosen, or comparing the novel with its author's previous works, in the apparent belief that each time the novelist writes a new book his object is to make it as much as possible like those preceding it, and that when he has failed to do so his attention should be called to the oversight.

It appears to be purely optional with the critic whether he shall relate the story of the novel (or what he calls its "plot"), or shall simply tantalize the reader by such chance allusions as: "If Betty had not left her golf-clubs in Dolly Fitzroy's motor, things might have turned out very differently for little Mrs. Bertie Lester," passing from this to general considerations on the handling of a theme to which he gives no farther clue. Sometimes, instead, he carefully summarizes the narrative, and, his summary concluded, turns without comment to the discussion of a minor episode, or the analysis of a character whose relation to the tale he has forgotten to mention, or has perhaps neglected to observe. If he is of the older tradition he is of course still much concerned with plot, that complicated and arbitrary combination of incidents which, in the English novel of the nineteenth century, replaced the absent logic of life. The critic of this school appears to regard the plot as something extraneous which may be fastened on to the author's subject like false hair, false teeth or any other artificial aid to loveliness, and to regard his choice of a particular "transformation" or "set" as purely accidental. To this school of critics the ending of the tale is, in particular, a matter on which the novelist is free not to decide till the last page. It must be owned that many works of fiction still give colour to this idea; but the pity is that critics trained in the tradition of the plot continue to seek (and to find) it indiscriminately in every novel offered to their notice.

Those of the younger school, who have found out that the detachable plot is no longer generally worn, and that the novelist's present concern is to depict life in unadorned naturalness, are earnestly bent on showing their sense of the innovation. They are disposed to seek out with zeal, and estimate conscientiously, the author's "view of life"; but too often they gather it from the conversation of his characters rather than from the mute evidence offered by his way of dealing with his subject. It would be easy to multiply such instances; it is a theme on which the harrowed novelist can furnish countless variations. But it seems useless to record them, since they all proceed from one fundamental deficiency: the absence of any clear notion as to how, and on what grounds, a work of fiction should be judged.

There seem to be but two primary questions to ask in estimating any work of art: What has the author tried to represent, and how far has he succeeded?—and a third, which is dependent on them: Was the subject chosen worth representing—has it the quality of being what Balzac called "vrai dans l'art"?[8] These three inquiries, if duly pressed, yield a full answer to the aesthetic problem of a novel. Outside of them no criticism can be either relevant or interesting, since it is only by viewing the novel as an organic whole, by considering its form and function as one, that the critic can properly estimate its details of style and construction. In any genuine attempt at the presentment of life all these details should be predetermined by the subject itself. As the conclusion of the tale should be contained in germ in its first page, so its length, its language, the successive illuminating incidents into which it flashes, should be implicit in the subject, and should therefore be judged only in relation to that subject, and not by comparison with the author's previous books or previous manner. Above all, the general conclusions which disengage themselves from the tale—as they must from any contemplation of life that goes below its surface—these conclusions must be sought, not in the fate of the characters, and still less in their own comments on it, but in the kind of atmosphere the telling of their history creates, the light it casts on questions beyond its borders. Some one once said of Tolstoi's characters that they go on doing things after their story is told; and the greatness of the novel may perhaps be measured by the width of this luminous zone. These are the first principles the critic should learn; and having learned them, he should try to make them the sole tests of the fiction he is called upon to appraise.

The novelist, of late, has been challenging his reviewer to the consideration of new theories of novel-writing. The reviewer should be ready and eager to examine and understand these theories, but to do so fruitfully he is bound to hold fast to the three points above indicated. Two principal perils seem, in fact, to lurk for the new novelist. One is consequent on the shock of his sudden release from the white-washed cell of conventions into the daylight and the outer air. To the poor Casper Hauser[9] of the pen everything in this grimy noisy rough-and-tumble outer world is so new and of such amazing interest that he is solicited with equal urgency by facts and instances that are not always of equal value. "Life" has suddenly shaken her immense cornucopia into his lap, and in scrambling for its richest and ripest gifts his hand sometimes roams and hesitates. This natural indiscrimination has been justified, and made to appear an artistic instinct, by the almost simultaneous production of unabridged versions of the two great Russian novelists. Here are Tolstoi and Dostoievsky seizing phenomena with as seemingly random a grasp, and producing, by the huge heaping up of their accumulated spoils, an overwhelming, an unapproachable impression of the sheer weight and mass of life. The argument seems indisputable, and it is irresistible to cry out: "This then is the real way at last!"

It is the critic's affair to deal discriminatingly with these new facts, to point out and insist upon the superior permanence and beauty of the subject deeply pondered, discerned, and released from encumbering trivialities, and to show that vague bulk may produce less impression of weight and solidity than a firmly outlined form. It is for the critic, farther, to show that the great Russian novelists—and Tolstoy in particular—may have produced their effects in spite of, and not because of, their seeming wastefulness of method, and that, in the case of Tolstoy at any rate, the wastefulness will nearly always be found to have served a deliberate artistic purpose. Lastly, in dealing with these or any other great representatives of their art, it is the critic's office, and his peculiar honour, to dwell most on the nature of their highest gift, on that divining and life-evoking faculty which, whatever method it resorts to for expression, is the very foundation of the novelist's art, and the result, not of this or that rule or theory, but of the intense and patient pondering on the depths of life itself.

Times Literary Supplement (London), 14 May 1914

[1] James's essay "The Younger Generation" (reprinted later that year in *Notes on Novelists*, in considerably expanded and revised form, as "The New Novel"), led the 19 March and 2 April 1914 issues of the *Times Literary Supplement* (London). The first part began by observing, "We feel it not to be the paradox it may at the first blush seem that the state of the novel in England at the present time is virtually very much the state of criticism itself; and this moreover, at the risk of perhaps some added appearance of perverse remark, by the very reason that we see criticism so much in abeyance." It is intriguing that Wharton's essay should open in response to the only work in which James refers to her own fiction, devoting a long, characteristically meandering paragraph to *The Custom of the Country*. As she remarked sardonically to Fullerton, "After being bracketed in Henry's article with Galsworthy & [Robert] Hitchens (wasn't it?) I feel that my niche in the Hall of Fame is in the most fashionable of its many mansions" (*L*, 316). It was not with Hitchens, however, but with Maurice Hewlett, one of the popular novelists whose work she had herself previously reviewed, that Wharton is linked by James, who later spoke highly of Wharton's own essay, which appeared as she was returning from her first trip to North Africa: "I took up my Lit. Supp. to find you in such force over the subject you there treated on that so happy occasion that the beautiful firmness & 'clarity,' even if not charity, of your nerves & tone clearly gave the lie to any fear I should entertain for the effect of your annoyance. I greatly admired by the same token the fine strain of that critical voice from out the patch of shade projected upon the desert sand, as I suppose, by the silhouette of your camel. Beautifully said, thought, felt, inimitably *jeté*, the paper has excited great attention & admiration here—& is probably doing an amount of missionary work in savage breasts that we shall yet have some comparatively rude or ingenuous betrayal of" (Powers 284).

[2] In "The Contemporary Novel," published in *Fortnightly Review* in 1911, H. G. Wells (1866–1946), English novelist and critic, discusses "the theory that the novel is wholly and solely a means of relaxation," what he calls "the Weary Giant theory": "The reader is repre-

sented as a man, burthened, toiling, worn. He has been in his office from ten to four, with perhaps only two hours' interval at his club for lunch; or he has been playing golf; . . . or he has been disputing a point of law; or writing a sermon; or doing one of a thousand other of the grave important things which constitute the substance of a prosperous man's life. Now at last comes the little precious interval of leisure, and the Weary Giant takes up a book." Interestingly, Wells calls this "the man's theory of the novel rather than the woman's. . . . I do not think that women have ever quite succumbed to the tired-giant attitude in their reading. Women are more serious, not only about life, but about books."

[3] Charles-Augustin Sainte-Beuve (1804–69), illustrious literary critic; Anatole France, pseudonym of Jacques-Anatole-François Thibault (1844–1924), novelist and critic; Jules Lemaître (1853–1914), dramatic critic for the *Journal des Débats*, much of whose criticism is collected in *Les contemporains*, 7 vols. (1885–99), and in *Impressions de théâtre*, 10 vols. (1888–98); and Emile Faguet (1847–1916), literary critic and historian, also for twenty years a dramatic critic for the *Journal des Débats*.

[4] Wells had reprinted the aforementioned article earlier in 1914 in *An Englishman Looks at the World* (American title, *Social Forces in England and America*). According to the passage Wharton has in mind, "Whenever criticism of any art becomes specialised and professional, whenever a class of adjudicators is brought into existence, those adjudicators are apt to become as a class distrustful of their immediate impressions, and, anxious for methods of comparison between work and work, they begin to emulate the classifications and exact measurements of a science. . . .They develop an alleged sense of technique, which is too often no more than the attempt to exact a laboriousness of method, or to insist upon peculiarities of method which impress the professional critic not so much as being merits as being meritorious."

[5] Again in "The Contemporary Novel," Wells claims to find "something profoundly vulgar about Thackeray. It was a sham thoughtful, sham man-of-the world pose he assumed."

[6] "Wherever you seize it, it's interesting"; declared by the Merry Person, referring to the scope of human life, in the prologue to Goethe's *Faust* (l. 169), a favorite and frequently quoted line in Wharton's essays, letters, and fiction.

[7] Remarking in the same essay that "[t]he novel has been treated as though its form was as well defined as the sonnet," Wells declares, "I rejoice to see many signs to-day that that phase of narrowing and restriction is over, and that there is every encouragement for a return towards a laxer, more spacious form of novel-writing. The movement is partly of English origin, a revolt against those more exacting and cramping conceptions of artistic perfection . . . and a return to the lax freedom of form, the rambling discursiveness, the right to roam, of the earlier English novel."

[8] See n. 2 to "Mr. Sturgis's *Belchamber*."

[9] Reference to the mysterious figure who suddenly appeared in Nuremberg in 1828, at the age of eighteen, after emerging, barely able to articulate his thoughts, from the isolation of the cramped cell in which he had spent most of his life; subject of the novel *Caspar Hauser oder die Trägheit des Herzens* (1908), published a few years before Wharton's article, by Jakob Wasserman (1873–1934).

The Architecture of Humanism

The Architecture of Humanism: A Study in the History of Taste.
By Geoffrey Scott. London: Constable, 1914.

Mr. Geoffrey Scott's design in this brilliant and discriminating book has been to treat of architecture in its twofold aspect, as a purely plastic problem and as an appeal to imaginative associations, and also to show to what extent there is a traceable relation between these aspects.[1] To this task he brings two qualities not often combined—that of being a practising architect and that of having a mind unwilling to rest in accepted formulas.

His first intention—as his preface explains—had been to formulate the chief principles of classical design in architecture; but as his plan developed it became more and more clear to him that "in the present state of criticism, no theory of art could be made convincing, or even clear, to anyone not already persuaded of its truth." And he continues:—

> There may, at the present time, be a lack of architectural taste: there is, unfortunately, no lack of architectural opinion. Architecture, it is said, must be "expressive of its purpose" or "expressive of its true construction" or "expressive of the materials it employs" or "expressive of the national life" (whether noble or otherwise) or "expressive of a noble life" (whether national or not); or expressive of the craftsman's temperament, or the owner's or the architect's, or, on the contrary, "academic" and studiously indifferent to these factors. It must, we are told, be symmetrical, or it must be picturesque—that is, above all things, unsymmetrical. It must be "traditional" and "scholarly," that is, resembling what has already been done by Greek, Roman, Medieval or Georgian architects; or it must be "original" and "spontaneous," that is, it must be at pains to avoid this resemblance; or it must strike some happy compromise between these opposites; and so forth indefinitely.

Clearness in the matter, Mr. Scott concludes, is to be obtained only through an inquiry into the true relation of taste to ideas; and to facilitate and limit this inquiry he has centred it on the architecture of the Italian Renaissance, combining an essay toward an understanding of aesthetic enjoyment in general with an acute and illuminating analysis of that particular phase of art.

Mr. Scott begins by showing that the Renaissance architects, more than any others, treated their art as a problem in abstract design; and that utilitarian, religious, and mechanical conditions were constantly subordinated by them to a conscious aesthetic ideal. In order, therefore, to estimate their achievement it is necessary to possess an aesthetic standard of architectural design. But modern criticism, as Mr. Scott points out, is based not on any reasoned theory or theories of design, but on a confused mass of plausible yet contradictory axioms. He therefore proceeds (and this is the second element in the book) to investigate the origin and credentials of these axioms. Dealing first with what he calls "The Romantic Fallacy," he defines Romanticism in general as a "high development of poetic sensibility towards the remote, as such," and points out that its irresistible tendency to judge plastic art through literature and literary conceptions makes it, of necessity, a misleading guide in the study of purely plastic problems.

> In transporting romance from poetry to architecture, it was not considered how different is the position which, in these two arts, the romantic element must occupy. For, in poetry, it is attached, *not to the form but to the content*. Coleridge wrote about strange, fantastic, unexpected, or terrible things, but he wrote about them in balanced and conventional metres. He presented his romantic material through a medium that was simple, familiar, and fixed. But in architecture this distinction could not be maintained. When the romantic material entered, the conventional form of necessity disappeared. "Quaint" design and crooked planning took its place. For here form and content were practically one.

Mr. Scott next proceeds to examine the origin of the later and more persistent "mechanical fallacy," the tendency "to judge the aesthetic value of architecture by its visible relation to construction." He regards this theory as the inevitable result of the mid-nineteenth century movement of scientific investigation, and points out how for a time "every aspect of things which eluded mechanical explanation became disregarded, or was even forced by violence into mechanical terms." He proceeds to analyse the weakness of "the argument from structure," and to trace to their source, with the impartiality which characterizes his book, the causes of the resulting confusion.

> Weight and resistance, burden and effort, weakness and power, are elements in our own experience, and inseparable in that experience from feelings of ease, exultation, or distress. But weight and resistance, weakness and power, are manifest elements also in architecture, which enacts through their means a kind of human drama. Through them the mechanical solutions of mechanical problems achieve an aesthetic interest and an ideal value. Structure, then, is, on the one hand, the technique by which the art of architecture is made possible; and, on the other hand, it is part of its artistic content. But in the first case it is

subject to mechanical laws purely, in the second to psychological laws. This double function, or double significance, of structure is the cause of our confusion. For the aesthetic efficacy of structure does not develop or vary *pari passu* with structural technique. They stand in relation to one another, but not in a fixed relation. Some structural expedients, though valid technically, are not valid aesthetically, and *vice versa*.

In the chapter on the "Ethical Fallacy," Mr. Scott takes pains to point out that, though in some respects this attitude toward the problem of artistic appreciation has become obsolete, yet its influence still lingers, under strange disguises, in the vocabulary of modern art criticism. Here his impartiality is even more commendable. While showing the absurdity of the attempt to make a moral issue of "the use of false eggs and darts," he nevertheless recognizes and insists on the existence of an emotional element in every serious appreciation of art.

> In the last resort, great art will be distinguished from that which is merely aesthetically clever by a nobility that, in its final analysis, is moral; or, rather, the nobility which in life we call "moral" is itself aesthetic. But since *it interests us in life as well as in art*, we cannot—or should not—meet it in art without a sense of its imaginative reaches into life.

Mr. Scott has sought to reach anew the obscure sources of that "delight" which (in the phrase forming the text of the book) Sir Henry Wotton calls the third "condition of well-building."[2] In the chapter called "Humanist Values" he treats this part of his problem with remarkable clearness and impartiality. "Architecture, simply and immediately perceived, is," he points out, "a combination...of spaces, of masses, and of lines....These appearances are related to human functions....We look at a building and 'transcribe ourselves into terms of architecture.'" He goes on to state the complementary truth that "the whole of architecture is, in fact, unconsciously invested by us with human movements and human moods," and that, consequently, we also "transcribe architecture into terms of ourselves"; and in his last chapter he sums up his suggested criterion of architectural values, and justifies his choice of the Italian architecture of the Renaissance as the best illustration of his argument in the following striking passage:—

> Architecture that is spacious, massive and coherent, and whose rhythm corresponds to our delight, has flourished most, and most appropriately, at two periods—antiquity, and the period of which antiquity became the base—two periods when thought itself was simple, human,

and consistent. The centre of that architecture was the human body; its method to transcribe in stone the body's favourable states; and the moods of the spirit took visible shape along its borders, power and laughter, strength and terror and calm. To have chosen these nobly, and defined them clearly, are the two marks of classic style. Ancient architecture excels in perfect definition; Renaissance architecture in the width and courage of its choice.

Mr. Scott is nevertheless aware that a danger no less to be dreaded than that of abstract speculation lies in wait for the art critic attracted to the method of physio-psychology. He makes ample acknowledgment of his indebtedness to Lipps's theory of the unconscious influence of the physical memory in aesthetic judgments, and to its concrete application in Mr. Berenson's studies of Italian painting;[3] but at the same time he warns us against the mistake of expecting too much of a purely aesthetic interpretation of artistic enjoyment.

> In the last resort, as in the first [he writes], we appreciate a work of art not by the single instrument of a specialized taste, but with our whole personality. Our experience is inevitably inclusive and synthetic. It extends far beyond the mere reaction to material form.

For lack of bearing this in mind the modern critic has begun to write of art as if it were a materia medica, and to note the patient's reactions before Titian's Venus or the Church of the Salute as though they were exactly analogous with those produced by the absorption of a sedative or a cathartic. It is one of the most signal merits of Mr. Scott's book that it analyses this new danger as discriminatingly as it dissects the old fallacy of judging architecture in terms of conduct.

It would give an incomplete idea of his book to leave it without alluding to his gift for vivid phrasing and happy definition. Mr. Scott is never led away by his images, but they are always meeting him at the right point and flashing on his subject the very light it needs; as, for instance, when he calls the eighteenth century at its close "that great finished issue and realized pattern," or says that during the phase of the Gothic revival, Renaissance architecture came to be treated "like the villain in the melodrama as a mere foil to the medieval myth."

Times Literary Supplement (London), 25 June 1914

[1] Geoffrey Scott (1883–1929), English architect and critic, first met Wharton a year earlier, joining her and Walter Berry on their return to Paris from a trip to Italy. "When I first knew Geoffrey Scott," she later recalled, "he was still practising as an architect, and not long afterward

he brought out that perfect book—or shall I say, that perfect introduction to a book?—'The Architecture of Humanism.' My interest in the Italian architecture of the Renaissance, and the styles deriving from it, created one of the first links between us, and led to many delightful pilgrimages" (*BG*, 328). Scott would later marry, to Wharton's chagrin, the widow of her old friend Bayard Cutting, Jr. A further moving reminiscence of Scott, and an account of his premature, lonely death, helps conclude Wharton's memoirs (*BG*, 375–78).

    2 "Well-building hath three conditions: Commodity, Firmness, and Delight"; a line from *The Elements of Architecture* (1624), by Sir Henry Wotton (1568–1639), English poet, diplomat, and humanist, whose long service as ambassador to Venice fostered in him an unusually sophisticated taste in painting and architecture. Scott begins his volume with this quotation.

    3 Theodor Lipps (1851–1914), German psychologist best known for his two-volume *Aesthetik* (1903–6); Bernard Berenson (1865–1959), art historian and critic, and one of Wharton's closest friends, who numbered Scott among his protégés.

REVIEWS AND ESSAYS,
1920–1934

Henry James in His Letters

The Letters of Henry James. Selected and edited by Percy Lubbock.
Two vols. London: Macmillan, 1920.

I. The Friend

Talent is often like an ornamental excrescence; but the quality loosely called genius usually irradiates the whole character. "If he but so much as cut his nails," was Goethe's homely phrase of Schiller, "one saw at once that he was a greater man than any of them."[1] This irradiation, so abundantly basked in by the friends of Henry James, was hidden from those who knew him slightly by a peculiarity due to merely physical causes. His slow way of speech, sometimes mistaken for affectation—or, more quaintly, for an artless form of Anglomania—was in truth the partial victory over a stammer which in his boyhood had been thought incurable. The elaborate politeness and the involved phraseology that made off-hand intercourse with him so difficult to casual acquaintances probably sprang from the same defect. To have too much time in which to weigh each word before uttering it could not but lead—in the case of the alertest and most sensitive of minds—to self-consciousness and self-criticism; and this fact explains the hesitating manner that often passed for a mannerism.

It is matter of rejoicing to the friends of Henry James that his letters should so largely show the least familiar side of his manifold nature.[2] The solemn and somewhat finicking person he sometimes passed for bore no likeness to the real man. Simplicity of heart was combined in him with a brain that Mr. Lubbock justly calls robust, and a sense of humour of the same fibre. This simplicity and robustness are everywhere visible in the Letters. His tender regard for his friends' feelings was equalled only by the faithfulness with which he gave them his view of their case when they asked for it—and sometimes even when they did not. But his frankness was tempered by so quick a comprehension, so warm a sympathy, that the letters glow rather than they cut, and the flourish of his blade flashes light instead of drawing blood.

Henry James's memory of the heart was unfailing. Again and again in writing to the fellow-novelists he most admired—to Stevenson, M. Paul Bourget, Mr. Howells, Mr. Wells—he interrupts an outburst of praise or an elaborate literary analysis to ask after the individual members of the author's family (each invariably named and characterised), or to allude with a searching precision to some small particularity of his correspondent's life. In such matters, moreover, he had a miraculous way of preserving his friends' perspective, instead of being subject to that common law of optics which situates other people's troubles or interests in the safe middle distance of our vision. He never minimised or hurried over anything that concerned them—the look of their houses, the names of their servants and dogs, the flowers in their gardens, the most private anniversaries in their lives. In all their inmost convolutions they were as real to him as the people in his books.

One of the charms of his correspondence is his habit of putting himself at once in the presence of the person addressed by means of some vivid personal allusion, some swift evocation of the habitual setting of their talks.

> This will reach you about Christmas time, and I imagine you reading it at a window that looks out upon the snow-laden pines and hemlocks of Shady Hill. —You flash your many-coloured lantern, over my small grey surface, from every corner of these islands . . . and I get the side-wind of the fairy-tale. —That dear little Chilworth Street vision of old lamplit gossiping hours . . .

And that this is no mere artifice of the practised correspondent his reiterated yearning cries to Stevenson attest:

> You are too far away—too invisible, inaudible, inconceivable . . . you have become a beautiful myth, a kind of unnatural uncomfortable un-buried *mort*. You put forth a beautiful monthly voice, with such happy notes in it; but it comes from too far away, from the other side of the globe, while I vaguely know that you are crawling like a fly on the nether surface of my chair . . . [and in another letter] Your chieftains are dim to me; why shouldn't they be when you yourself are?

Almost every letter written after the flight to Samoa contains a wistful allusion to the loss caused ("to my imagination . . . not to my affection") by the fact of not being able to see his friend in the setting of their early friendship.

In the greater number of the letters the revelation of Henry James's yearning affection is the most striking quality. Others of course abound—flashes of brilliant portrayal, as when he says of Mrs. Kemble[3] that she is *"tout d'une pièce*, more than any one, probably, that ever lived; she moves in a mass, and if she does so little as to button her glove it is the whole of her 'personality' that does it"—with the characteristic comment: "Let us be flexible, dear Grace; let us be flexible!"—or of John Bright[4]: "He reminds me a good deal of a superior New Englander, but with a *fatter, damper nature* . . ."

and such touches as the early impressions of Ruskin, and of the beautiful Mrs. William Morris ("with a pre-Raphaelite tooth-ache")[5], written in the freshness of his observation, when correspondence was still an opportunity for expression.

Nevertheless, these "bits" are perhaps fewer than the general reader will have expected, and far fewer certainly than glowed forth, for his friends, in the great swirls and floods of his talk. Some one said of the "Letters" that "one heard him talk in them"; but though they speak with his voice they do not approach the best that he could say. The reasons are obvious. In the first place, his manner, even in youth, was never terse. To no one more completely than to him might Coleridge's apophthegm, "Genius is always subtle, but never keen,"[6] have been applied. His style was not lax, but it was always ample; he took a great deal of space to turn round in. And it was in allusion and comment, above all in reminiscence, that he excelled; whereas the modern letter is usually a mere bald summary of facts. Henry James has put it on record that interesting letters should be published; but his own were certainly not written with such a view. All are intimate, improvised, and rapid; all were meant solely for the person addressed. Henry James, in dashing them off, was certainly never thinking of his attitude before an eventual public, nor of himself in any way, except in so far as he counted for his correspondent. If so many of the letters begin with an enumeration of his physical disabilities, it is only because he wants to show why he has delayed writing, or can write so little, or is in other ways so deficient a correspondent. Once past this preliminary, he makes straight for what matters—the situation and the preoccupations of his correspondent. And whether he is writing to Stevenson or W. D. Howells or Mr. Gosse[7] on the "métier" that so constantly engrosses them, or to some friend unable to share in any of his intellectual interests, the completeness of his self-abandonment is the same. His one effort is to identify himself with the person addressed, to commune, in an almost mystic sense, with the friend whom his passionate imagination brings so near, whether the substance shared be the food of the gods or the humblest domestic fare.

His letters, therefore, give mere hints and fragments of his talk; the talk that, to his closest friends, when his health and the surrounding conditions were favourable, poured out in a series of images so vivid and appreciations so penetrating, the whole so sunned over by irony, sympathy, and wide-flashing fun, that those who heard him at his best will probably agree in saying of him what he said of M. Paul Bourget: "He was the first, easily, of all the talkers I ever encountered."

It used to be one of the joys of his familiars—I had almost said, one of their sports—when they were grouped with him about some friendly fireside, in the intimacy that showed him at his realest and rarest, to say: "And now tell us about the So-and-sos." Leaning back in the widest armchair in reach, or standing before the fire with his hands behind him and his shoulders against the mantelshelf, he would survey his audience with a preparatory twinkle, and then, shifting his weight from one foot to the other, and padding about the room like a leisurely elephant in a cane-brake, he would throw out a series of ejaculations and disconnected sentences, of allusions, cross-references, and parenthetical rectifications and restatements, till not only his hearers' brains but the room itself seemed filled with a palpable fog. And then, suddenly, by some miracle of shifted lights and accumulated strokes, the So-and-sos would stand out in their habit as they lived: drawn with a million filament-like lines, yet as sharp as an Ingres, as dense as a Rembrandt; or, to call upon his own art for an analogy, as minute and as massive as the people of Balzac. It mattered not if the So-and-sos were a group of Albany cousins, or the family of some world-renowned genius; that evocation immortalised them, made them for ever the property of his listeners.

Evocations so vivid are rare in the letters, and never have the richness of his spoken pictures. Since modern letters are seldom written for publication, or even for the "handing around" which, till the end of the 18th century, placed upon the distinguished correspondent the responsibilities of a journalist and an essayist, it is obvious that their editing necessitates the elimination of needless repetitions and of allusions to matters of purely personal interest. But in this respect Mr. Lubbock's task must have been beset with difficulties. Not only is it almost impossible to "edit" paragraphs that proceed with all the tackings, returns, digressions, and surprises that marked the talk of Henry James, but such elimination is almost sure to cut out some swift aphorism or memorable picture embedded in coils of explication. Mr. Lubbock has therefore undoubtedly chosen the wisest course in leaving the letters almost as they poured from the writer's pen.

But one of the things impossible to preserve because so impossible to explain, with whatever fulness of footnotes, was the quality of fun—often of sheer abstract "fooling"—that was the delicious surprise of his talk. The letter to Mr. Walter Berry "on the gift of a dressing-bag" is almost the only instance of this genial play that it has been possible to keep. From many of the letters to his most intimate group it has been necessary to excise long passages of chaff, and recurring references to old heaped-up pyramidal jokes, huge cairns of hoarded nonsense. Henry James's memory for a joke was prodigious; when he got hold of a good one, he not only preserved it piously, but raised upon it an intricate superstructure of kindred nonsense, into which every addition offered by a friend was skilfully incorporated. Into his nonsense-world, as fourth-dimensional as that of the Looking Glass, or the Land where the Jumblies live, the reader could hardly have groped his way without a preparatory course in each correspondent's private history and casual experience. The merest hint was usually enough to fire the train; and, as in the writing of his tales a tiny mustard-seed of allusion spread into a many-branched "subject," so his best nonsense flowered out of unremembered trifles.

One of his tricks was to seize on a chance phrase and juggle with it for hours and days. I remember that once, on a motor-trip, we were overtaken by hot weather at Poitiers, and Henry James set forth to purchase a more seasonable hat. His companions naturally proposed the most fantastic head-gear that the local trade could show; and after he had indignantly rejected each suggestion, and insisted that he wanted a hat "like everybody else's," I said: "Well, then, ask for the hat of *l'homme moyen sensuel*." To his visualising mind this called up an object superlatively comic; and the shape of the hat of *l'homme moyen sensuel*, and the vision of himself in that character, applying to a Poitiers hatter for suitable head-gear, recurred in his talk for months afterward.

On another occasion we were motoring through Dymchurch, near Rye, and some one said that there ought to have been a mid-Victorian novel about the Dymmes of Dymchurch. He threw himself upon the idea, built up in a trice the genealogy of the Dymmes, and let us into all the details of their history; how one branch lived at Dulwich, how the German governess's name was Fräulein Dumm (alas, I've lost the French tutor's), and how one enterprising Dymme had married into the Sparkle family, and been blessed with a daughter called little Scintilla Dymme-Sparkle.

My third reminiscence is of still another motor-trip, among the hills of Western Massachusetts—the corner of New England that he preferred. We had motored so much together in Europe that allusions to Roman ruins and Gothic cathedrals furnished a great part of the pleasantries with which his mind played over what he has called "the thin empty lonely American beauty"; and once, when his eye caught the fine peak that rises alone in the vale between Deerfield and Springfield, with a wooden barrack of a "summer hotel" on its highest ledge, I told him that the hill was Mount Tom, and the building "the famous Carthusian monastery." "Yes, where the monks

made Moxie," he flashed back, referring to a temperance drink that was
blighting the landscape, that summer, from a thousand hoardings.

Slight and scant instances these, scarce worth recording to those whose
better memories have kept richer examples of his fun; but at least they give
a clue to what was going on behind that grave and impressive demeanour,
and into what regions of happy fooling the twinkle of his eye and the twitch
of his mouth invited one.

Mr. Lubbock has justly said that only in the letters written during the war
did Henry James give the full measure of his character and genius. "He gave
us what we lacked—a voice"; and those who were with him during the autumn days of 1914 will never forget the transfiguration of the whole man. It
was as if he who, as long ago as in his thirties, had definitely classified himself as an observer, now suddenly leapt into participation; as if at last the one
void in him had been filled.

The letter on Rheims which found so thrilling an echo in French hearts is
only one of many into which he poured his whole self;[8] broke, as it were,
again and again, the precious box of ointment that he seemed to have preserved for this supreme libation. The man who so early said of himself: "It
would be hard to imagine a life with less chiaroscuro in it than mine," had in
reality depths under depths of shadowy unexplored feeling; and it may
never be known by what accident it remained in bondage to his art till the
great breaking-up of the foundations of the world.

II. The Man of Letters

From the early days when his brother William sternly admonished him on
the "bad business" of having introduced the supposed portrait of "a Miss
Peabody" into "The Bostonians,"[9] to the end of his long life, Henry James
lived in the intellectual loneliness that is the lot of all originators. He once
wrote of himself that it was the fate of the Cosmopolitan to be lonely; but this
was a superficial diagnosis. He was not lonely because he lived in a country
not his own, and at heart he knew it; he was never as lonely as in America.
His sense of solitude was founded on his fundamental *differentness*; and he
was different not only from the amiable great people whom he has painted
in "The Death of the Lion," but also from the fellow-craftsmen among whom
he so yearningly sought for understanding.

It was not that Henry James was cut off from the friendship and sympathy
of his kind. Of a novelist who spent his youth in the company of Flaubert,

Daudet, and Turgeniev, and his old age in appreciative communion with Mr. Kipling, Mr. Conrad, Mr. Wells, and many of the younger English novelists; who had talked with George Eliot, was the friend of George Meredith, and the life-long correspondent of Stevenson, W. D. Howells, Sir Sidney Colvin,[10] and Mr. Edmund Gosse, it may be said that he had the best his day could give. Sympathy was never denied him, either in his affections or in his intellectual labours; and the few whose approbation he valued gave it unstintedly to his books. But the deep central loneliness persisted. His eager admiration of what others had done and were doing in their respective lines was always shadowed (though never diminished) by the feeling that even the best among them did not understand what he was trying for. It was well enough to tell himself (as he doubtless did) that the immediate success of a work of art is always in inverse ratio to its originality. He knew the penalty, he was ready to pay it; but he could never wholly overcome the longing, not to be bought by the many but at least to be understood by the few.

The evidence of this constant longing to be understood—so pathetically shown in one of his letters to Howells: "Nothing more delightful, or that has touched me more closely, even to the spring of tears, has befallen me for years, literally, than to receive your beautiful letter, so largely and liberally anent 'The Wings of the Dove.' Every word of it goes to my heart." This evidence of his craving for recognition may be as surprising to many readers as his solicitous tenderness for his friends. In truth, the two feelings are akin; Henry James was a solitary who could not live alone. Mentally and sentimentally, he needed understanding; and there are few sadder letters in the book than the one which answers Stevenson's sick protest at the "Portrait of a Lady"—the peevish entreaty that James should "never do it again."[11] James had a deep affection for Stevenson, and an equal admiration for his genius. He could not see how so vigorous a creative faculty, combined with so sensitive an artistic feeling, could be unsustained by any general theory of art; how it could be only a vague Planchette-like state of possession. He credited Stevenson with a critical sense equal to his creative power; and that the critic who had joyously welcomed "Roderick Hudson," "Daisy Miller," and the "Princess Casamassima" (which he appears to have valued chiefly for its Dickens-like pictures of "low life"!) should condemn "The Portrait of a Lady" was incomprehensible, and heart-breaking, to James. In later years the explanation may have occurred to him—that the picture of poor Ralph Touchett was simply unendurable to Ralph Touchett's fellow-victim. But to an artist of Henry James's quality it can never be comprehensible that a fellow-artist should form his aesthetic judgments emotionally, should "hate" anything in a work of art but its intrinsic worthlessness, whether of subject or of execution.

The recurring wonder at this stage of mental confusion finds expression in a letter to Mr. Gosse on the Letters of Meredith, whose literary judgments were a perpetual perplexity to Henry James.

> Meredith speaks a couple of times of greatly admiring a novel of Daudet's, "Numa Roumestan," with the remark, twice over, that he has never "liked" any of the others; he only "likes" this one! The tone is of the oddest, coming from a man of the craft — even though the terms on which he himself was of the craft remain so peculiar, and such as there would be so much more to say about. To a fellow-novelist who could read Daudet at all (and I can't imagine his not, in such a relation, being read with curiosity, with critical appetite), "Numa" might very well appear to stand out from the others as the finest flower of the same method; but not to take it as one of them, or to take them as of its family and general complexion, is to reduce "liking" and not-liking to the sort of use that a spelling-out schoolgirl might make of them.

From his youthful protest to his brother William (in reply to fraternal strictures on the exquisite tale of "The Europeans"), "I think you take these things too rigidly and unimaginatively—too much as if an artistic experiment were a piece of conduct," to the passages inspired, years later, by George Meredith's correspondence, Henry James continually stated and restated his theory of composition. The writing of fiction was still, when his career began, an unformulated art in English-speaking countries. Only in France, and among men but slightly his elders, had an attempt been made to define the story-teller's main purpose and guiding principles, to enlarge and to define his field. Henry James applauded, in this French group, "the infernal intelligence of their art, form, manner," but at once perceived their scheme to be too narrow and superficial. Yet the "floods of tepid soap and water which under the name of novels are being vomited forth in England" seemed to him infinitely less "an honour to our race."

From the first, he had an unshaken faith in his conception of the novelist's art. In 1876, when as a young and untried author he meets Flaubert, crowned with achievement, he writes: "I think I easily—more than easily— see all round him intellectually." This implied no depreciation of Flaubert's art, which he then deeply admired, but an instant perception of the narrowness of his philosophy of life. Henry James was always insisting on this point.

For him every great novel must first of all be based on a profound sense of moral values ("importance of subject"), and then constructed with a classical unity and economy of means. That these two requisites should not be regarded as the measure of every work of fiction worth measuring was unintelligible; it was the inability of many of his most appreciative readers to apply the test either to his own books, or to those of others, that so bewildered and discouraged him. Subject and form—these are the fundamentals to which he perpetually reverts; and of the two (though he would hardly have admitted that they could be considered separately) subject most concerned him.

There is an inveterate tendency on the part of the Anglo-Saxon reader to regard "feeling" and "art" as antithetical. A higher sensibility is supposed by the inartistic to inhere in artless effort; and every creative writer preoccupied with the technique of his trade—from grammar and syntax to construction—is assumed to be indifferent to "subject." Even the French public, because Flaubert so overflowed to his correspondents on the importance of form and the difficulties of style, seems not yet to have discovered that he also wrote: "Plus l'idée est belle, plus la phrase est sonore."[12] Still, in France careful execution is not regarded as the direct antithesis of deep feeling. Among English-speaking readers it too commonly is; and James is still looked upon by many as a super-subtle carver of cherry-stones, whereas in fact the vital matter for him was always *subject*, and the criterion of subject the extent of its moral register.

I remember his once saying, after we had seen, in Paris, a play by a brilliant young dramatist, consummate master of *la scène à faire*,[13] but whose characters, whatever their origin or education, all wallowed in a common *muflerie*: "The trouble with eliminating the moral values is that almost all the dramatic opportunites go with them," since, where there is no revolt against the general baseness, the story, however scenic, remains on the level of what the French call a *fait divers*.[14]

But Henry James had as keen an eye for the plastic value of "subjects" as for their moral importance. In this connexion, I remember once getting an enlightening glimpse of his ideas. We were discussing Flaubert, for whom his early admiration had cooled, and for whose inner resonance I accused him of having lost his ear. James objected that Flaubert's subjects were not worth the labour spent on them; to which I returned: "But why isn't Madame Bovary as good a subject as Anna Karénine? Both novels turn upon a woman's love affairs." "Ah," he said, "but one paints the fierce passions of a luxurious aristocracy, the other deals with the petty miseries of a little *bourgeoise* in a provincial town."

In spite of the violent fore-shortening of the retort I understood what he meant, and was glad to come upon an interesting development of the idea in one of the letters to Howells, who had been pleading the boundless artistic possibilities of the local American subject, as containing "the whole of human life."

> It is on manners, customs, usages, habits, forms [James replied], upon all these things matured and established, that a novelist lives—they are the very stuff his work is made of; and in saying that in the absence of those "dreary and worn-out paraphernalia" which I enumerate as being wanting in American society, "we have simply the whole of human life left," you beg (to my sense) the question. I should say we had just so much less of it as these same "paraphernalia" represent, and I think they represent an enormous quantity of it. I shall feel refuted only when we have produced (setting the present high company—yourself and me—for obvious reasons apart) a gentleman who strikes me, as a novelist, as belonging to the company of Balzac and Thackeray.

It would be a mistake to think that Henry James valued the said paraphernalia for their scenic qualities, as a kind of Wardour Street setting for his situations. His meaning is best given by that penetrating phrase in "The American Scene": "It takes a great deal of history to make a little tradition, and a great deal of tradition to make a little taste, and a great deal of taste to make a little art."[15] In other words, the successive superpositions of experience that time brings to an old and stable society seemed to him as great an asset to the novelist as to the society itself. Yet he never ceased to preach that the novelist should deal only with his own "scene," whether American or other; and there is as much sincerity as irony in the close of the same letter to Howells:

> I must add, however, that I applaud and esteem you highly for not feeling it; i.e. the want of paraphernalia. You are certainly right— magnificently and heroically right—to do so, and on the day you make your readers—I mean the readers who know and appreciate the paraphernalia—do the same, you will be the American Balzac.

Next to subject, and conterminous with it, is the great question of form. When Henry James began to write, it had not yet dawned upon English-speaking novelists that a novel might be anything other than a string of successive episodes—a "sum in addition," as he called it. It was one of his profound originalities to feel, and to illustrate in his own books, the three-dimensional qualities of that rich art which had hitherto, even in the great pages of Balzac and Thackeray, been practised only in the flat.

For the application of the new method two things were essential: the choice of a central situation, and of what might be called centripetal incidents. To put it in another way: the tale must be treated as a stellar system, with all its episodes revolving like "the army of unalterable law"[16] round a central *Reason Why*.

> There is, to my vision [he writes to Mr. Wells], no authentic and no really interesting and no *beautiful* report of things on the novelist's, the painter's part, unless a particular detachment has operated, unless the great stewpot or crucible of the imagination, of the observant and recording and interpreting mind, in short, has intervened and played its part.

The way of attaining this centralised vision is, as he tells Mrs. Humphrey Ward,[17] to select, among the characters of a projected novel, a reflecting consciousness, and to

> "make that consciousness full, rich, universally prehensile, and *stick* to it—don't shift—and don't shift *arbitrarily*—how, otherwise, do you get your unity of subject or keep up your reader's sense of it?" To which, if you say: "How then do I get Lucy's consciousness?" I impudently retort: "By that magnificent and masterly *indirectness* which means the *only* dramatic straightness and intensity. You get it, in other words, by Eleanor." "And how does Eleanor get it?" "By everything! By Lucy, by Manisty, by every pulse of the action in which she is engaged and of which she is the fullest—an exquisite—register. Go behind *her*—miles and miles; don't go behind the others, or the subject—i.e. the unity of impression—goes to smash."

And when his seemingly bewildered correspondent objects that Tolstoi and Balzac do not keep to one "consciousness," he patiently explains:

> The promiscuous shiftings of standpoint and centre of Tolstoi and Balzac for instance (which come, to my eye, from their being not so much big dramatists as big painters, as Loti is a painter[18]), are the inevitable result of the *quantity of presenting* their genius launches them in. With the complexity they pile up they *can* get no clearness without trying again and again for new centres.

The rule of composition is, in short, never to be applied from the outside, but to be found in germ in each subject, as every vital principle of art must be; the one preliminary requisite being that the novelist should have the eye to find, and the hand to extract. From this stand Henry James never swerved.

> What I said above [he goes on] about the "rule" of presentation being, in each case, hard and fast, *that* I will go to the stake and burn with slow fire for—the slowest that will burn at all. I hold the artist must (infinitely!) know how he is doing it, or he is not doing it at all. I hold he must have a perception of the interests of his subject that grasps him as in a vice, and that (the subject being of course formulated in his mind) he sees *as* sharply the way that most presents it, and presents most of it, as against the ways that comparatively give it away. And he must there choose and stick and be consistent—and that is the hard-and-fastness and the vice. I am afraid I *do* differ with you if you mean that the picture can get any *objective* unity from any other source than that.

Again and again, to Mr. Wells in particular, he reiterates his horror of "that accurst autobiographic form which puts a premium on the loose, the improvised, the cheap, and the easy." And again, in developing the same argument to Mr. Compton Mackenzie:[19]

> In presence of any suchlike intention I find I want a subject to be able quite definitely to state and declare itself—*as* a subject; and when the thing is communicated to me (in advance) in the form of So-and-So's doing this, that or the other, or Something-else's "happening," and so on, I kind of yearn for the expressible idea or motive, what the thing is to be done *for*, to have been presented to me; which you may say perhaps is asking a good deal. I don't think so, if any cognisance at all is vouchsafed one; it is the only thing I in the least care to ask.

The prefaces to the Definitive Edition deal exhaustively with subject and construction, but they do so with a scattered magnificence. They were the work of an ill and weary man, whose pen wanders disconcertingly from personal reminiscence to the theory of composition, and all but the most patient are left more bewildered than enlightened. I had often urged Henry James to let one of his friends—the task was meant for Mr. Lubbock—detach from those packed pages, and place in proper sequence, the chief passages on the art of fiction. The idea interested him, and should still be carried out; but meanwhile those for whom the mining of the prefaces is too arduous will find in the Letters a clearer and more accessible, if less deeply reasoned, compendium of his theory.

Henry James, as his years advanced, and his technical ability became more brilliant, fell increasingly under the spell of his formula. From being a law almost unconsciously operative it became an inexorable convention; and to turn the difficulty created by his growing reluctance to "shift the consciousness" he invented the "chorus" of unnaturally inquisitive and ubiquitous hangers-on, the Assinghams and others, who, oddly resuscitated from the classic drama (*via* Racine and Dumas *fils*) snoop and pry and report in "The Wings of the Dove," "The Sacred Fount," and "The Golden Bowl." These pages are not concerned with the ultimate results of his art, but only with a summary of its principles as set forth in his letters; but it should at least be borne in mind that no reader who takes the theories of a great artist too literally is ever likely to surprise his secret.

One thing is certain: however much Henry James, toward the end of his life, formalised his observance and disciplined his impulses, in the service of the Genius he once so movingly invoked, he continued, to the end, to take the freest, eagerest interest in whatever was living and spontaneous in the work of his contemporaries. "I do delight in Wells; everything that he does is so alive and kicking," he once said to me; and on another occasion, speaking of Loti: "Oh, well, you see, I love Loti's books so, even when I don't like them." So his rich nature comes full circle, the intellectual and the "affective" sympathies meeting in a common glow of human kindliness and human understanding.

If every one of his books should perish, and their memory be wiped out, this great man of letters would live always in the hearts that knew him as a great character and as a great friend.

Quarterly Review, July 1920

[1] Quoted in the entry dated 17 January 1827 from the famous *Conversations with Goethe* (1836–48) of Johann Peter Eckermann (1792–1854), close associate of the poet during Goethe's later years.

[2] Shortly after his death in 1916, James's niece and nephew, Margaret Mary ("Peggy") James and Henry James III, two of his brother William's children, began to assemble a selection of their uncle's letters. Asked for her advice, Wharton encouraged them to appoint as its editor Percy Lubbock (1879–1965), English critic and biographer, and disciple of James (*L*, 375–81). Later she was invited to review the collection by George Prothero, editor of the *Quarterly Review* and, along with his wife, a good friend of James.

[3] Frances Anne ("Fanny") Kemble (1809–93), English actress, author of dramas, poems, and volumes of memoirs, and longtime friend of James.

[4] John Bright (1811–89), British Radical statesman and orator, closely associated with the Reform Act of 1867.

[5] Jane Burden, wife of William Morris (1834–96), English Victorian poet, utopian writer, and innovative printer.

[6] "Few men of Genius are keen; but almost every man of genius is subtle"; Coleridge's remark is recorded in the 26 October 1831 entry of *Table Talk* (1835), a report of his conversations on philosophy and religion posthumously assembled by his nephew.

[7] Edmund Gosse (1849–1928), English man of letters, librarian of the House of Lords, prolific literary historian and biographer, and London friend of James.

[8] In Lubbock's transcription, James's letter to Wharton of 21 September 1914 begins, "Rheims is the most unspeakable and immeasurable horror and infamy—and what is appalling and heart-breaking is that it's *'for ever and ever.'* But no words fill the abyss of it—nor touch it, nor relieve one's heart nor light by a spark the blackness; the ache of one's howl and the anguish of one's execration aren't mitigated by a shade, even as one brands it as the most hideous crime ever perpetrated against the mind of man." A translation of these and the next five sentences, by Wharton's friend Alfred de Saint André, was recited at a session of the Académie Française on 9 October 1914 and published the following day in the *Journal des Débats*; it was later reprinted in Marie-Reine Garnier's *Henry James et la France* (Paris, 1927). Lubbock also includes the 17 October 1914 letter in which James remarked to Wharton, "Of the liveliest interest to me of course the Débats version of the poor old Rheims passage of my letter to you at the time of the horror—in respect to which I feel so greatly honoured by such grand courtesy shown it, and by the generous translation, for which I shall at the first possible moment write and thank Saint André." (Initially, it seems, the destruction to Rheims Cathedral was not as catastrophic as James's letter suggests.) For more accurate and fully annotated transcriptions of both letters, see Powers 302–3, 310–11.

[9] At the time of its serialization in 1885–86, it was widely assumed in Boston that James had based his portrayal of the befuddled and ineffectual Miss Birdseye in *The Bostonians* on Elizabeth Palmer Peabody (1804–94), Hawthorne's sister-in-law active as a leading reformer.

[10] Sir Sidney Colvin (1845–1927), art critic, director of the Fitzwilliam Museum, and keeper of the department of prints at the British Museum.

[11] After expressing his admiration of James's earlier novel, *Roderick Hudson*, Stevenson admitted, "I must break out with the news that I can't bear the *Portrait of a Lady*. I read it all, and I wept too; but I can't stand your having written it; and I beg you will write no more of the like." In the reply to which Wharton refers, James declared, "My dear Louis, I don't think I follow you here—why does that work move you to such scorn—since you can put up with Roderick, or with any of the others? As they are, so it is, and as it is, so they are. Upon my word you are unfair to it—and I scratch my head bewildered. 'Tis surely a graceful, ingenious elaborate work—with too many pages, but with (I think) an interesting subject, and a good deal of life and style. There! *All* my works may be damnable—but I don't perceive the particular damnability of that one."

[12] Flaubert to Mademoiselle Leroyer de Chantepie, 12 December 1857; the phrasing differs slightly: "Plus une idée est belle, plus la phrase est sonore."

[13] Term coined by Francisque Sarcey (1827–99), powerful drama critic for *Le Temps*, to denote the high point in the hero's fortunes or the culminating moment of the hero's greatest triumph, a prototypical feature of the nineteenth-century *pièce bien faite* (well-made play), theatrical form perfected by Augustin-Eugène Scribe (1791–1861) and Victorien Sardou (1831–1908). James's abiding interest in such conventions of French drama would have been well known to Wharton.

[14] I.e., news item, usually brief.

[15] James's phrasing, in "New York: Social Notes," one of the essays in *The American Scene* (1907), is even more sweeping: "it takes an endless amount of history to make even a little tradition, and an endless amount of tradition to make even a little taste, and an endless amount of taste, by the same token, to make even a little tranquillity."

16 "Around the ancient track marched, rank on rank, / The army of unalterable law"; concluding lines of "Lucifer in Starlight" (1883), sonnet by George Meredith (1828–1909), English poet and novelist.

17 Mary Augusta Ward (1851–1920), popular English novelist and friend of James, who refers to her novel *Eleanor* (1900).

18 Pierre Loti, pseudonym of Louis Marie Julien Viaud (1850–1923), French novelist on whom James wrote a couple of searching essays.

19 Edwardian English novelist, author principally of *Sinister Street* (1913–14).

The Great American Novel

What exactly is meant by that term of "American novel" on which American advertisers and reviewers lay an equal and ever-increasing stress—a stress unparalleled in the literary language of other countries?

To European critics the term "great English" or "great French" novel signifies merely a great novel written by an English or a French novelist; and the greatest French or English novel would be the greatest novel yet produced in one or the other of these literatures. It might be, like "La Chartreuse de Parme" (assuredly one of the greatest of French novels), a tale of eighteenth-century Italian life; or, as in the case of "Lord Jim" or "Nostromo" or "Kim," its scene might be set on the farther side of the globe; it would none the less be considered typical of the national genius that went to its making, as, for example, "La Tentation de Saint Antoine" and "Salammbô" of Flaubert are so considered, though the one is situated in Egypt in the sixth century of the Christian era and the other in Carthage, B.C. 150, or as "The Wrecker" or "The Ebb-tide" must be regarded, though the life described in them has so largely an exotic setting.¹ In the opinion of European critics only one condition is needful to make a novel typical of the country of its origin: that its writer should possess, in sufficient richness, the characteristics of his race. "John Inglesant" is not considered less typically English than "Lorna Doone" because it ranges through a cosmopolitan world reaching from the Tiber to the Thames while the other tale concerns the intensely local lives of a handful of peasants in the west of England.²

It would appear that in the opinion of recent American reviewers the American novelist must submit to much narrower social and geographical limitations before he can pretend to have produced *the* (or *the greatest*, or even simply *an*) American novel; indeed the restrictions imposed appear to differ only in kind from those to which a paternal administration subjects drinkers of wine, wearers of short skirts, and upholders of the evolutionary hypothesis. The range allotted is so narrow that the feat of producing the "greatest" American novel, if ever accomplished, will rank the author with the music-hall artist who is locked and corded into a trunk, and then expected to get out of it in full view of his audience.

First of all, the novelist's scene must be laid in the United States, and his story deal exclusively with citizens of those States; furthermore, if his work is really to deserve the epithet "American," it must tell of persons so limited in education and opportunity that they live cut off from all the varied sources of culture which used to be considered the common heritage of English-speaking people. The great American novel must always be about Main Street, geographically, socially, and intellectually.

In an address made not long ago Mr. Kipling cited the curious fate of certain famous books which, surviving the conditions that produced them, have become to later generations something utterly different from what their authors designed, or their original readers believed, them to be.[3] The classic examples are "The Merchant of Venice," a rough-and-tumble Jew-baiting farce to Shakespeare's contemporaries, and "Don Quixote," composed by Cervantes, and accepted by his public, as a gently humorous parody of the picaresque novel of the day; but Mr. Kipling found a still more striking instance in "Gulliver's Travels," fiercest and most brutal of social satires when it was written, and now one of the favorites of the nursery.

Some such fate, in a much shorter interval, has befallen Mr. Sinclair Lewis's "Main Street," that pioneering work which with a swing of the pen hacked away the sentimental vegetation from the American small town, and revealed Main Street as it is, with all its bareness in the midst of plenty. The novel was really epoch-making; but the epoch it made turned into something entirely different from what its author purposed. Mr. Lewis opened the eyes of the millions of dwellers in all the American Main Streets to the inner destitution of their lives, but by so doing apparently created in them not the desire to destroy Main Street but only to read more and more and ever more about it. The dwellers in Main Street proved themselves to be like the old ladies who send for the doctor every day for the pleasure of talking over their symptoms. They do not want to be cured; they want to be noticed.

It must not be regarded as diminishing Mr. Lewis's achievement to remind his readers that he was not the first discoverer of Main Street. Over thirty years ago, Robert Grant situated "Unleavened Bread" in the same thoroughfare; and so, a little later, did Frank Norris his "McTeague," and Graham Phillips his "Susan Lenox"—and they were all, as it happens, not only "great American novels," but great novels.[4] But they came before their time, their bitter taste frightened a public long nurtured on ice-cream soda and marshmallows, and a quick growth of oblivion was trained over the dreary nakedness of the scene they had exposed. It was necessary that a later pioneer should arise and clear this vegetation away again, and if Mr. Lewis had done no more than demolish the tottering stage-fictions of a lavender-scented New England, a chivalrous South, and a bronco-busting West he would have rendered a great service to American fiction. This having been accomplished, however, it is permissible to wonder whether, as a theme, Main Street—in a literary sense—has not received as much notice as its width and length will carry, or even more. The difficulty is that it is now established as a canon, a first principle in the laws of American fiction; and thence it will be difficult to dislodge it.

The term is of course used to typify something much more extended, geographically, than Mr. Lewis's famous thoroughfare. "Main Street" has come to signify the common mean of American life anywhere in its million cities and towns, its countless villages and immeasurable wildernesses. It stands for everything which does not rise above a very low average in culture, situation, or intrinsic human interest; and also for every style of depicting this dead level of existence, from the photographic to the pornographic—sometimes inclusively.

The novelist's—any novelist's—proper field, created by his particular way of apprehending life, is limited only by the bounds of his natural, his instinctive interests. The writer who sees life in terms of South Sea cannibals, as Herman Melville did, will waste his time (as, incidentally, Melville did) if he tries to depict it as found in drawing-rooms and conservatories;[5] though this by no means implies that the cannibal is intrinsically a richer and more available subject than the inhabitant of drawing-rooms. No subject is foreign to the artist in which there is something corresponding to a something within himself. The famous theory of the "atomes crochus"[6] is as true of affinities between novelist and subject as of those between one human being and another. To the creator the only needful preliminary to successful expression is to have in him the root of the matter to be expressed.

Nevertheless, there remains—there must always remain—the question of the amount and quality of material to be extracted from a given subject. Other things being equal, nothing can alter the fact that a "great argument"[7] will give a greater result than the perpetual chronicling of small beer. And the conditions of modern life in America, so far from being productive of great arguments, seem almost purposely contrived to eliminate them.

America has indeed deliberately dedicated herself to other ideals. What she has chosen—and realized—is a dead level of prosperity and security. Main Street abounds in the unnecessary, but lacks the one thing needful. Inheriting an old social organization which provided for nicely shaded degrees of culture and conduct, modern America has simplified and Taylorized[8] it out of existence, forgetting that in such matters the process is necessarily one of impoverishment. As she has reduced the English language to a mere instrument of utility (for example, by such simplifications as the substituting of "a wood," or, mysteriously, "a woods," for the innumerable shadings of coppice, copse, spinney, covert, brake, holt, grove, etc.), so she has reduced relations between human beings to a dead level of vapid benevolence, and the whole of life to a small house with modern plumbing and heating, a garage, a motor, a telephone, and a lawn undivided from one's neighbor's.

Great as may be the material advantage of these diffused conveniences, the safe and uniform life resulting from them offers to the artist's imagination a surface as flat and monotonous as our own prairies. If it be argued that the greatest novelists, both French and English, have drawn some of their richest effects from the study of narrow lives and parochial problems, the answer is that Balzac's provincial France, Jane Austen's provincial England, if limited in their external contacts compared to a Main Street linked to the universe by telephone, motor, and wireless, nevertheless made up for what they lacked in surface by the depth of the soil in which they grew. This indeed is still true of the dense old European order, all compounded of differences and *nuances*, all interwoven with intensities and reticences, with passions and privacies, inconceivable to the millions brought up in a safe, shallow, and shadowless world. It is because we have chosen to be what Emerson called "mixed of middle clay"[9] that we offer, in spite of all that patriotism may protest to the contrary, so meagre a material to the imagination. It is not because we are middle-class but because we are middling that our story is so soon told.

Another reason is to be found precisely in that universal facility of communication, the lack of which might seem to have made the life of Balzac's narrow towns all the narrower. In fact, that life was not only fed from the deep roots of the past, the long confused inheritance of feudalism, burgherdom, diocesan and monastic influences, the activities of the guilds, the dogged labors of the peasants, and the fervors of an ornate religion; it had, besides, the concentrated flavor which comes of long isolation. Bad roads, slow communications, dangers from flood and foe, all these factors, for generations, for centuries, combined to make of each little town a hot-bed for its own idiosyncrasies. Even in the English novels of Trollope's day, a day so much airier and more sanitated, the weight of a long past, and the comparative isolation of each social group, helped to differentiate the dull people, and to give a special color to each of their humdrum backgrounds. Only when mediocrity has achieved universal diffusion does it become completely unpaintable.

Nothing is less easy to standardize than the curve of an artist's secret affinities; but literary criticism in modern America is a perpetual incentive to standardization. The public (as everywhere and always) likes best what it has had before; the magazine editor encourages the young writer to repeat his effects; and the critic urges him to confine himself to the portrayal of life in the American small town—or in New York or Chicago as viewed from the small-town angle.

Still more insistent is the demand of reviewers that the novelist shall deal only with what the wife of one of our late Presidents touchingly described as "just folks."[10] The idea that genuineness is to be found only in the rudimentary, and that whatever is complex is unauthentic, is a favorite axiom of the modern American critic. To students of natural history such a theory is somewhat disconcerting. The tendency of all growth, animal, human, social, is towards an ever-increasing complexity. The mere existence of art as a constant form of human expression, the recurring need of it shown by its reappearance in every age of history, proves man's inherent inability to live by bread alone. Traditional society, with its old-established distinctions of class, its pass-words, exclusions, delicate shades of language and behavior, is one of man's oldest works of art, the least conscious and the most instinctive; yet the modern American novelist is told that the social and educated being is an unreality unworthy of his attention, and that only the man with the dinner-pail is human, and hence available for his purpose.

Mr. Van Wyck Brooks makes much of Howells's resonant but empty reply to Henry James's complaint that there was little material for the novelist in a rudimentary social order: "There is the whole of human nature!"[11] But what does "human nature" thus denuded consist in, and how much of it is left when it is separated from the web of custom, manners, culture it has elaborately spun about itself? Only that hollow unreality, "Man," an evocation of the eighteenth-century demagogues who were the first inventors of "standardization." As to real men, unequal, unmanageable, and unlike each other, they are all bound up with the effects of climate, soil, laws, religion, wealth—and, above all, leisure. Leisure, itself the creation of wealth, is incessantly engaged in transmuting wealth into beauty by secreting the surplus energy which flowers in great architecture, great painting, and great literature. Only in the atmosphere thus engendered floats that impalpable dust of ideas which is the real culture. A colony of ants or bees will never create a Parthenon.

It is a curious, and deeply suggestive, fact that America's acute literary nationalism has developed in inverse ratio to the growth of modern travelling facilities, and in exact proportion to the very recent Americanism of the majority of our modern literary leaders.

Like all Anglo-Saxons, the old-time Americans came of a wandering, an exploring stock; unlike the Latins, we have never been sedentary except when it was too difficult to get about. Old New York and old New England (owing to this difficulty) sat chiefly at home, and, as Henry James somewhere has it, brightened their leisure by turning the pages of a volume of Flaxman Outlines in a bare parlor looking out on a snowy landscape;[12] but in those steamless and wireless days Poe was letting his fiery fancy range over all heaven and earth, Melville was situating his tales in the tropics, and Hawthorne coloring his with the prismatic hues of a largely imaginary historic past. Our early novelists were, in fact, instinctively choosing those scenes and situations which offered the freest range to their invention, without fear of being repudiated as un-American if they wandered beyond the twelve-mile limit.

America's sedentary days are long since past. The whole world has become a vast escalator, and Ford motors and Gillette razors have bound together the uttermost parts of the earth. The universal infiltration of our American plumbing, dentistry, and vocabulary has reduced the globe to a playing-field for our people; and Americans have been the first to profit by the new facilities of communication which are so largely of their invention and promotion. We have, in fact, internationalized the earth, to the deep detriment of its picturesqueness, and of many far more important things; but the deed is done, the consequences are in operation, and it is at the very moment when America is pouring out her annual millions over the old world that American reviewers and publishers are asking for a portrayal of American life which shall represent us as tethered to the village pump.

It seems as though it would not only be truer to fact but would offer far more lights and shades, more contrasts and juxtapositions, to the novelist, if he depicted the modern American as a sort of missionary-drummer selling his wares and inculcating his beliefs from China to Peru, with all the unexpected (and, to the missionaries, mostly unperceived) reactions produced in the societies thus edified. It is not intended to suggest that the wandering or the expatriate American is the only fit theme for fiction, but that he is peculiarly typical of modern America—of its intense social acquisitiveness and insatiable appetite for new facts and new sights. The germ of European contacts is disseminated among thousands who have never crossed the Atlantic, just as other thousands who have done so remain blissfully immune from it; and to enjoin the modern novelist to depict only New Thermopylae in its pristine purity is singularly to limit his field.

It is doubtful if a novelist of one race can ever really penetrate into the soul of another, and hitherto the attempts to depict foreign character from the inside have resulted in producing figures very much like the Englishman of the French farce, or the Frenchman of "Punch." Even Meredith, James, and Trollope never completely achieved the trick, and their own racial characteristics peep disconcertingly through the ill-fitting disguise. But there is another way of "catching the likeness" of the foreigner, and that is as his idiosyncrasies are reflected in the minds of the novelist's characters who are of the latter's own kin. This is the special field which the nomadic habits of modern life have thrown wide open to the American novelist. Thirty years ago, in attempting this kind of reflected portraiture, he was hampered by the narrowness of the reflecting surface. The travelling American of that day was almost always a mild dilettante en route for the Coliseum or the Château of Chillon; and his contacts with the indigenous were brief and superficial. Now innumerable links of business, pleasure, study, and sport join together the various races of the world. The very novelists who still hug the Main Street superstition settle down in the Quartier Latin or on the Riviera to write their tales of the little suburban house at number one million and ten Volstead Avenue. And the exploring is no longer one-sided. The same motives which send more and more Americans abroad now draw an annually increasing number of foreigners to America. This perpetual interchange of ideas and influences is resulting, on both sides of the globe, in the creation of a new world, ephemeral, shifting, but infinitely curious to study and interesting to note, and as yet hardly heeded by the novelist. It is useless, at least for the story-teller, to deplore what the new order of things has wiped out, vain to shudder at what it is creating; there it is, whether for better or worse, and the American novelist, whose compatriots have helped, above all others, to bring it into being, can best use his opportunity by plunging both hands into the motley welter. As the Merry Person says in the

Prologue to "Faust": "Wherever you seize it, there it is interesting"—if not in itself, at any rate as a subject for fiction, as a new opening into that "full life of men"[13] which is the proper theme of the novelist's discourse.

The "great American novel" continues to be announced every year; in good years there are generally several of them. But as a rule they turn out to be (at best) only the great American novels of the year. Moreover, the proof of their greatness (according to their advertisers) is usually based on the number of copies sold; and this kind of glory does not keep a book long afloat.

Of really great novels we have hitherto produced fewer than the future traveller from New Zealand will be led to infer from a careful study of our literary statistics; but we have perhaps half a score to our credit, which is something; and another, and the greatest, may come at any moment.

When it does, it will probably turn out to be very different from what the critics counsel, the publishers hope, or the public is accustomed to. Its scene may be laid in an American small town or in a European capital; it may deal with the present or the past, with great events or trivial happenings; but in the latter case it will certainly contrive to relate them to something greater than themselves. The ability to do this is indeed one of the surest signs of the great novelist; and another is that he usually elaborates his work in quietness, and that when it appears there is every chance that it will catch us all napping, that the first year's sales will be disappointingly small, and that even those indefatigable mythomaniacs, the writers for the jackets, may for once not be ready with their superlatives.

Yale Review, July 1927

[1] *The Wrecker* (1892) and *The Ebb-Tide* (1894), novels of Robert Louis Stevenson (1850–94).

[2] *John Inglesant* (1880), by Joseph Henry Shorthouse (1834–1903), historical romance set in seventeenth-century England and Italy; *Lorna Doone* (1869), by Richard Doddridge Blackmore (1825–1900), among the most popular English novels of the nineteenth century.

[3] Kipling's address was delivered to the Royal Literary Society in June 1926 and later published, under the title "Fiction," in *A Book of Words* (1928).

[4] Less well known than *McTeague* (1899), by Frank Norris (1870–1902), *Unleavened Bread* (1900), by Robert Grant (1851–1940), jurist and friend of Wharton, portrays the fortunes of a ruthlessly ambitious woman, while *Susan Lenox: Her Fall and Rise* (1908), by David Graham Phillips (1867–1911), prolific topical novelist, charts its heroine's ascent from prostitution to a successful career on the stage.

[5] As in, say, Melville's novel *Pierre; or, The Ambiguities* (1852).

[6] Term derived from Democritus, referring to atoms that hook onto one another in forming organisms; used figuratively to denote profound or spontaneous feelings of affinity or sympathetic identification, as when Wharton, later recalling the start of her friendship with Theodore Roosevelt, remarks that "we had never 'hooked' (in the French sense of the *atômes crochus*) until after the publication of 'The Valley of Decision'" (*BG,* 312).

[7] Like that of Milton's *Paradise Lost,* book 1, l. 24.

[8] Reference to the influential methods of "scientific management" developed around the turn of the century by Frederick Winslow Taylor (1856–1915) to accelerate factory production and efficiency.

[9] "Mortal mixed of middle clay, / Attempered to the night and day, / Interchangeable with things, / Needs no amulets nor rings"; opening lines of Emerson's poem "Guy" (1847). "Mortals Mixed of Middle Clay" was one of Wharton's working titles for her first volume of tales (*L*, 36).

[10] Photographed with her husband, Warren G. Harding, on the front porch of their home in Marion, Ohio, during his successful presidential campaign in 1920, Florence Kling Harding explained, "I want the people to see these pictures so that they will know we are just folks like themselves."

[11] The exchange in which Howells famously responded to James's dissatisfaction with the denuded, undeveloped social landscape of the United States, and with its unsuitability to the novelist, is recounted by Van Wyck Brooks (1886–1963), prominent American literary historian and critic, in *The Pilgrimage of Henry James* (1925), a study on which Wharton elsewhere similarly commented (*L*, 493, n. 3).

[12] Wharton has in mind a long passage from the third chapter of *Hawthorne* (1879) in which James expatiates on a remark in an earlier biography of his subject: "There is another little sentence dropped by Mr. [George Parsons] Lathrop in relation to this period of Hawthorne's life, which appears to me worth quoting, though I am by no means sure that it will seem so to the reader. It has a very simple and innocent air, but to a person not without an impression of the early days of 'culture' in New England, it will be pregnant with historic meaning. The elder Miss Peabody, who afterwards was Hawthorne's sister-in-law and who acquired later in life a very honourable American fame as a woman of benevolence, of learning, and of literary accomplishment, had invited the Miss Hathornes to come to her house for the evening, and to bring with them their brother, whom she wished to thank for his beautiful tales. . . . 'His hostess brought out Flaxman's designs for Dante, just received from Professor Felton, of Harvard, and the party made an evening's entertainment out of them.' This last sentence is the one I allude to; and were it not for fear of appearing too fanciful I should say that these few words were, to the initiated mind, an unconscious expression of the lonely frigidity which characterised most attempts at social recreation in the New England world some forty years ago. . . . The initiated mind, as I have ventured to call it, has a vision of a little unadorned parlour, with the snow-drifts of a Massachusetts winter piled up about its windows, and a group of sensitive and serious people, modest votaries of opportunity, fixing their eyes upon a bookful of Flaxman's attenuated outlines." John Flaxman (1755–1826) was an English neoclassical draftsman and sculptor whose set of designs for illustrations to Dante were widely noted.

[13] I.e., "volle Menschenleben," the phenomenon to which the Merry Person is referring in the prologue to Goethe's *Faust* (ll. 167, 169).

A Cycle of Reviewing

A cycle is defined by the Oxford Dictionary as "a time between two beginnings," and therefore the word, as used in this brief attempt to plot the curve of fiction reviewing within my own experience,[1] should really be written in the plural. It is twenty-nine years since I threw my first infant to the wolves; and I might echo the remark of Browning's Ogniben: "I have known four-and-twenty leaders of revolts."[2]

Certainly it would appear that in the last quarter of a century there have been more frequent changes of opinion, more contradictory attempts to set up new principles of fiction writing (and reviewing) than in the previous corresponding interval. I say "it would appear" because one must allow for the inevitable tendency to see the past in uniform stretches, the present in microscopic corrugations; but I doubt if the novelists contemporary with Scott and Jane Austen, or those of the succeeding generation, had quite as many contradictory rules laid down for them as those of my day.

In saying this I am, of course, not alluding to the inevitable curve of condescension, praise, dithyrambic enthusiasm and gradual cooling off, which any novelist who has run a twenty-years' career should be prepared to meet with Marcus Aurelius's "Everything is fruit to me which thy seasons bring, O Nature."[3] Whoever offers his wares for sale in the open market should accept rose wreaths or rotten eggs with an equal heart; but what I have in mind is not the author's susceptibility to criticism, but the critic's.

The last twenty years have produced an incessant fluctuation of opinion, both as to what a work of fiction should be, and as to how it should be written. If there has been one thing constant in this series of critical upheaval it is the conviction of the reviewers that they can enlighten novelists on both these points; and it is because I believe they could if they were prepared for their task that I think the question worth examining. I am convinced that the reviewer should be as helpful to the author as to the reader; and what he can be to the latter is still to be learned from Sainte-Beuve, and those minor successors of his who continue to maintain in France the tradition that a work of art is something worthy of the attention of a trained intelligence. "Trained" is the word on which my argument turns.

I have never before written a line on the subject of my own treatment at the hands of the reviewers, because I considered the subject of minor interest to myself, and of none to others; but my literary life has now been long enough to offer a curious example of the zigzag course of modern reviewing. My experience is probably fairly typical, and at any rate to me the most available, since one more often remembers criticism of one's self than that meted out to others—unless one has had a hand in the meting. I, therefore, offer no excuse for using myself as the vile body in the case.

When I published my first volume of stories, one of the earliest reviews of it began: "When the author has mastered the rudiments of her craft she will know that *all short stories should open with dialogue.*" Inexperienced as I was, the dogmatism of that left me unmoved, for I was already obscurely aware that any story, long or short, should begin as its subject ordains; that, in fact, the only rules to be considered in art evolve from the inside, and are not to be applied ready-made from without.[4] But my experience of ready-made reviewing did not cease there.

My succeeding novels were indulgently received, but the critics almost all deplored in them the regrettable absence of "plot." As this criticism also seemed to me ready-made and applied from the outside it did not affect my course any more than the other. I continued to let my tales shape themselves in obedience to their inner organism; and the day finally came when, still indulgently, I was urged to emancipate myself from the incubus of "plot" which (it was pointed out) was the curse of all my generation of novelists.

While deploring the absence of plan in my earlier works, the critics had thus far agreed in praising their so-called "brilliancy." There is nothing I have ever hated more than "brilliancy" pinned on like a trimming; but I wrote as I could, and was naturally happy to be praised. Experience, how-ever, subdued my natural tendency to "put things" pointedly, and I became conscious—and happily conscious—of having reduced my style to a more even and unnoticeable texture. It was at this time, however, that the critics again joined in a chorus of reproof. What a pity, they said, that novels which might otherwise, etc., etc., should be disfigured by the fatiguing brilliancy, the shower of epigrammatic fireworks, which, etc., etc. This time they were right—but they were chastening me for a youthful foible which middle age had automatically cured. Only it happened that in the interval my label had been stuck on me; and no efforts of mine can shake it off. Gradually, mean-while, from being a defect this absent quality has once more become a merit. I am again praised for scintillating, encouraged to be more dazzling; I am also applauded (oh, marvel!) for my indubitable skill in the composition of the novel. If only my gift as a story teller "were equalled by, etc., etc.," I should at last have fulfilled all the requirements of my judges. So that my once deplorably plotless fiction, from having been at one time afflicted by too much plot, is now redeemed only by a skilfulness of plot which if. . . . And all the while, I am persuaded that the reader heroic enough to survey the ground I have travelled would find that I had gone telling my tales in the same old way (which happened to be my way), without, as far as I can see, ever modifying my method [save][5] as my subject required.

But of late a far more serious charge has been brought against me. It is that I write only about the rich! I will not pause to controvert this by giving a list of my tales, which deal with divers classes of people; my point is other. Supposing I *did* write only about the rich—what then? If I did, the chances would be that it was because they happened to be the material most "to my hand." Twenty years ago the same charge was brought against a man of genius: it is no secret that a leading review rejected *Du Côté de chez Swann*, because Proust dealt in it with the fashionable, and tales of the fashionable were not then in demand.[6]

Here, I believe, one puts one's finger on the two chief weaknesses of modern reviewing: the idea that the reader wants only a certain "line of goods," and must have it, and the idea that certain categories of human beings are of less intrinsic interest than others. Doubtless when the *style noble* was the proper wear there were critics to tell Jane Austen that *Rowena* was more intrinsically interesting than *Emma*;[7] now the opposite view prevails, but it is no more valid as criticism. Subjects differ from one another in scope and in plastic interest; but not categories of people. Moreover, novelists also differ in their "reach," and in their faculty for visualizing categories and situations. In the House of Art are many mansions, and the novelist's business is to stick to the one in which he feels himself at home. Only the giants can range over the whole area, and do the "big bow-wow" and the chatter at Miss Bates's with equal mastery.[8]

I believe the failure to recognize this is the chief flaw in much modern reviewing, and the chief source of bewilderment, if not discouragement, to the budding novelist. However little importance he may attach to the verdict on an individual book, yet, if he is at all interested in the processes of his art, he cannot but be curious as to the standards on which such a verdict is based. And I am persuaded that all artists should be interested in the processes of their art, if not articulately, as the French are, yet at least inwardly, cogitatively, with the desire that some one who *is* articulate should try to divine and formulate the principles stirring in them. These principles for the novelist, seem to me to be, first, that he should write of any class of people who become instantly real to him as he thinks about them; secondly, that his narrative should be clothed in a style so born of the subject that it varies with each subject; and thirdly, that the unfolding of events should grow naturally out of the conflict of character, whether (technically speaking) plotlessness or plotfulness results.

A novel is good or bad in proportion to the depth of the author's nature, the richness of his imagination, and the extent to which he is able to realize his intention. If the reviewers would judge novels by those criteria they would render services greater than they guess to the writer who thirsts to know how much of the inward vision he has succeeded in making visible to others.

Spectator, 3 November 1928

¹ Wharton undertook this "brief attempt" after the London *Spectator* requested an article in August 1928.

² The concluding line of Browning's drama, *A Soul's Tragedy* (1846), set in sixteenth-century Italy. The line, delivered by the Pope's legate, actually reads *"four*-and-twenty leaders," to distinguish it from Ogniben's earlier declaration, "I have known three-and-twenty leaders of revolts," and thus to reflect his cynicism at the latest reactionary *volte-face* on the part of another would-be extremist whose ideological allegiances fluctuate as unpredictably as the aesthetic principles of the critics and reviewers whom Wharton has in mind.

³ From the *Meditations*, part 5, sec. 23, of Marcus Aurelius (121–80), Roman emperor strongly influenced by the philosophy of the Stoics.

⁴ For Wharton's later account of this incident, and her reaction, see *A Backward Glance*, 113–14.

⁵ Correction specified in EW to *Spectator*, 7 November 1928 (Yale).

⁶ Wharton is presumably referring to the *Nouvelle Revue Française*, which initially rejected the first volume of Proust's vast novel, in a decision for which Gide, one of its founders, later remorsefully apologized.

⁷ Referring to a character in *Ivanhoe* (1820), by Sir Walter Scott (1771–1832), and to the eponymous heroine of Austen's 1816 novel.

⁸ Wharton refers to the terms in which Scott famously distinguished himself from Austen in the 14 March 1826 entry of his *Journal*, first published in 1890: "That young lady had a talent for describing the involvement and feelings and characters of ordinary life, which is to me the most wonderful I ever met with. The Big Bow-wow strain I can do myself like any now going; but the exquisite touch, which renders ordinary commonplace things and characters interesting, from the truth of the description and the sentiment, is denied to me." By "the chatter at Miss Bates's," Wharton has in mind, of course, one of the pivotal scenes in *Emma*.

Visibility in Fiction

Visibility: the condition of being visible. —*New English Dictionary*

No one interested in the art of fiction can have failed to reflect on the mysterious element which seems to possess, above all others, the antiseptic quality of keeping a novel alive. One reader may wish to prove this quality to be one thing, another reader another. "Style," that undefinable yet so plentifully defined attribute, is perhaps most often invoked—and "style" (in the sense of the selective quality which shapes substance as well as form) can in fact embalm a tale: that is, give it an enduring semblance of vitality. Style can arrest the air of lifelikeness; but it cannot really keep the characters alive, and the aliveness of the characters seems the novel's one assurance of prolonged survival.

In the attempt to probe this mystery of visibility one ends by having to put aside all theories, all the reasons one's personal preferences might dispose one to invoke as decisive. It may or may not be possible to find out why the power of giving life is the novelist's only assurance against dissolution; the facts declare it to be so. One need only enumerate the small number of novels which, outliving both their first success and their inevitable subsequent depreciation, have again floated to the surface, and held their place there, to see that however different they are in kind, however difficult it seems to discover their common denominator, they have one, and it is this. Or rather, to be still more accurate, they have two, seldom coexistent, but on the contrary mutually exclusive. These privileged books, in fact, are sometimes just "good yarns," in the old simple sense of the tale of adventure—the tale in which the characters remain subordinate to their experiences, exist only in function of what happens to them, though these happenings may be so vividly depicted as to reflect the light of life upon their faces. It was necessary to open a parenthesis for the inclusion of the stories which have achieved this kind of immortality, or the reader would have cried: "And 'Rob Roy'? And 'Moby Dick'? And 'Lord Jim'?"; but they can hardly be included in the present inquiry, which concerns rather the fictitious people who remain vivid to us through some animating principle distinct from the adventures that befall them—characters so present in the minds of generations of readers that they have acquired an historic personality, and go on living with the substantiality of the famous people of the past.

A good story has enthralled readers from the beginning of time, and will doubtless always do so. The recent craze for the detective novel is the inevitable result of the modern novelist's growing tendency to situate the experiences of his characters more and more in the region of thought and emotion; but the people in most novels of adventure live with a mere vegetable life compared with the vital flame which animates the figures depicted in great novels of character or of manners. No one, for instance, would be likely to claim for the actors in the best of such tales—"Robinson Crusoe," the vividest of the Dumas series, even the most successful among Scott's— the acute visibility which makes the heart throb and the marrow tingle at the flesh-and-blood aliveness of Tolstoi's Prince Andrew and Natasha, of Beatrix Esmond and the Fotheringay, of Père Goriot, old Grandet, Madame Marneffe, or the incomparable Madame de Rênal of "Le Rouge et le Noir."

Three cases, indeed, there are wherein adventure and character-drawing so closely overlap that it would be rash to maintain that the tales owe their survival to the one element rather than the other. These exceptions are, of course, to be found in the novels of Scott, Stevenson, and Conrad, the only novelists of adventure who have quite successfully defended the individuality of some of their characters against the overwhelming encroachment of events. Some; not all; but more at least than Dumas, whose Chicot, indeed, pleads to be excepted, but whose other characters linger in memory only as cleverly drawn but one-dimensional figures compared with the living beings of the great novelists of character. It is certain, at any rate, that the novel of manners or of character (and all the greatest novels belong in one or the other of these groups) must stand or fall with the degree of lifelikeness of the characters. To the axiom thus narrowed down, few exceptions will be found save the somewhat awkward one of the phantasmagoric world of Dickens. This world, indeed, is tremendously alive; it has entered into all our lives; yet on surveying it attentively, one perceives that the aliveness is not always lifelike, and that it is always larger than life. These overwhelming exuberant people, who, whenever they appear, go through the same tricks of speech or gesture, as though bouncing out of the wings at the call of their cue, are, in fact, the people of the stage, that other-dimensional land where attention must be focussed and character defined by devices of representation as different from the novelist's as sculpture is from painting.

The startling visibility of Dickens's characters is indisputable; they are "close-ups" before the cinema. And there is no doubt, either, that in spite of the elaborate machinery of his plots, Dickens takes rank, and high rank, among the novelists of character, and as such only has survived. Yet his characters live but the oddly restricted lives of people in plays (in all plays but the greatest): that is, they live only *in their story*, as the people of a drama live only in its dramatic conventions. To accept the reality of these characters one must first accept the artificial conditions in which they exist; and that Dickens can constrain most of his readers to do this is proved by the survival of his novels. Mrs. Nickleby, at first sight, seems as much alive as any character in "War and Peace"; not until the history enshrining her is at an end does one perceive that she lives only in its pages, can breathe only its peculiar air, whereas the Princess Mary, Natasha, the wonderful Rostov family, and all the rest of the characters in "War and Peace," live as we live, in time and space, live a life independent of the narrative in which they figure, a life overflowing the bounds of even the vast scene which their creator conceived for them.

Scott, Stevenson, Conrad, though first of all tellers of good tales rather than psychological novelists, have, nevertheless, given to some of the characters peopling their pages a deeper reality than Dickens ever gave to his. What they have failed in is to meet the supreme test: they have animated episodical characters, but their central figures (only perhaps excepting Conrad's Nostromo) have remained abstractions or puppets. Dugald Dalgetty and Andrew Fairservice are real flesh-and-blood; Rob Roy, Waverley, the Master of Ballantrae, brave figures as they are, yet seem fabricated out of a surprisingly lifelike substance which faintly suggests the most expensive embalming.

But it is, after all, of greater interest for the critic (and still more, of course, for the novelist) to try to detect what makes for visibility in character-drawing than to speculate on the mysterious reasons why such visibility keeps a book afloat while all the other fairy godmothers who attend its launching— beauties of style and of description, intellectual insight and moral ardor— cannot save it from going to the bottom.

The only novels that live are those whose characters the reader calls by name. Emma (whether Woodhouse or Bovary), Père Goriot, Rastignac, Anna Karenina, Vronsky, Barry Lyndon, Clive Newcome, Jos Sedley, Becky Sharp, Lord Steyne, Daisy Miller—what reader ever hesitates over their identity, or would think of citing their names in quotation marks? They have broken away from the printed page and its symbols, they mix with us freely, naturally; and so do a host of minor figures who have mostly escaped out of the same tales. For the gift of giving visibility to the characters of fiction is the rarest in the novelist's endowment, and one can almost count on ten fingers the creative artists who have possessed it.

To get a general consensus as to who they are would not be difficult, so rare and so compelling is this art of conferring visibility; but the beginning of wisdom would be to find out how it is done. At first that, too, seems not impossible; one inclines to ascribe the result to the trick of associating, in the reader's mind, the characters depicted with a certain set of idiosyncrasies of word, gesture, conduct, or else to the degree of visual intensity with which the author has evoked them—or to the combination of both procedures, as in Balzac. But is this explanation adequate? Does the most profoundly real visibility obey the call of such recurrent artifices? Is it not the result of a combination of arts much subtler and less self-conscious than these?

Let us take the people whom the novelist tries to make visible by associating them with catchwords and ascribing to them, whenever they appear, the same physical or mental oddities. Dickens excelled in this art, and to Zola and the French "naturalists" it became an accepted device of the craft, their chief short-cut to realization. Whoever sneezed or squinted on the first page, sneezed or squinted at each subsequent appearance. Whoever stuttered, spoke every sentence in his rôle with a stutter; whoever had a grotesque pronunciation, pronounced every word grotesquely. The most horrid and nerve-racking examples of the use of this device are to be found in Balzac, where everything is to be found, of best and worst, that the novelist's art can make use of. But the artifice seldom results in complete visibility; it merely suggests it, as the sound of a snore through the wall of a hotel bedroom suggests that there is someone sleeping next door. The characters thus described remain, as it were, concealed behind their idiosyncrasies.

Sometimes one is inclined to think that visibility is achieved simply by the author's own intense power of seeing his characters in their habit as they lived, and by his ability to reproduce the color of his vision in words. No novelist has ever possessed this power to the same degree as Tolstoi. That lifted upper lip of the poor little wife of Prince Andrew, Maslova's squint, Karenin's way of cracking his dry finger joints—though so little emphasized in comparison with the tricks of Dickens's people, they haunt us like Becky's sandy hair and green eyes, like the sultry splendor of Beatrix Esmond. Undoubtedly, this rare gift of passionate contemplation and vivid picturing does help to make bodily visible the characters of these two supremely equipped novelists; but what of certain other novelists who did not possess it, and yet confer visibility on their creations? Do we any of us really know what Mrs. Proudie looked like, or Archdeacon Grantley or even the great Lady Glencora? Who ever actually *saw* a Dostoevsky or a Turgenev character with the eyes of the flesh? And as for Jane Austen's, one almost wonders if she ever saw them bodily herself, so little do their physical peculiarities seem to concern her.

The fact is that on all sides perplexity awaits us. We certainly do not think of Jane Austen's characters as disembodied intelligences, though she has favored us with such scant glimpses of their physical appearance; while George Meredith, who has spent the richest of epithets and epigrams on his personages, though some of them have the appearance of life, has evoked none as tangible, substantial, solidly planted on the earth that we ourselves tread, as the least of Jane Austen's creations. Trollope, again, is perplexingly careless in the matter of physical word-painting. The portraits of his men are reduced to a minimum (though the touches he gives are vigorous); while the colors he uses to portray his women, and more especially his heroines, are out of the same scantily supplied paint-box which served Scott, Jane Austen, and all their lesser contemporaries. Yet, if we have a nodding acquaintance with the lavishly portrayed Meredithians, the Hardings, Grantleys, and Pallisers are our very kin! How, then, is the magic wrought?

It is a truism to say that it all depends on the measure of the novelist's genius. Of course; but what is the particular faculty of genius that produces, by means so different, the identical effect of visibility? Sometimes one inclines to ascribe it to a quality of *quietness*; almost to that slow taking of pains which was once thought the fundamental attribute of genius. Certainly the great novelists, even those (chiefly those) who packed their pages with immortality while the printer's devil waited in the passage, seem never to have written in a hurry. There were days when, obviously, they had no time to correct their grammar or make sure of their syntax; hardly ever a day when they could not let their characters ripen and round themselves under the sunlight of a steady contemplation. It must be, then, surely, this mysterious faculty, something so intimate and compelling, so much like a natural process, that outward accidents, the hurry and worry of the surface, can never check, can seldom even distort it. Once called into life the beings thus created continue their dumb germination in the most tormented mind, if the mind be a great novelist's; and by the time they are born into the book which is their world they are such well-constituted organisms that they live on in our world after theirs has ended.

No one, perhaps, has exhibited as completely as Tolstoi the result of the novelist's intense absorption in his creatures. All those who have attempted the art of fiction, or even considered it critically, know the initial difficulty of making the reader of a thickly populated novel immediately distinguish between the various characters as they first appear. Experience, of course, helps the novelist in this respect; he will avoid crowding his opening pages; he will be careful to give his readers time to get used to one character before he "brings on" another; he will, above all, sternly exclude the supernumeraries who are forever clamoring for an engagement, attracting attention by their antics, and trying to persuade him of their eventual usefulness. These principles are elementary—but look how the great men defy them! Tolstoi, especially, juggles with this particular difficulty. Re-read "Resurrection" with this technical problem in mind, and admire the way in which, as he follows Prince Nekludov from point to point in his long hunt after Maslova and his own soul, Tolstoi indulges himself in the delight of calling into rounded visibility each judge, juryman, lawyer, prison official, turnkey, soldier, prostitute, convict, or provincial magistrate or administrator, with whom Nekludov comes into contact in his agonizing pilgrimage from St. Petersburg to Siberia! Tolstoi knew that most of these people, whose physical appearance, clothes, voices, and tricks of speech he so carefully reproduces, would appear only once in the course of his tale; but he knew also that they were not supernumeraries, but "stuff o' the conscience"[1] to the tortured Nekludov, and therefore he painted them as vividly as his unhappy hero saw them. Perhaps no other novelist has achieved just this *tour de force*; and it is of interest as showing the creator's power of identifying himself with his creature, and visualizing with terrible completeness every face and figure burnt upon Nekludov's "lidless eyes in Hell."[2]

But it is a harder task to sustain visibility than to evoke it for a moment; and here again Tolstoi is equalled only (and never surpassed) by Jane Austen, Balzac, Thackeray—and at times by Stendhal, Flaubert, and Trollope. Can anyone, for instance, after seeing Emma Bovary under the umbrella opened against the spring shower, in the first pages of her life history, forget for a moment how she looked, and who she was? The survival of her name is there to attest her visibility. But though Charles Bovary, M. Homais, Madame de Rênal, Count Mosca, the Duchess de Sanseverina, and many of Trollope's people have escaped out of their books and still live with us, their number is small compared with the throng of friends and companions with whom the four greatest of life-givers have blessed us.

Balzac, Jane Austen, Thackeray, Tolstoi: almost invariably, when these touched the dead bones they arose and walked. Not only stood, struck lifelike attitudes, did the Madame Tussaud business with an uncanny air of reality, but actually progressed or retrograded, marked time or spurted forward, in our erratic human way; and came out at the end of their tales disfigured, altered, yet still the same, as we do when life has thoroughly dealt with us. These four novelists alone—with Proust perhaps as an only fifth—could give this intense and unfailing visibility to their central characters as well as to the episodical figures of the periphery; and it is plain that, though their results are identical, and Mr. Woodhouse is as warm to the touch as Henry Esmond, the procedure in each case was profoundly different.

To say this is perhaps to acknowledge that the problem is insoluble, the "trick" not to be detected; yet we may still conjecture that a common denominator is, after all, to be found in the patient intensity of attention which these great novelists concentrated on each of their imagined characters, in their intimate sense of the reality of what they described, and in some secret intuition that the barrier between themselves and their creatures was somehow thinner than the page of a book.

Yale Review, March 1929

[1]"Though in the trade of war I have slain men, / I hold it very stuff o' the conscience / To do no contrived murder"; Iago's lines, from Shakespeare's *Othello* (act 1, sc. ii, ll. 1–3).

[2] From the closing line of "Inconclusiveness" (1869), sonnet 63 of *The House of Life*, by Dante Gabriel Rossetti (1828–81), Victorian English poet.

Tendencies in Modern Fiction

The moral and intellectual destruction caused by the war, and by its far-reaching consequences, was shattering to traditional culture; and so far as the new novelists may be said to have any theory of their art, it seems to be that every new creation can issue only from the annihilation of what preceded it. But the natural processes go on in spite of theorizing, and the accumulated leaf-mould of tradition is essential to the nurture of new growths of art, whether or not those who cultivate them are aware of it. All the past seems to show that when a whole generation misses the fecundating soil stored for it by its predecessors its first growth will be spindling and its roots meagre. So one waited; one hoped; one watched tenderly over every shoot that seemed to have sap in it.[1]

This waiting has now lasted for nearly a generation. Enough time has elapsed for the critic to take stock of the new fiction, and for its creators to take stock of themselves; and it begins to look as though the rejection of the past—accidental, enforced at first, but now, it must be supposed, deliberate—had definitely impoverished the present. I believe the initial mistake of most of the younger novelists, especially in England and America, has been the decision that the old forms were incapable of producing new ones. No work based on the determination to be different seems to have a principle of life in it; genius is always "different" (that is, individual) in spite of itself; but never merely for the sake of being so.

For these reasons it is difficult, in judging the new tendencies, to find a common ground for criticism. The artist who rejects the past *en bloc* should at least offer some sort of new criterion, some view of life, some general conception of the validity of the creative act, by which his work may be measured. It is doubtful if such considerations have ever troubled the greater number; but, since the same sort of experiment necessarily leads to the same results, the new novelists have picked out of the ruins involving the older culture the odds and ends of some of the very principles they ignore.

In the early days of the art most of the characters in fiction were either "stylized" abstractions or merely passive subjects of experiment, or both. In the novels of character the figures were little more than the Lover, the Siren, the Miser, and so on; in the novel of adventure of the same period they were the Aunt Sallies of the village fair, perpetually set up to be knocked down by outward happenings. Both these sets of characters were virtually suspended in the void; their names were often reduced to initials, and the reader was at most allowed to know that the heroine had a brow of ivory, and the hero a frank, ingenuous eye. But presently someone—I suppose the merit is due first to Fielding and next to Scott—noticed the impact of surrounding circumstances on every individual life, the professional distortions, the religious and atmospheric influences, and those subtler differences produced by the then scarcely apprehended law of variability. The individual character burst the shell of the novelist's abstraction, and from the day of Scott and Balzac readers began to talk of this or that personage in a favorite novel as though he or she had been a living human being—as in the world of imagination, which is only a transposition of the other, they actually were.

This growth of individuality in the people of fiction led, about the middle of the nineteenth century, to the experimenting with new theories, perhaps necessary as a means of transition, though it turned out that they could never be more. The imagination, it was decided, was not a powerful enough medium; it was to be superseded by direct observation. The novelist exchanged his creative faculty for a kodak. Visible, palpable details of dress, of background, of bodily peculiarities, replaced the free drawing of character; statistics crowded out psychology. The "realists" had hit on a convenient device; they had discovered that it is much easier, whenever a given character appears, to put the same phrase on his lips, or to call the reader's attention to the same physical infirmity, a squint, a stammer, an odd pronunciation (a means of identification cruelly over-used by Balzac), than to build up, stroke by stroke, the shape and growth of his soul. Whatever, as Henry James once put it, could be smelt, seen, tasted, or touched,[2] was given precedence over mental and moral characteristics. But it remained to be discovered that this device led back, by another road, to the old stock types of the earlier fiction—save that the character who used to be merely the Miser was now the man whose left eyelid twitched, or the siren the young woman who was always preceded by a whiff of "White Rose."

Gradually the born novelists found that such short-cuts did not lead them where they wanted to go, and the more gifted took another path, in the wake of the great Russians, while the feebler beat their brains out against the blank wall of "Naturalism." Transmutation is the first principle of art, and copying can never be a substitute for creative vision.

Many of our younger novelists seem innocently to have rediscovered the facile effects which Zola's generation had worn so threadbare; but in their opinion the generation which invented the "slice of life" had not the full courage of its method. Though the novelists of that day tore their slice from the lump, and served it up uncooked, they felt all the while the obligation to account for having chosen one particular slice and not another; and this obligation is precisely what the new novelists disavow. They profess (or would seem to) that any slice is equally to their purpose, if they do not scornfully reject any notion of a purpose. The mid-nineteenth century group selected; the new novelists profess to pour everything out of their bag. Maupassant ended his "slices" with a climax (if this appalling metaphor may be forgiven); Katherine Mansfield tore hers off when they had filled so many pages—or so her imitators appear to believe. But every ending, as well as every beginning, is arbitrary and therefore selective. No bag has yet been found big enough to hold the universe, and the contents of the biggest bag is only, in the last resort, a selection. Yes; but it is, or would appear to be, an accidental selection; and as such it might be regarded, if only the creative intelligence were not always irresistibly sorting and rejecting. The experiments of the new novelists, and the comments of their docile interpreters, have proved, in spite of both, that any lasting creative work must be based on some sort of constructive system; the creator must have a conviction to guide him. The conviction of the new group is that there should be none; but this, too, is a system. And just as they have had to put together a sort of unconscious philosophy of life to support the fabric of their tales, so in method many of them have gone back to the "slice of life," and renamed it (perhaps because they did not know the experiment had already been made) the "stream of consciousness." Any such generalization must admit of notable exceptions; nevertheless the trend of the new fiction, not only in America and England, but on the continent, is chiefly toward the amorphous and the agglutinative. The novelists most in view reject form not only in the structure of their tales but in the drawing of character. They reduce to the vanishing point any will to action, and their personages are helpless puppets on a sluggish stream of fatality. That many commit acts of violence does not disprove this: they drift into them like somnambulists, and the onlookers or participants are as spectral as the fugitive apparitions of a dream. The reader, at the moment, may be deceived by such artifices; but the book closed, he seems to stand on the scene of a drunken revel "whence all but he have fled"[3]—so rapidly have the wraiths he has been reading about vanished from his memory.

To counteract this evanescence, the younger novelists attempt to give substance to their creations by an exaggerated physical realism, and by recourse to such superficial disguises as singularities of dialect and slang. To facilitate their realism, they naturally incline to situate their tales among the least developed classes; and in America, for instance, our young novelists are frequently praised for choosing the "real America" as the scene of their fiction—as though the chief intellectual and moral resources of the country lay among the poor whites of the Appalachians, or their counterparts in other regions.

Is there not some simpler explanation for this choice? It is obviously much easier to depict rudimentary characters, moved from the cradle to the grave by the same unchanging handful of instincts and prejudices, than to follow the action of persons in whom education and opportunity have developed a more complex psychology. For the same reason it is easier to note the confused drift of subconscious sensation than to single out the conscious thoughts and deliberate actions which are the key to character, and to the author's reason for depicting that character. I have often wished, in my "Sister Anne" watch for the coming great novelist, that these facilities did not so temptingly concord with the short-cut in everything which is the ideal of the new generation, with the universal thirst to surpass the speed-record in every department of human activity. The way of the young novelist used to be steep and difficult. The publishers rejected him, the public turned from him to names already known, and methods already familiar; the critic reviewed him in batches, as the "minor poets" are still dealt with. But nowadays all this is changed. Important prizes are offered for the "First Novel" (before it has even been tested by print), publishers advertise the work of the unknown as though being unknown were a quality and not merely a quantity; and every inducement is offered to seize the first short-cut to notoriety and pecuniary benefit.

To a generation agreed that the past is not the soil of the future, such simplification of method was almost irresistible. The choice was probably unconscious, and the novelists left it to the critics to justify them, and to supply the key to a philosophy of art which did not yet exist.

Luckily the story-telling gift is a tough plant, and will survive the indiscriminate praise of the present day as it did the qualified approval of less accommodating critics. It will struggle through the chaos of present conditions in life and art, it will find out that difficulties are not meant to be avoided but to be mastered, it will develop the patience to explore and depict the enduring characters of human nature under the shifting surface of slang and sexuality, and it will gradually find methods of expression more pertinent to such a theme.

I have my white stone ready to mark the day when I see a young novelist slowly and doggedly rowing up-stream instead of slipping down the current with the cheering crowd; for I believe that he is already training for the inevitable effort.

Saturday Review of Literature, 27 January 1934

[1] Wharton was both skeptical of, and unsettled by, the methods of many postwar novelists, but she recognized their significance, and expressed as early as 1928 a desire to publish some kind of comment on their work. Responding, for example, to Desmond MacCarthy's invitation to contribute an article to *Life and Letters*, Wharton declared, "I want to do one called 'Deep Sea Soundings' on this tiresome stream-of-consciousness theory which is deflecting so much real narrative talent out of its proper course" (EW to Desmond MacCarthy, 17 October 1928 [Yale]). Although she never published an essay in *Life and Letters*, three years later her interest in writing such a piece was still strong: upon reading Faulkner's *Sanctuary*, she remarked, "I have been much interested and amused, and am more than ever determined to write my article 'Wuthering Depths' on the new school of fiction" (EW to Edward Sheldon, 8 June 1931 [Yale]). Two years later, Henry S. Canby, editor of the *Saturday Review of Literature*, finally provided her with a more timely occasion on which to work out her thoughts on the subject, and she decided to write an essay on the new generation of writers, noting, "I would rather deal with modern fiction in a general way than write anything like a study of one or two given authors." In a sign of the shape that her ideas had begun to assume, Wharton added, "If you like I should probably be able to send you two articles, one to be called 'Documentation' and the other 'Permanent Values in Fiction'" (EW to Henry S. Canby, 13 October 1933 [Yale]). Indeed, the manuscripts among her papers at Yale include an essay, "Documentation in Fiction," that represents a substantially identical draft of "Tendencies in Modern Fiction"; in the published article, apart from deleting two brief passages, Wharton simply rearranged the order in which the sections of her argument had unfolded in the earlier version. Sending him the article around five months after she had accepted his suggestion, Wharton informed Canby, "I fear you will be disappointed at my not having dealt individually with the work of more of the younger novelists; but it was impossible to do so in such a limited space, . . . and if I were to say what I think of a good many of the younger writers, I should be regarded simply as a novelist of the old school incapable of understanding the new generation" (EW to Canby, 15 March 1934 [Yale]). Apart from a brief reference to Katherine Mansfield, Wharton's article is indeed fairly unspecific, shooting from the hip in many directions at many, not necessarily compatible, targets. She would not explicitly mention figures like Joyce, Woolf, or Lawrence until the next essay, "Permanent Values in Fiction," which was obviously conceived as a companion to its predecessor and which followed "Tendencies in Modern Fiction" in the *Saturday Review* by a couple of months.

[2] See n. 6 to "Maurice Hewlett's *The Fool Errant*."

[3] Reference to the opening lines of "Casabianca," best-known shorter poem by Felicia Hemans (1793–1835), popular English poet: "The boy stood on the burning deck / Whence all but he had fled."

Permanent Values in Fiction

Much as I dislike, in so brief an article, to go back to origins—though those of modern fiction are comparatively recent—I can hardly avoid beginning with the question: What constitutes a novel? To the generation which read Dickens and Thackeray, Balzac and Stendhal, the problem hardly presented itself. The answer floated, so to speak, on the surface of the enquiry: a novel is a work of fiction containing a good story about well-drawn characters.

To a generation nurtured on Mr. Joyce and Mrs. Woolf such a definition would seem not only pitifully simple, but far from comprehensive. The real preoccupations of some modern novelists seem so unrelated to the form they have chosen that one is almost driven to wonder if practical interests have not tempted them to expand the scope of the novel. Supposing a brilliant essayist, a literary critic, or a historian, wishes to get a wide hearing for his ideas, and a remunerative market for his prose; if he asks himself in what form his work will reach the largest public, the obvious answer is: in the form of a novel. This was discovered long ago by the pleaders of special causes— Harriet Beecher Stowe, Charles Reade, Mrs. Gaskell, for example—who produced (often with immensely remunerative results) that unhappy hybrid, the novel with a purpose.[1] But they did at least respect the accepted view of the novel, as being a vehicle for the telling of a story, and simply told their stories in terms of the moral they wanted to enforce, instead of letting their characters follow unhindered the devious ways of experience.

The modern writer with a purpose (no less a purpose because no longer a moral one) is unhampered by such restrictions. Whatever ideas or views he deals in, he barely troubles to manufacture mouthpieces for them, even of the most rudimentary sort; and the characters in modern fiction are often (as, for instance, in the novels of D. H. Lawrence) no more differentiated than a set of megaphones, through all of which the same voice interminably reiterates the same ideas.

It is true that there is still an ineradicable undergrowth of writers instinctively convinced that the novelist's job is to tell a tale and to mirror human nature; and whenever they have the ability to accomplish one or both of these difficult feats, the general public seizes on their books with avidity, and even the most severely selective find excuses for enjoying and applauding them. But for the present the trend of serious criticism turns more and more from this conception of the novel, whatever talent may go to its making.

The novel in its most serious form is tending to become a sort of anthology of the author's ideas; and to those who object that a given book, labeled a novel by its author, is really only a literary hold-all, the author, and most of the critics, condescendingly reply that the book in question is, on the contrary, a new form of novel—an answer which sounds final, but obviously begs the question. The attempt to define the modern novel was anticipated, a generation ago, by the witty Mrs. Bell of Boston. A bucolic friend presented Mrs. Bell with a sucking pig so remarkably pink and pleasing that, instead of eating it, she kept it as a household pet as long as it was small enough for the part. But at length, for all its endearing qualities, it outgrew the drawing-room; and on being questioned as to its subsequent fate, Mrs. Bell sadly said: "Oh, we just keep it to put things in."[2]

I do not for a moment assume that essayists and historians are turning themselves into novelists from motives mainly commercial, or at least consciously so. I wish they were; for I believe the real cause to be a much more harmful one—the belief that new "forms" are recurringly necessary in all the arts. It is less dangerous for an artist to sacrifice his artistic instincts to the pursuit of money or popularity than to immolate them to a theory; and I know no theory more contrary to the free action of genius than the persuasion that a given formula—alphabet, language, or any generally accredited form of expression—is worn out because too many people have used it. When I hear this asserted by critics, and see it tremblingly accepted by would-be creators, I am reminded of a distressed millionairess who once said to me: "My husband and I want to build a country house, but we don't know what style to choose, for one of my brothers-in-law has already used the Ionic order, and the other the Corinthian—and the Doric is really too simple!"

Since the world began, and man pictured his first stories on the walls of prehistoric caves, forms have been unceasingly and irresistibly modified by having new life poured into them; for what my distraught millionairess did not know, but what critics of any of the arts should surely remember, is the incessant renovation of old types by new creative action. There is no fear of monotony while the creative springs perpetually bubble up in new intelligences; and I doubt if, for instance, it would have occurred to any really great creative writer that the old rules of syntax were too narrow for his genius, unless he had been told so by the non-creative. The acceptance of such theories certainly shows a temporary decline of the inventive faculties; but the human imagination is fed from sources far below the reach of surface droughts, and the arrested currents will flow again, and the permanent values eventually declare themselves.

Meanwhile one must turn to the past to learn what these permanent values are in the field of fiction; for it is not always easy to ascertain, if one tries to discover them in one's contemporaries. There is a law of mental optics which makes it difficult, in all the arts, to separate surface novelty from real originality; but few are conscious of this optical incapacity, and some (it must be remembered) are not afflicted by it. In spite of the *Quarterly* a handful of Keats's contemporaries knew what he had given them;[3] and in every generation there has been an eye adjusted to focus the eternal at short range.

In general, however, when the range is too close, the object contemplated tends to become either blurred or monstrously enlarged; and it is only necessary to study that master of all the critics, Sainte-Beuve, to find countless instances of the unreliability of contemporary "close-ups."[4] Perhaps only one great creative artist can discern the supreme qualities of another; as Napoleon did when he saw Goethe, as Balzac did when he read Stendhal.

Taking this difficulty into account, I am inclined to think that the best way of estimating contemporary writers is by extracting from the whole body of fiction some evidence of what its lasting qualities are; to find out what "keeps" and what does not. Though in all the arts it is admitted that contemporary judgments are often temporary, we agree to assume that the verdict of time is final. And that verdict, where the writing of fiction is concerned, seems to say that two qualities alone survive the test. One, and the principal, is the creating of characters which so possess us with the sense of their reality that we talk of Anna Karenina, Becky Sharp, the Père Goriot, and Tess, as of real people whom we have known and lived with; and the other is the art of relating these characters to whatever general law of human experience made the novelist choose to tell their tale rather than another.

In examining the work of recent novelists it is somewhat disconcerting to find how seldom either of these points seems to have engaged their attention. They may perhaps be said to have dismissed them as irrelevant to the new theory of the novel; but I wish they had not discarded what are, and must always be, the two things most difficult of achievement. I am always suspicious, in creative work, of modifications which avoid difficulties; and nothing in the novelist's task puts his ability to the test as does the creating and keeping alive of his characters, and, next to that, the reasoned relating of their individual case to the general human problem. A tale in which the characters drift by like figures in a film is much easier to reel off than one in which a deeper significance is sought, and makes itself felt to the end.

Two perils beset the average reader: he is apt to be taken either by sheer sentimentality, or by what one might call a cultured mediocrity; and if left to himself would swing contentedly between the two. But the appalling facilities for the dissemination of pseudo-culture, the virtual impossibilty of escaping from the current literary contagions, have disturbed the pleasant somnolence of the majority. They are told every morning, by wireless and book-jacket, by news-item and picture-paper, who is in the day's spotlight, and must be admired (and if possible read) before the illumination shifts; and every passing fad and experiment in their favorite field of letters is pressed on them with bewildering rapidity. All this tends to make popular judgments more unreliable than ever; but it is the more instructive to note that when a Babbitt struts on the stage the thin shadows take flight before his sturdy flesh-and-blood, and a deep laugh of appreciation encircles the world.

Mr. Lewis is not the only creator of live people among modern novelists, but I choose him as a symbol because the line he follows—while it is in some danger of becoming a rut—seems to me to be the true one. In his quest of material he has conformed to Goethe's counsel, and plunged his hand into the thick of average human nature;[5] and I believe the greatest error of the younger novelists, of whatever school, has been to imagine that abnormal or highly specialized characters offer a richer field than the normal and current varieties. Emily Brontë was a woman of genius; but if she had lived longer, and attained to a closer contact with reality, she might have made, out of the daily stuff of life at Haworth parsonage, a greater and more deeply moving book than by picturing a houseful of madmen. Dostoievsky, in "The Idiot," also essayed the study of abnormal people; but he blent them with the normal, as life itself does—and thus, incidentally, showed that their chief interest, for the reader, lies not in their own case, but in its tragic and destructive reactions on the normal. And readers who, in spite of their admiration for "Wuthering Heights," sometimes find it difficult to disentangle Heathcliff from Earnshaw, and the two Catherines from one another, will not easily forget the living presence of Prince Myshkin, and his strange vigil with the murderer beside the dead body of Nastasia.

The general reading public, suggestible though it is, and anxious to follow the hints given by the selective minority, is yet irresistibly drawn to any book based on genuine observation of character, and embodied in consecutive and significant narrative. Sinclair Lewis's success is probably due far more to the fact that he has drawn people with recognizable faces, and told their stories with a vigorous simplicity, than because of any general perception of his rare gift of tragic irony. A long course of cinema obviousnesses and of tabloid culture has rendered the majority of readers insensible to allusiveness and to irony, but they still rouse themselves when they see "a likeness" to flesh-and-blood in the people they are asked to read about; and I believe this instinct is a sound one, and that such books as Sinclair Lewis's and Theodore Dreiser's have more of the lasting stuff of good fiction in them than dozens of works dressed up in a passing notoriety.

Saturday Review of Literature, 7 April 1934

[1] Charles Reade (1814–84), popular English author of topical novels and novels of sensation; Elizabeth Gaskell (1810–65), prominent Victorian social novelist.

[2] Helen Choate Bell (1830–1918), celebrated Boston social personality and wit.

[3] Reference to John Croker's infamous attack on *Endymion* in the April 1818 issue of the powerful *Quarterly Review*.

[4] Wharton has in mind Sainte-Beuve's failure to appreciate the work of contemporaries like Balzac, Stendhal, and Baudelaire.

[5] An allusion to the Merry Person's declaration about "Menschenleben" in the prologue to *Faust* (l. 169), "Wo Ihr's packt, da ist's interessant [Wherever you seize it, it's interesting]," a line Wharton quotes in two earlier essays (and elsewhere as well).

A Reconsideration of Proust

The request of the Editor of *The Saturday Review of Literature* to send him within a very brief time-limit an article on Proust found me on an autumn holiday in the West Highlands, far from the long shelf which holds my "Recherche du Temps Perdu," farther still from the atmosphere in which Proust had the only being conceivable to him.[1] Mr. Buchan's "Massacre of Glencoe" had formed my most recent reading, and the calm, ruddy faces of Highland chieftains and their wives, as portrayed by Raeburn and the far greater Allan Ramsay, filled every corner of my mental picture gallery.[2] It was impossible to be more remote from Proust and all the implications of his tormented genius, and I had already written a cable of refusal when it suddenly struck me that, if I *could* fish up and reconstitute Proust (*my* Proust, that is, for such evocations are necessarily subjective) out of the bottom of a dark Scottish loch, or a Jacobite cavern on a stormy moor, I should have applied a far severer test to his genius than if his books were under my hand, and the Parisian air in my lungs.

No sooner had the thought presented itself than its ramifications drew me on, and I tore up the cable and got out my fishing-line. For, after all, what constitutes the ultimate proof of creative genius but the degree to which it penetrates and becomes a part of the intelligence on which it acts? If I can succeed in fishing Marcel Proust up alive out of the depths of my mind I may have performed a more interesting feat than any "study" I might have written after conscientiously rereading him. The residue he has left in me is the crystallizing of a million stray reactions produced while the volumes were in my hand, and it is with this quintessential Proust, who must obviously be the lasting one, that I will try to deal.

Any one who attempts this fishing-up of authors not recently reread will be struck by the difference in the weight and vitality of what they capture. Sometimes the line comes up all too lightly, a thin wraith dangling from the hook; sometimes the hook has only a name on it; but, more rarely, the line tugs, and a living, bounding presence leaps into sight. Those are the writers who have what one may call mass, or four-squareness; and of this small company Proust is preëminently one. Let us bend above his glittering, palpitating flanks.

It is necessarily from the novelist's point of view that I make the experiment. Inevitably, novels make a different impression on the minds of novelists, provoke in them reactions more intense and complex than those produced on the non-creative mind. There is an active participation in the reading of novels by novelists which either lifts the reader to creative rapture or—makes the work fall from his languid hand. Therefore what I say of Proust must be regarded as the view of a fellow-craftsman, however remote from his genius.

Genius he had, and to a prodigious degree. Fortune had perhaps endowed him more lavishly with natural gifts than any French writer of fiction since Balzac. If he had known how to use them as the far less lavishly gifted Flaubert used his—and the "Education Sentimentale" offers many available points of comparison—Proust might have been the new Balzac, the great master he just failed of becoming.

As the years pass, and my view of him falls more and more into perspective, I find it but little changed in its main lines. I thought then, and I think now, that his intellectual speculations hampered his genius as a story teller, and that the mist of Bergsonian metaphysics, which now and then thickens to a fog, not only impedes the progress of his tale but frequently blurs the vivid faces of his protagonists. Looking back on his work as a whole I am more and more of this opinion; and every encounter with the small group of fervent Proustians—the readers who really know their way about in that puzzling labyrinth of human experience—fortifies my conviction that Proust's real claim to greatness is the fact of having called into being so immense a number of lifelike characters. Whenever two Proustians meet the references exchanged are always, inevitably, to his people, not to his philosophy; and the names of Aunt Léonie, of Madame de Villeparisis, of the Duc de Guermantes, of the tragic Swann, the immortal Verdurin group, and the ineffable Monsieur de Norpois, are instantly on their lips. It must not be understood that I am uninterested by Proust's abstract speculations, or indifferent to his philosophy of life. I am convinced that no storyteller, however great his gifts, can do great work unbased on some philosophy of life. Only the author's own convictions can give that underlying sense of values which lifts anecdote to drama, drama to tragedy. Proust's fault lay in not restraining this sense of values, in too often letting his philosophic speculations crowd his people and their actions from the foreground.

But what, after all, does that matter, when, however often he pushes them out of the way, their uncanny vitality always forces them back into their rightful place? The jaded novel reader, accustomed to seeing the characters in whose vitality he has been asked to believe, fade away after the first pages, and die on the author's hands, stands amazed at this rebounding vitality of the Proustian people. Again and again they reappear in the crowded, tossing pages, almost like drowning people clutching at a raft—and almost invariably they regain their footing on it, shouting, gesticulating, possessing themselves of their square foot or two of space in that packed world, and making it vibrate with reality. A great gift—the greatest and the rarest in the storyteller's complex equipment. We forgive everything else to the magician who makes us believe in his imperious people, not only once but a hundred times calling them to passionate life, and at each reappearance showing us that, in the interval, they have not dangled on a hook in his property-shop, but have maintained activities of their own behind the scenes, growing, changing, maturing, withering, or ripening, as the case may be, but always following the rich curve of life's transformations. In this respect I know nothing, in the greatest novelists, to surpass the evolution of poor Swann's dreamy, vacillating character, the coarse, unimaginative thickening of Odette's, the zig-zag course of Saint Loup's uneven nature, the persistence, in the Duchesse de Guermantes, of her old racial inheritance, and the peasant simplicity underlying her social sophistication.[3]

The investigation of Proust's one or two glaring failures—his inability to put life into such painfully elaborated characters as the wretched wraith

Albertine and the simply non-existent violinist over whom he vainly expended so many pages[4]—belongs to another view of the author and of his work, and one which may be excluded from a survey of his results as a creator of character. Every creative novelist, for one reason or another, has such failures; certain characters (perhaps those too near to his own to be properly focussed) obstinately refuse to come to life; but how little it matters, in the case of Proust, whose successful evocations were so many!

It is in the number of these living creations that he so far surpasses all but the supreme novelists. And this particular gift is the best worth studying in the attempt to allot him a definite place among his peers. That the gift was nourished by his incessant brooding on the sources of our sensibility I should be the last to deny. He has gazed upon his people as the seer gazes on his crystal. He has never been satisfied to disguise a pack of dummies under a few showy tags of reality: tricks of speech, of gesture and thought. All these people are really living, growing, changing before our eyes; and to achieve this result Proust had first to live in them, to *be them*, with each one of their sudden and often brief reappearances to force his way into them again and feed with his own blood the currents of their tangled personalities. Perhaps there is no better way of summing up the mysterious process than Flaubert, avowedly most "objective" of novelists, found when some idiot asked him: "Dear master, who actually *was* Madame Bovary?"—"Madame Bovary? Why, myself, of course." That is Proust's answer as we go back to him.

I have said that, in returning to Proust after a considerable interval, I have found little to modify in my first estimate of his genius. But in one respect I have changed my opinion; and this change I believe has been experienced by most of his early readers.[5] When "Du Côté de chez Swann" gave us its first electrical shock I suppose we all thought: "Here is an innovator! Here is new wine in a new bottle!" But, though there is a certain sense in which genius is always new, the great originators draw as much from the past as from the present—and Proust was no exception. Indeed it is truer to say of him—though few would have said it when his first volumes appeared—that he ends the long and magnificent line of nineteenth century novelists, than that he opens a new era. Even his method, new as it seemed at first, is only a somewhat careless combination of the traditional forms of fiction; and every line that he wrote shows that he belonged to a generation of novelists who were more interested in the inward drama of life than in its outward accidents.

Nearly a generation has gone by since Proust, on his deathbed, wrote the last, profoundly moving pages of "Le Temps Retrouvé"—that stormy "Testament of Beauty"—and it is now possible for his readers not only to revise their personal impression of his genius, but to ask what mark he has made on the generation succeeding him.

To the latter question the answer must be: None! On the general tendencies of modern fiction Proust appears to have had no action whatever. It is even difficult to find a trace of his influence in any of the "little chapels," as the more theoretical experimenters with the art are called in France. Proust has founded neither a popular nor a highly specialized school; in neither category has he either disciples or imitators. There are several reasons for this. It will not suffice to say that he is not imitated because he is not read; though this is partly true. But he has always had a small following of devoted readers, whose admiration increases with the lapse of time; and I believe the fundamental cause of his isolation is that the only thing that interested him was the drama of the soul. The outward incidents he recorded, however brutal, and often repellent, concerned him only as manifestations of the inner life; and nothing interests the modern novelist and his readers less than the inner life. In spite of Proust's individual antecedents his traditional world was still essentially a Christian and Catholic one; the moral and intellectual conflicts arising in such a society alone seemed to him worth recording. It is this which divides him from his successors in the pitifully shrunken field of his art.

At one time it seemed that only the length of his tale stood between himself and popularity. But this has long since been disproved. After exhausting the delights of "tabloid" fiction the reader (and the publisher) now clamor for long books, and modern fiction does not fear to drape itself in sagas and epics as long as the longest tales of Richardson and his prolix school. But the modern reader, in demanding length, does not ask for depth; in fact he absolutely rejects it. The modern novel must be long, but it must be beaten out thin; mental effort must be reduced to a minimum, and the reader enabled to travel as easily over his thousand pages as the pedestrian slipping along on an escalator.

It is impossible to imagine any works of fiction offering fewer of such facilities than those of Marcel Proust. He is all in depth; and he will have to wait for full recognition till the surface of life is once more discovered to be of interest only in proportion to its inner significance. Meanwhile, for the few who still hold to this belief, each sounding of his deep pages will continue to render up new treasures.

Saturday Review of Literature, 27 October 1934

[1] Henry S. Canby's request had been occasioned by the forthcoming Random House re-issue, in four volumes, of C. K. Scott-Montcrief's translation of *A la recherche du temps perdu*.

[2] John Buchan (1875–1940), Scottish novelist and journalist, had published *The Massacre of Glencoe* a year earlier; Sir Henry Raeburn (1756–1823) and Allan Ramsay (1713–84), Scottish portrait-painters.

[3] Mentioning the same characters, along with "the invalid aunt in the pale twilight of her provincial bedroom, and the servant François who waits on her," as well as "the great, the abject, the abominable and magnificent Monsieur de Charlus," Wharton had applauded their "tough vitality" in much the same terms some years earlier: "Ah, how they all live, and abound each in his or her own sense—and how, each time they reappear (sometimes after disconcert-ingly long eclipses), they take up their individual rhythm as unerringly as the performers in some great orchestra!" (*WF*, 158–60).

[4] Reference to the character Charles Morel.

[5] As early as 1925, Wharton had in fact already registered this change of opinion, and antici-pated the remarks that follow, in her earlier essay on Proust, discussing what she called the "series of experiments" that had "unsettled" "the conception of the art of fiction" some time after his novel began to appear in print: "An unexpected result of the contradictory clamour has been to transfer Proust, who ten or twelve years ago seemed to many an almost unintelligible innovator, back to his rightful place in the great line of classic tradition" (*WF*, 153).

TRIBUTES AND EULOGIES

Frederic Bronson

To the Editor of The Evening Post:

Sir: It must be a matter of surprise to those who knew the late Frederic Bronson that in the newspaper notices of his death so much more space should have been given to the fact that he was interested in the development of sport than to the enumeration of the many ways in which he was of more serious service to his fellow-townsmen.[1] This inadequate presentment may have been partly due to Mr. Bronson's unassertive character; but it does not speak well for any community, or at least for its standards as represented by the press, that a man who fills, however modestly, such a place as Mr. Bronson occupied, should be known chiefly for tastes which he regarded as a mere relaxation from his real interests.

He was, in fact, a man who might in many ways be cited as an example to a society where, of all the arts, none is less understood than the intelligent use of leisure. Rich men's sons among us are still, as a rule, either trained to go on adding to their wealth, or suffered to squander it without sense of civic obligations. Mr. Bronson presented an instance of the man of means who ennobles his leisure by devoting it to the service of the community. To name the many good works with which he was connected would give but a slight idea of the extent of his beneficence. In such cases the good a man does is not to be measured by the number of charities to which he contributes, but by the amount of personal aid he gives to each. It was Mr. Bronson's merit to dedicate to such duties the time, the energy, the patient and unremitting care that most men reserve for the advancement of their private interests. Thus, he was among the most active organizers of the City Club, he devoted himself for many years to the work of the House of Refuge, and his unwearied efforts to raise a fund for the enlargement of the Lying-in Hospital are too recent to need recalling.[2] It would be easy to multiply such instances; but it is more important to record that Mr. Bronson doubled the efficacy of what he did by the simple and spontaneous way in which he did it.

He had, to an unusual degree, what might be called the civic conscience; and all that he was as a private person—the loyal friend, the sound adviser, the perfectly just and upright man—he had the rarer merit of being as a citizen. For this reason it seems fitting that he should be known and commemorated beyond the limited circle of those who had the opportunity of esteeming him personally in both characters.

New York Evening Post, 2 April 1900

¹ Frederic Bronson (1850–1900), treasurer of the New York Life Insurance and Trust Company, and a director of the Savings Bank for Merchants' Clerks. Although he is not mentioned in her memoirs, Bronson presumably belonged to the group of elders (like Bayard Cutting, Robert Minturn, and John Cadwalader) of whom Wharton later offered a more ambivalent account: "The best class of New Yorkers had shaken off the strange apathy following on the Civil War, and begun to develop a municipal conscience, and all the men I have mentioned were active in administering the new museums, libraries and charities of New York; but the idea that gentlemen could stoop to meddle with politics had hardly begun to make its way, and none of my friends rendered the public services that a more enlightened social system would have exacted of them" (*BG*, 95).

² City Club, on West Forty-fifth Street, founded in 1892 for the purpose of promoting social interaction among civic-minded men interested in encouraging the efficiency of city government and the election of suitable leaders to municipal office; House of Refuge, a reformatory for boys under eighteen, located at Randall's Island near 125th Street; the Lying-in Hospital, at Second Avenue between Seventeenth and Eighteenth Streets, provided free relief and care to destitute women in childbirth.

George Cabot Lodge

It would be impossible, I think, for any friend of George Cabot Lodge's to write of the poet without first speaking of the man; and this not only because his art was so close to his life, but also, and chiefly, because, to those near enough to measure him, his character, his temper, the "virtue" in him, made his talent, distinguished as it was, a mere part of an abounding whole.¹

Abundance—that is the word which comes to me whenever I try to describe him. During the twelve years of our friendship—and from the very day that it began—I had, whenever we were together, the sense of his being a creature as profusely as he was finely endowed. There was an exceptional delicacy in his abundance, and an extraordinary volume in his delicacy.

All this, on the day when he was first brought to see me—a spring afternoon of the year 1898 in Washington—was lit up by a beautiful boyish freshness, which, as the years passed, somehow contrived to ripen without fading.² In the first five minutes of our talk he *gave* himself with the characteristic wholeness that made him so rare a friend: showing me all the sides of his varied nature, the grave sense of beauty, the flashing contempt of meanness, and that large spring of kindly laughter that comes to many only as a result of the long tolerance of life. It was one of his gifts thus to brush aside the preliminaries of acquaintance and enter at once, with a kind of royal ease, on the rights and privileges of friendship; as though, one might think, with a foreboding of the short time given him to enjoy them.

Aside from this, however, there was nothing of the pathetically predestined in the young Cabot Lodge. Then—and to the end—he lived every moment to the full, and the first impression he made was of a joyous physical life. His sweet smile, his easy strength, his deep eyes full of laughter and visions—these struck one even before his look of intellectual power. I have seldom seen any one in whom the natural man was so wholesomely blent with the reflecting intelligence; and it was not the least of his charms that he sent such stout roots into the earth, and had such a hearty love for all he drew from it. Nothing was common or unclean to him but the vulgar, the base and the insincere, and his youthful impatience at the littleness of human nature was tempered by an unusually mature sense of its humours.

I might pause to speak of the accomplishments that made his society, from the first, so refreshing and animating: for he was an admirable linguist, a good "Grecian," a sensitive lover of the arts, and possessed, on the whole, of the fullest general "culture" I have ever known in a youth of his age. But even as I number his gifts I see how suffused they were for me by the glow of his beautiful nature, and how little what he knew ever counted in comparison with what he was; unless it be exacter to say that it counted precisely in proportion to what he was. At any rate, his attainments did not, even in those days, single him out as much as his unusual gift of sympathy, and the range of his response to the imaginative call. As his voice—that beautiful medium of fine English speech—could pass from the recital of Whitman or Leconte de Lisle[3] to the vivid mimicry of some exchange of platitudes overheard in street or train, so his mind flashed through the same swift transitions, and the boy who was dramatizing the broad humours of a *tournée de Montmartre* would break off to tell how, at the end of a summer night in London, he had gone down to await the dawn on Westminster Bridge,

When all that mighty heart was lying still.[4]

One is accustomed, in enjoying the comradeship of young minds, to allow in them for a measure of passing egotism, often the more marked in proportion to their sensitiveness to impressions; but it was Cabot Lodge's special grace to possess the sensitiveness without the egotism. Always as free from pedantry as from conceit, he understood from the first the give and take of good talk, and was not only quick to see the other side of an argument but ready to reinforce it by his sympathetic interpretation. And because of this responsiveness of mind, and of the liberating, vivifying nature from which it sprang, he must always, to his friends, remain first of all, and most incomparably, a Friend.

It was in the year of our meeting that "The Song of the Wave, by George Cabot Lodge," was published by Charles Scribner's Sons. When this earliest volume appeared, the young author (who had taken his degree at Harvard in 1895) had but lately returned from Paris, where, in close comradeship with his friend Joseph Stickney,[5] he had spent two years in linguistic and historical studies at the Sorbonne.

Perhaps, if measured with his later works, the most distinctive thing about "The Song of the Wave" is its title. All his life long, George Cabot Lodge was a lover of the sea.

> "Come," said the Ocean, "I have songs to sing,
> And need thine utterance."

This is the voice of his "call," to which henceforth he always lent a yearning ear, and which was soon to find a more individual utterance in "The Greek Galley," the best poem of his second volume (published in 1902),[6] and to break into its fullest expression in the beautiful "Tuckanuck" sonnets of "The Great Adventure" (1905). The sea was no mere symbol to him, nor his love of it a literary attitude. Living from childhood on the rocky New England coast, and spending long weeks of his dreaming studious youth on the lonely beach of Tuckanuck Island, off Nantucket, he had as close a kinship as Whitman's with the element he sang, and sailing and swimming were the forms of exercise in which he most delighted. The sea is a great inspirer of song, but she has been sung so often and so long that she may be pardoned for sometimes repeating an old refrain in the ears of her new lovers. It was inevitable that George Cabot Lodge, like other young poets, should pass through the imitative stage of which his first three volumes give occasional proof, and equally inevitable that the voices of Whitman and Swinburne should be those oftenest heard in them. "N'écoute pas"—Gounod once wrote in a letter to a friend—"N'écoute pas ceux qui te disent qu'il ne faut pas imiter les maîtres, ce n'est pas vrai; il ne faut pas en imiter un, mais les imiter tous. . . .*On ne devient grand maître qu'à condition d'être le parent des autres.*"[7] And the same argument is put more forcibly in Goethe's cry to Eckermann: "Originality? What do people mean by originality? From the moment of our birth the world begins to react on us, and the only thing we can call our own is our energy, our power, our will"[8]—in other words, our reaction on the world.

The first opportunity to test himself in this respect came to Cabot Lodge, as it comes to so many, through a private grief—the death of his friend

Stickney; and in the sonnets commemorating this loss his verse first sounds a distinctly personal note.

The one beginning:

> "At least," he said, "we spent with Socrates
> Some memorable days, and in our youth
> Were curious and respectful of the Truth,"

has a gallant ring of young defiance, but a more sustained level of beauty is reached in "Days."

> Still on his grave, relentless, one by one,
> They fall, as fell the mystic, Sibylline
> Sad leaves, and still the Meaning's secret sign
> Dies undeciphered with each dying sun—

To wrest from life the secret of that meaning was the problem that haunted Cabot Lodge; and the insistency with which his verse reverts to it is saved from sameness only by the varied notes it wrung from him.

He had already, in the year preceding the publication of "The Great Adventure," attempted to give the subject an ampler and more philosophic expression in the long dramatic poem called "Cain." In this volume his fine sense of rhythm finds its first large opportunity, and the blank verse is of a variety and an *envergure* remarkable in a first effort of such length. Nevertheless, intellectually and imaginatively he traversed a great distance in the year between "Cain" and "The Great Adventure," and three years after the latter book he brought out another dramatic poem—"Herakles"—in which the image he had so patiently sought to shape emerged at length from the marble. The theory that the artist should sacrifice much to produce little—the "sculpte, lime, cisèle" of Gautier[9]—seems sometimes to be confused with the notion that abundant production is proof of mediocrity. Mediocrity, alas, is often fertile; but so, almost always, is genius. Taken by itself, abundance, in the sense of capacity for sustained expression, is a hopeful sign; and it is well that a young poet should measure himself with a long task. Cabot Lodge, in "Herakles," certainly proved the value of the effort. It freed him from the tendency to draw all his effects from his inner experience, and roused him to a perception of dramatic values. The subject he chose was magnificent: the labours of Herakles, like the "passive resistance" of Prometheus, offer an inexhaustible theme to the poetic imagination. A page from Diodorus Siculus sums up the argument; but the author, indifferent to archaeology, uses the legend as the symbol of the long labour of the soul of man, "dissatisfied, curious, unconvinced at last," and ever, in Goethe's phrase, going "forward over graves."[10]

As regards the growth of Cabot Lodge's art, perhaps the most interesting thing in the volume—aside from the more complex harmony of the verse—is the drawing of Creon's character. Hitherto the poet's personages had been mouth-pieces, but in the Theban King he created a man, and the ease with which he "exteriorized" Creon's good-humoured disenchantment and tolerant worldly wisdom gave promise of a growing power to deal with his themes objectively. This promise is reaffirmed in "The Noctambulist," one of the long poems of "The Soul's Inheritance," the volume to which Cabot Lodge had put the finishing touches just before his sudden death. The protagonist of the poem is not, like Creon, a character antithetical to his creator. He is a version of the poet's own personality, but a new version, and one rendered *from the outside*. This power of dissociation, and the ability to project one['s] self far enough for the other to focus it, is the very mainspring of the dramatizing faculty; for to draw one's neighbour is a much easier business than to draw *one's self as seen by one's neighbour*.

The Noctambulist is he who, having "been all the rounds of repetition" in "the same old adventure of the mind," has reached the point when

> "Swift as passion, brutal as a blow,
> The Dark shuts down. . . .
>   And, O, the truth
> Is terrible within us!—for at last
> We touch our bounds—we fill, in every gyre,
> In all its pearly mansions, wondrously,
> Up from what blind beginnings, long-evolved—
> The unfinished shell of our humanity."

He has reached that point; has felt—

> "Walled round and prisoned in the senseless dark—
> How little we are free! . . ."

And has gone on to the farther discovery that

> "The Night is best!—for only when we fill
> The total measure of our human ken,
> And feel in every exercise of being
> The bondage of our fixed infirmities,
> Are we assured that we, in every cell

And nerve, respond to all life's whole appeal,
Known and unknown, in sense and heart and brain. . . ."

This is the writer's maturest conception of life, and his verse rose with it in an ampler movement. Such memorable passages abound in "The Noctambulist," and in its harmony of thought and form it remains perhaps the completest product of Cabot Lodge's art.

An increasing beauty of versification marks this latest volume. His was not the lyric muse. He "knew to build the lofty rhyme,"[11] and the measured pace of blank verse, and the balanced architecture of the sonnet, best fitted the expression of his reflective and discursive mind. It is indeed a defect of some of his earlier verse that it deals too exclusively with general ideas expressed in abstract terms; but with the rounding of his nature he had grown more sensitive to the appeal of the visible world. The awakening of this sense expresses itself in "Unison," another poem contained in the last volume.

So, in the mind's resolvent unity,
All powers and phases of the natural world
Showed the one urge within, and we discerned
In the rich tissue of apparent things
The secret sense which is not theirs but ours.

The quality of the last lines shows to what degree his verse was in process of being enriched by this sensibility to external beauty. Already it had given him not only new images, but a new simplicity and directness of phrase. The lines:

The mountain rose in power beneath our feet,
Vestured in basalt *and the endless grass*

have a concreteness and a colour undiscoverable in his earlier volumes. And a higher simplicity is reached in the poem called "Strength and Solitude."

We have laid down our ear to the dumb sod—
We who are man and mortal as all things,
And more and yet not otherwise than they—
We have laid down our ear and heard the earth
Of graves and the innumerable grass
Whisper to us. . . .

Here the beauty of visible things speaks no longer in images, but directly, without need of interpretation, in that fusion of thought and sense which makes the magic of poetry.

From the first, Cabot Lodge had shown a preference for the sonnet. Its structural severity appealed to his sense of form, and to the seriousness of his poetic mood. In every volume from the "Poems" to "The Soul's Inheritance," he gave this shape to some of the best expressions of his thought; and, as with his blank verse, so in the metric of his sonnets, the beauty of form grew with the growing richness of content. All through the sonnets there are fine passages, such as:

> O Memory, Lord of broken and broadcast
> Fragments of life, like scattered Cyclades
> Set in the dark illimitable seas
> Of Time—

and

> May we . . . discern how earth and sky and sea,
> And love and life and death and destiny,
> Are wrought of one eternal element,
> Quarried in dim deep strata of the soul,

and single lines of insistent beauty, like the picture of Love:

> With eyes of silence and with lips of song,

and the magnificent apostrophe to Silence:

> Lord of the deserts 'twixt a million spheres.

As his work progressed, the scattered graces were more often knit into a homogeneous whole, and one comes on sonnets of such completeness as "Questions," "Only the Dark!" or "Cor Cordium"—the latter marked by a beautiful inversion of the familiar sea-shell metaphor:

> Then, as it were against the inward ear,
> We hold, in silence, like a chambered shell,
> The dazed one human heart—and seem to hear
> Forever and forever rise and swell
> And fail and fall on Death's eventual shore,
> Tragic and vast, Life's inarticulate roar!

In "The Soul's Inheritance" each of the longer poems leads up to a stately portico of sonnets, in whose intercolumniations the gravely moving pentameters lose themselves like the garlanded figures of some Greek procession. Almost all these sonnets are fine; and it is at once tragic and consoling for those who loved him and watched his progress with a jealous care, to note that the latest are the finest. Intellectually and plastically, he was nearing completeness in this form of verse; and how close he had come to it such a poem as this remains to prove.

> Earth, sea and sky are not as once they were
>> To us: there is no aspect of all things,
>> No pulse of heart or brain, no whisperings
>> Of truth's grave music to the inward ear,
> Unaltered or unglorified: the mere
>> Being of life, intense as song-swept strings,
>> Is like a breathless sense of soaring wings
>> Loosed in the spirit's boundless atmosphere! . . .
> We are not as we were! Our feet have ranged
>> The summits of imperishable hours;
>> Life is a lordlier hope; and we, estranged
> In secret and at heart from all control,
>> Walk in the wide new futures of the soul,
>> Charged as with incommensurable powers! . . .

To part with him on this note is to preserve his image as it lives in the hearts that cherish him. To the end he travelled, seeking "new ranges for the feet of song," and one leaves him on a height, with his face to the morning. For he, who had so many gifts, had above all the gift of life; and that is the best, since it gives all the others their savour.

Scribner's Magazine, February 1910

[1] George Cabot ("Bay") Lodge (1873–1909), American poet and dramatist, son of the powerful senator from Massachusetts; works mentioned by Wharton include *Cain: A Drama* (1904), *The Great Adventure* (1905), *Herakles* (1908), and the posthumously published *The Soul's Inheritance* (1909).

[2] It was through Walter Berry that Wharton met "Bay" Lodge, to whom she became extremely close, and whom she later remembered as "one of the most brilliant and versatile youths I have ever known" (*BG*, 149). Evidently, Wharton first considered writing two separate memorial essays on Lodge; in the third in a series of anguished letters to his widow, Elizabeth Frelinghuysen Davis (Bessy) Lodge, Wharton had written, shortly after his death in August 1909, "I want very much to write something about Bay's work, if you & his parents wd. like me to. . . . My idea would be to do a short article for the Literary Supplement of the London Times, which is on the whole the best thing of its kind in England, & something longer for any American magazine you may prefer. My first thought was the Atlantic [Monthly], but I should like to reach a larger public" (EW to Bessy Lodge, 16 September [1909] [MHS]). The poet's father promptly wrote to express his approval and encouragement, while two months later the posthumous publication of Lodge's last volume of poems moved Wharton to exclaim to his widow, "How much I want to say of them!" (EW to Bessy Lodge, 16 November 1909 [MHS]). By the

end of November, she had evidently decided upon a single essay, to appear in *Scribner's Maga-zine*, and sent it to Bessy with unusually expansive comments: "I have been so happy in writing it that I hope you will feel I have given some impression of what he was to his friends. As regards the critical part, I have simply given my personal view, as I often put it to him. . . . I hope you will like the choice of quotations, which I tried to make as characteristic & as varied as I could.—I wanted to say much more, but I think this kind of article gains in some ways by being short—&, even if I didn't, the inexorable magazine limits are there!" (EW to Bessy Lodge, 30 November [1909] [MHS]). Elsewhere, however, Wharton gives some sense of certain addi-tional constraints under which she composed her tribute to Lodge, whose verse lacked "any real sense of 'visible beauty,'" as she had put it to Sara Norton, adding, "'He doesn't see things in images'" (qtd. in Lewis 171). To Brownell, soon after publishing her eulogy, she was more evocatively candid: "I was especially glad that you liked what I wrote about Bay Lodge. It was doubly difficult to do, first because I loved & admired him so much, & secondly because I felt that he had never, in his poetry, 'given' all that was in him, or even a large part. So I had to walk on a narrow rope above an abyss, & it was reassuring to learn that you thought I had kept my balance" (EW to W.C. Brownell, 9 April [1910] [Amherst]). Brownell was not alone in admiring the essay; briefly referring in his *Life of George Cabot Lodge*, a year later, to the poet's friend-ship with "Edith Wharton, whose unerring taste and finished workmanship served as a correc-tive to his youthful passion for license" in verse, Henry Adams cites several passages from "[h]er fine appreciation" of Lodge, and observes that "the. . .simple quality of the truest art runs through the whole of Mrs. Wharton's painting. . . . Every touch of her hand takes the place of proof." Since her own essay "gave practically no 'biography,' because that. . .seemed to me less important in an article like this," as she admitted to Bessy Lodge (30 November [1909] [MHS]), Wharton had looked forward to Adams's work: "I am waiting eagerly to see what Mr. Adams writes" (*L*, 216–17). Late in life, she felt free to offer a more critical appraisal of Lodge (*BG*, 149–51).

³ Charles-Marie-René Leconte de Lisle (1818–94), French poet, leader of the Parnassian school of anti-Romantic verse.

⁴ "Dear God! the very houses seem asleep; / And all that mighty heart is lying still!"; con-cluding lines of Wordsworth's sonnet "Composed upon Westminster Bridge" (1807).

⁵ Joseph Trumbull Stickney (1874–1904), known more as a classicist despite the publication of *Dramatic Verses* (1902) and remembered after his premature death as an exceptionally prom-ising poet by Lodge and their friend William Vaughn Moody (1869–1910), with whom he co-edited Stickney's *Poems* (1905).

⁶ *Poems (1899–1902)*.

⁷ "Don't listen to those who tell you that you must not imitate the masters, it's not true; you must imitate not one but all of them. . . . One becomes a great master only in being the parent of others"; characteristic remark of Charles Gounod (1818–93), French composer.

⁸ As quoted in the 12 May 1825 entry from the famous *Conversations with Goethe* (1836–48) of Johann Peter Eckermann (1792–1854), Goethe's close associate toward the end of his life.

⁹ "Sculpte, lime, cisèlle; / Que ton rêve flottant / Se scelle / Dans le bloc résistant!"; conclud-ing stanza of "L'art," from *Émaux et camées* (1852), perhaps the most famous collection of Théophile Gautier (1811–72), French poet, novelist, and essayist. The poem is often thought of as one in which Gautier distilled his aesthetic credo. Interestingly, in his lengthy essay on Gautier in *French Poets and Novelists* (1873), James quotes in its entirety the same "singularly perfect little poem which closes the collection of chiselled and polished verses called 'Émaux et Camées,'" describing it as "a charming example of Gautier at his best," and concluding, "These admirable verses seem to us to be almost tinged with intellectual passion" and mark "a case of an aesthetic, an almost technical, conviction, glowing with a kind of moral fervour." Wharton did not perhaps share James's conflation of the moral with the aesthetic, or his unqual-ified enthusiasm; Culwin, the malevolent aesthete in "The Eyes" (1909), remarks that an aspir-

ing writer among his mistreated protégés "wanted the laurel and not the rose, and he kept on repeating Gautier's axiom, and battering and filing at his limp prose till he'd spread it out over Lord knows how many hundred pages" (*CS*, 2: 128).

[10] Diodorus Siculus (c. 40 B.C.), Greek writer whose *Bibliotheke Historike* remains valuable as a repository of ancient myths. Describing a trip on which his son August died in Rome and was buried in the Protestant Cemetery, Goethe concludes a letter of 23 February 1831 to Karl Friedrich Zelter (1758–1832), composer and close friend, with the exclamation, "Und so, über Gräber, vorwärts! [And so forward, over graves!]."

[11] "[H]e knew / Himself to sing, and build the lofty rhyme," from Milton's "Lycidas" (1638), ll. 10–11.

Jean du Breuil de Saint-Germain

We saw each other quite rarely—we always got along![1]

I do not know if there is better proof than that of a truly amicable relationship. Those made for understanding one another will get along so much the better if the opportunities to exchange ideas, to compare experiences, to get accustomed to one another's ways of judging things and men, are multiplied. The friendship that Jean du Breuil inspired in me was not nourished by that sort of daily intimacy: sometimes I would not see him for weeks. But each time we met, I felt this current of reciprocal understanding, which gives one the impression of living in someone's intimacy, immediately re-establish itself.

Jean du Breuil had to the highest degree the gift of creating that impression. He took such a lively interest in others' ideas, and not only in their ideas but in their ways of feeling, of envisioning life, and all its joys and all its sadnesses, that in meeting with him again, even after a long absence, one never lost a moment in the exchange of empty and useless words. At once he would seat himself next to you, and would begin, with a laughing look which sometimes veiled such a great depth of sadness, to speak of interesting things. And he was interested in so many things! All questions concerning the development of civilization excited him. He, who perhaps passed in certain circles for an idle and worldly creature, devoted a great deal of his time to the study of social problems. And it was not as a dilettante that he concerned himself with them; it was not only the large historical panorama that deeply interested him, but the practical information that came from it. He wanted everyone's well-being, he wanted it ardently and intelligently, and he proved it not only in his writings, his addresses at the Molé Conference[2] and elsewhere, but in the unwavering devotion with which he hurried everywhere when asked to speak about matters that rankled him. He spared no efforts, sold neither his time nor his work, traveled from one end of France to the other to speak in public meetings where the thought of the new generation was being formed.

Yet, through modesty, and perhaps also a bit of contempt, he carefully hid this side of his existence from those who did not share his enthusiasms. What good was it to display his zeal in front of those who were indifferent? An open spirit, an ironic and indulgent observer of the spectacle of life, he knew how to draw all the amusement possible from the various circles he frequented, without ever confusing a temporary diversion with the large preoccupations that filled his heart and his mind.

A distinguished professor who knew him as a young boy, and for whom he had always nursed an admiring friendship, recently wrote of him: "I knew him when he was a child, *but already original and bold.*" These two epithets admirably sum up this spirit in one stroke, in which one recognized the proud vigor of his tall profile and of his vigorously drawn features.

As a child, he dreamed of becoming a naval officer, attracted no doubt by a fascination with distant horizons. For he always possessed the insatiable curiosity of great travelers, not that of simple countryside explorers, but that of a man for whom nothing human is indifferent. He wanted to see everything, observe everything, of human life.

Then philosophy and history seized his imagination. He dreamed of being a writer; but ultimately he followed the example of many of his contemporaries and attended Saint-Cyr.[3] There, the dreamer who had wished to dedicate his life to study became the best cavalryman in the school, already displaying that multitude of talents which sometimes prevents a too-gifted man from choosing early enough and definitively enough among the different careers that attract him. For ten years he was a soldier, and a good soldier, a dragoon commander whose fine military qualities were recognized and praised by his superiors. But this anxious and searching spirit was not made for garrison life. He needed action, the decisive gesture, intellectual or moral. At the time of the Boer War, he resigned and went to Africa to join up with Colonel Villebois-Mareuil.[4] Although the latter died before he arrived, du Breuil nonetheless offered his services to the French squadron. In one of his lectures he drew a picturesque sketch of this band of cosmopolitan roughnecks. "One met there all types of uprooted peoples and the most varied specimens of humanity, drawn down there by the dual attraction of the war and of gold. . . . I remember the philosophical spectacle of a defrocked Trappist and of an ex-friend of 'la belle Otero,'[5] relating with some melancholy their experiences, both equally undeceived by heaven and earth. . . ." A short time afterwards, he left the French commando to join that of the Russians, with whom he fought until the surrender of Pretoria. He brought back to France beautiful souvenirs of his great cavalcades across the veldt—and a profound admiration for the English against whom he had fought. I believe that the Boer War remained one of the most striking experiences of his life.

Before returning to France, he traveled again to Madagascar, and shortly thereafter he set out again, this time for Chile and Peru. Then he visited Colombia and Central America; and it is after his return from this voyage that he began to take an interest in the questions which would come, little by little, to dominate his time and his thought.

It was toward politics that his mind more and more directed itself. Not toward party politics, but toward a more impartial and therefore less conspicuous sort, whose unique goal is the improvement of society. If he had lived, he would certainly have played a role in the legislative world, and this role would have been that of a man above all personal ambitions, and dedicated to the service of the broadest and most independent ideas. The all-too-sparse writings that he left behind—lectures or pamphlets—bear witness to this clearly enough. He was solitary and independent. He cared neither about success nor about popularity. What was most striking in him was the high impartiality of his judgments. He was not—far from it!—a "moderate": a sad and mediocre character in between everyone! What he wanted he wanted passionately; but this passion did not blind him. On the contrary, it shed light equally on each side of the complicated problems he wished to resolve. It was thus that, in an address given at the Molé Conference, he said:

> Those among you who believe most sincerely that Catholicism is fading on history's horizon should say to yourselves: "We are witnessing the decline of one of humanity's most beautiful religious days. . . . " The example of progressive societies seems quite typical to me in this respect. . . . Look at Australian, American, Scandinavian statesmen. Do you think that they are highly religious men, men imbued with any dogmatic religious truth whatsoever? I do not think so. But . . . these men never miss an opportunity to affirm publicly their concern for religious truth, whatever it may be, Catholic or Protestant. These men, by nature, by an old liberal and Protestant inheritance, are profoundly convinced *that one must respect souls*, that it serves no purpose to violate them, and that a statesman in the presence of that mysterious fermentation of popular spirit, must adopt a respectful attitude. . . . Allow me to conclude by simply but urgently counselling intellectual modesty. . . .

I think it unnecessary to have a personal opinion on the questions raised in order to recognize the fairness and generosity of such a declaration. Here are the words of a proud intellectual spirit. And never did the attitude of Jean du Breuil betray them. He searched everywhere for the truth, and he proclaimed it even when it seemed to run counter to his dearest convictions. His moral ardor was always backed by that noble patience which distinguishes a true statesman from a parliamentary *arriviste*.

This constant disdain for popularity manifested itself in the devotion with which he served the feminist cause. That is not the quickest way for a French politician to advance his career! There is no question less exciting for the Latin imagination. Woman? But she is adored, spoiled, in Latin countries! Let a few million frustrated old maids agitate themselves up there, to the north, in the land of fog, or in puritanical and hypocritical England; we French, more chivalrous and at the same time more sincere, have given the French woman, as wife and mother, a position too privileged to be rejected by her for the sad honor of meddling in political struggles. . . . No! It is not at all about that, cries Jean du Breuil. It is not a question of privileged women! They form only a small minority next to the great army of those who, from birth to death, are pursued by the darkest misery. And it is neither for "chivalrous" motives, nor for reasons of an intellectual order, that Jean du Breuil asks that women be enfranchised in France: it is because there are, in this beautiful country "where they always talk of women's grace and charm, and never of their rights," several million women, widowed or single, who depend solely upon themselves, and whose wages do not exceed an average of 450 francs per year; and that, among these women, there are large numbers working at home who scarcely earn an average of 0 fr 90 per day![6] Jean du Breuil had ascertained the horror of that situation, he had been haunted by the vision of the woman of the people, "at first a young girl, then married, then a poor old woman, but always filled with bitterness, soundly beaten and dying of hunger," and he understood that the only practical way to come to her aid was to obtain for her the right to vote. One must read his admirable paper, "Woman's Social Misery and Suffrage," to see with what lucidity of mind and by what diverse means he conducted the inquiry that led him to this conclusion.

It is Jean du Breuil who opened my eyes to a question of which—I admit it to my shame—I had not until then understood the immense social implications. In a few words, he made me see that the only thing that matters, in the feminist movement, is the fate of those women "whom the brutal economic law of big-city life waits to devour," of those poor hard-working women who accept their long misery with an animal fatalism because they do not know that they have a right to a more humane existence. In short, one would be tempted to say that women who argue for the right to vote could very well do without it, but it is necessary for those women, so much more numerous, who do not even know what it is, or why others are demanding it in their name!

I have tried to speak of the good man who, the further he matured, made himself more and more the champion of unpopular causes and obscure miseries. How much easier and sweeter it would be for me to speak of the dependable friend, the charming comrade, whose image I recall whenever I hear his name!

We got along from our very first meeting; but perhaps we would have remained mere acquaintances if a trip that we took together by chance to Spain had not revealed to me his original and spontaneous nature. It was the first time that I traveled to the north of Spain: he had covered it by train, and knew the chief cities; but he was unaware of all that the slow trip by car can reveal about a country. It was an exquisite journey. The weather was beautiful, and all of Castile's small cities—Palencia, Valladolid, Salamanca, Avila— warmed their old red walls in the blaze of a golden sun. This rugged and dusky land, its vast desert plains, the macabre framework of its mountains, everything that this bare and meagre countryside has in it of the old Spanish soul, struck the lively imagination of Jean du Breuil. But it was especially in the cities that his curiosity was aroused. I had always traveled with persons who experience, as I do, the enchantment of beautiful landscapes, of old monuments, without seeking to attach this visual emotion to the feelings of those who, formerly, had looked at these horizons and walked these streets, those for whom this dreamscape had framed everyday life. Jean du Breuil, by contrast, re-lived especially, between these old walls, the joys and the anguish, the struggles and the defeats of long generations of the dead; and his heart beat for them with the same ardor, the same *thirst for justice*, that he placed at the service of his fellow citizens.

I will never forget a morning spent with him in the Prado. We had gone down to the ground floor, into the rooms where the works of minor Spanish painters were shown, and where one sees, among the somber Virgins and the taciturn Christs, the small, very animated canvases of Juan de Borgoña,[7] those scenes from the life of San Domingo de Guzman that form the most curious and realistic picture of sixteenth-century Spanish customs.[8] It was in front of the painting of the auto-da-fé of San Domingo that du Breuil began to speak, with his fine enthusiasm, about a book little-known, I believe, in

France, *The History of the Inquisition* by that great scholar, that admirable historian, Doctor Henry Lea, of Philadelphia.[9] I have often been struck, moreover, by the range and the variety of his readings. Possessing an admirable command of the English language, he had indefatigably explored our literature in every direction, just as he loved to explore new countries; and here also, as before monuments and works of art, what he especially sought, what he always discovered, was the expression of the human soul, of the obscure soul of the masses, with its blind-man's groping and its tireless surges toward liberty and light.

Little by little, in writing these lines, I have happened to evoke the living image, the actual presence of this dear friend. . . . and now it is no longer about his noble intelligence and his generous ambitions that I speak, it is quite simply about *him*; and I would like to be able to capture here, in a few strokes, the vision of this touching personality. Yes, as I re-read his articles, as I look over the addresses and the fragments of letters that I have in front of me, all these written and printed words come to life like the bones in the valley of the dead, and I see standing before me the one who gave them importance and color, I hear his warm voice, I see his thin, slightly mournful smile, and especially the look in his eyes, those eyes that listened and asked, that seemed always thirsty for sympathy and understanding. . . .

In a beautiful article on the final days of Gordon (published in *l'Action Française* on December 1, 1902), Jean du Breuil unconsciously drew a picture of his own personality.[10] The words inspired in him by the magnificently useless end of the defender of Khartoum reveal what was most generous and profound in his own soul. "Few men," he wrote, "come across as many scenes of blood and destruction in their lives, have mixed with as many primitive and barbarous peoples. Far from being hardened to it, the heart of this soldier seems to have been, throughout his life, *the prey to a perpetual emotion*"—and, in these last lines, the friends of Jean du Breuil entirely recognize him. . . .

He had dreamed of doing many things, he had accomplished a few; but one felt that his life was only just beginning to take form. He was among those, rather rare in Latin countries, whose character matures slowly, whose maturity is full of promise. . . . I believe that he himself knew this, that he saw opening before him a future of beneficent activity. But a pressing duty called. He went to the front, and there, during the dreary months of waiting, he revealed once again his remarkable military aptitude. "Lieutenant du Breuil was a warrior," his commander wrote, "he was a brave man among brave men." He was made, obviously, for the war of the past, for the great journeys across the veldt, the rough cavalry charges, the movement, the initiative, the whims of combat. "I love risk and war," he wrote to me from the trenches. But the long wait, the oppressive monotony of his life under the crushing Flemish sky, in the cold and the mud, how all of that must have saddened that impulsive and bold nature! Nevertheless, he wrote to us from there that he was "full of spirit and gaiety." He had made himself into a spirit of hope, of duration.

His fine speech on the three years law,[11] at the Molé Conference, is the most complete expression of that clear-sighted and patriotic soul. After having spoken about the Republic, which "rose haggard and stumbling from the ruins of Sedan," which "raised the flag to the top of the mast, rescued honor, grew, affirmed itself," he added: "We were told that a new military success would disturb it. I believe that it could on the contrary consolidate it definitively. But if it is written that she must disappear, if her work is done, French citizens from all parties, our hatreds abolished and forgetting our discords, hope at least at this hour that, born one evening from defeat, the Republic will have the good fortune to die one morning by French victory. . . . "

So spoke, last year, Jean du Breuil; and eighteen months later he himself had the "good fortune" to die for his country, on a morning already lit by the next French victory. We would have wished that he had lived, he who could have rendered so many other services to his country! But since he had to die for her, listen to this description of his death and tell me if he had not accomplished all. "It was in a superb gesture that he was struck, wanting to look for one of his wounded men close to the Germans. He went straight ahead, without the slightest hesitation and the least worry of danger, and he was spotted by some Prussians lying in ambush in the willows. He took a bullet in the heart and another under the shoulder-blade; he took five or six steps, saying: 'Hit in the chest,' and he fell. His second-in-command lay down next to him and dealt him the deathblow, and aided by a man was able to bring his body back to the trenches. He was remarkable for his extraordinary sang-froid and courage, leading his men, by whom he was adored, but never taking any precautions for himself."[12]

At the bottom of the picture sent in his memory, his family inscribed this verse of Saint Matthew, who, in fact, seems to have written it for him: "Blessed are those who hunger and thirst for righteousness, for they shall be filled." Yes . . . but perhaps he would have judged the promise of a reward, even of the highest sort, useless. Because for souls like his it sufficed to have known that divine thirst. . . . It sufficed to have, like him, always loved and sought justice.

Revue Hebdomadaire, 15 May 1915

[1] Jean du Breuil de Saint-Germain (1873–1915), sociologist and military officer, killed in action near Arras on 22 February 1915. He had a particularly strong and sympathetic interest in feminism and women's issues, as shown in his essay "De l'intérêt qu'ont les hommes au suffrage des femmes" (1913) and in the essay mentioned by Wharton, "La misère sociale de la femme et le suffrage." A selection of his articles and lectures was posthumously assembled under the title *In memoriam Jean du Breuil de Saint-Germain*. Wharton's description of their visit to Spain is considerably more precise and evocative than her later account (*BG*, 330). By the time he left for battle, du Breuil seems to have become romantically attached to Bessy Lodge, who had resettled with her children in Paris after the death of her husband, the young poet whom Wharton had eulogized in an earlier essay. Wharton's consideration of the essay on women's social misery is quoted at length in Grosclaude, "Jean du Breuil de Saint-Germain, 1873–1915," *Anthologie des écrivains morts à la guerre*, 5 vols. (1924–26), 3: 94–95.

[2] Prestigious lawyers' debating society founded in the nineteenth century, connected with the Paris bar and named after a distinguished family of lawyers going back to the sixteenth century. Evidently, many young lawyers, especially those with political aspirations, developed their rhetorical skills, and established a reputation, by joining the society's debates.

[3] The Ecole spéciale militaire de Saint-Cyr, military college originally founded by Napoleon in 1808 at Fontainebleau and later moved to Saint-Cyr, a small town near Versailles.

[4] Georges Henri Anne Marie Victor, the comte de Villebois-Mareuil (1847–1900), legendary figure of the Boer War, renowned as "the Lafayette of South Africa" for his role in mobilizing first the corps of French volunteers and then the International Legion against the British; he fell at Boshof on 5 April 1900.

[5] Popular name of Caroline Otero, born Augustina Carolina Iglesias (1868–1965), Spanish cabaret dancer and singer, one of the more notorious performer-courtesans of the *belle époque*.

[6] I.e., ninety centimes, well below the poverty level.

[7] Juan de Borgoña (1495–1536?), influential painter active at Toledo, principally responsible for transmitting to Spanish painting the style of the Italian Renaissance.

[8] Wharton refers to the series of paintings by Pedro Berruguete (1440–1504) of a chief figure of the Spanish Inquisition, including his portrait of "Santo Domingo de Guzmán Presiding over an Auto-da-Fé."

[9] Henry C. Lea (1825–1909), publisher and historian, author of *A History of the Inquisition in the Middle Ages*, 3 vols. (1888), and of *A History of the Inquisition of Spain*, 4 vols. (1906–7).

[10] "Les derniers jours de Gordon Pacha," *l'Action Française* 7 (1 December 1902): 900–26. Charles George Gordon (1833–85) was, of course, the famed English military figure killed in the fall of Khartoum.

[11] The Three Year Law, which proposed to lengthen the term of French military service from two to three years, had provoked much debate in 1913.

[12] In response to her own message of condolence, Wharton had also received a moving letter about du Breuil from the comte de Séguier, captain of artillery. She sent a copy of the letter, "which seems to me one of the noblest things I ever read," to James, who had earlier declared, "Another pang was your mention of Jean du Breuil's death. . . . I didn't know him, had never seen him; but your account of the admirable manner of his end makes one feel that one would like even to have just beheld him" (Powers, 336, 331; for the text of de Séguier's letter, see 393–94).

William C. Brownell

I

The most discerning literary critic of our day is dead.[1]

I have carefully weighed this estimate, and see, on reflection, no reason to qualify it—unless by the elimination of "literary." Since M. Paul Bourget's early "Etudes de Psychologie Littéraire," since Henry James's "French Poets and Novelists," and his later "Notes on Novelists," I know of nothing in modern French or English literary criticism possessing the range, the substance, the quality of being at what Matthew Arnold called "the centre," to the same degree as William Brownell's three or four volumes.[2] But his mind, though in all ways formed to compare and to choose, and above all to exercise that subtlest critical function of detecting differences where most observers see only a resemblance, was perhaps at its best in sounding the springs of human character. One need but open "French Traits," that masterpiece of forty years ago which is a masterpiece still, to understand why the art of criticism has been called creative.

The critic of society brings to the appreciation of letters all the added power acquired in the larger field; Brownell's "Victorian Prose Masters" and "American Prose Masters" would scarcely have been the books they are had not his analysis of the French soul preceded them. America produces numerous critics of life who have found out that there is something wrong with Main Street, but do not know the remedy because they have never really studied the alternatives. Such intellectual uneasiness is the first step to good criticism, but it does not lead far unless supplemented by the intellectual range and detachment needful for the survey of culture "from the centre all round." This sense of perspective, this power to comprehend and relate to each other different traditions and alien ideals, was the beginning of William Brownell's art; and no great critic has ever been able to do with less.

II

"French Traits," published in 1888, was at once recognized by the few French readers who came across it as an astonishingly penetrating estimate of the national character. That it is not better known in France, that it has never been translated into French, is perhaps partly due to the difficulty of rendering the author's nervous and subtle language, but much more to the incuriousness of France as to foreign judgments on things French. Never

was a race more impenetrably enclosed in its own great tradition than the
French before 1914. "French Traits," if written to-day, would have been
translated hot from the press, and have run into many editions. But though
known only to the discerning few, by them it was appreciated from the
outset. Several years before the war one of Brownell's greatest admirers,
M. André Chevrillon, spoke to me of the book's amazing vitality, and of his
wish to make it known to his compatriots by an article accompanied by the
translation of typical selections.[3] I hope this may still be done, for a recent
re-reading proves to me that the intervening world-upheaval has not diminished the vitality which had struck M. André Chevrillon. As an attempt to
define the fundamentals of French character the book is the truest ever
written by a foreigner; and only those who have lived long in France can
know how little of real importance it leaves unsaid, and how little of what it
says requires to be modified in the light of conditions which look, on the
surface, so new.

What most struck Brownell about the French was the stability of character which seems formed to sustain the shock of the revolutions and catastro-
phes provoked by that indefatigable engine, the French intellect. Twenty
years before Mr. Kipling sang of France that she was "first to follow Truth,
and last to leave old truths behind,"[4] Brownell had said: "France has most
conspicuously of all nations changed with the epoch; in those successive
readjustments which we call progress she has almost invariably been in the
lead. She was the star of the ages of faith as she is the light of the age of
fellowship. The contrast between her actual self and her monuments [*i.e.*,
the symbols of her past] is, therefore, most striking; but at the same time it
is superficial only and perfectly explicable. And its explanation gives the key
to the French character; for there is one instinct of human nature, one aspi-
ration of the mind, which France has incarnated with unbroken continuity—
since there was a France at all France has embodied the *social instinct*."

I should like to quote the whole development which follows, and, wandering from page to page, to cite fresh proofs of the dexterity with which our
traveller from the new world takes apart the machinery of the old. But space
permits only a few examples. "Society [in France] takes moral errors much
more lightly than it does with us. . . . The main consideration is to have the
heart right; until it is corrupt nothing occurs which can be called irrepara-
ble." . . . "Temperance is the most universal rule in speech, demeanor, taste,
and habits. Nothing is less French than eccentricity. . . . The normal attitude
is equipoise. . . . Their gaiety itself is consciously hygienic. Pleasure is their
constant occupation mainly because they can extract out of it everything,

and make it such an avowed motive. . . ." "Frugality is noticeable every-where. It is the source of the self-respect of the poor. . . ." "It never occurs to a Frenchwoman to regret her sex. . . ." "Their rarer quality for dealing with subjects whose native realm is the borderland between the positive and the metaphysical. . . . Here their touch is invariably delicate and intuitively just. . . . They show immense tact . . . in treating of that entire range of topics the truth concerning which seems so accessible and is yet . . . so elusive— the nebulae lying, as it were, within the penumbra of perception, neither quite outside its range in the clear light nor wholly within the shadow . . . where logical conclusion is divined to be incomplete and misleading . . . where scores of practical questions concerning love, marriage, manners, morals, criticism are to be discussed without dogmatism, and the clearest view of them is seen to have qualifications. . . . This field they never mistake for the positive. They are no more unconsciously vague here than in the positive. . . ."

The sight which could probe so deeply into another race's characteristics has left little for later analysts to amend.

III

In 1902 came "Victorian Prose Masters." Among lovers of letters it excited an immediate interest; and I well remember the stimulus it was to my own imagination. Now, on re-reading it, I find that it "dates" more than the com-panion volume, perhaps because it is mainly concerned with figures still too august for clear discernment. Certainly, with much that is admirable, it con-tains judgments which time might have modified—doubtless did—and on the whole is less spontaneous and original than "American Prose Masters," which appeared in 1909. I thought at first that the diminished interest of the Victorian volume might be due to the fact that, dealing mainly with fiction, it omits all reference to the great Russian portent which was already filling the heavens. How situate Thackeray or even Balzac in those heavens with-out reference to the pole-star of Tolstoy's genius? But this argument falls, because—to my mind at least—the "George Eliot" and the "Meredith" con-tain the book's best pages. The "Thackeray," strangely enough, though the most "convinced" is the least convincing. I am impressed neither by the defense of Thackeray's buttonholing manner, nor by the curious deprecia-tion of Balzac which is employed to throw the English novelist's genius into stronger relief.[5] I agree in the estimate of Thackeray's almost unique natural endowments, but not with the proofs adduced.

But this, apropos of George Eliot: "It is the temperament, not the thinking, of men and women, that is permanently and rewardingly interesting in
. . . fiction" . . . this, of George Meredith: "He is often heavy-handed, but
always in the pursuit of deftness"—what beautiful foreshortenings they
are, and how "modern," as we so oddly say in praise of things unaffected by
time!

Such treasures, not rare in the Victorian volume, abound on every page of
its successor. The writer's critical faculty had matured, and with it his sense
of relative values. The firmness with which he situates his authors, without
fear or favour, exactly where each belongs, makes the book unique in American criticism. My one quarrel with it is that a boy's happy memories of
Leatherstocking perhaps give too rosy a glow to the appreciation of Cooper.
But the "Hawthorne" and the "Poe" are models of serene impartiality, and
yet those two were the authors most difficult for an American to judge objectively twenty-five years ago—Hawthorne because, for some mysterious reason, every old literary *cliché* still sprang full-armed to his defense whenever
his name was mentioned, Poe because of the factitious prestige lent to him
by the genius of Baudelaire in the very country whose intellectual judgments were the source of Brownell's.

Of "The Marble Faun" he says: "Probably its admirers considered that the
treatment poetized the moral. But a truth is not poetized by being devitalized." . . . Of "The House of the Seven Gables": "There is detail enough, but
of singular thinness and an almost gaseous expansion"; and of the novels in
general: "Hitherto, at all events among ourselves, their lack of substance has
been deemed a quality instead of a defect." And of Hawthorne himself: "He
unquestionably dwelt apart, and partly, perhaps, for this reason his soul was
believed to be like a star. . . . His genius was a reflective one. . . . Revery was
a state of mind which he indulged and applauded, and there can hardly be
a more barren one for the production of anything more significant than con-
ceits and fancies" . . . and he adds that all this is "not convincing to those who
believe *that the artistic synthesis of nature should be more rather than less
definite than its material."* (I italicize this as a singularly happy summary of
a central principle of creative art.)

The "Poe" is equally remarkable. "Foreign recognition sets such traps for
our naïveté that it is prudent to be on our guard. . . . The theory that the
foreign estimate previsages posterity's is open to some question" . . . and
this: "He had no sense of awe. The sense of awe was a plaything to him. . . .
He used it as one of the tools of his trade—to create his effects, to harrow his

reader's nerves." . . . "Crime undoubtedly furnishes apposite material to the novelist of character as well as to the portraitist of manners, and is a personal as well as a social factor in human life. But this aspect of it Poe, *whose criminals are only criminals*, completely ignores. . . ."

Though I have quoted only depreciatory passages from these two chapters it must not be thought that Brownell felt the qualities less than the defects of the authors he dealt with. But Hawthorne and Poe had been mummified by undiscerning admiration; their cult was in danger of becoming a superstition, and Brownell's fearless hand merely swept away the flummery accumulated about their images. I know of nothing as honest and independent as his criticism of these two writers since the young Emerson's reverent but lucid estimate of the Lake Poets.[6]

From the chapter on Emerson much might be quoted which would show that Brownell could praise as delicately and discerningly as he criticised; that in praise and depreciation he remained equally fearless and impartial. But when a book forms a series of reasoned judgments, and not a mere string of detachable epigrams, the only way to do justice to it is to read it.

The same may be said of all Brownell's books, including the little volume entitled "Criticism" (1914), and the remarkable "Genius of Style" which appeared only four years ago. In all his writings he showed his essential quality: enthusiasm guided by acumen. He could not have been so great a critic had he not had so generous a nature.

IV

How can I end without one personal word of the friend who was even wiser than the critic? I wonder to how many beginners it happens to be met on the threshold by two such guides as Brownell and Edward Burlingame, his colleague in the house of Scribner? I do not think I have ever forgotten one word of the counsels they gave me. Edward Burlingame's were often lapidary; as when, in the attempt to stem the first outrush of my fiction, he said to me one day, with his exquisite gentleness: "And now, wait awhile. You musn't run the risk of becoming *a magazine bore*."[7]

Mr. Brownell would not have needed to say that; he made me feel it. As in criticism he achieved the difficult feat of setting up a standard which was classical without being academic, so in his spoken counsels the eagerest open-mindedness was combined with an unwavering perception of final values. Rarely as I saw him—alas, too rarely!—the sense of his wisdom and sympathy was always with me, like a guiding touch on my shoulder. Even now that light hand remains, to stimulate and restrain—surely the two chief offices of friendship. In thinking of him to-day I again give thanks for them.

Scribner's Magazine, November 1928

¹ William Crary Brownell (1851–1928), prominent, judicial, relatively conservative literary and cultural critic with whom Wharton initially corresponded in his additional capacity, since the mid-1880s, as "literary consultant" to Scribner's, her first publisher. Immediately after his death, Wharton received from Robert Bridges, editor of *Scribner's Magazine*, an urgent request for a brief essay, which she completed by mid-summer 1928. Although proud to have it lead a volume of tributes to Brownell the following year, Wharton later claimed that she had "found it difficult to convey the exquisite quality of the man" in the article, in which "I tried to put . . . something of my deep admiration for the scholar and critic," whom she still described as "[o]ur most distinguished man of letters" and as "one of the rarest intelligences I have ever known" (*BG*, 144–45).

² Paul Bourget (1852–1935), French novelist and critic, whose *Essais de psychologie contemporaine* had appeared in 1883; James's two volumes were published in 1873 and 1914, respectively. In "The Literary Influence of Academies," from *Essays in Criticism* (1865), describing England as "a nation with no centre, no intellectual metropolis like an Academy," and which stresses the cultural importance of "a centre of correct information," "a centre of correct taste," and a "centre of intellectual and urbane spirit," Arnold cites a passage from Bossuet, the seventeenth-century French theologian and philosopher, as an illustration of "prose without the note of provincialism—classical prose, prose of the centre."

³ André Chevrillon (1864–1957), French literary critic and historian (and nephew of one of Wharton's early influences, Hippolyte Taine), with whom she had become acquainted in Paris around 1908, describing him to Charles Eliot Norton as "a man of the finest *quality* all through" (*L*, 131), and later remembering him as "the author of a number of delightful books on English literature. . . . [I]t was Monsieur Chevrillon who first made not only Ruskin but Kipling known to French readers" (*BG*, 287–88). Wharton had in fact played an instrumental role on Brownell's behalf in the episode to which she refers. Twenty years earlier, she had informed Brownell, "In a few months you make your appearance in the Revue de Paris, with two chapters of 'French Traits' . . . , preceded by an introduction by André Chevrillon in which he will give an 'appreciation' of the book, & of your whole 'oeuvre'. . . . Much as I should have liked to see the whole book translated & published in a volume, I have now seen enough of the French literary 'coulisses' to know the immense advantage of being presented in this way, in the *best* review, by the *best* literary critic (as Chevrillon undoubtedly is)" (EW to Brownell, 8 March [1908] [Amherst]). Wharton was to have assisted in the translation of the passages from his work, declaring to him in the same letter, "I'm so glad, & *so* proud to have had the least tiny part in it!" Soon thereafter, she asked Sara Norton, "Did I tell you my great joy over the fact that Mr. Chevrillon, who is certainly now the first literary critic in France, is to write an 'appreciation' of my dear Brownell in the Revue de Paris, & that an old friend of mine . . . is to translate with me two chapters of 'French Traits,' to be published with the article? . . . I know the work will be well done; & it will mean honour and recognition for Brownell, such as he has never had in his own country" (*L*, 136–37). For reasons never clarified, Chevrillon evidently abandoned the idea, and Wharton had to tell Brownell, a year and a half later, "I have been told that he goes through queer neurasthenic phases, & he must have been in one last year, when he so suddenly & unaccountably 'chucked' his *own* project of writing about you in the Revue de Paris. I hope you understood at the time—I was so furious & disgusted I may not have made it clear—that

when I wrote you on the subject the whole thing was absolutely *settled*, & that I had his express authority for telling you so!—I should never have mentioned the matter to you if it had not been spoken of as definitely arranged. . . . I know it all matters very little to you, but to me it is a lasting pang" (EW to Brownell, 9 October [1909] [Amherst]). Answering his reply the following spring, Wharton added, "I appreciated very much also what you said . . . about the Revue de Paris episode. You don't know what a bitter disappointment it was to me; & all the more so because the whole thing came from Chevrillon, & was not in any sense cooked up or 'promoted' by me. . . . I had felt so confident of the outcome, & so proud in having a share in making you known to French readers—through my help in the translation—that I am still unconsoled & disgusted!" (EW to Brownell, 9 April [1910] [Amherst]).

⁴ Sixth line of Kipling's poem "France" (1913).

⁵ "When Thackeray is reproached with 'bad art' for intruding upon the scene," Brownell remarks in the essay that opens *Victorian Prose Masters*, "the reproach is chiefly the recommendation of a different technic. . . . But it may also be said that for the novel on a large scale, the novel as Thackeray understood and produced it, Thackeray's technic has certain clear advantages. In order to deal with life powerfully, persuasively, and successfully, the direct method is in some respects superior to the detached. . . . If Thackeray's 'subjectivity' destroyed illusion it would indeed be inartistic. The notable thing about it is that it deepens illusion. The reality of his 'happy, harmless fable-land' is wonderfully enhanced by the atmosphere with which his moralizing enfolds it. . . . Nothing could establish the edifice of his imaginative fiction on so sound a basis as those confidences with the reader—subtly inspired by his governing passion for truth—in which he is constantly protesting that it is fiction after all." As for the contrast that Wharton found so unconvincing, Brownell later observes, "The framework of 'The Newcomes' would include three or four of Balzac's most elaborate books, which, compared with it, indeed, seem like studies and episodes, lacking the large body and ample current of Thackeray's epic. . . . Taken as a whole, it is true, Thackeray's human comedy is less comprehensive than Balzac's, with which alone it is to be compared in the world of prose fiction. Taken as a whole, it lacks that appearance of vastness and variety which Balzac's has. . . . Considered, that is to say, purely as a world of the imagination, Thackeray's is the more circumscribed. But it is born of less travail; it is constructed with the effortless ease of greater spontaneity; its preliminary simplification has been carried farther; and, if less complicated and ingenious, less speculative and suggestive, it is far more real. Its philosophy is more human, more winning, more attaching, and in a very deep sense more profound."

⁶ As expressed in the first chapter of *English Traits* (1856), in which Emerson recalls his encounters with Wordsworth and Coleridge during his first visit to England.

⁷ Wharton later repeated this recollection of Edward Livermore Burlingame (1848–1922), editor of *Scribner's Magazine* from its inception in 1887 to 1914, who shepherded into print many of her early works (*BG*, 145–46).

Memories of Bourget Overseas

As I was reading the obituaries devoted to Paul Bourget in all the great French dailies, as well as in the journals, I was struck by the uniformity of these "portraits" of the master.[1] Whatever their judgments of his literary achievements, and his political convictions, all of these writers, without exception, were agreed in representing the man just as one too frequently saw him in his works: the intransigent moralist, the unsmiling pedagogue. Now I have known many men of letters in whom one would immediately discern a fundamental link between the person and the writer; but for those who knew Bourget intimately it was truly difficult to discern this link in him; because the true, the living Bourget, such as I knew him, overflowed on all sides the narrow person whom his young admirers have constructed since his death with elements drawn from his work.

At first, then, I was surprised by the uniformity of all these "portraits" of the great man; then I realized that among the close friends of his youth and of his brilliant maturity, many had disappeared, and that the writers who speak of him today can offer to their readers only the rigid effigy of an old Bourget burdened with honors and prejudices, he who, little by little, was substituted for the brilliant and relaxed friend of my youth. In fact, I knew Bourget closely from the time of his visit to the United States the year after his wedding; and nothing resembles less my dear friend of old, so bustling and full of gaiety, an "older brother," who played for so many years such a large role in my life, than the pompous and severe character who is in the process of becoming the Bourget of the future.

Alas, all that is quite natural, because there are very few survivors of the time when Bourget truly reached the peak of his intellectual development, without yet having lost his freedom of mind. It is for that that I wished to bring to my old friend the tender homage of those old memories—notes, scattered and quite incomplete, on a friendship that stopped only when, after the death of his wife, he voluntarily separated himself from most of those in whose intimacy he had lived up to that point. . . .

II

It was in 1893.

The year before, Bourget had married the exquisite and gentle Minnie David, and had taken her away to Greece on their honeymoon—a trip from which both of them returned intoxicated by the beauty of that countryside which resembles no other, and by the splendor of the works of art with which men have adorned it. Like all of those who make this pilgrimage he dreamed only of renewing it, when the following summer, Gordon Bennett, owner of the *New York Herald*, and an old friend of Bourget, proposed that he make a visit to report on the United States at the expense of the great daily.[2]

At that distant period the French were not great travelers. The idea of going to America would have made a more intrepid explorer than Bourget hesitate, and I do not really know what made him decide to take, with his young wife, this great leap into the unknown. But he accepted the *Herald*'s offer, and when his friends in Paris learned that his decision was made, they hastened to give him letters of introduction for New York, Boston, Washington, etc.

From the time of his beginnings in Paris, Bourget was linked with the Ridgways, originally from Philadelphia but settled for some time in Paris. He discovered that the old Mrs. Ridgway, whose children had married in France, was the first cousin of my father-in-law, and my husband, as a result, the relative of the enchanting Henry Ridgway who was the model for the elegant "clubman" of Bourget's earliest novels. Thus it was that, when Bourget set out on the discovery of the New World, the young Mrs. Henry Ridgway, daughter of the Parisian banker Munroe, decided to offer him a letter of introduction to her Wharton cousins.

At that time, my husband and I spent our summers in Newport, the most *"fasionable"* (as Bourget always called it) resort in the New World. Bourget was very eager to see the worldliness of this overseas Deauville[3] up close, and as soon as he arrived he left us the letter of introduction that our Ridgway cousin had given him.

What an emotion for a young woman passionate about literature, but never even dreaming of the possibility of becoming herself a member of the illustrious fraternity of writers! Naturally, I had read all of Bourget's books, and although, even at that time, I did not like his novels very much, I had, on the contrary, the keenest admiration for his *Essais de Psychologie contemporaine*, of which the first volume had by then appeared.

At the time we met I knew almost no men of letters. I had always led a purely social life, and the thought of receiving a great French writer into my own home intimidated me at least as much as it flattered me. Not sharing my husband's taste for the frivolous and monotonous Newport life, I did not realize the documentary attraction that a kind of life which seemed to me to be a hopeless banality could hold for a foreigner as fond of novelty as Bourget. I did not know whom to invite to meet the illustrious writer, and I was much too timid to imagine that he might rather have shared a family meal than attend a formal luncheon.

But I had to comply, and, somewhat reluctantly, I invited the household to lunch with six or seven friends. "At least," I thought, "they will be able to enjoy our incomparable view of the sea" (for we lived on the top of a cliff that overlooked the Atlantic) "for want of taking part in interesting conversations."

I had forgotten that everything interests travelers, and especially those of Bourget's quality. I do not know if, that first day, his myopic vision reached as far as the dazzling sea spread out at his feet; but I know that our house and our guests interested him enormously. My guests had been hand-picked, for it was not easy at Newport to find guests likely to be interested in the intellectual life. But what Bourget wanted was to see chosen representatives of high society as one understood it at the time in my country; and from that point of view he certainly made some interesting relations at my home.

Yet what especially surprised and interested him, he later told me, was finding in this ultra-frivolous milieu a house filled with books. He expected it so little that he returned, with his wife, as often as possible, enchanted by the contrast between the peaceful library of Land's End, with its great bay windows opening onto the immensity of the Atlantic, and the Casino life and the life of sports, yachting, bridge, sumptuous dinners, and elegant dance-parties, which constituted the Newport "season." At that time, when the villas standing in line along the cliffs were almost all inhabited by the old families of New York—the Astors, the Van Alens, the Goelets, the Winthrops, the Chanlers, the Cushings, etc., this resort season still had a wholesome elegance; but the agreeable people who constituted that small society were, with very few exceptions, hermetically closed to the intellectual and artistic movement which, in Paris and in London, had reached even the most frivolous milieux. In Newport it was not yet necessary to appear to be interested in ideas.

I will always remember that first meeting with the celebrated writer and his young wife.[4] Bourget's beautiful head, with its solemn and tormented features, with its cheerful smile, its eyes ever alert, resembled one of those lifelike and vigorous busts of a Roman senator that one sees in the Capitoline Museum. As for his wife, she had the slightly antiquated grace of a Winterhalter portrait,[5] and her large, soft eyes seemed lost in a mysterious distance where one felt she lived her real life, her profound life. One could even say that in certain respects she was all depth, and he all external, multiple, and insatiable curiosity. She was very shy, or rather, I think, little inclined to make friends easily, to strike up casual friendships, whereas Bourget, tireless explorer of the human soul, could have taken for his motto the poet's *Homo sum*.

Both of them, however, immediately felt at home at Land's End, where the eighteenth-century Italian furniture that my husband and I had brought back from our numerous travels recalled to Bourget his own excursions in Tuscany and Umbria. It is thanks perhaps to my library and my Venetian consoles that we were immediately at ease with each other, and that I do not remember having had to go through with them that tedious initial stage which so often precedes true understanding. It seems to me that we understood and loved one another from the very first day.

I have often noticed that these "love-at-first-sight" friendships are in general the prelude to a lasting attachment, without shadows and without exhaustion. This was the case with us. From our first meeting, I knew that I had two new friends upon whom I could always rely, and who were probably going to play a great role in my life. There were so many questions upon which we agreed, so many tastes that we shared, so many subjects we could endlessly discuss!

III

The Bourgets, who had come to Newport for a few days, stayed there a whole month. Leafing through the first few pages of *Outre-mer* (which I had not re-read since 1894), I perceive the interest that the smallest details of this life of elegant men and women of leisure could have for the author. But I also realize that he did not escape the error common to almost all the sociologists coming from old Europe to study American customs. For Bourget, as for all the other Europeans, North America was especially, before all, the land of dollars. Now this conception, which, since then, has become, alas, only too exact, was not true, forty years ago, for the old eastern cities. In New York, especially, wealthy families were most often composed of persons of mediocre intelligence but agreeable manners who, for several generations, had been living on private incomes. The prodigious increase in the value of real estate in New York had created a small, rich society, idle and closed, where only very few representatives of the new western classes, of no more than modest origins, but having earned in mines and railroads the millions that would soon eclipse the fortunes of old New Yorkers, had insinuated themselves. In the milieu in which I lived (and which formed, in my youth, the small New York "society" of that time), one never heard talk of Wall Street, and most of the men spent their leisure in sports and hunting. In my circle—father, brothers, uncles, cousins—nobody was "in business," except one of my mother's brothers, who, wishing to provide for a large family, had accepted the presidency of one of the new western railroads that were beginning to attract American investors.

It was after he left Newport that Bourget undertook, with the household of John Gardner of Boston, an extensive trip through the western states. It is probable that he already knew Mrs. Gardner,[6] who owned a palace in Venice, and each year made long visits to Paris and Italy. Very friendly with John Sargent,[7] and other painters of the era, and with the great collectors of Paris and London, Mrs. Gardner was one of the celebrities of Boston, which she would endow with her beautiful collection of Italian paintings and art-objects. To house these treasures she erected a mansion in the style of a Venetian palace, with a white-hot windowed courtyard, where camelias and bougainvilleas bloomed in the dead of winter, and where hundreds of birds sang freely, while the snow piled up in the streets of Boston swept by a glacial Canadian wind.

This mansion, filled with precious paintings and beautiful furniture of the Italian Renaissance, became, at the death of the woman who had created it, the Isabella Gardner Museum; but I believe that when Bourget came to Boston it was not yet built, and that the Gardners lived in a private dwelling in the winter, and in the summer in their country home in the vicinity of the city. The Bourgets soon became friends with the couple, but when I next saw Bourget I learned, not without surprise, that for him the truly interesting one in the household was not the brilliant and capricious Mrs. Gardner, but her calm and silent spouse. John Gardner, in fact, of old Boston stock, offered to the avid collector that Bourget was the perfect example of a "gentleman" businessman. At that time the species was still rather rare here, and completely unknown in France. In my youth, the descendants of old "colonial" families took very little interest in business, and if they were very rich, it was chiefly because the land they had inherited, in New York, in Boston, in Philadelphia, had increased fabulously in value.

But with the construction of the great western railways, the men of this old milieu, especially the bankers and the big lawyers, were drawn to this new Eldorado, which was soon to present more marvelous opportunities to grow rich than those of the California gold mines. It was the western railroads that unsettled our little New York society by introducing not only the harsh desire for profit, and an immense increase in wealth, but also the new element of big businessmen who, until that time, had been kept apart from the old society. It is from that time that New York high society, while parading its uncommon extravagance, lowered itself little by little to the social and intellectual level of the newcomers.

But we must return to Bourget, and to his journey across the United States. He returned after several months, having seen much and noted much. But what strikes us most in re-reading his book is to see him dumb-founded and overwhelmed by the rapidity and the tumult of a journey which would seem to us, today, like a slow walk through a peaceful and sleepy Arcadia!

IV

I do not believe I saw the Bourgets again before they left America, but it was probably the following year that we met with them again in Paris. It seems to me that at that time they were still living in their small apartment on the rue Vaneau, where Bourget had lived before his marriage; but a short time later they moved to rue Barbet-de Jouy, into the quiet apartment they were never to leave. In any case, after their voyage to America, my husband and I never let a year go by without paying them a visit, either in Paris or in the lovely Plantier de Costebelle, which they purchased, I believe, a few years after renting the apartment on rue Barbet-de-Jouy.

Each year we came to spend the end of winter and the spring in France and in Italy and soon fell into the pleasant habit of taking a small trip every year with friends to whom we were bound by truly fraternal affection. Some-times we met in Milan, to visit the small towns of northern Italy; at other times we joined our friends at one of the numerous spas that Bourget, always preoccupied with questions of therapy, already judged indispensable to his health and that of his docile spouse. I remember several visits to Pougues, two weeks in Ragatz (right in the middle of the Dreyfus affair!), and other watering-place encounters, one in Royat, to which he took a great fancy after the coming of the automobile allowed him to discover the alpine beauties of Auvergne.

It was thanks to us in small part that Bourget, always cautious and hesitant when it was a question of the slightest change in his habits, became rather swiftly a devotee of the road. But our first trips to Italy precede the coming of the automobile. We generally went to stay in either Milan, or Turin, or Venice: then we would rent a large coach to make excursions into the sur-rounding areas. My husband, on a bicycle, went ahead as a scout, reserved our rooms at the inn and ordered our meals, while we followed behind at the slow trot of our tired old horses through the ravishing bergamasque coun-tryside or the Piedmont's alpine valleys.

But what joy when the automobile, allowing us to stretch these explora-tory journeys, enabled us to discover small, forgotten corners, such as the magical village of Sabbioneta, Lake Iseo, Madonna di Tirano. The Bourgets were perfect traveling companions. Dear Minnie, whose exquisite visual sensibility made her a valuable collaborator on *Sensations d'Italie*, particularly enjoyed what one could call the hidden beauties of our travels: a beautiful Renaissance villa lost in a remote valley, splendid retables asleep in the silence and humidity of a large abandoned church. For her, as for me, the catalogued riches of museums and galleries possessed less charm than these beautiful forgotten things in the unknown corners of a country too rich to count its treasures.

V

And in the evening, back at the inn after a joyous day of salutary fatigue, what did we talk about, sitting down to spaghetti and chianti? About everything, it seems to me, so open was Bourget's mind, so vast his culture, his memory well stocked with recollections of his literary and social beginnings. Unlike most of his French contemporaries, he had traveled a great deal, not only in the United States, but in Italy, England, Ireland (where he often went to visit an old, highly cultivated French friend, who had inherited a beautiful estate there). It is thanks to Henry James, the great novelist, that he made in England, in literary, academic, and social circles, so many interesting connections, a few of which turned into lasting friendships. In the Bourget of that period there was nothing of the intense intellectual and cultural "nationalism" which characterizes certain French men of letters, and which always reminds me of Kipling's famous verse: "How can they know England, who only England know?"[8]

In fact, it is only in seeing other countries, in studying their customs, reading their books, associating with their inhabitants, that one can situate one's own country in the history of civilization; and despite Bourget's more and more sedentary way of life, these numerous journeys left him not only with precious memories of art, and the friendship of some elite men, but also, and especially, an openness of mind, and an objectivity in his judgments of men and things, that would certainly surprise those who knew only the old Bourget of these last years.

I have often noticed that friendships between two persons of different countries who have the same intellectual and artistic tastes have an exceptional quality in the very fact that they are troubled by none of the fondnesses or antipathies which exist between people from the same milieu. What good is it to tell stories about a neighbor to someone who knows nothing about him or his circle? One is compelled to take refuge in general ideas, or questions of art and literature. Instead of relishing the latest society and salon gossip, one speaks of Tolstoy or Proust, of Wagner or Debussy; and on questions of general interest one mutually projects the light of a curiosity free of all constraints.

To confirm this point of view I have only to recall my frequent, my endless discussions with Bourget on the subject of the Dreyfus affair, and especially the Rennes trial.[9] We found ourselves near the Bourgets at Ragatz at that time, and naturally we talked about it, he and I, from morning to night. I say "he and I," because he had asked me not to make the slightest allusion to it in front of his wife, who did not believe that one could consider this burning question in a purely objective way. Bourget, on the other hand, understood it very well, and as soon as we were alone we resumed our discussion. Like most of my compatriots I did not at all share his point of view, or rather that of his circle; for he always told me that personally he had no fixed opinion on Dreyfus' guilt. For him, what was most important was the political duty to defend the army, by whatever means possible. I was far from being of his opinion, but he never became angry in listening to my arguments; and I can say that nothing gave me a higher idea of his intellectual independence than this stay with him at a time when many of the French, and of the most intelligent, yielded in spite of themselves to the pressures of an ambiance overheated by political hatreds.

But the "Affair" was not our sole topic of conversation during our stay at Ragatz. I remember that the day we arrived, Bourget came to meet us, overjoyed at a discovery he had just made. The son of the Duchess of Langeais was staying at our hotel!

That night, at the restaurant, Bourget pointed him out to me: he was a very pale, withered, little old man who, seated by himself at a table in a distant corner of the dining room, paid no attention at all to the bathers surrounding him. . . . The son of the Duchess of Langeais! To understand the emotion aroused by this discovery, one had to have known that Bourget passionately worshipped Balzac, and all of Balzac's work—an adoration shared, moreover, by most of his contemporaries for the one that James called "the father of us all."[10]

The appalling tale of the Duchess of Langeais was based (everybody knew) on an affair of a certain Duchess of X . . . ,[11] and the old man seated opposite us was the son of the woman who had played such an important role in the scandalous chronicle of Restoration salons.

I rarely saw Bourget as moved, as delighted, as he was at the idea of conversing with the son of a woman Balzac had immortalized! He had

already written to a friend in the Faubourg Saint-Germain[12] requesting a
letter of introduction to the old Count de . . . ; and he awaited the arrival of
that letter with feverish impatience.

The next day, he received it. His correspondent warned him that the
Count de . . . was an "old recluse," firmly determined not to make any new
acquaintances; but she had urgently begged him to make an exception for
the great French novelist, and Bourget, at the height of his fame, was convinced that such a request would be favorably received.

That very day, he left the letter with his card for the Count. "You will see,"
he told me, as we went down to dinner, "he will come speak to me. . . . I will
introduce you to him. . . . "

Alas, the son of the Duchess of Langeais did not bother to come and greet
us. He did not even glance in the direction of our table. The next day, he was
content to leave a card for Bourget with the concierge; and during all the
rest of his stay at Ragatz, he continued to stare icily at the poor novelist who
had dreamed of long, impassioned conversations with the son of Mme de
Langeais.

I should say that Bourget was the first to laugh at his mishap. At that time
he laughed easily. Every aspect of the human comedy aroused his insatiable
curiosity, awakening in him a sense of humor or of irony; but he remained all
the same a little vexed at this quite unexpected rebuff.

VI

Bourget, when traveling, very easily made friends with people he met along
the way. These chance encounters diverted him a great deal and provided
him with an inexhaustible supply of amusing anecdotes. But he also brought
himself into contact with people able to facilitate his historical and archeo-
logical inquiries, or who, quite simply, interested him as so many choice
specimens of a foreign society. Thanks to him I made very agreeable acquaintances in the countries we visited together. It was he who led us to old
Prince Trivulzio in his Milanese palace, where I was delighted to examine
at my leisure the incomparable treasures that surrounded him in that magnificent abode, one of the most perfect examples of the residence of a great
Italian lord whose ancestors, for three hundred years, had dedicated their
wealth to the acquisition of a collection of masterpieces.

In the Milanese church where the Trivulzio princes are buried, I remember that Bourget had us notice that the tombs of the royal family were situated, in marble-covered alcoves, "au premier," that is, above the arcade

upon which rests the central dome of the church. "Even dead, the Trivulzios must be lodged on the *piano nobile*," he said, smiling.

It is also thanks to him that I met the great composer Boito, that charming and courteous man of the world, who was so helpful to me when I wrote a book on Italian villas.[13] But it would be impossible for me to name all the relations I formed in Italy thanks to Bourget. I remember above all that it was a letter from him that brought me into contact with Miss Violet Paget (the famous writer "Vernon Lee") whose books on Italy—*Euphorion, Belcaro*, etc.—were the delight of the generation initiated by Ruskin and Walter Pater into the beauties of the great Italian primitives.[14] Miss Paget, who long outlived the great art critics of our youth, always received distinguished foreigners visiting Florence in her small villa, the "Palmerino," and for many years she was very close to the Bourgets. As readers of Anatole France know, she appeared in *Le Lys rouge*, under the name of Miss Bell,[15] and she was one of the last representatives of that world before the war, where one gathered with friends to talk about beautiful paintings and beautiful music, without suspecting under what mortal blows this peaceful society was soon to crumble.

VII

But it was especially in Paris and in Costebelle that I spent long days with the Bourgets. As he grew older, he became more sedentary and less inclined to travel. I often tried to carry him away by car to Spain, or northern Italy, but he let himself be immobilized by the slow tyranny of routine, and his wife, who had the traveling spirit, did not dare cross him in his habits. For many years they always made the journey from Paris to Costebelle by automobile, and I, who traveled the same route twice a year, always urged Bourget to vary his itinerary by describing to him the countless wonders that lined the various roads leading from Paris to the Mediterranean. Bourget listened with genuine interest to my descriptions of Albi, Moissac, Souillac, Tournus, to name only a few of the towns he could have visited without going too far out of his way; but each year, he regularly retraced the same steps: Sens, Moulins, Lyon, Avignon, and I do not even believe that he saw the exquisite chapel of Saint-Gabriel, near Tarascon, or the Merovingian baptistry of Vénasque, because he would have had to make a small detour to get there.

He was the first to make fun of this impossibility of modifying his itinerary: but it persisted, and like all whims, this one became more tyrannical with age. No more trips to Italy, to Germany, to England: no more spontaneous excursions; everything was settled in advance, and above all, one could do only the *already done*.

After the war, having sold my country house in the United States, I settled in France for good. For the summer, I had purchased a small property near Montmorency, and for the winter I stayed in an old house on the rocky heights that overlooked the "old village" of Hyères. These two plans greatly annoyed Bourget, for reasons that my readers will scarcely be able to guess. It was Bourget himself who had shown me my future abode in Hyères, an old abandoned dwelling. We climbed there on foot from the old town, and I was immediately enchanted by the splendid view from the terrace, which overlooks all the sea, from Cape Bénat to the roads of Toulon. But when I told Bourget that I wanted to buy that house, he was dismayed because no one had lived there for fifty years, and he was certain that the local merchants would never climb up there (it was five minutes from the marketplace and the main street)! He implored me not to commit such a piece of folly, and when I ignored him, and moved into the restored and modernized house, the Bourgets, for at least two years, always left their automobile at the entrance to the estate and climbed on foot the long path that led to the house. As for my little house in the northern suburbs, they went two years without seeing it, because Bourget had never ventured north of Paris by automobile! It is perhaps thanks to the habit that he finally made of coming to Saint-Brice that he chose much later to settle in Chantilly—a decision he certainly would not have dared to make in the first years after the war!

At Hyères he knew only three routes, one that led through the Gapeau valley to the old charterhouse of Montreux, one by the Fort of Bréganson, and one by Toulon. Once he had been forced to take a lovely drive, he talked about it for a long time and asked only to take it again; the great difficulty lay in deciding to risk a first attempt. When he moved to Plantier the household had (unbelievably!) two saddle horses, and Bourget and his wife went riding every morning—but without ever straying from the trail that the old Comte de Beauregard had made for his race-horses, between La Capte and the Gien peninsula.

When he formed the habit of taking an annual cure at Royat, he ventured with a thousand precautions onto the beautiful mountainous roads of Auvergne; and as I had traveled over that region in all directions, we often discussed it. One day Bourget alluded to la Chaise-Dieu,[16] and I told him of my regret at having never visited it.

Gracefully, he expressed his surprise:

"How is it, my dear friend, that you who live on the highways, who constantly run after new discoveries, do not know this wonder of wonders, one of the most beautiful monuments in France, and one that is so close to my home?" (He always boasted of being from Auvergne!)

Completely abashed at my oversight, I did not fail to make the pilgrimage to La Chaise-Dieu the following summer. When I saw Bourget after that visit I had to confess to him my slight disappointment. In spite of all the archaeological interest of the renowned abbey-church, it impressed me less than its glorious rivals of Puy, Clermont-Ferrand, and even Issoire and Brioude.

"Is it because your descriptions of it to me were too eloquent? I don't know . . . but . . . "

Bourget interrupted me.

"Ah! What luck!" he said with his mischievous smile. "Since you were disappointed, I won't need to go see it!"

And he laughed like a child, delighted at having made me believe that he had studied on the spot all of the architectural details of the abbey.

*   *   *

I have wanted, in these few remarks, to speak not of the writer but of the friend. I believe that a foreigner's opinion of a body of work as well-known as Bourget's holds only slight interest for his compatriots: and yet I realize that it is impossible to postpone any longer the painful admission that I never much liked his novels. It is particularly difficult for me to admit that, because he did me the great honor of writing a very beautiful preface for the French translation of my first novel, *The House of Mirth*. It is even thanks to him that my friend Charles Du Bos (whom I did not know at the time), made his literary debut in translating my novel; and I will always be grateful to Bourget for having done me this friendly service.[17]

My admiration for his critical essays has always been very great; but why was it that the qualities which made the conversationalist so captivating— the gaiety, the irony, the lively and easy manner in which he related an anecdote or mimicked a conversation—why was it that everything that made his talk so brilliant and so delectable vanished every time the novelist took up his pen?

We spoke often of the art of the novel, for the technique of our trade interested both of us deeply; and I soon realized that Bourget's ideas were entirely opposed to my own. From the moment he began a novel, Bourget mounted the pulpit; he had to make each character a pawn in a game cleverly contrived beforehand, and from which the unforeseen or disconcerting in life was utterly banished. Having discovered that our theories would never agree, we wisely resolved no longer to discuss our respective works; but, in return, we never tired of telling one another the subjects of our future books.

We both saw the irony and sadness of the human lot in the same way; each incident supplied us, him as well as me, with a new subject, and we spent hours telling them to each other. Bourget would always chide me because in my books I did not sufficiently explain my characters; I replied that he underestimated the intelligence of his readers in supposing that he had to analyze in advance, at great length, the spring of every action, almost of every utterance, instead of letting them reveal themselves in the speech and actions of his characters.

Needless to say, these debates never left the interlocutors with the slightest rancour toward each other. Nothing altered Bourget's affectionate good nature toward his friends. One could tease him, make fun of him, even scold him a bit, without offending him. During the long years of a nearly fraternal friendship, I never saw in him the slightest shadow of impatience or resentment.

Bourget was, moreover, the trustiest and the most indulgent friend whom one could imagine. I realized this after the war upon learning, not without surprise, of the treasures of indulgence he laid up for his old German and Italian friends. Among the latter, especially before Italy entered the war, there were those who, in spite of the delightful welcome they had always received in Paris, in both the literary and social circles, did not hesitate to proclaim their hatred for France and the French. Bourget knew this well; but what I could not bring myself to forget, he made a point of quickly forgiving.

"Ah, poor M . . . ," he would say, "we can't hold it against her, because she had to make a living . . . " (The person in question was a journalist.)

Or else: "Ah! the Countess X . . . has doubtless been poorly informed; and besides, she has German relatives. . . ."

His heart was filled to the bottom with good-will, and many are the young men of letters who are indebted to him for his sage advice and generous encouragement. Even when he did not share their opinions, he was always ready to do them a service; and many are those who, without admiring the writer, would honor the literary integrity of the man.

One day I had very moving proof of this literary probity. It was at the time of Tolstoy's death. A long time before, the great Russian novelist had become the object of Bourget's contempt and hatred. Always very personal in his judgments, and strongly influenced, while growing old, by the opinions of those in his circle, he had come to deny the literary genius of the writer because he scorned, with good reason, his vague social theories. Quite often I had made him notice that the novelist's genius had remained intact in spite of the intellectual poverty of the man. Bourget always replied:

"But no, my dear, you are mistaken: this Tolstoy was never a great novelist. What are *Anna Karenina, War and Peace, Resurrection?* A jumble of crude theories, unconnected scenes, without beginning and without end. . . ."

The day of Tolstoy's death, we took up this discussion again, and I have never heard Bourget express himself with more injustice and violence. But that very day a great newspaper asked him for an article on Tolstoy. In order to do it, he had to take a good look at the novels that he had certainly not re-read in years; and, having done so, Bourget wrote on the Russian novelist, whom he had in fact never ceased to admire, one of the most beautiful and generous articles that one artist has ever dedicated to the memory of another.[18]

All of Bourget is in this story: his fundamentally generous nature, his sudden changes of opinion, and above all his magnificent professional integrity.

It is that Bourget, the great honest man, who always admired, often in spite of himself, everything that was great in art and thought, whom his friends will always remember, it is that Bourget whom they will not cease to mourn.

Revue Hebdomadaire, 21 June 1936

---

[1] Paul Bourget (1852–1935), French novelist and critic, "one of the most stimulating and cultivated intelligences I have ever met, and perhaps the most brilliant talker I have ever known" (*BG*, 123); among his works mentioned by Wharton are *Outre-mer: Impressions of America* (1895), *Sensations d'Italie* (1892), and *Essais de psychologie contemporaine* (1883). Informing Gaillard Lapsley that she was "engaged (for the Revue des Deux Mondes) on some reminiscences of Bourget, as I knew him—written after reading the numerous 'articles necrologiques' written by various young or middle-aged 'parties' who knew only the old stuffy Academician," Wharton claimed to have "suggested this to [René] Doumic [director of *Revue des Deux Mondes*] in a moment of exasperation at the inadequacy of all these official portraits, & as Doumic jumped at the idea I'm in for it!" (*L*, 590–91). Objecting to several cuts and various other alterations that Doumic had made in the proofs (EW to René Doumic, 16 May 1936 [Yale]), Wharton withdrew the article, which promptly appeared in the *Revue Hebdomadaire* instead.

[2] James Gordon Bennett (1841–1918), editor, inherited the ownership of the *New York Herald* from his father and namesake, who had founded the newspaper in 1835.

[3] Popular resort in northern France.

[4] Wharton's brief earlier account dwells poignantly on Minnie Bourget, "a being so rare, so full of delicate and secret vibrations, yet so convinced that she had been put on earth only to be her husband's attentive shadow, that I never knew by what happy accident I penetrated what might be called her voluntary invisibility, and found myself made free of her real self" (*BG*, 104–5).

[5] Franz Xaver Winterhalter (1806–73), fashionable nineteenth-century German portraitist.

[6] Isabella Stewart Gardner (1840–1924), art collector and Boston socialite, who established in 1903, on land she had purchased in the Fenway, the museum that bears her name.

[7] I.e., John Singer Sargent (1856–1925), the distinguished portrait painter and muralist.

[8] From Kipling's poem, "The English Flag" (1891): "But what should they know of England who only England know?" (l. 2). Cited elsewhere to corroborate her claim that any writer requires "an accumulated wealth of knowledge and experience," Kipling's line, according to Wharton, "might be taken as the symbolic watchword of the creative artist" (*WF*, 19).

[9] Alfred Dreyfus (1839–1935), army officer whose trial and conviction for treason in 1894 provoked one of the celebrated controversies of the Third Republic, was retried before a new court martial at Rennes in 1899. On the part of many anti-Dreyfusards (like Bourget) among the French intelligentsia, "l'Affaire" aroused a particularly virulent anti-Semitism.

[10] The original text of Wharton's article misquotes in italicized English the phrase from "The Lesson of Balzac" (1905) in which James acknowledges the novelist as "the master of us all."

[11] The heroine of *La Duchesse de Langeais* (1833–34) was evidently based on the coquettish Marquise de Castries, with whom Balzac had a brief unconsummated liaison.

[12] Heart of French aristocratic society, situated on the Left Bank in Paris.

[13] Arrigo Boito (1842–1918), Italian composer; *Italian Villas and Their Gardens* (1904).

[14] See n. 6 to "The Three Francescas."

[15] Vivian Bell, portrayed as a pre-Raphaelite Englishwoman, is a character in *Le lys rouge* (1894) of Anatole France (1844–1924), French novelist and essayist.

[16] Medieval Benedictine abbey near Auvergne.

[17] Bourget had recommended Charles Du Bos (1882–1939), who would become a prominent critic and literary biographer, for the task of translating *The House of Mirth*; Du Bos's important and illuminating memoir of Wharton, with whom he and his wife became close friends, is quoted at length in Percy Lubbock's *Portrait of Edith Wharton*. Bourget's preface to *Chez les heureux du monde*, which was serialized in the *Revue de Paris* in 1907 and published in book form the following year, has been translated by Adeline Tintner (*Edith Wharton Review* 8 [Spring 1991]: 19–22).

[18] "L'Erreur de Tolstoï" (1910), reprinted in the second volume of Bourget's *Pages de critique et de doctrine* (1922).

On Sir Louis Mallet

To the Editor of the Times:

Sir:

It will soon be a month since Sir Louis Mallet died, and I have waited till now in the hope that some voice more authorized than mine would complete your analysis of his public career by a word about the man who was so much else, and so much more, than an accomplished diplomatist and public servant.[1]

But no one has spoken; perhaps because, even to those who knew him best, Louis Mallet was a man difficult to define, and elusive of classification. Yet there must be many who would not willingly let him go without some expression of love and regret, some attempt to record the qualities which gave him a place apart in the ranks of friendship; and for them I venture to speak.

Louis Mallet, in fact, was in most respects a man apart. Some of the finest characteristics of two races lived in him without contending: he was tenaciously English, yet irrepressibly and discerningly French. Thanks to this double heredity his view of life was larger and more liberal than most men's, and his judgment of public affairs refreshingly independent. I have never known any one who combined the astringent quality of moral indignation with a greater charity toward human infirmity; and his quick perception of underlying motives made him the most understanding of friends.

He was kept young by his perennial interest in life, and his tastes and curiosities ranged from international politics to horticulture, from travel to the fastidious arranging of houses and gardens, from wide reading in history and travels to a truly French enjoyment of conversation. Nothing escaped him; nothing missed him; he had, even when he was silent, the Gallic gift of promoting good talk, and if he had not been so much besides it might almost have been said of him that he was above all a brilliant listener.

For all this, and for his untiring sympathy and eager responsiveness, his friends dearly cherished him; yet nothing now expresses their sense of loss as truly as Montaigne's poignant "parce qu'il était lui, et que j'étais moi"[2]— that knell which goes sounding on through the quiet hours when a friend leaves us whom no other can quite replace.

St-Brice-sous-Forêt, August 24th, 1936

[1] Sir Louis Mallet (1864–1936), English diplomat who served in Brazil, Rome, and Cairo before becoming assistant under secretary for foreign affairs (1907–13) and ambassador to Turkey (1913–14). He had retired in 1920 and settled in southern France. On the grounds that it

had arrived too long after Mallet's death, the *Times* of London never printed the letter, of which a typescript lies among Wharton's professional correspondence at Yale.

    [2] "Because it was he, because it was I," from "Of Friendship," book 1, chap. 28 of the *Essais* (1580) of Michel de Montaigne (1533–92), explaining the close attachment that he had developed, while serving in the Parlement of Bordeaux, with Etienne de La Boétie, whose death overshadows the early essays.

On Bayard Cutting, Jr.

I have been asked to do a thing I have long wished to do: to set down a few recollections and impressions of the friend to whom these memorial pages are devoted;[1] yet now that I am face to face with my opportunity I am arrested by the difficulties it presents. It is probable that the facility of characterising a friend is in inverse ratio to the degree of one's friendship or rather, perhaps to the rareness of its quality. Where the relation has been one determined, or at least stimulated, by outward accident, by pleasant propinquities, by affinities of place or pursuit rather than of inner feeling, these at once provide a frame for the picture, a scaffolding to support the rising monument.

    There are as many kinds of friendship as of minds, and many are built up in a definite hard bright pattern, where dates and days, and things seen and done, fit into the memory like the coloured cubes of a mosaic. But where the tie has been an irresistible one of shared perceptions and curiosities, a spiritual, mental atmosphere making times and places indifferent to those who breathed it, the task of definition becomes more difficult and infinitely more dissatisfying.

    I cannot recover any connected impression of the stages of time and the degrees of intimacy between my first knowing Bayard Cutting—in his boyhood, his pre-Harvard days, it must have been—and the period, shortly after his marriage, when, accidentally thrown together for a few weeks (and here again, I fail to remember where), we found ourselves at once and securely and completely friends. I can only say that from the first the understanding between us was so deep and sure as to preclude—certainly on my part, and I think on his—the least consciousness of the difference in our ages. We seemed to be of the same age just as we were of the same mind. This was perhaps partly due to the fact that, when we thus discovered each other, Bayard Cutting was already touched by illness. To say that it had not yet clouded his spirit or lessened his buoyancy is to imply that it ultimately did so; whereas, to the close of his short eager intensely living life, the last impression he ever produced was that of being under any kind of physical disability. Yet it may be that, even when I first began to know him, the fact of his having been thrown back on his intellectual interests, to the exclusion of the bodily activities he had so naturally rejoiced in, had given him a riper mind, a wider vision, and above all a greater faculty of imaginative sympathy, than one commonly finds in the type of healthy happy youth to which he intrinsically belonged.

It might almost be said that the only way in which he betrayed his lack of strength was in his constant untiring struggle to live as if he were unaware of it: to be forever up and doing with the careless unconsciousness of health. The effort to crowd so much endeavor, so many impressions, so much work and so much enjoyment into his measured days confessed, perhaps, to a haunting sense of their brevity; yet there was nothing feverish or rebellious in his haste. Seldom, indeed, has any one borne with a better grace, with fewer apologies and less impatience, the ever-increasing restrictions of ill-health. He never seemed to wish to disguise the fact that he was an invalid; but he remembered it in such a way as to make everyone else forget it.

Here, again, there was nothing studied, nothing calculated in his attitude: he no more struck the pose of Stoicism than that of Christian resignation. The impression one had to the end was that, though he knew he was gravely ill, and had early had to make his terms with that knowledge, yet he knew so many other things more interesting, more impressive and more immediate, that his individual plight was quite naturally dismissed to the remoter planes of consciousness.

The unusual range of his interests must indeed have saved him from ever feeling that plight too intolerably. He had so many windows of escape from his own case! Perhaps the distinctive thing about him, in this respect, was that his tastes were so inwoven with his personality. I have never known an intelligence in which the play of ideas was so free, yet their reaction so tinged by the elusive thing called "character." Coolness of thought and ardour of moral emotion dwelt together in him to their mutual enrichment. His activities flowed naturally into channels which often narrow the current of the mind. He cared passionately for politics, economics, all manner of social and sociological questions, and cared for them practically, reformingly, militantly. Yet he contrived—young as he was—to keep a part of himself aloof from the battle and above the smoke, and to look down on the very conflict he was engaged in.

Two gifts of his rich nature helped him to this impartiality: his love of letters and his feeling for beauty. Nothing so clarifies the moral sense as a drop of aesthetic sensibility. To delight in all the noble superfluities, the "by-products" of the great human ebullition, is perhaps the finest way of proving that the labour and strife are not in vain.

As an instance of the intensity of his delight in such manifestations I may cite his discovery of the Comédie Humaine. I do not know by what happy hazard he who had sailed so far and wide on the seas of literature had reached the age of twenty six or seven without more than sighting this vast continent; but happy the hazard assuredly was, since the adventure was thus reserved for the long imprisoned days when his mind had to make up, by wider flights, for the ever closer bondage of the body. I shall never forget the cry of joy that announced his discovery; or the way in which, in the long letter retailing it, his critical appreciation kept itself clear of his not infrequent moral antagonism. In this case, as in so many others, the intellectual estimate was singularly pondered and mature, and the moral judgment—the judgment on Balzac as a critic of life—coexisted with the freest admiration of his power of creating it.

This ceaseless intellectual curiosity was fed by familiarity with many tongues. It seemed to Bayard Cutting a perfectly natural and simple thing to learn a new language for the sake of reading a new book; and he did it, as the French say, "in playing." His gift of tongues undoubtedly contributed to his open-mindedness and increased the flexibility of his sympathies. It was the key to different points of view, and that key he was never weary of turning.

It played so smoothly in its many wards, and there was so little creaking or straining of locks and hinges, that his erudition and his accomplishments never overshadowed his personality. He was so much more remarkable than anything he knew or did!

This affirmation brings me to the most delicate point in my attempted picture of him: the point where the imponderable undefinable thing called "the likeness" must be caught. Here was a young man without health or its glow of animal spirits, without any specially developed and exercised "talent," without even the showier social gifts: what was it that made him so remarkable?

Not his learning or his accomplishments, assuredly; or even the mind which so delightfully employed them. Interesting as his mind was, even that did not, or did not wholly, explain the rare quality that all who knew him recognized. One is driven, in defining him, to say that it was his "nature," the essence of him, that was rare.

It was, at any rate, something subtler and deeper than mere brain or mere heart: a happy mingling, perhaps, of qualities and faculties which, even when they coexist, are seldom fused. The result was a receptiveness of mind and a tolerance of heart that produced the impression not of a too early maturity but of youth in its mellowest prime. This mellowness was marked in him. Even when his bodily weakness increased, and he became more and more the slave of the invalid's routine, one never felt that he was missing anything, he gave one no sense of mental or physical privation. His ill-health seemed, toward the end, just the quiet corner from which, quite soberly and deliberately, he had chosen to look on at the great exuberant spectacle of things.

And perhaps, in some not remote way, it was just this—the pitiful accident of his doomed youth—that gave him his rareness and his brightness, that was the undefinable essence of his soul. It was this, perhaps, which at once made life so glorious to him, and beauty so divine, and pity so natural, and his friends so dear; and which also, in its mysterious efficacy, gave him the time to give to all these things—as though, conscious of having so few days to spend in the mixed business of living, he chose to spend them all on what was finest and best.

W. Bayard Cutting, Jr.: 1878–1910 (1947)

[1] [William] Bayard Cutting, Jr. (1878–1910), son of one of the most successful and cultivated railroad tycoons of the Gilded Age; his father had been one of Wharton's New York friends of the older generation. Admired and beloved by his teachers and classmates, the younger Bayard left Harvard before his senior year to serve in London as private secretary to Joseph Choate, U.S. ambassador to England, where in 1901 he married Lady Sybil Cuffe (who would survive him and go on to marry first Geoffrey Scott and then Percy Lubbock). After a couple of years in California, where he edited a local newspaper from 1903 to 1905, Cutting journeyed widely abroad before becoming vice consul at Milan in 1908. Soon retiring in ill-health from the diplomatic service, he died of consumption in 1910. Although its opening sentences suggest that she composed it not long afterward, Wharton's eulogy was not published until 1947, a decade after her own death, when it was chosen to conclude a small, privately printed collection of tributes and reminiscences prepared by Cutting's family and including obituaries in the *Harvard Bulletin* and the *Grotonian*, as well as letters of condolence from one of his teachers at Harvard, George Santayana. Since it carries a preface by Cutting's father, who died only two years after his son, the booklet must have been substantially ready by 1912, and Wharton's essay is likely to have figured among the original items; indeed, the only contribution that would have been at all recent at the time the booklet appeared is an excerpt from Grotonian Ellery Sedgwick's *The Happy Profession* (1946). Why the family waited over thirty years to publish the collection is something of a mystery; even Cutting's daughter, the accomplished literary biographer Iris Origo, makes no mention of the project (quoting a couple of passages from Wharton's tribute without referring to its publication) in the chapter on her father in her memoir, *Images and Shadows: Part of a Life* (1970). Wharton's untitled essay is considerably fuller than her other account of Cutting (*BG*, 151–52).

PREFACES, INTRODUCTIONS, FOREWORDS

Translator's Note to *The Joy of Living*

The translation of dramatic dialogue is attended with special difficulties, and these are peculiarly marked in translating from German into English.[1] The German sentence carries more ballast than English readers are accustomed to, and while in translating narrative one may, by means of subordinate clauses, follow the conformation of the original, it is hard to do so in rendering conversation, and virtually impossible when the conversation is meant to be spoken on the stage. To English and American spectators the long German speeches are a severe strain on the attention, and even in a translation intended only for the "closet" a too faithful adherence to German construction is not the best way of doing justice to the original.

Herr Sudermann's dialogue is more concise than that of many other German dramatists; yet in translation his sentences and speeches need to be divided and recast: to preserve the spirit, the letter must be modified. This is true not only of the construction of his dialogue but also of his forms of expression. Wherever it has been possible, his analogies, his allusions, his "tours de phrase," have been scrupulously followed; but where they seemed to obscure his meaning to English readers some adaptation has been necessary. Apart from these trifling changes, the original has been closely followed; and such modifications as have been made were suggested solely by the wish to reproduce Herr Sudermann's meaning more closely than a literal translation would have allowed.

The Joy of Living, by Hermann Sudermann, 1902

---

[1] Wharton was commissioned by the famous English actress Mrs. Patrick Campbell, born Beatrice Stella Turner (1865–1940), to translate *Es lebe das Leben* (1902), then the latest play of Hermann Sudermann (1857–1928), German dramatist and novelist. Mrs. Campbell had first appeared in New York early in 1902 as the lead in *Magda*, the English title of Sudermann's play *Heimat*; after seeing the production, Wharton declared to Sara Norton, "Mrs. Campbell struck me the other night as a great ranting gawk. How I hate English & American acting! It's like an elephant walking on the keyboard of a piano" (*L*, 56). Her disapproval did not prevent her from accepting Mrs. Campbell's commission, and *The Joy of Living*, as Wharton's translation was entitled, opened on 23 October 1902 and lasted only a short time on Broadway before touring the country and ending up in London by June of the following year. Published by Scribner's toward the end of 1902, the translation sold continuously well, to Wharton's amazement, for over twenty-five years. The assignment must have been a valuable one for Wharton, who had been much involved in dramatic writing around that time, having adapted *Manon Lescaut* with Charles Frohman (who directed the production of *The Joy of Living*) and attempted more than one play of her own. In her account of this episode, Wharton stressed her objections to the mistranslation of "the German title ('Long Live Life,' in its most bitterly ironic sense)" on which Mrs. Campbell settled (*BG*, 167–68).

Introduction to *A Village Romeo and Juliet*

I

The tale of which an English translation is here offered is taken from "Seldwyla People,"[1] that volume of Gottfried Keller's stories which Nietzsche called one of the four masterpieces of German prose.[2]

The point is one on which no one was better fitted to pronounce than the writer whose own prose rose to a height of beauty above any the language had yet reached; yet the author whom Nietzsche thus singled out was not a German but a Swiss.

Gottfried Keller, the son of a carpenter who died when his boy was four years old, was born in Zürich in 1819, and of the seventy-one years of his life fifty-two were spent in his native country, and for the most part in his native town. He did not leave Switzerland till he was twenty, and at the age of thirty-seven he returned there to remain until his death. In the interval, indeed, he had dipped into the art students' life of Munich (where he had gone to study painting), had matriculated at the University of Heidelberg, and had spent, in the vain attempt to win a living from literature, six tragic though not unfruitful years in Berlin. Between the Munich and Heidelberg periods he had again gone back to Zürich, and had lived there, under his mother's roof, for another six years—the "lost six years" of his life, as he called them. He had returned home, penniless and disheartened, after finally giving up his unsuccessful struggle to become a painter. According to certain of his contemporaries the attempt would have ended differently had he had better teaching and money enough to prolong his studies; but his biographer, Herr Jakob Baechtold, is probably nearer the truth in saying that though, in more favorable conditions, he might have done good work, it would not have been "what he exacted of himself."[3] At any rate, he was forced by sheer destitution to renounce what he then considered his true calling, and—bitterer still—at the age of twenty-three, to turn again to his mother for support.

Of this melancholy interlunar phase few details survive; but Keller, through sheer discouragement and humiliation—aggravated, no doubt, by the monotony of his narrow existence under his mother's roof—seems to have fallen into habits of convivial vagabondage. They persisted, with brief intervals of penitence, till, many years later, his native city, in recognition of his genius, appointed him to the high office of "Stadtschreiber"; but from that day to the end of his life he was an efficient civil servant and a model citizen.

His mother and sister were compelled, by their small means, to live with a frugality which seemed like discomfort to Keller. They did what they could for the unsuccessful genius and were probably not to blame if he felt the humiliation of his dependence on them; but they were plain illiterate women, incapable of sharing his thoughts or understanding his ambition, and the youth who returned to them burning with dreams and tortured with energies had had three years of a free student's life in the artistic centre of Germany. He came back from it, starving, to face a worse form of starvation. The contrast was too great and his wretchedness inevitable.

Fortunately his activity, in the course of time, found other outlets than the eloquence of the Rathskeller. In his despair he turned to letters and conceived the plan of the autobiographical novel which later, in Berlin, was to grow into his long romance, "Der Grüne Heinrich." The experiment was doomed to speedy failure. Great novels rarely flow from unpractised pens, and after a few days of helpless groping the young author was drawn away from his project by accidentally taking up a volume of Herwegh's poems.[4] The lyric spring was loosed and he turned poet. He was at the age of song, and it was no doubt as well that the novel was put aside. But fiction was his destined form, and after publishing, in 1848, a volume of verse which he afterward described as "characteristic of the restricted field in which it was produced," he drifted back to his pot-house idling. He was now nearly thirty, and still, as Herr Baechtold picturesquely puts it, "sat with his feet under his mother's table." By this time he had become known in his native town as an incorrigible wastrel; but a few people had already begun to suspect that he was also a genius. Among them were two German university professors, the chemist Jakob Löwig and the orientalist Hitzig.[5] They contrived to excite the interest of some of Keller's fellow townsmen, these in turn appealed to the municipality, and Zürich finally offered her prodigal son a travelling purse of eight hundred francs. He seized it, says his biographer, "in both hands," and started for Heidelberg. After much hesitation he had decided to become a dramatist.

II

After two years of study at Heidelberg (from 1848 to 1850) Keller, having received an additional stipend of a thousand francs from the municipality of

Zürich, made up his mind to go to Berlin, whither he was drawn by Varn-hagen von Ense's encouraging reception of his poems as well as by the op-portunity of theatrical training.[6] He had been greatly influenced by Hebbel, and he brought with him to Berlin a dramatic fragment called "Therese," a "bourgeois tragedy," which was obviously inspired by "Maria Magdalena."[7]

Keller, who had gone to Berlin with the intention of staying a year, re-mained for nearly six. They were years of bitter material privation and of steady intellectual growth. He haunted the theatres, saw many distin-guished and stimulating people, strove unsuccessfully to complete his play, was ill, starving, discouraged, and managed, the while, to produce the four volumes of "Der Grüne Heinrich," the work on which his eventual claim to greatness will probably rest. Few pages of fiction can surpass the freshness, the spontaneity, the young abundance of the chapters written while he was struggling with want, ill health and ill success. Berlin made him, though it nearly killed him in the making.

In 1854 he had published the first three volumes of his novel, and his publisher was clamouring for the fourth; but eighteen months elapsed be-fore it was ready for the press. The delay appreciably chilled the interest of his readers, and no doubt diminished the popularity of the book. But in the most favourable conditions it would hardly have attracted much notice. It was too new, too original, too much in advance of its time; and when Keller, shortly after the appearance of the last volume, wrote to ask if there were any demand for a new edition of the whole, his publisher, Vieweg, replied that of the thousand copies originally printed only a hundred and fifty had been sold.

The year after the appearance of his masterpiece, Keller wrote to his mother that he could hold out no longer in Berlin. He acknowledged that instability and laziness, and the incapacity to keep a firm hold on any pro-jected work, were the main causes of his failure. Art is a wayward growth, and Keller's genius may have needed this long stage of gestation; but he had to live, and his means were exhausted. So he went back to Zürich, humbled but not beaten, and still convinced that he could earn a living if only he "could work in peace."

Before leaving Berlin he had finished the first volume of "Die Leute von Seldwyla"—the volume which contains "A Village Romeo and Juliet" and the finest of his other tales—and it was published soon after his return to Zürich. It shared the fate of his novel. Recognised by a few as a work of exceptional beauty, it remained unread and unbought by the many. The purists carped at Keller's Swiss locutions, without (as Herr Baechtold says) perceiving that they were "of the essence of his subject," and the public saw nothing of interest in the little volume of half-humourous half-tragic peasant tales. Meanwhile Keller was already at work on a second volume and on two other collections of stories, "Die Sinngedichte," and "Sieben Christliche Legenden." But though, before leaving Berlin, he had contracted for the publication of two new volumes of tales, his incorrigible procrastination wore out his publisher's patience, and after four years of correspondence and postponement he was obliged to pay back the royalties advanced to him.

The stories, nevertheless, were taken up later and gradually completed; and when his genius had at length been recognised, and his appointment as Stadtschreiber had freed him once for all from financial cares, he published the "Sinngedichte" and the Christian Legends, and later (in 1886) another novel, "Martin Salander," which his most ardent devotees rank high among his works. But the wild freshness of morning clings to the two books written during the bitter years of Berlin. "Der Grüne Heinrich" and the first volume of "Die Leute von Seldwyla" contain the fullest and most enchanting expression of Gottfried Keller's extraordinarily personal gift, and while his admirers will probably long argue over the relative value of the two books, all would doubtless agree that neither of them is surpassed by any of his later works.

III

Though Gottfried Keller was born in Switzerland, and spent the greater part of his life there, it is among German writers that he must be classed. In his day Zürich, like Basel, was a nursery of German culture, and though purists may detect both incorrectness and provincialism in his language (a blessing he probably owed mainly to his escape from youthful over-education, and to his keen feeling for the savour of the soil), his work is nevertheless purely German in spirit and his best books were written under the direct influence of German culture. Happily, however, he drew their inspiration from his native soil, and celebrated, in his short stories as well as in his one great novel, the landscape and the people of his own corner of German Switzerland.

Keller, who died in 1890, rich in friends and honoured by the public esteem of his native town, has for years been regarded in German-speaking lands as a master of modern prose; but his fame, as yet, has hardly crossed their borders. This is no doubt partly due to the fact that the complicated beauty of his style—its number, its variety, its homely plodding strength and sudden lyric flights—make his books difficult to translate. Those who cannot read him in his own tongue will doubtless never understand why his work ranks so high in Germany; few styles have so much of the elusive beauty which defies translation.

"Indem ich sie so gewaltsam an mich gedrückt, hatten wir den Becher unserer unschuldigen Lust zu sehr geneigt: sein Trank überschüttete uns mit plötzlicher Kälte."

In English it runs: "We had tilted too abruptly the cup of our innocent desire, and the draught, overflowing, chilled us with a sudden cold." No substituted syllables could ever match the original cadence; yet the beauty of the image survives through the diminished harmony. It is this fact which justifies the attempt to translate Gottfried Keller: his best work is so full of sweetness and irony, so warm with humour, so radiant with poetic imagery, that even deprived of his magic language it still keeps much of its essential beauty.

The two volumes called "Seldwyla People" are usually regarded as Keller's completest work. Seldwyla is a small Swiss town—any small Swiss town—and its chronicler has peopled it with all the humorous, shrewd or tragic types that such a community produces; or rather not with "types" (save in the sense in which any rounded figure of fiction is one) but with living people whose characters develop, whose faces are individual and familiar, whose names and idiosyncrasies linger in the mind. Some readers may think that "Der Grüne Heinrich," in spite of its inequalities, and the marked decline of interest after the middle of the second volume, is a more considerable achievement than the Seldwyla tales; but the latter are undoubtedly the product of a maturer and more disciplined art. Even these, however, are unequal in quality, and of the number "A Village Romeo and Juliet" is perhaps the only one that attains perfection. Its rival, "The Three Just Comb-Makers" (said to have been the one which Wagner preferred), is but a trifling performance in comparison. The degree to which, in the last analysis, subject will always be found to count as an element of greatness, is well exemplified by the difference between these two stories. One is a microscopic analysis of small motives actuating trivial people, the other a study of the fundamental passions in hearts great enough to give them play. But aside from the greater importance of the subject, the treatment of "A Village Romeo and Juliet" is far ampler and stronger. The delightful choice of episode, the steady march of events, the vitality and significance of every detail, and the firm stroke with which the main line of the drama is nevertheless drawn through its rich tracery of incident—these qualities are to be matched only in tales of such completeness as "La Grande Bretèche" and "The Death of Ivan Ilitch."

There is nothing in "A Village Romeo and Juliet" to suggest comparison with these stories except the level of its achievement. In spite of its tragic theme it has a playful simplicity and a grace of desultory detail quite foreign to the genius of Balzac and Tolstoi. The tale suggests the heathery commons and blue pine forests of lower Switzerland: it "breathes and smells" of wild rose, whortleberry and resin. And the eerie figure of the Black Fiddler, demonic yet homely, is essentially a German evocation. Keller, in his opening paragraph—which might have been omitted to the advantage of the tale— explains that a few great themes are perpetually coming up again under the story-teller's pen. But the attempt to rewrite a famous story has not in general been successful, and it would be hard to find, in the range of fiction, another instance of an immortal tale retold in terms that will bear comparison with its prototype. One of the reasons of Keller's success is that he was too great an artist to make use of the incidents of the original tale. He simply took the central situation, and, transposing it into terms of Swiss peasant life, let it flower into a series of fresh episodes. The title of his story disarms criticism. His Romeo and Juliet are villagers; his Juliet a Gretchen, his Romeo a farmer's boy. But "the old woe of the world"[8] overhangs them, and their hearts are at the height of their adventure. The writer's skill is in the ingenious transposition of the tale, the way in which it is used as a pretext for endless original variations. In Keller's other work his touch is less sure. His talent was of the rarest, but most of his books have the defect of suggesting beautiful improvisations. There was something amateurish in all but his best work. Too often he either chose his subjects injudiciously, or failed to extract from them all they had to yield. He did not wrestle with them till the morning. This is peculiarly the case with "Der Grüne Heinrich," most moody, wilful and unequal of great novels. He had a magnificent subject—the adventures of a young village lad like himself, in quest of learning and experience—but he did not know *how to corner it*, and it escaped from him, leaving only its rainbow fringes in his grasp. In some of his finest short stories, on the contrary (and the "Comb-Makers" is an instance), he spent a sculptor's vigour on the proverbial cherry-stone. Alone, perhaps, among his works, "A Village Romeo and Juliet" stands above both of these criticisms. Here the scale of detail is exactly commensurate with the beauty of subject and the tale has the careless completeness of a cloud or a flower.

At what pains such careless completeness is achieved only he who has tried can tell. The construction of Keller's story deserves the closest critical analysis: it has the inspired ingenuity of great art. But its grace and simplicity and sombre beauty are as readily felt as the spell of a noble landscape; and some of its vignettes are like the tiny green dells in a bleak defile, or the cottage garden that surprises the traveller on a lonely road.

This mixture of ruggedness and gaiety is Keller's most marked characteristic. His tender or humorous episodes are as minutely rendered as the delicate flowers in the foreground of a Primitive painting, and set, as these often are, against a background of naked rock. His art, in fact, suggests that of the early Northern painters: it has a kind of smiling archaic gravity, an ingenuous preoccupation with small intimate daily things, as different as possible from the larger and more formalised lines of the classic tradition.

Keller had many of the characteristics of the great novelist, and among them the instinctive art of modifying his manner to suit his subject. His style could expand to a fresco-like sweep or contract to the minute enamelling of tiny surfaces. When he had a wall to cover, his treatment was large without being loose, when he painted a miniature his stroke was at once fine and strong. His gift of characterisation is equally remarkable. Few figures in fiction are more sturdily drawn than those of the astounding Frau Margret and her husband in "Der Grüne Heinrich," and all of Keller's secondary characters are vividly individualised. His backgrounds are always alive. The woman who buys poor Vrony's bedstead in "A Village Romeo and Juliet," even the boy who carries off the tester on his head, the village landladies who successively entertain the lovers during their long day of dream-like wandering, and the peasants and gipsies with whom they dance by moonlight under the vine-garlanded loggia, all are different and real—one feels that in the case of each of them the act of creation has been performed anew.

But Keller was above all a poet, and his great originality lay in the quality of his imagery and in his gift of extracting from the homeliest words and the most familiar situations their hidden element of poetry. The reader of "A Village Romeo and Juliet" will detect this faint irradiation in almost every page, and the first part of "Der Grüne Heinrich" is continually luminous with it. It was the fashion, in the eighteenth century, to divide the poetic view of things into the two categories of "fancy" and "imagination." This formal distinction is not without its uses in defining certain talents; but in Keller's case both points of view existed and were frequently merged. There is exquisite fancy in the story of Meretlein, the plaintive witch-child, in "Der Grüne Heinrich," and in the analysis of the little Heinrich's first attempt to puzzle out his relation to the world and its maker; and the highest quality of imagination in such pages as those which describe his wandering through the forest with Anna, in the chapter called "Evening Landscape." But for pure poetry nothing in Keller's work surpasses the last tragic scene in which Vrony and Sali exchange rings before starting on their flight through the mist-drenched fields to the river. Their words throb like violins: the reader catches the very beat of their tortured hearts.

It is in such moods of poetic divination that Keller is at his highest. He finds phrases which set free the imagination like Imogen's cry:

> But one that rode to's execution, man,
> Could never go so slow,

or like Keats's:

> So the two brothers *and their murdered man*
> Rode from fair Florence.[9]

When, for instance, Keller writes: "Even the soul of the evil-doer *rubs its invisible dark hands with joy* when it finds that others have dealt uprightly and kindly with it," one feels that no one else would have found precisely this image, and that no other could have been so expressive. In the sense in which poetic imagery is the violent foreshortening of experience, certain images of Gottfried Keller's rank with Shakespeare's.

A Village Romeo and Juliet, by Gottfried Keller, 1914

[1] *Romeo und Julia auf dem Dorfe*, finest of the novellas that compose *Die Leute von Seldwyla* (1856), a collection about residents of an imaginary town in Switzerland, and the work that established the fame of Gottfried Keller (1819–90), Swiss novelist. Other works of Keller discussed by Wharton include *Das Sinngedicht* (1881–82), a cycle of tales, *Sieben Legenden* (1872), a collection of religious stories set in the early Christian era, and *Der Grüne Heinrich*, the bildungsroman first written in 1855, then published in 1880 in an extensively revised version, and later alluded to by Wharton in *The Writing of Fiction*, where she speaks of "the zone of the unclassifiable" that contains "such enchanting hybrids as . . . that great Swiss novel, 'Der Grüne Heinrich,' in which fantasy, romance and the homeliest realities are so inimitably mingled" (67). This edition of *A Village Romeo and Juliet* was translated by Anna Bahlmann, her German tutor in Wharton's youth and her secretary since 1904. Around a year after proposing it to Scribner's, Wharton sent Bahlmann's translation of *A Village Romeo and Juliet* to Edward Burlingame with the remark, "It is such an enchanting thing that it ought to be known to English readers," only to offer a more hesitant appraisal a few weeks later: "It is very artlessly written, with frequent repetitions, & has little of the great literary beauty of 'Der Grüne Heinrich,' though it is so remarkable in structure and feeling" (EW to E. L. Burlingame, 20 September and 22 October 1913 [Princeton]). Long afterward, one of her latest secretaries informed an inquiring scholar that "the translation . . . was almost entirely rewritten by Mrs. Wharton" (EW to E.K. Brown, 1 September 1930 [Yale]).

[2] In section 109 of *The Wanderer and His Shadow* (1880), later incorporated in the second volume of the 1886 edition of *Human, All Too Human*. The other three "masterpieces" mentioned by Nietzsche (along with works of Goethe and his conversations with Eckermann) are

the *Aphorisms* of Georg Christoph Lichtenberg (1742–94), the first book of the autobiography of Heinrich Jung-Stilling (1740–1817), and *Nachsommer* (1856), a novel by Adalbert Stifter (1805–68).

[3] Jakob Baechtold, *Gottfried Kellers Leben: Seine Briefe und Tagebücher*, 3 vols. (1894–97).

[4] Georg Herwegh (1817–75), revolutionary German poet.

[5] Carl Jakob Löwig (1803–90), German chemist; Ferdinand Hitzig (1807–75), distinguished biblical scholar and Hebrew philologist, who became professor of theology at the University of Zürich in 1833.

[6] Karl August Varnhagen von Ense (1785–1858), German poet.

[7] Domestic tragedy (1844) of Friedrich Hebbel (1813–63), dramatist and lyric poet.

[8] "Why this is the old woe o' the world; / Tune, to whose rise and fall we live and die"; from "James Lee's Wife" (ll. 217–18), opening poem of Browning's *Dramatis Personae* (1864).

[9] See notes 10 and 11 to "The Three Francescas." (Here EW's emphasis, while "But" should read "Why," "murdered" should read "murder'd," and "from" should read "past.")

Preface to *Futility*

There are few novelists nowadays, I suppose, who will not readily acknowledge that, in certain most intrinsic qualities of the art, the great Russians are what Henry James once called Balzac,[1] the masters of us all.

To many readers of the western world, however, there was—there still is, despite the blinding glare which the Russian disaster has shed on the national character—a recurring sense of bewilderment in trying to trace the motives of the strange, seductive and incoherent people who live in the pages of Dostoievsky, Tolstoi, and their mighty group. In Balzac, at all times, the western mind is at home: even when the presentment is obviously a caricature, one knows what is being caricatured. But there are moments—to me at least—in the greatest of Russian novels, and just as I feel the directing pressure of the novelist most strongly on my shoulder, when somehow I stumble, the path fades to a trail, the trail to a sand-heap, and hopelessly I perceive that the clue is gone, and that I no longer know which way the master is seeking to propel me, because his people are behaving as I never knew people to behave.

"Oh, no: we *know* they're like that, because he says so—but they're too different!" one groans.

And then, perhaps, for enlightenment, one turns to the western novelist, French or English or other, the avowed "authority" who, especially since the war, has undertaken to translate the Russian soul in terms of our vernacular.

Well—I had more than once so turned . . . and had vainly hunted, through the familiar scenery of *vodka, moujik, eikon, izba* and all the rest, for the souls of the wooden puppets who seemed to me differentiated only from similar wooden puppets by being called Alexander Son-of-Somebody instead of Mr. Jones or M. Dupont.

Then I fell upon "Futility."[2] Some one said: "It's another new novel about Russia"—and every one of my eager feelers curled up in a tight knot of refusal. But I had a railway-journey to make, and the book in my bag—and I began it. And I remember nothing of that railway-journey, of its dust, discomfort, heat and length, because, on the second or third page, I had met living intelligible people, Sons-and-daughters-of-Somebody, as Russian, I vow, as those of Dostoievsky or Goncharoff,[3] and yet conceivable by me because presented to me by a mind open at once to their skies and to mine. I read on, amused, moved, absorbed, till the tale and the journey ended together.[4]

This, it seems to me, is the most striking quality of Mr. Gerhardi's book: that he has (even in this, his first venture) enough of the true novelist's "objectivity" to focus the two so utterly alien races to which he belongs almost equally by birth and bringing-up—the English and Russian; to sympathize with both, and to depict them for us *as they see each other*, with the play of their mutual reactions illuminating and animating them all.

There are lots of other good things in the book; indeed, it is so surprisingly full of them that one wonders at the firmness of the hand which has held together all the fun, pathos and irony of the thronged sprawling tale, and guided it resolutely to an inevitable conclusion. "It takes genius to make an ending," Nietzsche said;[5] and, perhaps partly for that reason, the modern novelist seems often to have decided that it is the trifle most conveniently dispensed with.

Mr. Gerhardi's novel is extremely modern; but it has bulk and form, a recognizable orbit, and that promise of more to come which one always feels latent in the beginnings of the born novelist. For all these reasons—and most of all for the laughter, the tears, the strong beat of life in it—I should like to hand on my enjoyment of the book to as many other American readers as possible.

Futility, by William Gerhardi, 1922

[1] In "The Lesson of Balzac" (1905), the lecture with which James toured the United States during his famous return visit of 1904–5.

[2] First novel of William Gerhardie (1895–1977), English novelist born in Petrograd of Russian and English parentage, who spelled his name Gerhardi for much of his career. Wharton was so enthusiastic about *Futility* that she wrote to Gerhardie to say, "Your novel seems to me so much the best thing that I've read about Russia since 'Oblomoff'—& I read that long ago— that I hope you will let me tell you how greatly I admire it. . . . I should not venture to thrust

this praise upon you if I admired your work only as an interpretation of Russia— It is because I feel in it so many of the qualities of the novelist born that I want to cheer you on to the next, in whatever field you mean to place it" (*L*, 456). Soon she allowed Gerhardie's English publisher to quote her letter in its advertisements, encouraged Duffield and Company to publish the American edition for which she provided her preface, and subsequently helped arrange a French translation of the novel. In another letter, she declared again, "I've just re-read 'Futility' and it's so very much better than anything else that's been done in England in years that I don't care how loud I am heard to shout it!" (qtd. in Dido Davies, *William Gerhardie* [Oxford: Oxford University Press, 1990], 123). The two later became friendly; see Gerhardie's *Memoirs of a Polyglot* (1931).

[3] Ivan Aleksandrovich Goncharov (1812–91), novelist whose *Oblomov* (1859) is his most famous work.

[4] According to Gerhardie's biographer, "A Cambridge don seeing her off on a long train journey had handed her *Futility*; she opened it reluctantly, but read on with growing zeal, because 'it made the journey seem as short as though I had been piloted by Amy,'" as she later expressed it to Gerhardie, referring to one of the characters in his novel (Davies 122).

[5] From Nietzsche's *Die fröhliche Wissenschaft* (1882; rev. version, 1886), sec. 281.

Introduction to *Gardening in Sunny Lands: The Riviera, California, Australia*

To the flower-lover from the north the first months of planning and planting on the Riviera are in the nature of a long honeymoon. In the thrill of his adventure he looks about him at other people's gardens, and sees, growing out of doors, and in unbelievable profusion, the plants he has had to cultivate under glass, or to coax through an existence of semi-invalidism in the uncertainty of the "sheltered corner"; he discovers still newer treasures in the catalogues of the local nurserymen, he summons them in consultation, he wanders through their nurseries; and every visit and every consultation results in the arrival of a cargo of fascinating novelties.

Only the second year does he learn his lesson. Then he discovers that, in the south, slight differences of soil, of exposure, of the degree of shelter available, seem to count far more than in more equable climes. Where the midday sun is so much hotter, proportionately great is the evening chill. Tender blossoms coaxed forth by a week of summer warmth will be cruelly nipped by a sudden blast off the snow-covered Alps; plants that crave sun in the north languish for half-shade in the south; others that under rainy skies thrive in a comparatively light soil need a damp crevice to nurse their roots through the southern summer.

Where conditions are so different and the caprices of the elements so incalculable, the newcomer's first cry is for guidance; and great is his wonder on learning that, though there have been many botanical books on Mediterranean and New-World flora,[1] the scattered knowledge of the Riviera horticulturists, which has created such wonderful gardens, has never yet been gathered up into a practical manual.

The pages that follow are an attempt to make this disseminated wisdom available to the beginner. The author's spoken counsels have already been so helpful in the making of my own garden that I feel sure my fellow-gardeners, and even those far more experienced than I, will welcome the appearance of such a book and find help in one or another of its stimulating suggestions.[2] As an authority on gardening in England, Mr. William Robinson said, ten years ago, in prefacing her book *The Herbaceous Garden*, that though he was happy to introduce her book, she was "well able to take her own stand among the flowers"; and though much of her own practical gardening has been done in England, I feel that his commendation may well be extended to her working knowledge of horticulture in southern gardens.

Mrs. Martineau has travelled extensively in southern California, and has lectured there on gardening. She has laid out and planted many gardens in the northern United States, and her experience in the south of France, which has been of many years' duration, has included, besides the laying out of gardens, much study of prevailing conditions of soil and climate all along the French Riviera and as far over the border as Alassio. To any who may think that this amount of experience and observation is not sufficient to justify the writing of even the following general suggestions on southern gardening, I can only say, as I know the author would: "May some resident southern gardener soon produce the comprehensive work we have all so long been waiting for!"

Meanwhile, since this little book, as an attempt to apply modern ideas of planning and planting to southern gardens, is apparently the first of its kind, I feel sure that, whatever its deficiencies or omissions, the soundness of its general principles, and the fact that the plain rules of practical flower and vegetable growing are combined in it with numerous suggestions for harmonious garden-design and schemes of colour-combination, will make it in a very literal sense the handbook of countless gardeners in southern lands.

Gardening in Sunny Lands: The Riviera, California, Australia,
by Mrs. Philip Martineau, 1924

---

[1] "Even E. Sauvaigo's encyclopaedia of exotic shrubs and plants grown on the Riviera (published at Nice in 1898) was never carried beyond the first volume. It has, moreover, long been out of print, and the modern reprint is not only abridged, but incomplete." (EW's note.)

[2] Alice Margaret (Vaughan-Williams) Martineau (1865?–1956), English horticulturist and author also of *The Herbaceous Garden* (1913) and *The Secrets of Many Gardens* (1924), had

often served as Wharton's consultant on such matters. During a visit from Martineau early in 1923, Wharton urged her to write a book about gardening in the south of France and tried to interest at least one publisher in the idea. At the end of her own foreword to *Gardening in Sunny Lands*, which includes a photograph of the novelist in her gardens at Ste. Claire, Martineau particularly acknowledged "Mrs. Wharton, but for whose steady encouragement and practical help this book would never have been written."

Preface to *Speak to the Earth:*
Wanderings and Reflections among
Elephants and Mountains

When you gave me *Out in the Blue*, dear Vivienne, I remember exclaiming after I had read it: "Oh, please write another book as enchanting as this one, but in which nobody wants to kill an animal, and they all live happily ever afterward!"[1]

A rash request, I thought on reflection; not that I doubted your ability to produce another enchanting book, but that I feared there might be little more to say about big game untroubled by human violence than about countries similarly blessed. . . .

Well, my fears were unfounded, and I ought to have known it; for after all (and unless you guessed it, I can't imagine why you chose me for this preface), after all, I, too, have lived that life and stammered that language, though my mountain tent was only the library lamp-shade, my wilderness a garden, my wildebeest stealing down to drink two astute and arrogant Pekingese; and as one of the initiated I was aware that those who know how to talk with animals know also how to talk about them.

And beautifully indeed you have proved it in these sunlit windswept pages. From the elephants romping with their friends, or twinkling at you ironically through the trees, to the least little bird hopping in at your hut door, they all had so much to tell that they had evidently been awaiting such a confidant for ages; and you would never have been able to pack all their yarns into one book if the Angel of Fire had not suddenly driven you out of the Paradise where you and they had lain down so happily around the Remington.

But what a pity that he drove you out so soon! I resent the too hurried reporting of those slow shy approaches to communion; I long for the subsequent history of creatures just glimpsed and lost again in your crowded pages, like the tantalizing acquaintances made and lost in the rush of travel. You had found—or so it seems to me—the exact language in which to tell us of these desert and mountain friendships; elusive, wary phrases, shifting and shimmering like their own forest leafage, and words held out to them like coaxing hands. Since Farrer's sylvan language I have met none that seemed so made for its subject;[2] and then, just as you were drawing nearer to the mysterious heart of your theme, as flower and bird and wild-hoofed creature were pressing about you to tell you their last secrets—just, in short, as you were about to "stroke the elephant's ear"—the crash came, the sky grew black, and the golden gates clanged shut. . . .

But luckily, thanks to you, not on us, your happy readers. For we are there again, in your innocent Bestiary whenever we open your book; or even without opening it, merely when we walk out and see through your eyes and hear with your ears the tireless messages of Nature.

Many will say this to you, many more will think it, and wish they had the courage to tell you. I count myself privileged to have been the first to walk with you in your wild places, and to have been asked to say what I found there, and invite in others to share my delight.

> *Speak to the Earth: Wanderings and Reflections*
> *among Elephants and Mountains*, by
> Vivienne de Watteville, 1935

[1] Vivienne de Watteville (1900–57), English writer, traveler, and naturalist, whose earlier book, *Out in the Blue* (1927), an account of the 1923–24 East African Expedition in which she participated with her father, is notable for its unsparing description of his death in Kenya from wounds suffered in a lion attack. *Speak to the Earth* is the record of her second African journey, in 1928–29, after which she married Captain George Gerard Goschen in 1930 and re-settled in England. As excerpted by Percy Lubbock in *Portrait of Edith Wharton* (1947), de Watteville's memoir of the novelist, recalling her sponsorship of *Speak to the Earth* and her eagerness to examine the proofs, offers a vivid portrayal of Wharton as a fastidious and demanding practical critic.

[2] John Reginald Farrer (1880–1920), traveler, botanist, flower painter, playwright, and author of *Alpines and Bog-Plants* (1908), *In Old Ceylon* (1908), and *On the Eaves of the World* (1917).

Foreword to *Benediction*

I

Kilmeny had been she knew not where—
Kilmeny had seen what she could not declare.[1]

Those two lines from the Ettrick Shepherd's only good poem were in my ears when I closed "Benediction"[2]—as they are whenever I touch the fringe of that other world into which only those who carry the wand-of-words can introduce us.

It does not happen often; but when it does, the boundaries of sense grow faint and we find ourselves mysteriously rapt "we know not where." The wand-wielders, among whom Claude Silve is so rare an adept, have various ways of carrying us with them, and varied and unrelated to each other are the sights and sounds they disclose, sights and sounds that, coming back to the world of clocks and calendars, we find we "cannot declare." Every magician must work his own magic in his own way; and those who seek for a glimpse of that kingdom are free to choose by which gate they would go in. Personally, I have always chosen a breach in the wall of reality, through which to peer and lean over the foam of perilous seas without losing my hold on the solidities of daily life. It is not that I am afraid of letting go, as it were, but that the contact of the plain earthly facts seems to give a special intensity to the other-world vision. And moreover (here the professional opinion intrudes) I have always suspected that it was far easier for the adept to cut his balloon and be off into the void than to let in his magic through the dark cottage, battered and decayed, of our plain human doings. And it is because Claude Silve has the art of keeping us, from the first word of her tale to the last, in our daily world yet not of it, that I have wanted to say a word of her delicate achievement.

Its great distinction, to my mind, is the author's success in acclimatizing real solid tangible people in her world of dream. Too often the dream-world novelist fills his shadowy domain with beings as vaporous as their setting; but as soon as we enter the château of Dampard we recognize its inhabitants as sturdy human beings, with sharp idiosyncrasies and latent violences, but seen through that faint haze of *otherness* in which the author is herself so visibly at home.

There are a few lines in "Lamia" which give me exactly the same stealing sense of flesh-and-blood reality in a dream-world.

> A place unknown
> . . . to any but those two alone,
> *And a few Persian mutes, who, that same year,*
> *Were seen about the markets. . . .*[3]

That is all; and because it is all, and we are instantly sure that the Persian mutes were never again seen about the markets, or anywhere else in our daylight world, their apparition in the loud glittering streets of Corinth is to me more shudderingly real and yet phantasmal than if Keats had dressed them in all the adjectives spent on the rest of the poem. And this reticence, this haunting allusiveness, is exactly what makes the magic of "Benediction."

In re-reading these paragraphs I find that my attempt to define the charm of the tale has led me, repeatedly but quite involuntarily, to borrow my analogies and illustrations from the English poets. Greater honour could not be paid to any book; and it confirms a feeling I have had since I first read the tale, that it may well make a more direct and intimate appeal to English readers than to those of its own tongue, among whom its unusual success is no doubt partly due to its being so oddly, bewilderingly un-French. Certainly, in the English version, there is about it that spell of the "lone sheiling,"[4] the veiled mountains and unquiet seas, which speaks familiarly to our old racial memories. The Latins, from Southern Italy to Northern France, have all received the stamp of Rome: classical statues under cloudless skies are a part of their cultural heritage, and they see people and things more sculpturally, more in the round, as it were, than the races for whom the long winter nights, the *Urwald*, and all the Nordic phantoms, have befogged the line between fact and dream.

II

I have spoken of "Benediction" as in some respects un-French; but this does not apply to the principal characters. Only the long French tradition, social and religious, could produce those unforgettable figures: the old Marquise, the Bishop, Adèle, the old housekeeper-maid, the venerable butler, and the Bishop's little satellite, M. Bonnefoy, who combines in his small obsequious person the functions of sacristan, valet and secretary. All these people, as I have said, are first of all real; if they have subterranean communications with that other world of Claude Silve's, only a word, a glance, a silence, now and then betrays them. Not so with the old Marquise's great-grandchildren, Eusèbe and Anna. Those two strange little beings seem to form the link—as children probably always do—between the dull world of grown-ups and that mysterious Kilmeny-land around and beyond it, and their listenings, their silences, their nearness and remoteness, show them to be still enveloped in the trailing clouds of glory.[5]

It is doubtless because of this that they, and they alone in the great cold arrogant house, are at ease and happy with the elfin guest whom their uncle Horace suddenly and inexplicably brings there; Madame Mancilia, the little creature with great eyes and a lute, and a box of fairy toys, who seems at home only with the children, and who vanishes as mysteriously as she has come, leaving Dampard outwardly unchanged, inexorable in its principles and its convictions, yet with one more light-footed ghost to flit down its corridors between dark and dawn.

One feels that Claude Silve is happiest in this society, that not a tremor of those faery lute-strings escapes her, and that she alone knows—and will perhaps tell us at some future time—whether, after all, Horace, though he forsook the inhospitable roof of Dampard in pursuit of his banished love, did not bring her back at last, with the lute and the exotic toys, to keep company with Anna and Eusèbe.

Benediction, by Claude Silve, 1936

[1] "For Kilmeny had been she ken'd not where, / And Kilmeny had seen what she could not declare"; from "Kilmeny: The Thirteenth Bard's Song," in *The Queen's Wake* (1813), long poem by James Hogg (1770–1835), English writer popularly known as "the Ettrick Shepherd."

[2] Novel of Claude Silve, pseudonym of Philomène de Laforest-Divonne (born 1887), member of "one of the leading ducal families" as well as "one of the better-known writers and journalists in France" (Lewis 438) and among Wharton's closest Parisian friends since before the war. Awarded the *Prix Femina* in 1935, *Benediction* was translated by Wharton's friend Robert Norton and published in the United States the following year, at her behest, by her publishers, Appleton. Its author's moving recollections of Wharton in her last years are quoted at length by Percy Lubbock in *Portrait of Edith Wharton* (1947).

[3] From Keats's *Lamia* (1820), part 1, ll. 388–91 (EW's emphasis); "those" should read "these."

[4] "From the lone sheiling of the misty island / Mountains divide us and a waste of seas; / Yet still the blood is strong, the heart is Highland, / And we in dreams behold the Hebrides"; ballad of exile (often thought to be a Canadian boat song) dating from the Scottish migration to Canada late in the eighteenth and early in the nineteenth century. "Sheiling" denotes a rude hut on a pasture.

[5] Allusion to the familiar lines from Wordsworth's "Ode: Imitations of Immortality from Recollections of Early Childhood" (1807): "Not in entire forgetfulness, / And not in utter nakedness, / But trailing clouds of glory do we come / From God, who is our home" (ll. 62–65).

Preface to *Eternal Passion in English Poetry*

Every anthology is always some one person's anthology—yours or mine or his; and the fact that no two can ever be alike ought to be a sufficient excuse for adding another to those already existing.

But in the present case the compilers feel that they need not even excuse themselves for not excusing themselves. As far as they know, their attempt is one of the first to gather between two covers a selection of the most beautiful (or what they believe to be the most beautiful) of English love-poems, lyrical and other.[1] Is it because almost all preceding anthologists have taken it for granted that, in the long line of selections of English poetry, there surely must be many devoted to this supreme category—that when sea and forest, open road and city street, the temple and the tavern, have all furnished their chosen specimens of inspiration, the mightiest of motive-powers could hardly have been forgotten? Or is it because an over-abundance of material was assumed, and the choice avoided as too arduous? At any rate, the field seems still relatively free, and the compilers feel themselves in a position to ask that the following selection of poems shall be given, till further notice, the unqualified title they have chosen for it.

The ruling motive of their selection has, of course, been that of personal preference. They offer to lovers of English verse what they believe to be a choice comprehending the most beautiful passages of love-poetry in the language. No antiquarian limitations, no pedantic search for the unfamiliar, no sense of the obligation to include such or such a poem because it has had the honours of previous selection, or to exclude another because it has been too often thus honoured, has been allowed to hamper their free choice. These are poems read aloud again and again by the winter fireside, and again and again found enchanting and satisfying to reader and listeners.

It may be of interest to add one word to this preliminary. The anthologists found with wonder, as they proceeded in their choice, that the rank taken by the love-poems in the total production of each poet is almost always in inverse ratio to the greatness of the poet. It may be open to discussion whether the rule applies to Shakespeare, because the Sonnets can be weighed only against fragments torn from the text of some mighty whole; one cannot, for instance, put any one sonnet in one scale, and the whole of *Romeo and Juliet* in the other, and say, "Choose!"

But in every other instance it seems to result from a careful winnowing of the field that in the work of the supremely great English poets the love-poem is not supreme. This is so obviously apparent in the case of Milton, Keats, Shelley, Coleridge, and Wordsworth (though he wrote one of the most perfect of English love-poems) that the point does not need pressing, and it is more curious to call attention to the constancy with which the reverse holds true, and the minor poets reach their highest height in the love-poem.

Just between the greatest and the less, astride on the two peaks, Robert Browning, in this category, proclaims himself, if not supreme, yet most abundant. His most beautiful poetry is certainly his love-poetry, and that he wrote more of it worth preserving than any one other English poet, will be found, on consulting the table of contents, to be the opinion of this particular group of anthologists.[2]

The problem of the relative importance of love-poetry in the whole work of a poet is too complex to be dealt with here; but perhaps a hint toward its solution may be found in the fact that the only emotion to which "all thoughts, all passions, all delights"[3] minister in the average man is but one among many in the breasts of those who, Admirals on the high seas of poetry, thrill to all the "tremors sent below by breezes striking the higher sails."

Eternal Passion in English Poetry, selected by
Edith Wharton and Robert Norton, 1939

[1] One of the seldom-discussed curiosities of her career, the selection assembled by Wharton and her friend Robert Norton, "with the collaboration of Gaillard Lapsley," originated as early as the mid-1920s, in the "poetry evenings" that became such a fixture of her life at Ste. Claire. According to the memoir that Norton supplied Lubbock, "In the first two winters, I remember, our reading was chiefly poetry, and lyric poetry above all. . . . We ransacked the 'Oxford Books' and other anthologies, and of her favourites she could stand endless reading and re-reading. . . . Two or three winters later, the evening occupation was the putting together of an Anthology of English Love Poetry. The idea arose during a reading of the last scenes of Antony and Cleopatra," as "one of the party exclaimed: 'There's real passion for you! how interesting to try and make a selection from English poetry of things of that intensity, taking it as our standard of comparison and admitting nothing that did not pass the test.' This started discussion, instances were suggested and weighed and a few nights later we were seriously at work compiling our list. I have it still—indeed Edith went so far as to have the poems typewritten with a view to publication; and then, owing, I suppose, to the pressure of her other work, she let it slide, to my regret. She was, of course, throughout, the chief contributor; I should imagine that at least two-thirds of the suggestions came from her" (Yale). Less than a year after her death, accepting from Lapsley "the type-script of the Anthology & Edith's Preface," Norton remarked, "Publishing is another matter; my recollection is that Edith made soundings in several directions & met with no encouragement whatever—the world is surfeited with Anthologies, she was told. How much the less chance now! I no longer know any publishers, & do not feel like hawking it about,

though I do think it's good enough to give the world—if only a title could be found to suggest the burning flame of passion which was our criterion!" (Robert Norton to Gaillard Lapsley, 6 June 1938 [Yale]). Presumably it was Lapsley, as Wharton's literary executor, who then made arrangements with Appleton, which published her anthology in 1939, under a title that does not entirely convey, perhaps, the intensity that Norton had described in his memoir and letter. As her opening remarks suggest, Wharton took great interest in the process of organizing such a volume, an interest that she expressed as far back as 1912, in thanking Berenson for his New Year's gift "in the shape of the Oxforder Buch Deutscher Poesie. . . . Thank you so much! It always interests me to see on what theory the anthologist works, & this Herr Doktor's ways are as mysterious as the Almighty's" (*L*, 266).

[2] Wharton included thirteen poems of Browning, exceeded only by her selections from Shakespeare, and three times as many as those of any of the other poets represented in the anthology.

[3] "All thoughts, all passions, all delights, / Whatever stirs this mortal frame, / All are but ministers of Love, / And feed his sacred flame"; opening lines of Coleridge's poem "Love" (1800). The entire stanza is quoted also in the conclusion to *French Ways and Their Meaning* (1919), as an illustration of what Wharton regarded as the good sense of the French, who "have refused to cut love in two" or "to regard it either as merely an exchange of ethereal vows or as a sensual gratification" and "frankly recognize its right to its own place in life." As his attachment to Halo Spear intensifies toward the end of *Hudson River Bracketed*, Vance Weston— whose discovery of Coleridge at Willows, home of one of her ancestresses, marks a turning point in his development, and who has written an essay on Coleridge in the meantime—decides that "his feeling for her included friendship, passion, love, desire, whatever thought or emotion, craving of sight and touch, a woman can excite in a man. All were merged in a rich deep communion; it was the element in which everything else in him lived. 'All thoughts, all motions [*sic*], all delights, Whatever stirs this mortal frame—' the poet whom Elinor Lorburn loved had summed it up long ago" (*HRB*, 432).

SELF-RECONSIDERATIONS

Introduction to *Ethan Frome*

I had known something of New England village life long before I made my home in the same county as my imaginary Starkfield; though, during the years spent there, certain of its aspects became much more familiar to me.

Even before that final initiation, however, I had had an uneasy sense that the New England of fiction bore little—except a vague botanical and dialectical—resemblance to the harsh and beautiful land as I had seen it. Even the abundant enumeration of sweet-fern, asters and mountain-laurel, and the conscientious reproduction of the vernacular, left me with the feeling that the outcropping granite had in both cases been overlooked. I give the impression merely as a personal one; it accounts for "Ethan Frome," and may, to some readers, in a measure justify it.[1]

So much for the origin of the story; there is nothing else of interest to say of it, except as concerns its construction.

The problem before me, as I saw in the first flash, was this: I had to deal with a subject of which the dramatic climax, or rather the anti-climax, occurs a generation later than the first acts of the tragedy. This enforced lapse of time would seem to anyone persuaded—as I have always been—that every subject (in the novelist's sense of the term) implicitly *contains its own form and dimensions*, to mark Ethan Frome as the subject for a novel. But I never thought this for a moment, for I had felt, at the same time, that the theme of my tale was not one on which many variations could be played. It must be treated as starkly and summarily as life had always presented itself to my protagonists; any attempt to elaborate and complicate their sentiments would necessarily have falsified the whole. They were, in truth, these figures, my *granite outcroppings*; but half-emerged from the soil, and scarcely more articulate.

This incompatibility between subject and plan would perhaps have seemed to suggest that my "situation" was after all one to be rejected. Every novelist has been visited by the insinuating wraiths of false "good situations," siren-subjects luring his cockle-shell to the rocks; their voice is oftenest heard, and their mirage-sea beheld, as he traverses the waterless desert which awaits him half-way through whatever work is actually in hand. I knew well enough what song those sirens sang, and had often tied myself to my dull job until they were out of hearing—perhaps carrying a lost masterpiece in their rainbow veils. But I had no such fear of them in the case of Ethan Frome. It was the first subject I had ever approached with full confidence in its value, for my own purpose, and a relative faith in my power to render at least a part of what I saw in it.

Every novelist, again, who "intends upon" his art, has lit upon such subjects, and been fascinated by the difficulty of presenting them in the fullest relief, yet without an added ornament, or a trick of drapery or lighting. This was my task, if I were to tell the story of Ethan Frome; and my scheme of construction—which met with the immediate and unqualified disapproval of the few friends to whom I tentatively outlined it—I still think justified in the given case. It appears to me, indeed, that, while an air of artificiality is lent to a tale of complex and sophisticated people which the novelist causes to be guessed at and interpreted by any mere looker-on, there need be no such drawback if the looker-on is sophisticated, and the people he interprets are simple. If he is capable of seeing all around them, no violence is done to probability in allowing him to exercise this faculty; it is natural enough that he should act as the sympathizing intermediary between his rudimentary characters and the more complicated minds to whom he is trying to present them. But this is all self-evident, and needs explaining only to those who have never thought of fiction as an art of composition.

The real merit of my construction seems to me to lie in a minor detail. I had to find means to bring my tragedy, in a way at once natural and picture-making, to the knowledge of its narrator. I might have sat him down before a village gossip who would have poured out the whole affair to him in a breath, but in doing this I should have been false to two essential elements of my picture: first, the deep-rooted reticence and inarticulateness of the people I was trying to draw, and secondly the effect of "roundness" (in the plastic sense) produced by letting their case be seen through eyes as different as those of Harmon Gow and Mrs. Ned Hale. Each of my chroniclers contributes to the narrative *just so much as he or she is capable of understanding* of what, to them, is a complicated and mysterious case; and only the narrator of the tale has scope enough to see it all, to resolve it back into simplicity, and to put it in its rightful place among his larger categories.

I make no claim for originality in following a method of which "La Grande Bretêche" and "The Ring and the Book" had set me the magnificent example;[2] my one merit is, perhaps, to have guessed that the proceeding there employed was also applicable to my small tale.

I have written this brief analysis—the first I have ever published of any of my books[3]—because, as an author's introduction to his work, I can imagine nothing of any value to his readers except a statement as to why he decided to attempt the work in question, and why he selected one form rather than another for its embodiment. These primary aims, the only ones that can be explicitly stated, must, by the artist, be almost instinctively felt and acted upon before there can pass into his creation that imponderable something more which causes life to circulate in it, and preserves it for a little from decay.

Ethan Frome, 1922 edition

[1] For Wharton's later account of its genesis, see *A Backward Glance*, 293–96.

[2] In "La Grande Bretèche" (1832), later described by Wharton as "that most perfectly-composed of all short stories," in which "Balzac showed what depth, mystery, and verisimilitude may be given to a tale by causing it to be reflected, in fractions, in the minds of a series of accidental participants or mere lookers-on" (*WF*, 92), the narrator hears three different accounts of the eponymous estate of a dead noblewoman; in Browning's narrative poem (1868–69), the same murder story is retold from a dozen different viewpoints.

[3] Wharton's introduction originated in a proposal from Charles Scribner, who was preparing "a handsome special edition of *Ethan Frome*" (Lewis 3) early in 1922 and who wrote to Wharton, "It has occurred to me that you might be disposed to write a few words of preface or introduction" (Scribner to EW, 16 March 1922 [Princeton]). Having lost most of her work since 1916 to Appleton, Scribner was perhaps eager to retain Wharton's patronage as much as possible. Although initially reluctant ("The idea is new to me, and as you know I have always disliked to talk about my work; but I do not wish to refuse, if you really think that such an introduction would be helpful"), Wharton complied with Scribner, who was able to assure her a few weeks later that "the preface is of unusual interest and adapted exactly to its purpose" (EW to Scribner, 30 March 1922, and Scribner to EW, 26 April 1922 [Princeton]). Her introduction has remained Wharton's best-known piece of critical writing.

The Writing of *Ethan Frome*

The conditions in which *Ethan Frome* originated have remained much more clearly fixed in my memory than those connected with any of my other stories, owing to the odd accident of the tale's having been begun in French.[1] Early in the nineteen hundreds I happened to be spending a whole winter in Paris, and it occurred to me to make use of the opportunity to polish and extend my conversational French; for though I had spoken the language since the age of four I had never had occasion to practise it for any length of time, at least with cultivated people, having frequently wandered through France as a tourist, but never lived there for more than a few weeks consecutively. Accordingly, it was arranged that I should read and talk for so many hours a week with a young French professor; and soon after our studies began he suggested that before each of his visits I should prepare an "exercise" for him.

I have never been able, without much mental anguish, to write anything but a letter or a story, and as stories come to me much more easily than letters, I timidly asked him if a story would "do," and, though obviously somewhat surprised at the unexpected suggestion, he acquiesced with equal timidity. Thus the French version of *Ethan Frome* began, and ploughed its heavy course through a copy-book or two; then the lessons were interrupted and the Gallic "Ethan" abandoned, I forget at what point in his career. The copy-book containing this earliest version of his adventures has long since vanished;[2] but a few years later Ethan's history stirred again in my memory, and I forthwith sat down and wrote it in English, reading aloud each evening what I had done during the day to a friend as familiar as I was with the lonely lives in half-deserted New England villages, before the coming of the motor and the telephone.[3] The legend that Henry James suggested my transposing the French "composition" into an English tale—a fable I have frequently come across of recent years—must be classed among the other inventions which honour me by connecting my name with his in the field of letters. I am not sure if he even saw the French beginning of the tale, but he certainly did not suggest its rewriting in English, and never read the story, or heard of it again, till it appeared in print in the latter language.

While I am on the subject of literary fables, I might as well destroy another which likewise concerns *Ethan Frome*. Not long since I read a thoughtful article on the making of fiction, in which the author advanced the theory that in a given case a certain perspective might be necessary to the novelist, and that one might conceivably write a better book about Main Street if one lived as far away from it as Paris or Palermo; in proof of which *Ethan Frome* was cited as an instance of a successful New England story written by some one who knew nothing of New England. I have no desire to contest the theory, with which, in a certain measure, I am disposed to agree; but the fact is that *Ethan Frome* was written after a ten years' residence in the New England hill country where Ethan's tragedy was enacted, and that during those years I had become very familiar with the aspect, the dialect and the general mental attitude of the Ethans, Zeenas and Mattie Silvers of the neighbouring villages. My other short novel of New England life, *Summer*, which deals with the same type of people involved in a different tragedy of isolation, might, one would suppose, have helped to prove to the legend-makers that I knew something at first hand of the life and the people into whose intimacy I had asked my readers to enter with me on two successive occasions.

Colophon, September 1932

[1] It was a report to this effect that led Elmer Adler, editor of the *Colophon*, to solicit an article from Wharton, who later incorporated part of "The Writing of *Ethan Frome*" in her memoirs (*BG*, 293–96).

[2] In fact, the "Black Book" survived and is housed among Wharton's papers at Yale; see W. D. MacCallan, "The French Draft of *Ethan Frome*," *Yale University Library Gazette* 27 (July 1952): 38–47.

[3] Wharton elsewhere identifies the friend as Walter Berry (*BG*, 296).

Foreword to *Ethan Frome: A Dramatization of Edith Wharton's Novel*

Not long ago, a friend, fulfilling one of the most sacred and cherished privileges of friendship, sent me the report of a lecture on American fiction in which the lecturer had done me the honour to include my name.

His reference to me (I quote from memory) was to the effect that *Ethan Frome* had some chance of surviving, though everything else I had written was destined to immediate oblivion. I took the blow meekly, bowed but not broken, and mindful that, though in my youth it would have been considered a discourtesy to fling such a verdict in the face of a faithful servant of English letters, other times (and especially other races) have introduced new standards of manners in my country.

Perhaps the lecturer was as right as he thought himself; but I presently extracted some comfort from the thought that Sainte[-]Beuve, probably the most acute literary critic who ever lived, went hopelessly and almost invariably astray in trying to estimate the work of his contemporaries; and that Madame de Sévigné, herself one of the most enchanting of stylists, in speaking of the greatest poet of her day and country, replied to a questioner: "Racine? Oh, he'll disappear as quickly as the craze for coffee."[1]

There are times when it is comforting, and therefore perhaps permissible, to compare small things with great; and if I have broken through my lifelong rule of never noticing any comments on my work, it is because, in reading the dramatization of *Ethan Frome* by Owen and Donald Davis, I found myself thinking at every page: "Here at least is a new lease of life for 'Ethan.'"[2] And the discovery moved me more than I can say.

It has happened to me, as to most novelists, to have the odd experience, through the medium of reviews or dramatizations of their work, to see their books as they have taken shape in other minds: always a curious, and sometimes a painful, revelation. But I imagine few have had the luck to see the characters they had imagined in fiction transported to the stage without loss or alteration of any sort, without even that grimacing enlargement of gesture and language supposed to be necessary to "carry" over the footlights.

I should like to record here my appreciation of this unusual achievement, and my professional admiration for the great skill and exquisite sensitiveness with which my interpreters have executed their task; and to add that, if, as I am told, *their* interpreters, the personifiers of Ethan, of Zeena and Mattie, and the minor Starkfield figures, have reached the same level of comprehension, then my poor little group of hungry lonely New England villagers will live again for a while on their stony hillside before finally joining their forbears under the village headstones. I should like to think that this good fortune may be theirs, for I lived among them, in fact and in imagination, for more than ten years, and their strained starved faces are still near to me.

Ethan Frome: A Dramatization of Edith Wharton's Novel,
by Owen Davis and Donald Davis, 1936

[1] See n. 4 to "Permanent Values in Fiction" and n. 1 to "*George Eliot.*"

[2] The "dramatization" of *Ethan Frome*, coauthored by Owen Davis and Donald Davis, followed "The Old Maid," by Zoë Akins, and Margaret Ayer Barnes's 1928 *The Age of Innocence* in a series of successful and lucrative stage adaptations of Wharton's work. What she called "the 'Ethan Frome' play" (*L*, 590) opened in Philadelphia in January 1936 and was published by Scribner's later in the year in a "special student's edition" for which Wharton was asked to supply a preface. As she admitted after completing the assignment, "I was rather handicapped by the fact that I have already twice told the story of my tale, and did not wish to repeat myself" (EW to Scribner, 15 January 1936 [Princeton]). Subtly different from those earlier statements, Wharton's poignant foreword offers yet another illuminating angle on her most familiar work.

Introduction to *The House of Mirth*

I

It seems like going back to the Pharaohs to try to re-enter the New York world in which *The House of Mirth* originated.[1] The book was written only thirty years ago, and the circle I described in it was that in which I had lived since my eleventh year, and which, in all essentials, had remained unchanged in the interval between my childhood and the writing of the book.

It is given to some novelists, even though they continue to ply their craft beyond middle age, to retain to the end an audience familiar with the life their tales depict, and still to a great extent leading that life. Thackeray and

Balzac, for instance, were spared the difficulty of having to readjust themselves to any marked modification in the point of view and the social habits
of their readers; whereas in Trollope's latest novels one feels the effort, remarkable if not always successful, of a painter of social life to adapt his vision
and its expression to conditions so abruptly modified that the resplendent
Duke of Omnium of Framley Parsonage would have seemed an almost legendary figure to the society described in *The Way We Live Now*, and *The
American Senator*.

Trollope's difficulty, however, was as nothing compared with that of the
novelist of manners whose first tales go back to the eighteen-nineties, and
who is asked to deal with one of them from the formidable vantage-ground
of 1935. To find an analogy, it would be necessary to imagine a French
novelist of manners the curve of whose work should bestride the cataclysmic
period from the execution of Louis XVI to the battle of Waterloo. Out of the
savage crimes and senseless destruction of those brief years a new world was
born, differing as radically from the old world which it destroyed as that
strange amalgam of new forces that grew out of the fall of the Roman Empire
differed from the civilization it overthrew; and great must have been the
difficulties of the humble story-teller seeking to reconstruct the setting of his
tales from the fragments of a shattered world. It is easy to see why Stendhal
dealt with, and dismissed, the battle of Waterloo in the first pages of *La
Chartreuse de Parme*, barely suffering his hero to skirt its periphery before
hurrying him on to a world as yet unaffected by such convulsions!

It may seem slightly out of scale to invoke the cosmos in dealing with the
fortunes of a social chronicler; but when there is anything whatever below
the surface in the novelist's art, that something can be only the social foundation on which his fable is built; and when that foundation totters, and is
swallowed up in a great world-convulsion, the poor story-teller's structural
problem is a hard one. No wonder that Benjamin Constant, and Goethe in
later life, hung their creations in the void, and that, for instance, all the
furniture, dresses, manners, and customs which make the first volume of
Wilhelm Meister so magically real, have vanished from its sequel, and from
the *Wahlverwandschaften*![2]

II

When I wrote *The House of Mirth* I held, without knowing it, two trumps in
my hand. One was the fact that New York society in the nineties was a field
as yet unexploited by any novelist who had grown up in that little hot-house

of traditions and conventions; and the other, that as yet these traditions and conventions were unassailed, and tacitly regarded as unassailable.

Why had no one written a novel of New York society? The answer is fairly obvious—most people thought it offered nothing worth writing about. I was very nearly of the same mind; yet I had always felt that the field might prove to be a rich one for any writer with imagination enough to penetrate below the surface.

I remember once saying to Henry James, in reference to a novel of the type that used euphemistically to be called "unpleasant": "You know, I was rather disappointed; that book wasn't nearly as bad as I expected"; to which he replied, with his incomparable twinkle: "Ah, my dear, the abysses are all so shallow."

Well, so they are; but at least they are always there, and the novelist who has the patience to dip down into them will find that below a certain depth, whatever his subject, there is almost always "stuff o' the conscience"[3] to work in. That is why, on reflection, I was not afraid of the poverty of my subject, but proceeded to attack it with the first fine careless valour of the inexperienced. And the subsequent career of the book would seem to justify my audacity; for, in spite of the fact that I wrote about totally insignificant people, and "dated" them by an elaborate stage-setting of manners, furniture and costume, the book still lives, and has now attained the honour of figuring on the list of the Oxford University Press.

The fact is that Nature, always wasteful, and apparently compelled to create dozens of stupid people in order to produce a single genius, seems to reverse the process in manufacturing the shallow and the idle. Such groups always rest on an underpinning of wasted human possibilities; and it seemed to me that the fate of the persons embodying these possibilities ought to redeem my subject from insignificance. This is the key to *The House of Mirth*, and its meaning; and I believe the book has owed its success, from the first, as much to my picture of the slow disintegration of Lily Bart as to the details of the "conversation piece" of which she forms the central figure.

Not that I consider the details in question without their value in giving substance and reality to the novelist's vision. Some readers may still recall Ruskin's savage invective against the school of painters who first substituted "drapery" for real clothes, with their buttons, tags and tucks, under the erroneous impression that vague folds of paint would "date" a picture less than a bustle or leg-o'-mutton sleeves.[4] Alas, the lapse of time was to prove that they date it far more; and a practised eye can easily tell exactly to what year of the eighties or nineties the professional beauties painted or photographed in "drapery" owe their dateless commemoration.

Of course bustles and leg-o'-mutton sleeves date! And what is more, they need not even be described by the novelist in order to figure in his pages as vividly as in contemporary portraiture. Everything dates in a work of art, and should do so; and to situate a picture or a novel firmly where it belongs in the unrolling social picture is to help it draw vitality from the soil it grew in. Jane Austen did not have to describe the attire of her shawled and ruffled heroines, nor the tight trousers and high stocks of their suitors; to bring them before us in their habit as they lived she had only to make her characters speak, move, behave, as people so clothed were in the habit of doing, instead of making them talk "drapery," after the manner of most heroes of fiction in her day.

Obviously, however, the other, and supreme, preservative of fiction is whatever of unchanging human nature the novelist has contrived to bring to life beneath the passing fripperies of clothes and custom. The essential soul is always there, under whatever disguise; and the story-teller's most necessary gift is that of making its presence felt, and of discerning just how far it is modified and distorted by the shifting fashions of the hour.

III

In my volume of reminiscences, *A Backward Glance*, I analysed, to the best of my ability, the origin of *The House of Mirth*, as viewed from what may be called the subjective side: the germination of the tale in the author's mind, and the reasons for its unfolding in the particular way it did.[5] Here, on the contrary, I should like to try to describe what happened to it when it entered other people's minds; for the strangest, and not the least interesting, adventure of any work of the imagination is the inevitable distortion it undergoes in passing from the mind of the writer to that of his readers. It was Mr. Kipling, I think, who cited as an extreme example of this curious transposition of values the fact that *Gulliver's Travels*, intended by its author to be the most savage of social satires, has long since settled down comfortably by the nursery fire as a wonder-tale for children;[6] and the same kind of transposition, though on a less startling scale, happens to every novel which attempts to go a little below the surface of life.

At the time of writing *The House of Mirth* I had too little literary experience to have taken note of this curious phenomenon, and great was my astonishment when the story which I had conceived as a simple and fairly moving domestic tragedy, was received with a loud cry of rejection and reprobation! The cry, to be sure, was not a general one; but the quarter from which it came made it peculiarly audible to me, for it proceeded from the

very group among whom I had lived my life and situated my story. If I had
been an older hand at my trade, this would not have surprised me; for the
attitude of the fashionable world towards those who try to catch its likeness
has invariably been one of surprise and resentment. One of the most acutely
observed scenes in Proust's *A la recherche du temps perdu* is that in which
the old Marquise de Villeparisis says to the young Marcel: "But do you really
consider Châteaubriand a genius? Why, he was an intimate friend of my
grandfather's, *et c'était de la très petite noblesse*."[7] My society critics took the
opposite attitude, but one based on the same anthropomorphic conception
of the work of fiction as something after all half real and half alive—like a
frightened child's idea of the terrifying stone water-gods glimpsed through
the mist of gushing fountains.

This supposed picture of their little circle, secure behind its high stockade
of convention, alarmed and disturbed the rulers of Old New York. If the
book had been the work of an outsider, of some barbarian reduced to guess-
ing at what went on behind the stockade, they would not so much have
minded—might have laughed over its absurdities, or, more probably, not
even have heard of its existence. But here was a tale written by one of themselves, a tale deliberately slandering and defiling their most sacred institutions and some of the most deeply revered members of the clan! And what
picture did the writer offer to their horrified eyes? That of a young girl of
their world who rouged, smoked, ran into debt, borrowed money, gambled,
and—crowning horror!—went home with a bachelor friend to take tea in his
flat! And I was not only asking the outer world to believe that such creatures
were tolerated in New York society, but actually presenting this unhappy
specimen as my heroine! And the people who surrounded her—dreadful
caricatures of this or that cousin or uncle or aunt (for of course my characters
were all immediately labelled, and some of them wore at least three different labels)—well, it was all so painful and surprising and unaccountable that
the best way, perhaps, was not to allude to the book in the presence of its
misguided author, but firmly to ignore the fact that she had committed this
deplorable blunder; a blunder which, like the book itself, would doubtless soon be forgotten.

IV

Less than twenty years later, if I had offered the same story to the same
readers as a study in social corruption, they would have smiled instead of
shuddering, and have wondered why I had chosen the tame and blameless

Lily Bart as a victim of avenging moral forces. I was certainly lucky in introducing her to the public at a moment when her venial lapses loomed gigantically against a sulphurous background; and looking back on her now, from the superior eminence of a world in which facilities for divorce and remarriage have kept pace with all the other modern devices for annihilating time and space, it seems incredible that the early success of *The House of Mirth* should in some measure have been one of scandal! But so it was, to my own amusement, and to the immense satisfaction of my publishers. Ah, golden days for the novelist were those in which a lovely girl could besmirch her reputation by taking tea between trains at a bachelor's flat! Thanks to this daring expedient, I had no reason for envying Octave Feuillet, who, years earlier, and perhaps as unwittingly, had achieved the same success by causing his hero (in *Le Roman d'un jeune homme pauvre*) to leap at the peril of his life from the top of a ruined tower, in order to shield the honour of a young lady with whom he had been accidentally shut up in that romantic trap![8] But I sometimes wonder if the novelists of the present day, so put to it to find new horrors in the domestic circle, do not envy *me*—if the brilliant leaders of the new fiction do not now and then sit down and wipe their dripping brows, and say to themselves: "Ah, how easy it must have been to tell a story when the mere appearance of lapsing from conventional rules of conduct caused far more scandal than we can produce after searching the medical encyclopaedias and the confessional manuals of eminent theologians for every known form of human perversity."

Yes—it was certainly easier; for the abysses, which were always so shallow, have grown even more so, now that they are on the itinerary of all the luxury-cruisers.

The House of Mirth, 1936 edition

[1] In spring 1935, Wharton received from London a letter in which H. S. Milford, of Oxford University Press, declared, "I have for a long time been anxious to have your work represented in the 'World's Classics,' and have been in communication with your publishers, as you might have heard, on the possibility of including 'The House of Mirth' in the series. . . . Do you think it would be possible for you to write an Introduction to this edition of the book? as short as you please though of course the longer the better" (H. S. Milford to EW, 15 May 1935 [Yale]). Her secretary replied on Wharton's behalf that "she would be very happy to have your work represented in the Oxford University Press, and that she hopes to be able to write an introduction for whatever book you choose within a few weeks," adding, however, "Mrs. Wharton is somewhat disappointed that you should have fixed upon the 'House of Mirth.' She thinks 'The Custom of the Country' a much better book, and suggests either that or 'Ethan Frome,' if you prefer a too-familiar title" (EW to Milford, 18 May 1935 [Yale]). Milford replied, "The choice of *The House of Mirth* was made not only perhaps because it is a favourite of mine, but also because it seems to have gone out of print in this country. As negotiations for *The House of Mirth* have gone so far with other publishers, I think it best to settle on that title, though I shall hope to

include others at some future date" (Milford to EW, 22 May 1935 [Yale]). It is regrettable that Wharton's death prevented them from pursuing this possibility, for her appraisal of her first best-seller is a fascinating document and deserves to be much better known.

² Benjamin Constant (1767–1830), French novelist known principally for *Adolphe* (1816), elsewhere admired by Wharton as one of the first "psychological" novels; *Elective Affinities* is the generally accepted English title of the second of the two Goethe novels mentioned by Wharton.

³ See n. 1 to "Visibility in Fiction."

⁴ Wharton seems to have in mind a passage from "Classic Schools of Painting," the third lecture in Ruskin's *The Art of England* (1884), regarding some portraits by Sir Joshua Reynolds and by some of his followers: "Nevertheless, I feel confident in your general admission that the charm of all these pictures is in great degree dependent on toilette; that the fond and graceful flatteries of each master do in no small measure consist in his management of frillings and trimmings, cuffs and collarettes; and on beautiful flingings or fastenings of investiture, which can only here and there be called a *drapery*, but insists on the perfectness of the forms it conceals, and deepens their harmony by its contradiction."

⁵ See *A Backward Glance*, 205–9.

⁶ See n. 3 to "The Great American Novel."

⁷ From *A l'Ombre des jeunes filles en fleurs* (1919), the second volume of Proust's novel.

⁸ Wharton refers to the popular 1858 novel of Octave Feuillet (1821–90).

Preface to *Ghosts*

"Do you believe in ghosts?" is the pointless question often addressed by those who are incapable of feeling ghostly influences to—I will not say the *ghost-seer*, always a rare bird, but—the *ghost-feeler*, the person sensible of invisible currents of being in certain places and at certain hours.¹

The celebrated reply (I forget whose): "No, I don't believe in ghosts, but I'm afraid of them," is much more than the cheap paradox it seems to many. To "believe," in that sense, is a conscious act of the intellect, and it is in the warm darkness of the pre-natal fluid far below our conscious reason that the faculty dwells with which we apprehend the ghosts we may not be endowed with the gift of seeing. This was oddly demonstrated the other day by the volume of ghost-stories collected from the papers of the late Lord Halifax by his son.² The test of the value of each tale lay, to the collector's mind, not in the least in its intrinsic interest, but in the fact that some one or other had been willing to vouch for the authenticity of the anecdote. No matter how dull, unoriginal and unimportant the tale—if some one had convinced the late Lord Halifax that it was "true," that it "had really happened," in it went; and can it be only by accident that the one story in this large collection which is even faintly striking and memorable is the one with an apologetic foot-note to the effect that the editor had not been able to trace it to its source?

Sources, as a matter of fact, are not what one needs in judging a ghost-story. The good ones bring with them the internal proof of their ghostliness; and no other evidence is needed. But since first I dabbled in the creating of ghost-stories, I have made the depressing discovery that the faculty required for their enjoyment has become almost atrophied in modern man. No one ever expected a Latin to understand a ghost, or shiver over it; to do that, one must still have in one's ears the hoarse music of the northern Urwald or the churning of dark seas on the outermost shores. But when I first began to read, and then to write, ghost-stories, I was conscious of a common medium between myself and my readers, of their meeting me half-way among the primeval shadows, and filling in the gaps in my narrative with sensations and divinations akin to my own.

I had curious evidence of the change when, two or three years ago, one of the tales in the present volume made its first curtsey in an American magazine. I believe most purveyors of fiction will agree with me that the readers who pour out on the author of the published book such floods of interrogatory ink pay little heed to the isolated tale in a magazine. The request to the author to reveal as many particulars as possible of his private life to his eager readers is seldom addressed to him till the scattered products of his pen have been collected in a volume. But when "Pomegranate Seed" (which I hope you presently mean to read) first appeared in a magazine I was bombarded by a host of enquirers anxious, in the first place, to know the meaning of the story's title (in the dark ages of my childhood an acquaintance with classical fairy-lore was as much a part of our stock of knowledge as Grimm and Andersen), and secondly, to be told *how a ghost could write a letter, or put it into a letter-box.* These problems caused sleepless nights to many correspondents whose names seemed to indicate that they were recent arrivals from unhaunted lands. Need I say there was never a Welsh or a Scottish signature among them? But in a few years more perhaps there may be; for deep within us as the ghost-instinct lurks, I seem to see it being gradually atrophied by those two world-wide enemies of the imagination, the wireless and the cinema. To a generation for whom everything which used to nourish the imagination because it had to be won by an effort, and then slowly assimilated, is now served up cooked, seasoned and chopped into little bits, the creative faculty (for reading should be a creative act as well as writing) is rapidly withering, together with the power of sustained attention; and the world which used to be so *grand à la clarté des lampes* is diminishing in inverse ratio to the new means of spanning it; so that the more we add to its surface the smaller it becomes.

All this is very depressing to the ghost-story purveyor and his publisher; but in spite of adverse influences, and the conflicting attractions of the gangster, the introvert and the habitual drunkard, the ghost may hold his own a little longer in the hands of the experienced chronicler. What is most to be feared is that these seers should fail; for frailer than the ghost is the wand of his evoker, and more easily to be broken in the hard grind of modern speeding-up. Ghosts, to make themselves manifest, require two conditions abhorrent to the modern mind: silence and continuity. Mr. Osbert Sitwell informed us the other day that ghosts went out when electricity came in;[3] but surely this is to misapprehend the nature of the ghostly. What drives ghosts away is not the aspidistra or the electric cooker; I can imagine them more wistfully haunting a mean house in a dull street than the battlemented castle with its boring stage properties. What the ghost really needs is not echoing passages and hidden doors behind tapestry, but only continuity and silence. For where a ghost has once appeared it seems to hanker to appear again; and it obviously prefers the silent hours, when at last the wireless has ceased to jazz. These hours, prophetically called "small," are in fact continually growing smaller; and even if a few diviners keep their wands, the ghost may after all succumb first to the impossibility of finding standing-room in a roaring and discontinuous universe.

It would be tempting to dwell on what we shall lose when the wraith and the fetch are no more with us; but my purpose here is rather to celebrate those who have made them visible to us. For the ghost should never be allowed to forget that his only chance of survival is in the tales of those who have encountered him, whether actually or imaginatively—and perhaps preferably the latter. It is luckier for a ghost to be vividly imagined than dully "experienced"; and nobody knows better than a ghost how hard it is to put him or her into words shadowy yet transparent enough.

It is, in fact, not easy to write a ghost-story; and in timidly offering these attempts of mine I should like to put them under the protection of those who first stimulated me to make the experiment. The earliest, I believe, was Stevenson, with "Thrawn Janet" and "Markheim"; two remarkable ghost-stories, though far from the high level of such wizards as Sheridan Le Fanu and Fitz[-]James O'Brien. I doubt if these have ever been surpassed, though

Marion Crawford's isolated effort, "The Upper Berth," comes very near to the crawling horror of O'Brien's "What Is It?"[4]

For imaginative handling of the supernatural no one, to my mind, has touched Henry James in "The Turn of the Screw"; but I suppose a ghost-novel can hardly be classed among ghost-stories, and that tale in particular is too individual, too utterly different from any other attempt to catch the sense of the supernatural, to be pressed into the current categories.

As for the present day, I have ventured to put my own modest "omnibus" under the special protection of the only modern ghost-evoker whom I place in the first rank—and this dispenses with the need of saying why I put him there.[5] Moreover, the more one thinks the question over, the more one perceives the impossibility of defining the effect of the supernatural. The Bostonian gentleman of the old school who said that his wife always made it a moral issue whether the mutton should be roast or boiled, summed up very happily the relation of Boston to the universe; but the "moral issue" question must not be allowed to enter into the estimating of a ghost-story. It must depend for its effect solely on what one might call its thermometrical quality; if it sends a cold shiver down one's spine, it has done its job and done it well. But there is no fixed rule as to the means of producing this shiver, and many a tale that makes others turn cold leaves me at my normal temperature. The doctor who said there were no diseases but only patients would probably agree that there are no ghosts, but only tellers of ghost-stories, since what provides a shudder for one leaves another peacefully tepid. Therefore one ought, I am persuaded, simply to tell one's ghostly adventures in the most unadorned language, and "leave the rest to Nature," as the New York alderman said when, many years ago, it was proposed to import "a couple of gondolas" for the lake in the Central Park.

The only suggestion I can make is that the teller of supernatural tales should be well frightened in the telling; for if he is, he may perhaps communicate to his readers the sense of that strange something undreamt of in the philosophy of Horatio.

Ghosts, 1937

---

[1] Wharton first "proposed that Appleton publish a volume of her early supernatural tales" (Benstock 424) as early as 1931. Out of a concern that such a volume would conflict on the market with her latest collection of short stories, the idea was postponed, and *Ghosts* did not appear until fall 1937, a couple of months after Wharton's death, consisting entirely of reprinted tales, except for "All Souls'" (the one new tale in the collection, and the last that she completed).

[2] *Lord Halifax's Ghost Book* (1936), assembled by the son of Charles Lindley Wood, second

viscount Halifax (1839-1934), was soon followed by *Further Stories from Lord Halifax's Ghost Book* (1937).

[3] This is not quite accurate as a paraphrase of the opening remark in "On Ghosts" (1935), by Osbert Sitwell (1892–1969): "Only by night do I believe in ghosts, and then more especially in a house that lies buried in the depth of the country and in which there is no electric light." The narrator of "All Souls'" repeats Wharton's paraphrase, referring to "a book by a fashionable essayist" (*CS*, 2: 879).

[4] "Thrawn Janet" (1881) and "Markheim" (1884), tales by Robert Louis Stevenson (1850–94); Joseph Sheridan Le Fanu (1814–73), Irish novelist and prolific author of ghost stories; Fitz-James O'Brien (1828–62), American poet and writer of fiction, known particularly for the tale "What Is It?: A Mystery" (1859); "The Upper Berth" (1894), story of Francis Marion Crawford (1854–1909), American novelist.

[5] Wharton dedicated *Ghosts* to Walter de la Mare (1873–1956), poet, novelist, essayist, and author of numerous ghost stories.

A Little Girl's New York

When four years ago I wrote the closing lines of my reminiscences, *A Backward Glance*, I thought of myself as an old woman laying a handful of rue on the grave of an age which had finished in storm and destruction. Now that I am older by only four years, I realize that my view was that of the sentimentalist watching the slow downward flutter of the first autumn leaves in still blue air, and talking with a shudder of forests stripped by winter gales.[1] For the succeeding years have witnessed such convulsions, social and political, that those earlier disturbances now seem no more than a premonitory tremor; and the change between the customs of my youth and the world of even ten years ago a mere crack in the ground compared with the chasm now dividing that world from the present one.

All elderly people feel the shock of changes barely perceptible to the generation that has had a hand in their making; but even centenarians can seldom have had to look back across such a barrier of new towers of Babel (or their ruins) as divides my contemporaries from the era of the New Deal; and I need no other excuse for beginning my old story over again than the growing mass of these obstructions. Everything that used to form the fabric of our daily life has been torn in shreds, trampled on, destroyed; and hundreds of little incidents, habits, traditions which, when I began to record my past, seemed too insignificant to set down, have acquired the historical importance of fragments of dress and furniture dug up in a Babylonian tomb.

It is these fragments that I should like to assemble and make into a little memorial like the boxes formed of exotic shells which sailors used to fabricate between voyages. And I must forestall my critics by adding that I already foresee how small will be the shells I shall collect, how ordinary their varieties, and the box, when it is made, what a mere joke of a thing—unless one should put one's ear to the shells; but how many will?

II

In those days the little "brownstone" houses (I never knew the technical name of that geological horror) marched up Fifth Avenue (still called "*the* Fifth Avenue*"* by purists) in an almost unbroken procession from Washington Square to the Central Park. Between them there passed up and down, in a leisurely double line, every variety of horse-drawn vehicle, from Mrs. Belmont's or Mrs. Astor's C-spring barouche to a shabby little covered cart drawn by a discouraged old horse and labelled in large letters: *Universal Exterminator*—which suggested collecting souls for the *Dies Irae*, but in reality designated a patent appliance for ridding kitchens of cockroaches.

The little brownstone houses, all with Dutch "stoops" (the five or six steps leading to the front door), and all not more than three stories high, marched Parkward in an orderly procession, like a young ladies' boarding school taking its daily exercise. The façades varied in width from twenty to thirty feet, and here and there, but rarely, the line was broken by a brick house with brownstone trimmings; but otherwise they were all so much alike that one could understand how easy it would be for a dinner guest to go to the wrong house—as once befell a timid young girl of eighteen, to whom a vulgar *nouveau-riche* hostess revealed her mistake, turning her out carriageless into the snow—a horrid adventure which was always used to point the rule that one must *never* allow a guest, even totally unknown, to discover such a mistake, but must immediately include him or her in the party. Imagine the danger of entertaining gangsters to which such social rules would expose the modern hostess! But I am probably the last person to remember that Arcadian code of hospitality.

Those were the days—à propos of Fifth Avenue—when my mother used to say: "Society is completely changed nowadays. When I was first married we knew everyone who kept a carriage."

And this tempts me to another digression, sending me forward to my seventeenth year, when there suddenly appeared in Fifth Avenue a very small canary-yellow brougham with dark trimmings, drawn by a big high-stepping bay and driven by a coachman who matched the brougham in size and the high-stepper in style. In this discreet yet brilliant equipage one just caught a glimpse of a lady whom I faintly remember as dark-haired, quietly dressed, and enchantingly pale, with a hat-brim lined with cherry color, which shed a lovely glow on her cheeks. It was an apparition surpassing in elegance and mystery any that Fifth Avenue had ever seen; but when our dark-blue brougham encountered the yellow one, and I cried: "Oh, Mamma, look—what a smart carriage! Do you know the lady?" I was hurriedly drawn back with the stern order not to stare at strange people and to remember that whenever our carriage passed the yellow one I was to turn my head away and look out of the other window.

For the lady in the canary-colored carriage was New York's first fashionable hetaera. Her name and history were known in all the clubs, and the name of her proud proprietor was no secret in New York drawing-rooms. I may add that, being an obedient daughter, I always thereafter *did* look out of the other window when the forbidden brougham passed; but that one and only glimpse of the loveliness within it peopled my imagination with images of enchantment from Broceliande and Shalott (we were all deep in the "Idylls of the King"),[2] and from the Cornwall of Yseult. She was, in short, sweet unsuspecting creature, my first doorway to romance, destined to become for me successively Guinevere and Francesca da Rimini, Beatrix Esmond and the *Dame aux Camélias*.[3] And in the impoverished emotional atmosphere of old New York such a glimpse was like the mirage of palm trees in the desert.

I have often sighed, in looking back at my childhood, to think how pitiful a provision was made for the life of the imagination behind those uniform brownstone façades, and then have concluded that since, for reasons which escape us, the creative mind thrives best on a reduced diet, I probably had the fare best suited to me. But this is not to say that the average well-to-do New Yorker of my childhood was not starved for a sight of the high gods. Beauty, passion, and danger were automatically excluded from his life (for the men were almost as starved as the women); and the average human being deprived of air from the heights is likely to produce other lives equally starved—which was what happened in old New York, where the tepid sameness of the moral atmosphere resulted in a prolonged immaturity of mind.

But we must return to the brownstone houses, and penetrate from the vestibule (painted in Pompeian red, and frescoed with a frieze of stencilled lotus-leaves, taken from Owen Jones's *Grammar of Ornament*)[4] into the carefully guarded interior. What would the New Yorker of the present day say to those interiors, and the lives lived in them? Both would be equally unintelligible to any New Yorker under fifty.

Beyond the vestibule (in the average house) was a narrow drawing-room. Its tall windows were hung with three layers of curtains: sash-curtains through which no eye from the street could possibly penetrate, and next to these draperies of lace or embroidered tulle, richly beruffled, and looped back under the velvet or damask hangings which were drawn in the evening. This window garniture always seemed to me to symbolize the superimposed layers of under-garments worn by the ladies of the period—and even, alas, by the little girls. They were in fact almost purely a symbol, for in many windows even the inner "sash-curtains" were looped back far enough to give the secluded dwellers a narrow glimpse of the street; but no self-respecting mistress of a house (a brownstone house) could dispense with this triple display of window-lingerie, and among the many things I did which pained and scandalized my Bostonian mother-in-law, she was not least shocked by the banishment from our house in the country of all the thicknesses of muslin which should have intervened between ourselves and the robins on the lawn.

The brownstone drawing-room was likely to be furnished with monumental pieces of modern Dutch marquetry, among which there was almost always a cabinet with glazed doors for the display of "bric-à-brac." Oh, that bric-à-brac! Our mothers, who prided themselves on the contents of these cabinets, really knew about only two artistic productions—old lace and old painted fans. With regard to these the eighteenth-century tradition was still alive, and in nearly every family there were yards and yards of precious old lace and old fans of ivory, chicken-skin, or pale tortoise-shell, exquisitely carved and painted. But as to the other arts a universal ignorance prevailed, and the treasures displayed in the wealthiest houses were no better than those of the average brownstone-dweller.

My mother had a collection of old lace which was famous among her friends, and a few fragments of it still remain to me, piously pinned up in the indigo-blue paper supposed (I have never known why) to be necessary to the preservation of fine lace. But the yards are few, alas; for true to my conviction that what was made to be used should be used, and not locked up, I have outlived many and many a yard of noble *point de Milan*, of stately Venetian point, of shadowy Mechlin, and exquisitely flowered *point de Paris*, not to speak of the delicate Valenciennes which ruffled the tiny handkerchiefs and incrusted and edged the elaborate *lingerie* of my youth. Nor

do I regret having worn out what was meant to be worn out. I know few
sadder sights than Museum collections of these Arachne-webs that were
designed to borrow life and color from the nearness of young flesh and
blood. Museums are cemeteries, as unavoidable, no doubt, as the other kind,
but just as unrelated to the living beauty of what we have loved.

III

I have said that the little brown houses, marching up Fifth Avenue like
disciplined schoolgirls, now and then gave way to a more important façade,
sometimes of their own chocolate hue, but with occasional pleasing alternatives in brick. Many successive Fifth Avenues have since been erected on
the site of the one I first knew, and it is hard to remember that none of the
"new" millionaire houses which, ten or fifteen years later, were to invade
that restless thoroughfare (and all of which long ago joined the earlier layers
of ruins) had been dreamed of by the boldest innovator. Even the old families, who were subsequently to join the newcomers in transforming Fifth
Avenue into a street of would-be palaces, were still content with plain wide-
fronted houses, mostly built in the 'forties or 'fifties. In those simple days
one could count on one's two hands the New York houses with ballrooms: to
the best of my recollection, only the Goelets, Astors, Butler Duncans,
Belmonts, Schermerhorns, and Mason Joneses possessed these frivolous ap-
pendages; though a few years later, by the time I made my first curtsy at
the "Assemblies," several rich couples, the Mortons, Waterburys, Coleman
Draytons, and Francklyns among them, had added ballrooms to their smart
establishments.

In the smaller houses a heavy linen called "crash," laid on the floors of two
adjoining drawing-rooms, and gilt chairs hired from "old Brown" (the Grace
Church sexton, who so oddly combined ecclesiastical and worldly duties)
created temporary ballrooms for small dances; but the big balls of the season
(from January to Lent) were held at Delmonico's, then, if I am not mistaken,
at the corner of Twenty-eighth Street and Fifth Avenue.

The Assemblies were the most important of these big balls—if the word
"big" as now understood could be applied to any social event in our old New
York! There were, I think, three Assemblies in the winter, presided over by
a committee of ladies who delegated three of their number to receive the
guests at the ballroom door. The evening always opened with a quadrille, in
which the ladies of the committee and others designated by them took part;
and there followed other square dances, waltzes and polkas, which went on

until the announcement of supper. A succulent repast of canvasback ducks, terrapin, foie-gras, and the best champagnes was served at small tables below stairs, in what was then New York's only fashionable restaurant; after which we re-ascended to the ballroom (in a shaky little lift) to begin the complicated maneuvers of the cotillion.

The "Thursday Evening Dances," much smaller and more exclusive, were managed by a committee of the younger married women—and how many young and pretty ones there were in our little society! I cannot, oddly enough, remember where these dances were held—and who is left, I wonder, to refresh my memory? There was no Sherry's restaurant as yet, and no Waldorf-Astoria, or any kind of modern hotel with a suite for entertaining; yet I am fairly sure we did not meet at "Del's" for the "Thursday Evenings."

At all dances, large or small, a custom prevailed which caused untold misery to the less popular girls. This was the barbarous rule that if a young man asked a girl for a dance or, between dances, for a turn about the ball-room, he was obliged to keep her on his arm until another candidate replaced him; with the natural result that "to him (or rather *her*) that hath shall be given," and the wily young men risked themselves only in the vicinity of young women already provided with attendant swains. To remedy this embarrassing situation the more tactful girls always requested their partners, between dances, to bring them back to their mothers or "chaperons," a somnolent row of stout ladies in velvet and ostrich feathers enthroned on a row of settees against the ballroom walls.

The custom persisted for some years, and spoilt the enjoyment of many a "nice" girl not attractive enough to be perpetually surrounded by young men, and too proud to wish to chain at her side a dancer who might have risked captivity out of kindness of heart. I do not know when the fashion changed, and the young men were set free, for we went back to Europe when I was nineteen, and I had only brief glimpses of New York until I returned to it as a married woman.

The most conspicuous architectural break in the brownstone procession occurred where its march ended, at the awkwardly shaped entrance to the Central Park. Two of my father's cousins, Mrs. Mason Jones and Mrs. Colford Jones, bought up the last two blocks on the east side of Fifth Avenue, facing the so-called "Plaza" at the Park gates, and built thereon their houses and their children's houses; a bold move which surprised and scandalized society. Fifty-seventh Street was then a desert, and ball-goers anxiously wondered whether even the ubiquitous "Brown coupés" destined to carry home belated dancers would risk themselves so far a-field. But old Mrs.

Mason Jones and her submissive cousin laughed at such apprehensions, and presently there rose before our astonished eyes a block of pale-greenish limestone houses (almost uglier than the brownstone ones) for the Colford Jones cousins, adjoining which our audacious Aunt Mary, who had known life at the Court of the Tuileries, erected her own white marble residence and a row of smaller dwellings of the same marble to lodge her progeny. The "Jones blocks" were so revolutionary that I doubt whether any subsequent architectural upheavals along that historic thoroughfare have produced a greater impression. In our little provincial town (without electricity, telephones, taxis, or cab-stands) it had seemed inconceivable that houses or habits should ever change; whereas by the time the new millionaires arrived with their palaces in their pockets Fifth Avenue had become cosmopolitan, and was prepared for anything.

IV

The lives led behind the brownstone fronts were, with few exceptions, as monotonous as their architecture. European travel was growing more frequent, though the annual holiday abroad did not become general until I grew up. In the brownstone era, when one crossed the Atlantic it was for a longer stay; and the returned traveler arrived with a train of luggage too often heavy with works of art and "antiques." Our mothers, not always aware of their aesthetic limitations, seldom restricted their purchases to lace and fans; it was almost a point of honor to bring back an "Old Master" or two and a few monsters in the way of modern Venetian furniture. For the traveler of moderate means, who could not soar to Salvator Rosa, Paul Potter, or Carlo Dolci (prime favorites of the day), facsimiles were turned out by the million by the industrious copyists of Florence, Rome, or Amsterdam; and seldom did the well-to-do New Yorker land from a European tour unaccompanied by a Mary Magdalen cloaked in carefully waved hair, or a swarthy group of plumed and gaitered gamblers doing a young innocent out of his last sequin. One of these "awful warnings," a Domenichino, I think, darkened the walls of our dining room, and Mary Magdalen, minutely reproduced on copper, graced the drawing-room table (which was of Louis Philippe *buhl*, with ornate brass heads at the angles).

In our country houses, collections of faïence, in which our mothers also flattered themselves that they were expert, were thought more suitable than pictures. Urbino, Gubbio, and various Italian luster wares, mostly turned out by the industrious Ginori of Florence, abounded in Newport drawing-rooms. I shall never forget my mother's mortification when some ill-advised friend arranged for a newly arrived Italian Minister—Count Corti, I think[5]—to visit her supposed "collection" of "china" (as all forms of porcelain and pottery were then indifferently called). The diplomatist happened to be a collector of some repute, and after one glance at the Ginori output crowding every cabinet and table, he hurriedly draped his surprise in a flow of compliments which did not for a moment deceive my mother. I still burn with the humiliation inflicted by that salutary visit, which had the happy effect of restricting her subsequent purchases to lace, fans, or old silver—about which, incidentally, she also knew a good deal, partly, no doubt, because she and my father had inherited some very good examples of Colonial silver from their respective forebears.

This fine silver and Sheffield plate may have called her attention, earlier than most people's, to the Colonial furniture that could then be had almost for the asking in New England. At all events, our house at Newport was provided, chiefly through old Mr. Vernon, the Newport antiquarian, with a fine lot of highboys and lowboys, and with sets of the graceful Colonial Hepplewhite chairs. It is a pity she did not develop this branch of her collecting mania and turn a deaf ear to the purveyors of sham Fra Angelicos and Guido Renis, who besieged the artless traveler from every shop door of the Lungarno and the Via Babuino. But even great critics go notoriously wrong in judging contemporary art and letters, and there was, as far as I know, only one Lord Hertford to gather up the matchless treasures of French eighteenth-century furniture in the arid days of the Empire.[6]

Most of the little brownstone houses in which the Salvator Rosas and Domenichinos gloomed so incongruously on friendly drawing-room walls still possessed the surviving fragments of "a gentleman's library"—that is, the collection of good books, well written, well printed, well bound, with which the aboriginal New Yorkers had beguiled their long and dimly lit leisure. In a world of little music and no painting, there was time to read; and I grieve to think of the fate of the treasures to be found in the "libraries" of my childhood—which still belonged to gentlemen, though no longer, as a rule, to readers. Where have they gone, I wonder, all those good books, so inevitably scattered in a country without entail or primogeniture? The rarest, no doubt, have long since been captured by dealers and resold, at soaring prices, to the bibliophiles of two continents, and unexpurgated Hogarths splendidly bound in crushed Levant are no longer outspread on the

nursery floor on rainy days, as they used to be for the delectation of my little Rhinelander cousins and myself. (I may add that, though Hogarth was
accessible to infants, *Leaves of Grass*, then just beginning to circulate among
the most advanced intellectuals, was kept under lock and key, and brought
out, like tobacco, only in the absence of "the ladies," to whom the name of
Walt Whitman was unmentionable, if not utterly unknown.)

In our New York house, a full-blown specimen of Second Empire decoration, the creation of the fashionable French upholsterer, Marcotte, the books
were easily accommodated in a small room on the ground floor which my
father used as his study. This room was lined with low bookcases where,
behind glass doors, languished the younger son's meager portion of a fine
old family library. The walls were hung with a handsome wallpaper imitating
the green damask of the curtains, and as the Walter Scott tradition still lingered, and there was felt to be some obscure (perhaps Faustian) relation
between the Middle Ages and culture, this sixteen-foot-square room in a
New York house was furnished with a huge oak mantelpiece sustained by
vizored knights, who repeated themselves at the angles of a monumental
writing table, where I imagine little writing was done except the desperate
calculations over which I seem to see my poor father always bent, in the vain
effort to squeeze my mother's expenditure into his narrowing income.

Luckily, once the unhappy consequences of the Civil War had worn off,
prosperity returned to us, as it did to the greater number of old New
Yorkers. To New York, in especial, it came with a rush; but in the difficult
years between my father must have had many anxious hours. My mother was
far worse than a collector—she was a born "shopper"; and the born shopper
can never resist a bargain if the object is in itself "good value," no matter how
little the purchaser may need it. Perhaps it was for this reason that my
mother's houses were always unfinished and that, for instance, a stately
conservatory, opening out of the billiard-room in our Twenty-third Street
house, remained an empty waste, unheated and flowerless, because the
money gave out with the furnishing of the billiard-room.

V

We had returned when I was ten years old from a long sojourn in Europe,
so that the New York from which I received my most vivid impressions was
only that tiny fraction of a big city which came within the survey of a much
governessed and guarded little girl—hardly less of a little girl when she
"came out" (at seventeen) than when she first arrived on the scene, at ten.

Perhaps the best way of recapturing the atmosphere of my little corner of the metropolis is to try to remember what our principal interests were—I say "our" because, being virtually an only child, since my big brothers had long since gone forth into the world, I shared either directly or indirectly in most of the household goings-on.

My father and mother entertained a great deal and dined out a great deal; but in these diversions I shared only to the extent of hanging over the stair-rail to see the guests sweeping up to our drawing-room or, conversely, my mother sweeping down to her carriage, resplendent in train, aigrette, and opera cloak. But though my parents were much invited, and extremely hospitable, the *tempo* of New York society was so moderate that not infrequently they remained at home in the evening. After-dinner visits were still customary, and on these occasions old family friends would drop in, ceremoniously arrayed in white gloves and white tie, with a tall hat, always carried up to the drawing-room and placed on the floor beside the chair of the caller—who, in due course, was regaled with the ten o'clock cup of tea which followed the heavy repast at seven-thirty. On these occasions the lonely little girl that I was remained in the drawing-room later than her usual bedtime, and the kindly whiskered gentlemen encouraged her to join in the mild talk. It was all very simple and friendly, and the conversation ranged safely from Langdons, Van Rensselaers, and Lydigs to Riveses, Duers, and Schermerhorns, with an occasional allusion to the Opera (which there was some talk of transplanting from the old Academy of Music to a "real" opera House, like Covent Garden or the Scala), or to Mrs. Scott-Siddons's readings from Shakespeare,[7] or Aunt Mary Jones's evening receptions, or my uncle Fred Rhinelander's ambitious dream of a Museum of Art in the Central Park, or cousin John King's difficulty in housing in the exiguous quarters of the New York Historical Society a rather burdensome collection of pictures bequeathed to it by an eccentric young man whose family one did not wish to offend—a collection which Berenson,[8] visiting it many years later, found to be replete with treasures, both French and Italian.

But the events in which I took an active part were going to church—and going to the theater. I venture to group them together because, looking back across the blurred expanse of a long life, I see them standing up side by side, like summits catching the light when all else is in shadow. Going to church on Sunday mornings was, I fear, no more than an unescapable family duty; but in the afternoon my father and I used to return alone together to the second service. Calvary Church, at the corner of Gramercy Park, was our parish church, and probably even in that day of hideous religious edifices, few less aesthetically pleasing could have been found. The service was "low," the music indifferent, and the fuliginous chancel window of the Crucifixion a horror to alienate any imaginative mind from all Episcopal forms of ritual; but the Rector, the Reverend Dr. Washburn, was a man of great learning, and possessed of a singularly beautiful voice—and I fear it was chiefly to hear Dr. Washburn read the Evening Lessons that my father and I were so regular in our devotions. Certainly it is to Dr. Washburn that I owe the discovery of the matchless beauty of English seventeenth-century prose; and the organ-roll of Isaiah, Job, and above all, of the lament of David over the dead Absalom, always come back to me in the accents of that voice, of which I can only say that it was worthy to interpret the English Bible.

The other great emotion of my childhood was connected with the theater. Not that I was, even at a tender age, an indiscriminate theater-lover. On the contrary, something in me has always resisted the influence of crowds and shows, and I have hardly ever been able to yield myself unreservedly to a spectacle shared with a throng of people. But my distrust of theatrical representation goes deeper than that. I am involuntarily hyper-critical of any impersonation of characters already so intensely visible to my imagination that anyone else's conception of them interferes with that inward vision. And this applies not only to plays already familiar to me by reading, but to any stage representation—for, five minutes after I have watched the actors in a new play, I have formed an inner picture of what they ought to look like and speak like, and as I once said, in my rash youth, to someone who had asked me if I enjoyed the theater: "Well, I always want to get up on the stage and show them how they ought to act"—a reply naturally interpreted as a proof of intolerable self-assurance.

However, in spite of my inability to immerse myself in the play, I *did* enjoy the theater in my childhood, partly because it was something new, a window opening on the foam of faëryland (or at least I always hoped to see faëryland through that window), and partly, I still believe, because most of the acting I saw in those early days in New York was really much better than any I have seen since. The principal theaters were, in fact, still in possession of good English companies, of whom the elders had played together for years, and preserved and handed on the great tradition of well-trained repertory companies, versus the evil "star" system which was so soon to crowd them out of business.

At Wallack's Theatre, still ruled by the deeply dyed and undoubtedly absurd Lester Wallack, there were such first-rate actors as old Mrs. Ponisi,

Beckett, Harry Montague, and Ada Dyas;[9] and when they deserted the classic repertory (Sheridan, Goldsmith, etc.) for the current drama, the average play they gave was about as good as the same type of play now acted by one or more out-of-focus stars with a fringe of obscure satellites.

But our most exciting evenings came when what the Germans call "guest-players" arrived from London, Berlin, or Rome with good repertory companies. Theater-going, for me, was in fact largely a matter of *listening to voices*, and never shall I forget the rapture of first hearing

> And gentlemen in England now abed
> Shall think themselves accursed they were not here,

in George Rignold's vibrant barytone, when he brought Henry V to New York.[10]

Again and again my father took me to see (or, I might better say, to *hear*) Rignold in Henry V; and it is through listening to him that I discovered the inexhaustible flexibility, the endless metrical resources, of English blank verse. To hear the great Agincourt speech, where the clarion call of mighty names—

> Harry the King, Bedford and Exeter,
> Warwick and Talbot, Salisbury and Gloucester,

is succeeded by the impetuous sweep of

> Be in their flowing cups freshly remembered,

and that in turn by the low still music of

> We few, we happy few, we band of brothers—

was to be initiated once for all into some of the divinest possibilities of English prosody.

Since those far-off days I have never heard of George Rignold (who was, I think, a Colonial), and have no reason to suppose that he ever made a name for himself on the London stage;[11] but I am sure he was a great interpreter of English verse, and in that play—the only one I ever saw him in—a great actor.

Only once, on another, later, occasion, did the theater of my childhood give me an emotional experience of such rare quality; and that was when a "*Gastspielerin*" from some distinguished German company appeared at the

Amberg Theatre in "Iphigenie auf Tauris," and I heard Iphigenia's opening speech

Heraus in eure Schatten, rege Wipflen[12]

spoken with the awed simplicity of a priestess addressing the divinity she served. When, by contrast, I remember the exasperation and disgust with which I assisted at the Salzburg production of "Faust" for the million,[13] I can only conclude that the nineteenth century, in spite of its supposed short-comings, knew more about interpreting poetry than we do.

In the way of other spectacles New York did not as yet provide much. There was in fact only the old Academy of Music, where Campanini, in his prime, warbled to an audience still innocently following the eighteenth-century tradition that the Opera was a social occasion, invented to stimulate conversation;[14] but my recollection of those performances is not clear, for, by the time I was judged old enough to be taken to them, the new Opera House was inaugurated, and with it came Wagner, and with Wagner a cultivated and highly musical German audience in the stalls, which made short work of the chatter in the boxes. I well remember the astonishment with which we learned that it was "bad form" to talk during the acts, and the almost immediate compliance of the box-audience with this new rule of politeness, which thereafter was broken only by two or three thick-skinned new-comers in the social world.

Apart from the Opera, the only popular entertainments I can recall were Barnum's three-ring circus (a sort of modern ocean liner before the letter)—and Moody and Sankey's revivalist meetings.[15] I group the two in no spirit of disrespect to the latter, but because both were new and sensational, and both took place in the old Madison Square Garden, at that time New York's only large auditorium, where prize fights and circuses placidly alternated with religious revivals, without any sign of public disapproval. But I must add that, sincere as no doubt the protagonists were, there was a theatrical element in their call to religion which, in those pre-Eddyan days, deeply offended the taste of many people; and certainly, among the throngs frequenting their meetings many avowedly went for the sake of Sankey's singing rather than of his companion's familiar chats with the Almighty. Though America has always been the chosen field of sensational religious performances, the New York of my childhood was still averse to any sort of pious exhibitionism; but as I was never allowed to assist at the Moody and Sankey meetings, my impression of them is gathered entirely from the comments of my father's friends, from whom I fear Saint Francis of Assisi and Savonarola would have received small encouragement. My mother, at any rate, gave none to the revivalists; and my father and I had to content ourselves with the decorous beauty of Evening Prayer at Calvary Church.

From all this it will be seen that the New York of those days was a place in which external events were few and unexciting, and little girls had mostly to

> be happy and building at home.

"Yet" (as Stevenson's poem continues)

> Yet as I saw it, I see it again,
> The kirk and the palace, the ships and the men,
> And as long as I live, and where'er I may be,
> I'll always remember my town by the sea—[16]

a town full indeed for me of palaces and ships, though the palaces came out of the "Tempest," "Endymion," and "Kubla Khan," and the ships were anchored on the schoolroom floor, ready to spread their dream-sails to all the winds of my imagination.

Harper's Magazine, March 1938

[1] Early in the last year of her life, Wharton had her secretary inform Eric S. Pinker—son of the famous literary agent James B. Pinker, and Rutger Jewett's successor as her representative—that she "has in contemplation an article called 'A Little Girl's New York'" (EW to Eric S. Pinker, 9 February 1937 [Yale]). Initially, it seems, she thought of the article as the first part of a larger project; having already begun to make arrangements for a sequel to *A Backward Glance*, tentatively entitled "Further Memories," Wharton's publisher assured her, shortly after she had written to Pinker, "We shall be honored to publish this volume when you have the manuscript ready for us" (John L. B. Williams to EW, 19 February 1937 [Yale]). Within a few weeks, Wharton finished "A Little Girl's New York," which Pinker accepted with enthusiasm but found unexpectedly difficult to place, confessing to its author in early May that the article had been rejected by *Cosmopolitan* and was under consideration at *Woman's Home Companion*, where it also failed to appear. By then, in any case, Wharton had abandoned her plan for "a second volume of Reminiscences," having "come to the conclusion," as her secretary notified Appleton, "that she has not enough material left to make this volume, and she will therefore publish an article summing up some of the aspects of Old New York which she omitted in 'A Backward Glance'" (EW to Williams, 17 March 1937 [Yale]). It is perhaps a sign of how badly her reputation had faded by that time that such an evocative and colorful essay, expatiating on the stage of her life covered in the earlier chapters of her memoirs, should have had to wait until several months after Wharton's death before finding a home in *Harper's Magazine*, which published "A Little Girl's New York" early in 1938.

[2] Tennyson's sequence of narrative poems, of which all but one had appeared by 1872.

[3] Celebrated 1852 play of Alexandre Dumas *fils* (1824–95).

[4] Principal work of Owen Jones (1809–74), English architect and ornamental designer, whose book considerably influenced the design of mid- and late-Victorian English wallpaper, carpets, and furniture.

[5] Count Luigi Corti (1823–88), Italian diplomat, foreign minister at the time of the Congress of Berlin, had been appointed ambassador to Washington in 1870.

[6] Richard Seymour Conway, fourth marquis of Hertford (1800–1870), whose private collection of paintings and furniture helped form the basis of the Wallace Collection in London.

[7] Mary Frances Scott-Siddons (1844–96), English-Indian actress, offered various readings in January 1876 at Steinway Hall and the Brooklyn Academy of Music, and then again in Brooklyn three years later.

[8] I.e., Wharton's close friend Bernard Berenson (1865–1959), the art historian and critic; her anecdote recalls the *donnée* of "False Dawn" from *Old New York* (1924).

[9] Lester Wallack (1820–88), nephew of James William Wallack the elder (1795?–1864) and the only member of the Wallack family born in the United States, had stage-managed for his father at the Wallack's Lyceum before becoming manager and principal star, until 1882, of the second Wallack's Theatre, which opened in 1861 in the theatre district then forming around Union Square and became one of the leading theatres in the country. Its major performers included Madame Ponisi, born Elizabeth Hanson (1818–99), an English actress who was long remembered for playing "first old women" roles in the stock company at Wallack's in the 1870s and 1880s; Harry Beckett (1839–80), known at Wallack's as its leading "low comedy" actor; Henry James Montague, born Mann (1843–78), an English actor whose debut at Wallack's in 1874 followed a successful London career and who became a matinee idol of the company; and Ada Dyas (1843–1908), the leading actress at Wallack's from 1874 to 1876.

[10] George Rignold (1838–1912) succeeded Charles Calvert in a famous production of Shakespeare's *Henry V* imported from the Theatre Royal of Manchester, scoring a success more, it appears, on the basis of his good looks than of his gifts as an actor. The spectacular revival ran triumphantly at Booth's Theatre in New York from 8 February through 24 April 1875 and returned the following season. Coincidentally, Henry James reviewed in the *Nation* not only this production but Rignold's later performance in *Macbeth*; see *The Scenic Art: Notes on Acting and the Drama, 1872–1901*, ed. Allan Wade, rpt. (New York: Hill & Wang, 1957), 26–27.

[11] Rignold had in fact already appeared in London in 1870 at the Queen's Theatre, Long Acre; in 1880, he would settle in Australia, where he managed Her Majesty's Theatre in Sydney from 1886 through 1895, mounting numerous Shakespearean productions.

[12] "Out here in your shadows, stirring tree-tops"; opening line of Goethe's blank-verse drama *Iphigenie auf Tauris* (1786).

[13] Max Reinhardt's spectacular open-air production, which would remain the most celebrated twentieth-century staging of Goethe's *Faust*, opened on 17 August 1933 at the Felsenreitschule in Salzburg, where Wharton traveled several days later to attend the music festival, describing the production to Gaillard Lapsley as "fit for a public abruti [stupefied] by cinema" (*L*, 567).

[14] Italo Campanini (1845–96), Italian tenor; he appeared as Radames in a production of Verdi's *Aida* at the New York Academy of Music on 26 November 1873 and in the role of Don José in the first New York performance of Bizet's *Carmen*, also at the Academy of Music, on 23 October 1878.

[15] Evangelist Dwight L. Moody (1837–99) and his music director, Ira D. Sankey (1840–1908), spear-headed the new wave of American religious revivalism of the 1870s and 1880s.

[16] From "Block City" (ll. 4, 21–24), in *A Child's Garden of Verses* (1885), by Robert Louis Stevenson (1850–94).

APPENDIX A

AN UNREPRINTED PARODY: "MORE LOVE-LETTERS OF AN ENGLISHWOMAN"

This brief item is a rare exercise in parodic writing on Wharton's part. A year earlier, she had composed, without publishing, "An Open or Shut Question," a rather labored pastiche of James's later style (Lewis 125–26). The following *jeu d'esprit*, which accompanied Frederic Taber Cooper's review of the anonymously written *An English Woman's Love-Letters*, is lighter and more successful, although its narrator is essentially a caricature of the sort of ostentatiously bookish woman later typically burlesqued in Wharton's fiction.

More Love-Letters of an Englishwoman

I

Ownest —— When I woke this morning my windows were covered with a thick, white frost, my bath-tub was an improvised skating-pond, and the mercury in the thermometer outside had forced a hole through the bulb at the base of the tube and disappeared. I was just dangling one timorous creamy magnolia-white foot over the edge of the bed, into the icy crackling void of circumambient cold, when the door opened and Juggins (that house-maid, Belovèd, is already pensioned against senility!)—Juggins brought me Your Letter—.

My Veriest—my Mortgage on Blessedness (as George Meredith might say—you *must* try to read him, Love!)—have you ever seen the sunrise steal suddenly with swift, amorous leaps from one ice-blue snow-peak to another? Have you seen the virgin bosom of the Alps flush beneath the hot, passionate kiss of Phoebus? (Don't be alarmed at my learning, dear! He's only the Norse Sun-god; you'll find him in the Vedda.) Well—*I* have, Sweet—(Aunty took me up the Rhigi once)—and just so the warmth and heat from your letter spread through my icy virginal room, like a forest fire devastating some primeval wilderness with the pent-up fury of a wild beast rending its defenceless prey. (Don't try to make out my metaphors, Darling; at least not till you've practised a little on Meredith first.) Ownest, think of it! Five hours had elapsed since I had heard from you. Letter No. 3659 had been delivered to me at midnight, as I stole up to bed through the silent house, with the glint of the moonlight shimmering ghost-like on the worn oaken stairs that your dear feet have caressed so often! (You've heard of the Scala Santa at Rome, my Demigod—the Sacred Stairs? Well, these are *my* sacred stairs— my heart goes up them on its knees to you, Ownest!) Midnight—think of it! And between then and breakfast, *no news of you* . . . and I still live! Oh, the endurance of the human heart! The bloodless inhumanity of our postal system!

II

Mine exclusively! Yesterday, in your absence, I called on your mother. She sent word that she had a headache, and begged to be excused, but I was firm. —Love, it is as I anticipated: she is an ignorant and arrogant old woman. But don't be afraid of my telling her so! To what depths of dissimulation would not love make me descend? I shall conceal my feelings; I shall influence her only by example. I could see that she was struck by my gown—the one I copied from Elaine's, in the *Idylls of the King*. (Tennyson, dear: I mean to read him to you next summer!) One can see that your mother has not had many artistic advantages; the drawing-room curtains are *too awful*; and sooner or later that bed of red geraniums by the front door will *have to go*. I made no allusion to the curtains beyond saying that I could not live in a room with aniline colours; for your sake, Darling, I was patient and forbear-ing. . . . Dearest! My one desire is to judge her leniently; but I happened to mention Meredith in the course of our talk, and her comments were so painfully wide of the mark that I thought it kinder to change the subject. It was not till just as I was leaving that I found out she thought I was referring to the late Lord Lytton![1]. . . Belovèd, that explains so much. . . .

P.S. You left your goloshes here yesterday, and—shall I tell you? Yes! I've kissed a little hole in one of them already!

III

Circumference of my Globe! This town is Pisa. Surely my Heart's Life does not need to be told that it is in Italy—not if he has read up the passages I marked in Baedeker before leaving? —Dear, since I have seen your mother

I realise how hard it must be for the love of the Beautiful to thrive in such an atmosphere—but surely you must have heard of the Leaning Tower of Pisa? Love, it is a melody in marble! O, how I pitied those of our party who were too ignorant and unimaginative to be thrilled by such a revelation! Don't laugh at me, Darling, and call me eccentric, original, romantic—but when Uncle asked me yesterday what I should like for a birthday present, I flung my arms about his neck and whispered—one of those little *Leaning Towers* in alabaster! Belovèd, I can never be thankful enough for having been born with an artistic nature. . . .

Bookman, February 1901

[1] Edward Robert Bulwer, first earl of Lytton (1831–91), statesman and poet who wrote under the pseudonym "Owen Meredith," and son of the novelist Edward Bulwer-Lytton. A line from his poem "Lucille" had provided the epigraph and title of Wharton's adolescent novelette, *Fast and Loose* (*BG*, 75).

APPENDIX B
AN UNPUBLISHED ESSAY:
"FICTION AND CRITICISM"

Both the Edith Wharton Collection at the Beinecke Rare Book and Manuscript Library, Yale University, and the collection of Wharton manuscripts at the Lilly Library, Indiana University, contain a number of unpublished essays, all of them relatively brief and most in various states of incompletion. Much of this fascinating material began to be put to use in Wharton scholarship as early as the pioneering studies of Black Nevius and Millicent Bell. Many of them contain echoes of insights and arguments reformulated elsewhere in Wharton's writing. For example, two undated fragments, each carrying the title "Adventures with Books" (Yale), one of them clearly drafted after the war, anticipate her recollections, in *A Backward Glance*, of her father's library and her own youthful reading. A somewhat fuller manuscript, "Italy Again" (Yale), introduces the distinction later developed—again in Wharton's memoirs—between the "cultivated amateur" (Pater, Symonds, and Vernon Lee) and the "trained specialist," reexamining the impact and relative value of each in the understanding of Italy and art. The fragmentary manuscript "Literary Tendencies" (Indiana) rehearses Wharton's later account of her first encounter with Harry Cust, editor of the *Pall Mall Gazette*, and of the dinner-table conversation in which they discussed "the most famous kisses in literature" (*BG*, 219), including additional examples like "the reluctant kiss that Julien Sorel forces himself to lay on Mme de Regnal's hand in the garden, as he sits beside her in the darkness" in *Le rouge et le noir*, while also parenthetically offering one reason why Henry James famously disliked Stendhal's novel ("Curious that H. James was almost insensible to the wonders of that great novel because he didn't believe that a callous arriviste like J.S. could really exist, and thought that, if he did, he was not worth writing a book about—this point defendable!"). The fragment contains also a brief and remarkable reminiscence of Yeats: "How I liked him on the one occasion we met! . . . I longed to talk to him about poetry, & his in particular, but he was all befogged with 'spiritualism,' and an astounding (!) medium who, as I remember it, when he (Yeats) thought of Goethe, had instantly quoted the 'ewig Weibliche—.' . . . "

From its title one guesses that "My Books—Literary Essays" (Indiana) was meant to begin a series. There survives only a typescript of the first section, entitled "I. Reading"; reflecting the conservatism of Wharton's tastes, it appears to belong to the same period as an article like "Permanent Values in Fiction." Also unfinished in manuscript, "Olifant" (Yale), a celebration of verse, explores "what I mean by the call of the Olifant," defined as a certain instant of epiphanic recognition: "When the lover of poetry, in one of the idle & delicious moments of estimation & comparison, has turned over all his heaped-up treasures, letting one after another drop into the golden cup of remembrance, he will catch, as certain of the jewels fall, a quite singular note, faint & quick as the whir of an insect's wing. . . . These mysterious collocations of syllables, lying so often outside of our considered choice of *the best*, yet so much closer to the heart, exert their spell through a double appeal to ear & memory." Even more intriguing are the outline and notes, carefully examined by scholars like Nancy Leach and Susan Goodman, on which Wharton planned to base her neverwritten essay on Whitman (Yale).

Among Wharton's papers at Yale, portions of two manuscripts are grouped under the same title as a typescript named "Fiction and Criticism"; across the top of the first page of the typescript, in Gaillard Lapsley's hand, is the observation, "3 disconnected fragments—they might be printed as such since they all deal with the same subject, but they would need a good deal of editing." Those in manuscript, however, appear to have belonged to different unfinished essays. One of them, referring to Leslie Stephen's "recent book on George Eliot" (and thus dating from 1902 or shortly thereafter), offers Wharton's fullest remarks on the historical novel, most of them quoted in Janet Goodwyn's recent study, and also looks ahead to "Visibility in Fiction" in its emphasis on "the visualizing power" of the novelist. The other fragment advances, while also enlarging upon, the comparison between French and Anglo-American literary criticism that underlies Wharton's powerful argument in "The Criticism of Fiction" (1914), and thus presumably belongs to a later date. On the other hand, the typewritten essay appears to be free-standing and addresses issues that do not figure in either of the manuscripts with which it is filed at Yale. Since it concludes with the intention of "citing a few well-known instances of novels" that serve her argument, followed by remarks on *Henry Esmond* as "the first example which presents itself," Wharton surely intended to offer additional illustrations. Even in its incomplete form, however, substantial excerpts from the essay have been quoted in recent studies like those of Goodwyn, Penelope Vita-Finzi, and Carol J. Singley. As Wharton's fullest treatment of the competing claims of the "moral" and the "aesthetic" in the writing and analysis of fiction, and as a sample of her unpublished critical prose, the undated typescript of "Fiction and Criticism," incorporating corrections Wharton inserted by hand, is printed here in its entirety for the first time.

Fiction and Criticism

Fashions in criticism change almost as rapidly as fashions in dress. Not many years ago the reviewers were disposed to think any novel great if it was depressing; now they insist that no novel which is depressing can be great.

The latter contention is in one sense true; for to the thoughtful reader no good piece of literary art can be depressing. This, however, is not the sense in which the reviewer wishes to be understood. A few years since, a writer in a well-known literary review thus naïvely summed up the popular theory of the art of fiction: "The truth about fiction just now is that it must be cheerful in order to be good. . . . Whatever else current fiction may contain, if it does not furnish sustenance, sunshine, comfort for the leisure hours of the middle-aged reader, it has failed in its elementary duty." Condensing the writer's "sustenance, sunshine, comfort" into the one word "happiness," one arrives at the formula of the average English and American critic. —"Fiction, to be good, must make the reader happy."

If the literary critic were forced to define his terms with the precision required of the scientific writer, this formula would have found less general acceptance, since its whole value obviously depends on the sense in which "happiness" is used. Unless the term be intended to represent the aesthetic emotion excited by a master-piece—be it Macbeth or the Decameron, Pickwick or Henry Esmond—the quality of exciting "happiness" can no more be required of a novel than of a Chinese porcelain. If the happiness demanded by the critic be a moral emotion, equivalent to that which we are supposed to feel in performing an unselfish action or witnessing a scene of innocent enjoyment, then it has no more to do with literature than with pottery.

It does not follow that great fiction should not communicate a moral emotion. Since fiction (to narrow Arnold's apothegm) is "a criticism of life,"[1] it must always, in proportion to its value, excite such an emotion; but that emotion, whether joyous or painful, must equally confer an aesthetic pleasure on the reader. This aesthetic pleasure is, in fact, quite independent of the incidental tendency of the work: Manon Lescaut should make the reader as "happy" as Lorna Doone.[2] The ultimate value of every work of art lies, not in its subject, but in the way in which that subject is seen, felt and interpreted. The writer's temperament, his point of view, his faculty for penetrating below the surface of his fable to the "inherences" which relate it to life as a whole: these are the determining factors in the creation of a work of art. It is needless to say that the imaginative writer will instinctively select a subject suited to his talent, depicting life from the point of view which best enables him to focus it; but whatever his subject, he will extract from it the elements of beauty, will show the microcosm in the atom. The only really "depressing" book, nay, the only really immoral book, is that in which the writer has not felt keenly enough the relation of the little fraction of life he represents to the eternal truths, to bring his subject into relation with the latter.

The immoral writer is, in other words, the writer who lacks imagination. Some of the greatest novelists have been, not immoral but *amoral*. Balzac, for instance, with all his vast psychological insight, was lacking in the subtler ethical perceptions, to the occasional detriment of his character-drawing: some of his models of virtue give utterance to sentiments a good deal more startling than the elucubrations of his villains. In Beyle [i.e., Stendhal, the French novelist Henri Beyle], even the primary "other-regarding" instincts were lacking: he was distinctly anti-social; yet both these writers by force of imagination, and by their magical divination of human motive, produced, in books like Le Père Goriot and Le Rouge et le Noir, studies of life so penetrating as to be profoundly moral.

There are only two classes of really immoral writers of fiction: those who write with the deliberate purpose of furnishing the locked book-case, and who are therefore negligible in a general survey of the subject; and those who though ambitious of describing life as it is, are not only restricted by narrow vision and defective imagination from seeing their subject "in the round," but are even unable to focus properly the objects within their limited field of vision—to "see life steadily and see it whole."[3] Unfortunately these are the writers who are least likely to be conscious of their limitations, and who therefore most often attempt subjects beyond their imaginative scope. In this way, they make for immorality, since they see the evil without its compensating readjustments, the bare incident without its complex antecedents.

The doctrine of "art for art's sake," of the fixed gulf between art and ethics, which was enunciated with so much confidence some thirty years ago, and is still a terror to the simple-minded critic, was merely a reaction against the tendency to sacrifice character-drawing to a thesis. It cannot be too often repeated that every serious picture of life contains a thesis; what differentiates the literary artist from the professed moralist is not a radical contradiction of purpose, but the fact that the one instructs by his observation of character, the other by the general deductions drawn from such observation. It must be remembered that, far as its roots strike back, the novel as it is now known is still a very recent form of art; and innovators are bound to be more or less explicit. It is therefore natural enough, that except in the case of a few astonishingly modern books, like Adolphe and Manon Lescaut, almost all the earlier novelists felt bound to interfere personally in the course of their narrative. As the reader grew more expert, he began to resent these asides and interruptions, and to demand that he should be allowed to draw his own conclusions from the facts presented. At length someone formulated this wish in the famous dictum of the impassivity of the artist, and such conviction did it carry with it, that Guy de Maupassant, in his interesting study of Flaubert, did not see the incongruity of declaring that "that impeccable artist should be called, not merely impersonal, but impassive," and that it was "an article of faith" with Flaubert that "every action, whether good or bad, is of interest to the author only as copy, without regard to its moral significance."[4]

The fallacy of this statement (which is peculiarly inappropriate when applied to Flaubert), is so self-evident that one is not surprised to find Maupassant, a few lines farther on, invalidating his position by the qualifying admission that, "if a book teaches a lesson, it must be in spite of its author, by *the mere force of the facts he narrates.*"

This is an excellent definition of a good novel. The novelist ceases to be an artist the moment he bends his characters to the exigencies of a thesis; but he would equally cease to be one, should he draw the acts he describes without regard to their moral significance. Maupassant, who understood the nature of Flaubert's art, though he was misled in the formula he deduced from it, goes on to say that the latter, though he attached considerable importance to the qualities of observation and analysis, "was still more concerned with the question of composition and style. By *composition,*" the writer continues, "he means that arduous effort which results in extracting their essence from the successive actions of a life-time, in selecting only the most characteristic traits, and grouping them in such fashion that they combine in the most perfect manner to produce the desired effects"; and Flaubert himself completes this exposition of a supposed "impersonal" method, by his statement that "there is nothing real but the relations of things, that is to say, *the connection in which we perceive them.*"[5]

In this phrase, which confesses the predominance of the personal equation, he has supplied the touchstone of good fiction.

It is not so much a sense of the smallness of man as of the vastness about him. The "realist" is never ironical; he is in deadly earnest; for it is impossible to be ironical without having a sense of the infinitudes. The chronicler of small beer, who thinks that drink the only brew, and has never suspected that, high overhead, the gods are quaffing nectar from cups of gold—that a story is of value in proportion to the quality of the author's perceptions (given, of course, the power of putting them into artistic shape). This truth seems obvious enough; yet it is the criterion by which the value of fiction is least often tried.

The sense of humour is the sense of proportion; and irony is the sense of humour *taken* from a higher point of survey—the "smile of the universe."[6]

To sum up, then: the immoral (or at least the harmful) novelist is he who handles a sombre or complex subject without sufficient power to vivify its raw material. "All the splendours and satisfactions of life, reflected in the dull consciousness of   , are as nothing compared to the   of Cervantes, writing Don Quixote in a cramped prison-cell."[7] This phrase of Schopenhauer's is the key to the inadequacy of so many would-be studies of life. In Middlemarch, when Dorothea, investing Doctor Casaubon with her own generous illusions, declares that he looks as she imagines Locke to have looked, Celia wonders drily "Whether Locke had a white mole   "; to which Dorothea makes the magnificent answer: "No doubt, when some people looked at him."[8] Dumas fils, in his preface to Manon Lescaut, has formulated the same theory: "Un chef-d'oeuvre n'est jamais dangereux, et toujours utile; le tout, c'est de savoir le lire."[9]

If it be objected that this is to view fiction from the critical or professional stand-point, and that the action of the tale is what, after all, the average reader bases his judgment on, the objection may best be answered by citing a few well-known instances of novels admittedly popular with the class of readers and reviewers most vehemently opposed to what they call depressing fiction.

Henry Esmond is the first example which presents itself. Judged by its story alone, it might be classed as one of the most depressing works in English fiction. Esmond sacrifices his aims and ambitions to benefit a group of trivial and ungrateful persons, whose use of their opportunities certainly cannot compensate him for the power he has renounced; and at the close of his lonely and disappointed youth, he marries an unloved woman who, besides being much older than himself, is actually the mother of the only woman he has ever loved! Setting aside the "equivocal" aspect of this situation (which would have been loudly enough denounced, had it been found in Balzac or Flaubert), it is evident that this is not the way in which, according to the modern reviewer, a hero of fiction should be left on the last page. In a novel written on conventional lines, the only "sad ending" permissible in such a case, would have been to leave Esmond unmarried and mourning for his lost love. Thackeray, however, being great enough to draw man as he is, with all his inconsistencies, his compromises, and the gradual blunting of his sensibilities, chose for his hero the infinitely more tragic dénouement of a loveless marriage with a narrow, jealous, faded and exacting woman.

This is the bare fable; but what is the book itself? By virtue of Thackeray's large vision and penetrating insight, of his realization of the truth that "even our failures are a prophecy," the impression left, if sad, is not mean, and the close of the story has the cold serenity of a winter sunset.

[1] Defined by Matthew Arnold as "[t]he end and aim of all literature" in "Joubert," from the first series of his *Essays in Criticism* (1865).

[2] *Histoire du chevalier des Grieux et de Manon Lescaut* (1731), novel by Antoine-François, abbé Prevost (1697–1763); *Lorna Doone* (1869), novel by Richard Doddridge Blackmore (1825–1900).

[3] Famous phrase of Matthew Arnold's sonnet "To a Friend" (1853), regarding Sophocles, "Who saw life steadily, and saw it whole" (l. 12).

[4] Maupassant's "Etude sur Gustave Flaubert" was published in 1885 as the preface to *Bouvard et Pécuchet*, in volume 7 of the Quentin edition of Flaubert's complete works.

[5] "Il n'y a de vrai que les 'rapports,' c'est-à-dire la façon dont nous percevons les objets" (Flaubert to Maupassant, 15 August 1878; EW's emphasis).

[6] Dante, *Paradiso*, canto 27, ll. 4–5.

[7] 'From the "Aphorismen zur Lebensweisheit," in volume 1 of *Parerga und Paralipomena* (1851), by Arthur Schopenhauer (1788–1860), German philosopher. In the spaces left blank in the typescript Wharton presumably meant to fill in the missing words "simpletons [Tropfs]" and "consciousness [Bewusstsein]."

[8] Again Wharton left incomplete (and uncorrected) her quotation of the passage from George Eliot's novel in which Celia asks her sister, "Had Locke those two white moles with hairs on them?" and Dorothea responds, "Oh, I daresay! when people of a certain sort looked at him." Elsewhere Wharton cites the same passage in discussing the structural aspects of the novel as a form (*WF*, 94–95).

[9] "A masterpiece is never dangerous, and always useful; what is most important is to know how to read it"; from the French dramatist's preface to an 1875 edition of *Manon Lescaut*.

APPENDIX C

"THE ART OF HENRY JAMES"

BY W. MORTON FULLERTON

"The Art of Henry James" originated in a lecture that William Morton Fullerton (1865–1952), American journalist and critic, delivered at Bryn Mawr in the fall of 1907, not long after the famous New York Edition of James's works had begun to appear. Native of Massachusetts, Harvard graduate, staff member of the London *Times*, and its Paris correspondent for around fifteen years, Fullerton seems to have met Edith Wharton in Paris the previous spring, having been instrumental in expediting the serialization of the French translation of *The House of Mirth*. Back home at the Mount by summer of 1907, Wharton learned from James himself (who had known him since the early 1890s), "Fullerton goes to the U. S. for a few weeks, & I am writing him to let you know where he is" (Powers 74). Thus prompted by the very subject of the lecture he planned to give, Fullerton obediently made arrangements to call at the Mount, for Wharton wrote by the middle of October to assure him, "We shall be delighted to see you here when you have pronounced your discours at Bryn Mawr (& do please bring me a copy of it, won't you?)," concluding her letter with the remark, "I am so glad you are going to talk about dear James at Bryn Mawr" (*L*, 116). Fullerton had returned to the United States primarily in order to visit his family in Massachusetts; and the engagement to lecture on James doubtless had something to do with the fact that one of the readers in English at Bryn Mawr happened to be Katherine Fullerton, who had been raised as his sister but had learned only a few years earlier that they were in fact cousins and not siblings. The revelation had already liberated, in both of them, certain feelings that emerged more openly than ever during his visit, and Fullerton left Bryn Mawr practically affianced to his cousin. Yet despite their understanding (and the chronic importunities of at least two other women in his life), it was his visit to the Mount a couple weeks later that quickly led to the extramarital affair that would remain one of the pivotal experiences of Wharton's life.

Enthusiastically celebrating the work of a treasured mutual friend, Fullerton's lecture would have provided an obviously convenient basis on which to rekindle their acquaintance, and "among the innumerable things he and Edith discussed" during his visit, according to Lewis, "was an essay he was completing on Henry James's fiction" (183). In fact, it would not be completed (at least in the form in which it was finally published) for another two and a half years, and his protracted, much-delayed efforts may be said to have accompanied the development of Fullerton's intimacy with Wharton, who took a correspondingly vital interest in the essay. As early as January 1908, while back in Paris, she wrote to her editor at *Scribner's Magazine*, Edward Burlingame, "I am trying to get Mr. Morton Fullerton to finish & send you an admirable article on Henry James which he has been writing, because I thought it would come out in the magazine so opportunely just now. He says just what I have always been wanting to say about the great man. —If the idea 'vous va' I will try once more to get him to give the last touches" (*L*, 127). She was somewhat more candid about the amount of work that remained to be done when she appealed also to her other literary advisor at Scribner's, William C. Brownell, a couple of weeks later, in support of "a very original article on Henry James which Mr. Morton Fullerton has written—or rather half-written. I am sure he would finish it at once if he thought the magazine would take it, but his 'Times' work absorbs him so much that it is hard for him to give any time to literary tasks unless there is a definite prospect of publication.... I am not sure, by the way, if I wrote this before to Mr. Scribner, or to Mr. Burlingame; but I venture to repeat it because I think the thing so 'worthwhile,' & because I see that Mr. Fullerton is so unlikely to finish it unless he is asked to" (EW to Brownell, 12 February 1908 [Princeton]). It was far enough along, even so, to allow Wharton to add, "The article has struck me very much, & I thought it might come à propos just now, coinciding with the appearance of the 'definitive' ... I want very much to have a ringing word said for H.J. just now, & I think this would attract a great deal of attention" (qtd. in Bell 271). Still persisting, and giving an initial idea of the extent to which she had not only prodded but also assisted Fullerton's efforts, she soon wrote again, "I am hoping to hear soon from Mr. Burlingame that he wants Mr. Morton Fullerton's article on James for the magazine, for I have taken a small fraction of a hand in it myself, & I want so much to have it published, just now when such stupid things are being written & said about the 'definitive' edition, & especially about the wonderful prefaces" (EW to Brownell, 2 March 1908 [Princeton]). The essay must have been submitted to *Scribner's* in some form soon thereafter, for Wharton intervened once again, writing to Burlingame near the end of March, "I have had a hand—or at least a small finger—in the article, & I think it's good. (Admire my modesty!) I *long* so to have someone speak intelligently & resolutely for James" (qtd. in Bell 272).

Evidently rejected by *Scribner's*, despite such strong and repeated endorsements, Fullerton's piece doubtless underwent further revision and polishing, and probably circulated further, before it was finally published, as a review of the New York Edition (signed "Morton Fullerton"), by James's old friend George Prothero in the spring of 1910 in the *Quarterly Review*—the very journal in which Wharton's own authoritative and substantial consideration of the same subject, her review of the James letters, would appear a decade later. By 1910, however, the New York Edition had already miserably failed, thereby depriving Fullerton's essay of much of its purpose. By that time, also, his affair with Wharton had greatly waned and seems to have essentially ended shortly thereafter; in the meantime, his cousin, increasingly distraught at Fullerton's vacillations and remoteness, had broken off their engagement in order to accept, in February 1910, a marriage proposal from Gordon Gerould, an English instructor at Princeton. Delivered as a lecture on the very trip during which he expressed his love to his cousin while starting to become adulterously involved with Wharton, and published at a time when both relationships were ending, the origin and the completion of Fullerton's essay on James thus frame a remarkably complex and debilitating episode in three briefly but tumultuously intersecting lives.

What James himself honestly thought of the essay is hard to make out. Only a couple of months after Fullerton's appearance at Bryn Mawr, he wrote to Katherine (later an estimable writer and critic herself), "Your report of the wondrous address showed a high benevolence as well as an unmistakeable wit," while mentioning that Fullerton had in fact met with him en route back to Paris and given James "a reading of his brilliant but delirious paper. It contains some admirable things & an admirable generosity—but I can't help wondering what even your 'brightest minds' made of it. It was written, moreover, obviously rather too much under the stress of motion & preoccupation & the inconvenience of scant time; so that though it sometimes (or constantly) does me much more than justice, it doesn't present at the best his admirable faculty (so trained & so expert) for orderly statement—& I have thus urged him to let it lie a while before he publishes it—& so take it in hand & chasten & *harshen* its 'partiality.' Which last, & the whole thing, infinitely moved me" (Henry James to Katherine Fullerton, 5 Dec. 1907 [Princeton]). By April 1909, presumably receiving from Fullerton a version of the article that had been rejected by *Scribner's*, James appears to have procrastinated in responding, as he admits to Wharton, with his usual hyperbolically apologetic flourishes, "You are a thousand times right to allude on a note of interrogation to Morton's article—& no note is sharp enough to pierce, I fully see, the apparent obscurity of my behaviour. All will be well, but there is a special explanation of—reason *for*—my having, lash myself as I would, been inevitably paralysed (that is embarrassed—up to now—fairly to anguish) over it. But that explanation I shall immediately, I shall in a day or two, make to him, if you will meanwhile lay me, all grovelling & groaning at his feet. Kindly assure him of my absolutely consistent affection & fidelity & ask him to have a very small further—a scrap of divine—patience with me" (Powers 111). In his next letter to her, toward the middle of May, he does claim, "I wrote a few days ago to Morton & shall very soon be writing him again" (Powers 113), but none of James's surviving letters to Fullerton dates, curiously enough, from the time at which he is discussing the essay with Wharton. The following April, with the article about to appear, James remarked, "I quiver & almost quibble over the imminent Quarterly," before confessing, less ambiguously, after its publication, "the bounty of the article is a joy to me" (Powers 157, 158). Learning in June that it had been picked up in the United States by *Living Age*, James further exclaimed to Wharton, "I rejoice in what you tell me of the Americanization of Morton's article" (Powers 163).

Whatever his own response to it, biographers both of James and of Wharton have had kind words for "The Art of Henry James." Leon Edel describes it as "a long and

full article on the Edition and on the significance of James's career in the history of
the novel" (*Henry James: The Master, 1901–1916* [Philadelphia: Lippincott, 1972],
418), while Lewis observes that Fullerton's original lecture "was expanded into a
long, appreciative and penetrating essay on the Edition and James's unique contributions to the art of the novel" (*L*, 117, n. 1), having earlier remarked that "this excellent
study . . . disclosed as nothing hitherto had done the great scope of James's major
theme: 'the clash between two societies,' American and European, as dramatized by
the invasion of Europe by American women" (Lewis 282). According to Lewis,
"Fullerton's discerning article had been timely" (299) even with regard to the unsuccessful campaign to secure the Nobel Prize for James. Finally, in introducing Wharton's correspondence with James, Lyall H. Powers refers to "the essay William
Morton Fullerton devoted to intelligent praise of the achievement of the New York
Edition of James's novels and tales" (Powers 5). Ultimately, however, one wishes that
Wharton had had more than "a small fraction of a hand," or at least a more discernible
hand, in the revision and preparation of Fullerton's lecture. Here and there one
detects clear traces of her guidance and interests. Late in the essay, Fullerton quotes
from Jules Jusserand, brother-in-law of one of her childhood friends, the same remark about Shakespeare that Wharton later cites in *The Writing of Fiction*; his reference to "the method . . . rigorously practised by the early French psychological novelists, the authors of such masterpieces as 'La Princesse de Clèves,' 'Adolphe,' or the
'Liaisons Dangereuses,'" echoes the vocabulary of Wharton's Hewlett review and
her review of Leslie Stephen's life of George Eliot, while citing her own favorite
examples of what she would later call "the novel of psychology" that "was born in
France" (*WF*, 61). At one point, Fullerton quotes the roll call of heroines in the
playful sonnet on James by Robert Louis Stevenson, whose complaints about *The
Portrait of a Lady* are sternly disputed in Wharton's review of the James letters. A few
years earlier, Wharton had alluded in "The House of the Dead Hand" (1904), as she
does in one of her unpublished essays, to the famous oak-tree image—invoked by
Fullerton early in his essay—from Wilhelm Meister's discussion of *Hamlet*. A point
of strong disagreement must have arisen when Fullerton applauds the "choral" function of the Assinghams in *The Golden Bowl* (a contrivance deplored by Wharton both
in her review of James's letters and in *The Writing of Fiction*); however, it seems
unlikely that he would have mentioned *The House of Mirth*, under any other circumstances, in the same breath with such works as *Anna Karenina*, *La Chartreuse de
Parme*, or *Vanity Fair*.

   Indeed, it might have been under her encouragement that Fullerton's article becomes even more heavily allusive than some of Wharton's own earlier reviews and
essays; yet his erudition, such as it is, does little to facilitate or enhance his argument
and fails to compensate much for its considerable stylistic excesses and irritations. As
Edel remarks, the essay "reads indeed as if the Master had inspired it. . . . If certain
sentences sound as if James himself wrote them, we must remember that Fullerton

had long been accused of writing his dispatches for the *Times* in a Jamesian style" (419). As a result, Fullerton's essay—although, for its time, an unusually penetrating and rigorous appreciation of the Jamesian aesthetic—grows more and more turgid, overwrought, and pretentious as it gathers steam. One wonders if their consultations on the James essay were as spirited, if not as successful, as the letter in which Wharton, commenting in 1912 on a draft of his next book, *Problems of Power*, complains to Fullerton about "all the heavy tin draperies of the Times jargon—that most prolix and pedantic of all dead languages" and implores him not to "let yourself be smothered in the flabby *tentacularities* of 'our own correspondent's' lingo. Drop 30 per cent of your Latinisms . . . , mow down every old cliché, uproot all the dragging circumlocutions, compress, diversify, clarify, vivify . . . " (*L*, 281).

Interestingly, his essay was not the first time Fullerton reviewed James's work. As far back as 1888, during his two-year stint, immediately following his graduation from Harvard, as literary editor of the *Boston Daily Advertiser*, he had contributed to its "Books and Authors" column, under the title "Balzac and Mr. James," a review of *The Aspern Papers* and of one of the volumes in Katherine Prescott Wormeley's ongoing translation of the *Comédie humaine*. Remarking that it is "[i]nto depths of life, where many are not willing to enter," that "Balzac passes . . . in the strongest contrast to the polite, well-bred pages of Mr. James," that James's "studies are episodic" and his "limitations are determinable," whereas "Balzac had none," and that "[t]he manner of Mr. James is Balzac's, but he uses it on but a small canvas" (*Boston Daily Advertiser*, 10 December 1888, 5), his earlier review establishes a distinction entirely reversed in James's favor by the time Fullerton reviews the New York Edition. Indeed, it is fitting that Balzac should be named or quoted, or paired with James, nearly a dozen times throughout "The Art of Henry James," for Bryn Mawr was one of the places where James had presented his lecture "The Lesson of Balzac," little more than two years before Fullerton's appearance, during his celebrated return visit to the United States in 1904–5 (a lecture dutifully cited by Fullerton near the end of his essay and from which he quotes, as Wharton does elsewhere, James's acknowledgment of Balzac as "the master of us all"). Ultimately, Fullerton is at pains to situate James not only with respect to a commanding predecessor like Balzac but also within the history and development of the novel as a form of literary art. To that extent, his essay, written by "one of the most promising of Henry James's younger friends and admirers" (Lewis 183), represents, if nothing else, a significant moment in the early stages of James's canonization, joining the work of more prominent "Jacobites" like Percy Lubbock (who had himself reviewed the New York Edition for the *Times Literary Supplement*). In Edel's words, "its insights make of this essay an important contemporary document in that it views critically the high originality of James's work—looks at it through the Edition as a totality, and assigns to James a role in the history of fiction which no one had hitherto done" (420). As one curious fruit of their tormented relationship, and as a work of criticism on which she obviously collaborated (to

whatever degree), "The Art of Henry James" is reprinted here for the first time since
its publication in 1910, serving as an appropriate coda to a volume of Wharton's own
critical prose.

The Art of Henry James

by W. Morton Fullerton

The Novels and Tales of Henry James. New York Edition.
In twenty-four volumes. London: Macmillan, 1907–1909.

The recent appearance of a definitive edition of Mr. James's novels offers to
his readers what he himself would call "a beautiful incentive" to take a general view of his work.

Mr. James's literary activity has extended over more than twenty years,
and during that time not only his language and manner, but the fundamental
theory of his art, has been modified in a way so curious and interesting as to
provoke continual discussion, and divide his readers somewhat sharply into
the champions of his earlier and his later styles. The publication of his "complete works" seems the opportune moment for summing up the arguments
on both sides, and trying to reach a general conclusion which shall more
clearly interpret the importance of his work; yet the reperusal of these volumes checks the very zeal it excites by making the reader pause and ask
himself, "What need has Henry James of champions or interpreters?" Why,
indeed, in such a case, "jostle the elbow of slow-fingering Time"?[1] Mr. James
has no need of such aid. He is bound to enter into his own; his final form is
indestructible. But if words in recognition of his eminence can serve no end
for him, they constitute an act which may have its uses for his public. They
have the purifying grace of a confession. We know where *he* stands. We do
ourselves a service in noting where *we* stand as well.

The opportunity of applying this test is abundantly aided by the prefaces
to the new edition. In these prefaces Mr. James has shed a vivid light on the
theory of his own work, and incidentally on the art of fiction in general. They
represent, in fact, the first serious attempt ever made in English to call upon
that bewildered art to pause and give a conscious account of itself; to present
its credentials and justify its existence. In these remarkable pages Mr. James
has again and again illustrated his general theory by taking to pieces before
the reader the complex machinery of his own fiction, and showing, with a
beguiling candor, how and to what end its intricate parts were combined.

The lesson is deeply instructive, though it may be questioned if it makes the process completely intelligible. The conjuror who shows his audience how a trick is done cannot impart the suppleness needed to execute it; he can display the successive gestures, not their moment of fusion. But Mr. James's confidences have at least the inestimable value of showing how *he* can do the work, and why he does it.

The early James, the painter of the single consciousness, with its more or less loosely grouped surrounding incidents, won a large measure of popular success by the distinction of his intelligence, the precision of his vision, the admirable freshness and flexibility of his style. But he was a James who, save in the very early tales (so personal in their romance), was still evidently under the influence of French comedy, French art, and Russian art, of Flaubert, Maupassant, and Turgénieff. The James of the second period—extending, one might roughly say, from "The Portrait of a Lady" to the great work of transition, "What Maisie Knew," and including such memorable volumes as "The Princess Casamassima" and "The Tragic Muse"—the artist of this period was simply disengaging and developing to the utmost the possibilities of expression latent in his first form of presentation. Taking up the hardly conscious theory of fiction where it had been left by Balzac—"the master of us all"—he had turned and twisted it about, and had shed on it at every angle the searching light of human experience. In the course of these experiments he had evolved, by a series of syntheses now clearly traceable in the collected edition, several principles tending to modify the whole theory of his art, and at last to break it down as the oak-roots, in Goethe's magnificent metaphor, burst the vase in which the acorn has been planted.[2]

The most fruitful of these innovations was the principle that the action of each narrative should be recorded in the consciousness of one or more of the actors rather than in the vague impersonal register of an *ex machinâ* storyteller. Mr. James had learned, in other words, that the only way of acquiring the objectivity necessary to artistic representation was to assume successively, and at the exact "psychological moment," the states of mind of the actors *through whom his story became a story*. This method had been rigorously practised by the early French psychological novelists, the authors of such masterpieces as "La Princesse de Clèves," "Adolphe," or the "Liaisons Dangereuses," where the drama had been either confined to one consciousness, or else—as in the novel of Choderlos de Laclos—presented, by means of letters, in different sharply divided layers. The same necessity had been intermittently recognized by Balzac and Stendhal, though the enlargement of their field, and the introduction of a human background, an "ambiance," for their principal figures, had greatly complicated and often obscured the problem. It was left to Mr. James to restate it in this infinitely more difficult form, to face the need of a definite solution, and lastly to find that solution in the art of passing, at the inevitable moment, from the consciousness of one character to that of another. The increased sureness and dexterity of these transitions constitute the other notable characteristic of what has here been called his second manner, and point the way to the fundamental change distinguishing the novels of his latest period.

The James of the second manner (when he was producing things in their kind the peer of the most excellent of their kind), before he had come to himself, *saw himself coming*. It needed not the prefaces to tell us this; but they bring beautiful corroboration of his early sense of the possibilities within him. It was perhaps this sense of what his art still concealed from him, of the amazing answer he was yet to wring from it, that kept him so single-mindedly to his path. There is no nobler example of intellectual probity in the world of letters; and the rarity of such phenomena is not difficult to account for. The great danger that besets the artist is the peril of popularity, and the all-too seductive appeal to outdo himself, to abound still more in the same sense. It is at his risk that he leaves his admirers in the lurch. What? just as they have begun to understand and "interpret" him he dares to perform a *volte-face* and show an aspect unknown to them? The secret of continued success is not to disturb the spectator's association of ideas. That is the lesson of any show-case of Tanagras. It is the principle so delightfully, if deliberately, exploited by Renan in the last fifteen years of his life.[3] It explains the abundance of the Henners, the Harpignies, even the Reynoldses, that stock the collections of our Adam Ververs. It requires courage to ignore this instant value of the trade-mark; for not only gratified vanity but uneasy self-criticism urges that the public may be right. Henry James had this high courage; and to it we owe the fact that he has become, throughout the English-speaking world of letters, one of those "premiers parmi les plus grands" with whom Hugo classed Balzac.[4]

It is first of all on the ground of form that this may be affirmed of him; yet he himself has shown, in divers passages of self-analysis, how "form" is in the last resort the outcome of the subject, as the subject is the outcome of the author's temperament. The arbitrary distinction between the two ought by this time to be classed among such metaphysical abstractions as the separateness of body and soul; and perhaps Mr. James's statement of the indivisibility of form and content may help to kill a mischievous literary superstition.

No one has spoken more authoritatively on the vexed point of "morality" of theme, on what Mr. James calls "the perfect dependence of the 'moral' sense of a work of art on the *amount of felt life* concerned in producing it." "The question" (he goes on in the same passage) "comes back thus obviously to the kind and degree of the artist's prime sensibility, which is the soil out of which the subject springs. The quality and capacity of that soil, its ability to 'grow' with due freshness and straightness any vision of life, represents, strongly or weakly, the projected 'morality.'" One might sum up the subject by saying that, as there is no color without vision, there is no "subject," good or bad, without contact with a given consciousness. In the domain of serious literature—the only one to be contemplated in such discussions—the so-called "badness" of a subject lies in reality in the inadequacy of the mind transmitting it. The dull or discolored mirror dims or disturbs the image it reflects.

The James of the third manner has surprised his most confident admirers by an evolution which even such a dispenser of aesthetic emotions as the creator of "Daisy Miller" and "Roderick Hudson," of "The Portrait of a Lady" and "The Tragic Muse," could not lead them to foresee, an evolution lifting him so far above himself, and above the prevision of those who thought they knew all that could be known about him, that he has been left somewhat ignored, less immediately accessible, and, in this period of democratic neglect of all the superiorities, more austerely aloof even than the best and most beautiful things have always been.

The charge oftenest brought against this new James is that of willingly cultivating a tantalising complexity of style. He is accused of seeing his own thoughts too long in advance, and, Hamlet-like, of pointing to the comet before it swims into our ken. He is said to be the prisoner of the whorl of the labyrinth, self-condemned to the arbitrary windings of a spiral ascent before reaching that luminous platform above the concentric hedges, whence there are restful vistas and wide horizons. Is it not rather that the mind of the modern reader, made myopic by the thin transcriptions of life which pass for fiction, has no perception of tone, depth, richness, and completeness of representation? All representation implies foreshortening; but that offered to the public by most of its favourites—who, as it were, pull their subject distortedly, absolutely to the surface, and flatten it out there so that it has nor form nor body—results in an outline as puerile as that of the figures in a pack of cards. It is as near an approach to "life" as a child's attempt to copy a Rembrandt etching by tracing its heavier lines through tissue paper; and how can eyes accustomed to such rudimentary adjustments develope an elasticity of function enabling them, not to measure, but even to see, a work of demiurgic art in rounded representation?

Passing from Mr. James's formula to the field in which he has illustrated it, one finds the same originality of choice, the same resolve to deal with the unattempted. It is chiefly on aesthetic grounds that this appreciation of his work has been based; yet, even if one adopts the habitual Anglo-Saxon way, and judges him by the matter of his work, the importance of his product will assuredly be admitted to be immense and very special. In the ninety-six separate stories, with their thousands of intensely individual figures, Mr. James has been many other things, no doubt, but he has first of all been the historiographer of that vast epic—the modern Iliad, when its peripatetic and romantic elements do not make it more like an Odyssey—the clash between two societies, the mutual call of two sundered worlds, with not one Helen but a thousand to create complications and to fire the chivalry of two continents. As a sociological phenomenon, no "Return of the Heracleidae," mythic or real, is comparable to the invasion of Europe by American women, backed by their indispensable heads of commissariat, the silent, clean-shaven American men. The emigration required its Homer, and Mr. James was there.

Nothing, assuredly, was ever better worth "doing," no finer, richer chance ever stared a great writer in the face. The very vastness of the subject has been his "beautiful incentive," and he has watched the shock of America with Europe on all its battle-fields, Venice, London, Paris, Rome, Geneva. Some of the episodes are more salient, some more engaging than others, but all are parts of the great poem of the new mingling of the races.

In such a general survey of Mr. James's theme it is impossible not to note the saliency, all along the line, of the feminine figure. From the outset he has devoted his most penetrating powers to the scrutiny of the inscrutable sex; and the women he has created, while certainly not less vividly real and really human than his men, are both more numerous and more varied. Few such galleries of great ladies are elsewhere to be found. He knows all the types, the most formidable and unfathomable as well as the safest and the most irresistible.

> Lo, how these fair immaculate women walk
> Behind their jocund maker . . .[5]

And since Stevenson filed his epithets for the slighted de Mauves, for Gressie the trivial sphinx, and Daisy and Barb and Chancellor, Mr. James has created Maisie Farange and Nanda Brookenham, Charlotte Stant and Mrs. Assingham and Maggie Verver.

> By what process of logical accretion [he asks, speaking of Isabel Archer, in the preface to "The Portrait of a Lady"] was this slight personality, the mere slim shade of an intelligent but presumptuous girl, to find itself endowed with the high attributes of a subject?

And he gives his answer thus:

> Challenge any such problem with any intelligence, and you immediately see how full it is of substance; the wonder being, all the while, as we look at the world, how absolutely, how inordinately, the Isabel Archers, and even much smaller female fry, insist on mattering. George Eliot has admirably noted it: "In these frail vessels is borne onward through the ages the treasure of human affection." In "Romeo and Juliet" Juliet has to be important, just as, in "Adam Bede" and "The Mill on the Floss" and "Middlemarch" and "Daniel Deronda," Hetty Sorrel and Maggie Tulliver and Rosamond Vincy and Gwendolen Harleth have to be; with that much of firm ground, that much of bracing air, at the disposal all the while of their feet and their lungs. . . . Now to see deep difficulty braved is at any time, for the really addicted artist, to feel almost even as a pang the beautiful incentive, and to feel it verily in such sort as to wish the danger intensified. The difficulty most worth tackling can only be for him, in these conditions, the greatest the case permits of. So I remember feeling here (in presence, always, that is, of the particular uncertainty of my ground), that there would be one way better than another—oh, ever so much better than any other!—of making it fight out its battle. The frail vessel, that charged with George Eliot's "treasure," and thereby of such importance to those who curiously approach it, has likewise possibilities of importance to itself, possibilities which permit of treatment and in fact peculiarly require it from the moment they are considered at all. There is always the escape from any close account of the weak agent of such spells by using as a bridge for evasion, for retreat and flight, the view of her relation to those surrounding her. . . ."Place the centre of the subject in the young woman's own consciousness," I said to myself, "and you get as interesting and as beautiful a difficulty as you could wish. Stick to that—for the centre; put the heaviest weight into *that* scale, which will be so largely

the scale of her relation to herself. Make her only interested enough, at the same time, in the things that are not herself, and this relation needn't fear to be too limited. Place, meanwhile, in the other scale the lighter weight (which is usually the one that tips the balance of interest); press least hard, in short, on the consciousness of your heroine's satellites, especially the male; make it an interest contributive only to the greater one. See, at all events, what can be done in this way. What better field could there be for a due ingenuity? The girl hovers, unextinguishable, as a charming creature, and the job will be to translate her into the highest terms of that formula, and as nearly as possible, moreover, into *all* of them."

It was thus, conjecturally, through his passionate interest in the presentation of the "frail vessel," and through the need of strengthening and fashioning it to contain the full measure of his theme, that Mr. James first learned to reflect his narrative in a central consciousness, and to select that consciousness for the multiplicity of its contacts.

Such a consideration leads back to the fact that the documentary value of Mr. James's work, unique as it is, is not his chief distinction. Far above it is his importance as an artist, as a creator of beautiful things. The primitive instinct of story-telling carries the novelist but a short way toward his goal. The art of fiction is other and more than the development of narrative; it is the most complete device invented for the representation of life. But there is representation and representation, and the way ultimately evolved and perfected, although not absolutely invented, by Henry James, is so unlike his earlier way that it constitutes the point of his lesson and the nature of his case. Only with Balzac may he be compared as to methods and to aims. Not that the methods of Balzac and Mr. James are the only ways of representing life. Tolstoi, for instance, is an incomparable story-teller, but Tolstoi deals only with the surfaces, is merely a deeper, richer Maupassant; his pictures recall the extraordinarily interesting narratives told by the kinematograph. They are what we call "life-like." No one can surpass him in realism, and no one has kept such realism up for so long a time. But such hypnotisation of vision, one might add, is almost pathological, and sure to end eventually in pessimism, since it is a vision that has revealed no secluded refuges where the artist can repose, and has little to do with that active creative insight that lifts the veil from the external aspect of things. Yet lifting the veil is a preliminary operation for the novelist, since his problem is to show what there is behind it, taken in connexion with all the aspects of his foreground.

To dominate one's material, to melt together all its elements in a fresh synthesis, in which nothing is left out, that is the whole operation of art. It is cerebral chemistry. Of the two highest activities of the human intelligence, art and science, the former alone puts in movement, agitates, the complete consciousness. And science itself is really fruitful and recompensing as an intellectual exercise only when, abandoning the *chemin de ronde* of the deductive method, it quits the syllogistic paths where the posters that indicate the way even to the most hurried of us spare us the pain of thinking, and pluckily allows itself to be lured towards new horizons by the will-o'-the-wisps of the imagination. Superior brains, like the brain of Henry James, alone achieve this higher synthesis, and thereby attain the steady serenity of their art, a serenity above individual preferences, which bestows the same care on each picture, each personage, each scene, because of the disinterested neutrality, the constant and perfect operation, of the registering organ.

But the great resemblance between the methods of Balzac and of Henry James must be qualified by an important difference. Balzac, the originator of "atmosphere" in fiction, presented his single figures in the round, worked as a *plein-airiste* in detail, but failed to give his whole case plastically. The latter achievement has been Mr. James's essential innovation. Before him the individual figure had had a back as well as a front, but the "situation" in which it was involved had always been a frieze, not a group, a flat pattern, not a circumnavigable globe.

Perhaps only those who have practised the trade—however modestly— can detect (though so seldom skilled to follow) the elusive *procédés* that lead to the achievement of the fully plastic effect.

> These [writes Mr. James, again in the remarkable preface to "The Portrait of a Lady"], these are the fascinations of the fabulist's art, these lurking forces of expansion, these necessities of upspringing in the seed, these beautiful determinations, on the part of the idea entertained, to grow as tall as possible, to push into the light and thickly flower there.

In comparing the growth of the novel to that of a plant, Mr. James has described the process by which his own stories grow, rather than that common to most works of fiction. For the plant, or the tree, branches out on all sides, and one must presuppose it, for its welfare, to be enveloped on all sides by opportunities for light and air; whereas the only "tree" which the average novel resembles is the flat diagram to which genealogists give that name. It is by seeing his situations thus more and more completely in the

round, and by enabling his readers' intelligence to circulate freely about
them, that Mr. James, in his latest novels, has most sharply separated himself, not only from his predecessors, but from the other novelists of his day.
Another important "lesson of the master" is that of the fundamental necessity of self-saturation. Mr. James has pointed out, in his lecture on Balzac,
that the latter's consummate artistic probity lay in his respect for the *liberty
of his subject*. But to set a subject free one must first have been its master.
The average novelist absorbs so little of the stuff he deals in that the subsequent process of pressing it out produces but the thinnest of trickles;
whereas with Balzac and Mr. James the sometimes overwhelming flow of
material proceeds from the opposite excess.

Balzac, in an admirable passage, notes that the artist's inevitable simplify-
ing of what he sees results in the objects of his vision becoming larger than
life. Thus he cannot avoid creating a type, and a type, being at once an
enlargement and a simplification, has in it an inevitable element of caricature. But the artist is the last person to be the dupe of this fact, and if he be
one of the great he tempers the crudity of the isolated representation by the
device of slipping in an "atmosphere," creating a "tone." Balzac and James,
by their elaborate treatment of all the circumstances surrounding their subjects, are toning down to the semblance of life figures which the method of
David or of Ingres, of Daudet or of Goncourt, would have left as so many
coloured silhouettes or grotesque accentuations. The amplitude of development necessary for the treatment *en relief* may result, for the mere story-
seeker, in a maze of confusing detail; but the alerter eye sees in it life's own
gradations of interwoven tone. A page of Mr. James's later novels is like
some vast, high-lifted park, exposing its densely-clad slopes to the rays of a
late sun, embossed with the domes of verdure of a hundred shades of green,
elms, oaks, and beeches contrasting with dusky pines and the slender silvery
poplars of France, the whole slope drinking, absorbing the light, blending
and fusing its myriad tones and shades. *Eidullia*, little pictures of an infinite
grace, come, as in Dante, to enhance the distinguished charm of the composition. They are the colour notes of the canvas, contributing to the general
impression of beauty, their presence *felt* by every one of taste, but not necessarily perceived in and for themselves save by the "restless analyst," to
whom, in "The American Scene," Mr. James so abundantly refers. These are
delicious devices of the art, these frequent enhancements of Mr. James's.
They make one wish for more space in which to dwell on the sense of the
noble sweetness of his sentiment—that ivory *patine* on his product—which
Dante shares with him, and which both share with certain painters of old

Italy. The quality of feeling in question is one of the rarest in human nature; for if there are enough puling sentimentalists in literature to fill a large asylum, this high grace, which is that of the loveliest natural compositions—a vision, say, of a long summer twilight in the Cyclades, or of the Cornice Road of the "Purgatorio"—has happened to bloom only at long intervals strangely sundered. Nowhere else indeed, unless it be in Dante, is there so much light, anything like the varied range of colour, *nuance*, tone.

It may be remarked in this connection that if Mr. James, like Balzac, has been less at his ease in the form of expression peculiar to the stage, it is doubtless partly because of the unwillingness of both to simplify to the verge of symbolism, as the dramatist must. Had these authors lived when the happy expedient of the Greek chorus still formed a part of dramatic expression, that subtle generator of atmosphere and tone might more often have induced them to give a dramatic form to their representations of life. In the case of Mr. James, at any rate, the inference is justified by the fact that he has used the device admirably in the novel—for what else is the *rôle* of the Assingham couple in "The Golden Bowl"?—and has defended it with ingenuity and eloquence in several passages of his prefaces.

If Shakespeare was rarely a writer of good plays, it was perhaps because he found simplification too dearly bought by the sacrifice of those effects of depth, density, colour-values, and perpetual interplay of light and shade by which alone the great artistic temperament can approximately express its tidal oscillations of emotion. This conjecture was certainly confirmed by the French version of King Lear played in Paris a few years ago. Thus stripped of the essential magic of poetic interpretation, and reduced to the lines of a sublimated melodrama, the greatest of tragedies might have passed (like much of Sophocles under the same conditions) for a masterpiece of that *genre rosse* with which M. Antoine shocked the nerves of Paris some years ago.[6]

The determination of Balzac and of James to make the art of the novelist a plastic art is virtually their refusal to forego, for the purpose of creation, *the use of any means of contact with life*. To exercise the fullness of this prerogative is the last triumph, as it is the supreme difficulty, of the novelist. The difficulty is inherent in the material at the writer's disposal. Most people think only in words, most people, at all events, of the Anglo-Saxon world; their whole conscious life is in words. The architect, the painter, the sculptor, the actor, the servants of all but the two muses of music and literature, have at their disposal signs and materials which make plasticity an essential result. To arrive at the same effect in prose literature is the mark of the highest art. Mr. James has achieved it in his later books, from "The Ambassadors" to "The Golden Bowl," and it is this achievement which makes them, in spite of the more accessible charm of his earlier novels, the significant and the original part of his work. The subtle blending of the material, the "effects" that have gone to the making of the firm, rounded rightness of such books as "The Wings of the Dove" and "The Ambassadors," are no doubt one with the processes of assimilation and utilisation for organic ends that take place within tree or animal. Mr. James evolves his creations by the same instinct as that of so-called unconscious "Nature"; and in this connexion one is led back to the intrinsic mystery of the work of art, the fact that it is always, in the last analysis, a product of individual conditions, and that no *novum organum* of criticism such as Taine devised[7] can ever explain or forecast it. Mr. James, in writing of the influence of the Concord *milieu* on Emerson, says, "He drew half his images, we recognise, from the revolution of its seasons and the play of its manners." But he goes on: "I don't speak of the other half, which he drew from elsewhere."[8] What a man draws "from elsewhere" is that element of personal inspiration—what Emerson himself called "the alien energy"[9]—which makes the inscrutability of his genius and its life-bestowing power. M. Jusserand has spoken of Shakespeare as "un grand distributeur de vie,"[10] and this strange vivifying faculty is the central mystery of art. In the great literary artist it results in the creation of things so living that they are actually beautiful to look upon. Books like "The Wings of the Dove" and "The Golden Bowl" may, in fact, be contemplated, looked at, and not only read.

Indestructibility of form is the inalienable mark of great work. It has hitherto, in English, at least, been the one superiority that great poetry, that of Milton, say, or Keats, has had over great prose utterance. But Mr. James has shown that prose may have not only as fine a form as verse, but even a more genuine, compacter plasticity, in which all the "effects"—of sound, of colour, of vision—are reciprocally inter-subordinate, marvellously fused as in some noble building or great music.

So deep is the unity of any fine work of art that one should never read Mr. James for a first, but only for a second, time. It takes time to read him at all, as it takes time to read anything, not merely the great thing. It is the happy "pull" that the painter or the architect has over the writer, that they can present their finished product whole to an eye capable of taking it in; whereas, foreshorten as he may, the novelist has to put up with the fact that he must transfer his emotions and his thought to a kind of map of Mercator's projection, and yet, amid all these essentially wrong perspectives, produce the right effect of roundness and solidity. Some of the great novelists shirk the problem altogether, others seem profoundly unconscious of it and go on *ad infinitum* mapping out longitudinally, as in the case of that supremely entertaining story, "Anna Karénine." There are none but purely artificial reasons why even such masterpieces as "Anna Karénine" or "The Chartreuse de Parme" or "The House of Mirth" or "Harry Richmond" or "Vanity Fair" should ever end.

Such books as "Eugénie Grandet" or "The Golden Bowl" are not the fruit of invention alone, but of imagination, an imagination nourished on that experience which puts the man or woman capable of it in possession of the faculty that made Lowell call Shakespeare "one of God's spies."[11] This imaginative sympathy—the love which, as Mr. James himself notes, Balzac had for his characters—enables the first-rate artist to feel *with* the creatures of his making, to see the world through their eyes. Balzac wrote in "Honorine":

> Les drames de la vie ne sont pas dans les circonstances; ils sont dans les sentiments, ou, si vous voulez, dans ce monde immense que nous devons nommer le monde spirituel.[12]

And, in Mr. James's case, the aspects of life most commonly present are its entanglements, its embarrassments. Fate is for ever stating problems, but seldom gives any clue to an answer. The chances it gives us all for throwing up the sponge a thousand times a day no doubt form the very warp and woof of our absurd existence. But they form as well the entire comic material of the tissue, and a man whose business it is to represent the spectacle of things can never tire of counting them. No phrase occurs more often—it is a sort of *leit-motiv* of composition—in a novel of Mr. James than the typical one marking his amused and wondering halt before each fresh case of the ubiquity, the inevitability of the human plight. The phrase is, "There you are!" If only "situations" and plights were regular decagons! But they all have so many facets, and the probity of the novelist is in being blind to none of them, and in turning his tale on its pivot in such a manner that as many as possible are presented to the reader's eye. An example of the difficulty and of its solution is given in such a cry as this, from the feminine leader of the chorus in "The Golden Bowl." "She doesn't deliberately intend, she doesn't consciously wish, the least complication," says Mrs. Assingham to her matter-of-fact husband, as they are speculating in real dismay on the possible consequences of Charlotte's unexpected arrival. "It's perfectly true that she thinks Maggie a dear—as who doesn't? She's incapable of any *plan* to hurt a hair of her head. Yet here she is, and there *they* are!"

When one recognises that so much of an artist's material is substance of
this expensive sort, it is a little easier to solve the question which Mr. James
himself raised in his lecture on Balzac, and which his own case puts just as
insistently, namely, how a man can find time, not merely to write so much
of such a quality, but, while writing so much, to see and study life. Mr. James
answers the question by saying that Balzac quarried his material within himself. But if the artist obtains this knowledge within himself, what guarantee
has the reader that he is getting the real thing, life itself? Obviously none,
save the tests that his own experience can bring to bear on the finished
representation. But it is just the mark of the great artists that they triumphantly meet this test and do what is called inspire conviction. That failure
to self-saturate is a mark of intellectual disloyalty, is just as much the lesson
of Mr. James as it is of Balzac or Shakespeare. And the fact of self-saturation
is the key to the mystery of a man's finding time to absorb so much life and
give it back in so many books. For the brain that "intends upon itself" instead of shifting about like a reporter with a note-book—granting it the initial gift of imaginative divination—that brain has only to sit quietly and to
record what it sees and knows. And it is precisely the brain of that special
stamp which, seeing and knowing a million things intuitively, where the less
endowed know only piecemeal and empirically, can dispense with the
cruder, slower methods of acquisition, since it is the brain of genius.

How much genius can "give" is a question in physico-chemistry, analogous with that of the "work" to be got out of an engine or a dynamo. An
infinitude of automatic reactions, syntheses, elaborations, may take place in
the subconsciousness; but evidently nothing takes place, or next to nothing,
if the machine is a poor one. The first distinction of superior minds is that
they not only see more alertly, instantly, untiringly, than the average intelligence, *but that they see a great deal more*, the word "see" possessing here no
figurative meaning, nor any sense more mystical than that implied by the
mere physical fact of vision. The second distinction is that they never *see*
anything without feeling it. This faculty of storing up in the brain a latent
emotive energy, a complex precipitate of perception in being, is what Mr.
James has called "the mystery and the marvel of experience," an accretion
that "may amount to an enormous sum, even when the figures on the slate
are too few and too paltry to mention. It may count for enrichment without
one's knowing why." With the average nerve-stuff of the crowd it ordinarily
counts for very little. The average human reactions are of a melodramatic
positiveness and an unironic sentimentality; and all these feelings hang grotesquely asunder, or, at best, are reciprocally attached by a very meagre set

of associative guide-ropes. In a mind like that of Mr. James, on the contrary, every element of the spectacle of life is an occasion for representation, and every representation a complex incentive to immediate artistic creation. The spectacle of Mr. James's intelligence at work, transmuting his experience into literature, might be compared with the mysterious processes of radio-activity. Nature, the world, life, impinge on, punctuate, his consciousness with a myriad of tiny unmeaning holes, and that consciousness has the magic capacity of transmuting these perforations, these nothings, into intelligible signs. The whole interior shiver determined by the ceaselessly beating waves of sensations, all the trembling consequences of each thud of the wave, its impact on the stored-up and beautifully classified images of his older sensations, all are automatically noted, translated and read out by this "restless analyst" as by a Pollak receptor.[13] A consciousness so completely alive is the rarest state of human activity. Operations of this nature have, of course, all their interest in proportion as the dim richness of the internal glow penetrates a larger and larger deposit of sensations.

When the mind in question glows with a larger number of stored-up images of anterior perceptions than are wont to be deposited in any save the most sensitive brain-stuff, every fresh onset of outside sensation produces a wondrously chromatic emotional atmosphere; and when that mind is the mind of a novelist, and of such a novelist as Henry James, his own account of his *feeling*, his report on the aspect of the shifting phenomena within, results necessarily in the ordered beauty of those complex renderings of life, his novels of the last ten years.

Quarterly Review, April 1910

[1] While waiting to see the increasingly disapproving Mr. Carteret at his estate, Nick Dormer, the aspiring painter in *The Tragic Muse* (1890), "sauntered about the church—it took a good while. . . . It struck him as a great pity such a pile should be touched: so much of the past was buried there that it was like desecrating, like digging up a grave. Since the years were letting it down so gently why jostle the elbow of slow-fingering time?"

[2] Image from book 4 (1783) of *Wilhelm Meisters Lehrjahre*, employed by the hero during his famous discussion of *Hamlet*: "An oak tree planted in a precious pot which should only have held delicate flowers; the roots spread out, the vessel is shattered [Hier wird ein Eichbaum in ein köstliches Gefäss gepflanzt, das nur liebliche Blumen in seinen Schoss hätte aufnehmen sollen; die Wurzeln dehnen sich aus, das Gefäss wird zernichtet]."

[3] Ernest Renan (1823–92), French historian, philologist, and theological writer best known for his controversial *Vie de Jésus* (1863).

[4] "First among the greatest," remark occurring in Hugo's eulogy, "Discours prononcé aux funérailles de M. Honoré de Balzac, 20 Août 1850," later published in *Actes et Paroles I: Avant l'exile* (1875).

[5] From "Henry James," sonnet of Robert Louis Stevenson (1850–94), English writer and friend of the novelist. Fullerton goes on to allude to the continuation of these lines: "and we

see / Slighted De Mauves, and that far different she, / Gressie, the trivial sphynx; and to our feast / Daisy and Barb and Chancellor (she not least!) / With all their silken, all their airy kin, / Do like unbidden angels enter in" (ll. 7–12). Stevenson's poem appears in *Underwoods* (1887).

[6] André-Léonard Antoine (1858–1943), innovative theater director, founder of the *Théâtre Libre* in 1887 and, with it, of the independent theater movement in France. Fullerton might have in mind Antoine's own 1904 production of *King Lear* as director of the Théâtre Antoine.

[7] Hippolyte Taine (1828–93), influential French critic and literary historian who famously emphasized the determining role of *race*, *milieu*, and *moment* in the production of literature.

[8] From "Concord and Salem," in *The American Scene* (1907).

[9] In "The Over-Soul," from *Essays: First Series* (1841): "When I watch that flowing river, which, out of regions I see not, pours for a season its streams into me, I see that I am a pensioner; not a cause but a surprised spectator of this ethereal water; that I desire and look up and put myself in the attitude of reception, but from some alien energy the visions come."

[10] "A great life-giver," from *The Literary History of the English People* (1905) by Jules Jusserand (1855–1932), for many years the French ambassador to the United States.

[11] James Russell Lowell (1819–91), American poet and literary critic; his remark alludes, of course, to the scene in which Lear reassures Cordelia, as they are about to be imprisoned, "We two alone will sing like birds i'th'cage. . . . And take upon's the mystery of things / As if we were God's spies" (*King Lear*, act 5, sc. 3, ll. 9, 16–17).

[12] "The dramas of life are not in circumstances; they are in feelings, or, if you like, in the vast realm which we should call the spiritual world"; from Balzac's novella "Honorine" (1843).

[13] Fullerton appears to be referring to one component of the Pollak-Virag Rapid Telegraph, devised a few years earlier by Hungarian inventors Antal Pollak and Jozsef Virag, which transmitted more that forty thousand words per minute and reproduced them, at the receiving end, in ordinary handwriting.

BIBLIOGRAPHY

CHECKLIST OF EDITH WHARTON'S
UNCOLLECTED CRITICAL WRITINGS AND
RELATED PROSE

Reviews, Essays, and Other Writings

"Newport's Old Houses." Letter. *Newport Daily News*, 8 January 1896, 8.

"Schoolroom Decoration." Lecture transcribed in "Education through the Eyes. Mrs. Wharton Addresses the Teachers on Art in the Schoolroom." *Newport Daily News*, 8 October 1897, 8.

"Frederic Bronson." Letter. *New York Evening Post*, 2 April 1900, 4.

"More Love-Letters of an Englishwoman." *Bookman* 12 (February 1901): 562–63.

"Impoverishing the Language." Letter. *New York Tribune*, 23 April 1901, 8.

"The Blashfields' *Italian Cities*." Review of *Italian Cities*, by Edwin H. and Evangeline W. Blashfield. *Bookman* 13 (August 1901): 563–64.

"Stephen Phillips's *Ulysses*." Review of *Ulysses: A Drama*, by Stephen Phillips. *Bookman* 15 (April 1902): 168–70.

"*George Eliot*." Review of *George Eliot*, by Leslie Stephen. *Bookman* 15 (May 1902): 247–51.

"The Theatres." Review of Minnie Maddern Fiske's performance in Lorimer Stoddard's dramatization of Thomas Hardy's *Tess of the D'Urbervilles*. *New York Commercial Advertiser*, 7 May 1902, 9.

"The Three Francescas." *North American Review* 175 (July 1902): 17–30.

"Mr. Paul on the Poetry of Matthew Arnold." Review of *Matthew Arnold*, by Herbert W. Paul. *Lamp* 26 (February 1903): 51–54.

"The Vice of Reading." *North American Review* 177 (October 1903): 513–21.

"Mr. Sturgis's *Belchamber*." Review of *Belchamber*, by Howard Sturgis. *Bookman* 21 (May 1905): 307–10.

"Maurice Hewlett's *The Fool Errant*." Review of *The Fool Errant*, by Maurice Hewlett. *Bookman* 22 (September 1905): 64–67.

"The Sonnets of Eugene Lee-Hamilton." *Bookman* 26 (November 1907): 251–53.

"George Cabot Lodge." *Scribner's Magazine* 47 (February 1910): 236–39.

"The Criticism of Fiction." *Times Literary Supplement* (London), 14 May 1914, 229–30.

"*The Architecture of Humanism*." Review of *The Architecture of Humanism*, by Geoffrey Scott. *Times Literary Supplement* (London), 25 June 1914, 305.

"Jean du Breuil de Saint-Germain." *Revue Hebdomadaire* 24 (15 May 1915): 351–61.

"Henry James in His Letters." Review of *The Letters of Henry James*, ed. Percy Lubbock. *Quarterly Review* 234 (July 1920): 188–202.

"The Great American Novel." *Yale Review*, n.s. 16 (July 1927): 646–56.

"William C. Brownell." *Scribner's Magazine* 84 (November 1928): 596–602.

"A Cycle of Reviewing." *Spectator* (London) 141 (supplement, 3 November 1928): 44–45.

"Visibility in Fiction." *Yale Review*, n.s. 18 (March 1929): 480–88.
"Tendencies in Modern Fiction." *Saturday Review of Literature* 10 (27 January 1934): 433–34.
"Permanent Values in Fiction." *Saturday Review of Literature* 10 (7 April 1934): 603–4.
"A Reconsideration of Proust." *Saturday Review of Literature* 11 (27 October 1934): 233–34.
"Souvenirs du Bourget d'Outremer." *Revue Hebdomadaire* 45 (21 June 1936): 266–86.
"A Little Girl's New York." *Harper's Magazine* 176 (March 1938): 356–64.
Tribute to Bayard Cutting, Jr. In *W. Bayard Cutting, Jr.: 1878–1910*. Privately printed: Marshlands, 1947. 47–56.

Prefaces, Introductions, Forewords

Translator's Note to *The Joy of Living*, by Hermann Sudermann, transl. Edith Wharton. New York: Scribner's, 1902. v–vi.
Introduction to *A Village Romeo and Juliet*, by Gottfried Keller, transl. A. C. Bahlmann. New York: Scribner's, 1914. v–xxvi.
Preface to *Futility*, by William Gerhardi. New York: Duffield, 1922. 1–3.
Introduction to *Gardening in Sunny Lands: The Riviera, California, Australia*, by Mrs. Philip Martineau. London: Cobden-Sanderson, 1924. 17–19.
Preface to *Speak to the Earth: Wanderings and Reflections among Elephants and Mountains*, by Vivienne de Watteville. London: Methuen, 1935. [vii–viii].
Foreword to *Benediction*, by Claude Silve (Philomène de Laforest-Divonne), transl. Robert Norton. New York: Appleton-Century, 1936. 1–6.
Preface to *Eternal Passion in English Poetry*, selected by Edith Wharton and Robert Norton, with the collaboration of Gaillard Lapsley. New York: Appleton-Century, 1939. v–vii.

On Her Own Work

Introduction to *Ethan Frome*. New York: Scribner's, 1922. i–v.
"The Writing of *Ethan Frome*." *Colophon*, pt. 11, no. 4 (September 1932), n.p.
Foreword to *Ethan Frome: A Dramatization of Edith Wharton's Novel*, by Owen Davis and Donald Davis. New York: Scribner's, 1936. vii–viii.
Introduction to *The House of Mirth*. Oxford: Oxford University Press, 1936. v–xi.
Preface to *Ghosts*. New York: Appleton-Century, 1937. vii–xii.

MANUSCRIPTS OF UNCOLLECTED ESSAYS

Foreword to *Benediction*. Holograph MS; setting TS. (Yale).
"A Cycle of Reviewing." Holograph MS; incomplete TS. (Yale).
"Documentation in Fiction." Draft of "Tendencies in Modern Fiction." Holograph MS. (Yale).
"A Further Glance." Draft of "A Little Girl's New York." Holograph MS. (Yale).

"George Cabot Lodge." MS. (Princeton).
"Permanent Values in Fiction." Holograph MS. (Yale).
"A Reconsideration of Marcel Proust." Holograph MS. (Yale).
"Souvenirs du Bourget d'Outremer." Untitled holograph MS. (Yale).
"Visibility in Fiction." Holograph MS; setting TS. (Yale).
"William C. Brownell." Holograph MS. (Yale).

Unpublished Critical Essays

"Adventures with Books." Incomplete holograph MS. (Yale).
"Fiction and Criticism." TS; two untitled, incomplete holograph MSS. (Yale).
"Italy Again." Holograph MS. (Yale).
"Literary Tendencies." Holograph MS. (Indiana).
"My Books—Literary Essays." Holograph MS; TS. (Indiana).
"Olifant." Holograph MS. (Yale).
Sketch of an essay on Walt Whitman. Holograph MS. (Yale).

The Fullerton Essay

Fullerton, W. Morton [in collaboration with Edith Wharton]. "The Art of Henry James." *Quarterly Review* 212 (April 1910): 393–408; *Living Age* 265 (11 June 1910): 643–52.

SELECTED SECONDARY SOURCES

Askew, Melvin W. "Edith Wharton's Literary Theory." Diss., University of Oklahoma, 1957.
Bell, Millicent. *Edith Wharton and Henry James: The Story of Their Friendship*. New York: Braziller, 1965.
Brown, E. K. *Edith Wharton: Etudes Critiques*. Paris: Librarie Droz, 1935.
Funston, Judith. "Macaws and Pekingnese: Vivienne de Watteville and Edith Wharton." *Edith Wharton Review* 7 (Spring 1990): 13–14.
Gooder, Jean. "Unlocking Edith Wharton." *Cambridge Quarterly* 15 (1986): 33–52.
Goodman, Susan. *Edith Wharton's Inner Circle*. Austin: University of Texas Press, 1994.
———. "Edith Wharton's 'Sketch of an Essay on Walt Whitman.'" *Walt Whitman Quarterly Review* 10 (1992): 3–9.
———. *Edith Wharton's Women: Friends and Rivals*. Hanover, N.H.: University Press of New England, 1990.
Goodwyn, Janet. *Edith Wharton: Traveller in the Land of Letters*. New York: St. Martin's, 1990.
Kaplan, Amy. *The Social Construction of American Realism*. Chicago: University of Chicago Press, 1988.
La Guardia, Eric. "Edith Wharton on Critics and Criticism." *Modern Language Notes* 73 (December 1958): 587–89.
Lawson, Richard H. *Edith Wharton*. New York: Ungar, 1977.

Lawson, Richard H. *Edith Wharton and German Literature*. Bonn: Bouvier Verlag Herbert Grundmann, 1974.

Leach, Nancy R. "Edith Wharton: Critic of American Life and Literature." Diss., University of Pennsylvania, 1952.

————. "Edith Wharton's Interest in Walt Whitman." *Yale University Library Gazette* 33 (October 1958): 63–66.

Lyde, Marilyn Jones. *Edith Wharton: Convention and Morality in the Work of a Novelist*. Norman: University of Oklahoma Press, 1959.

Nevius, Blake. *Edith Wharton: A Study of Her Fiction*. Berkeley: University of California Press, 1953.

Noack, Jeanette S. "Edith Wharton: Her Critical Theories of Prose Fiction, as Shown in Her Fiction and Her Criticism." Master's thesis. Stanford University, 1936.

Puknat, E.M., and S.B. Puknat. "Edith Wharton and Gottfried Keller." *Comparative Literature* 21 (Summer 1969): 245–54.

Singley, Carol J. *Edith Wharton: Matters of Mind and Spirit*. Cambridge: Cambridge University Press, 1995.

Tintner, Adeline R. "Wharton's Forgotten Preface to Vivienne de Watteville's *Speak to the Earth*: A Link with Hemingway's 'The Snows of Kilimanjaro.'" *Notes on Modern American Literature* 8 (Autumn 1984): Item 10.

Tuttleton, James W. "Edith Wharton: Form and the Epistemology of Artistic Creation." *Criticism* 10 (Fall 1968): 334–51.

Valdivia, Olga Avendaño de. "Edith Wharton: Chapter II." *Andean Quarterly* (Summer 1943–44): 39–40.

Vita-Finzi, Penelope. *Edith Wharton and the Art of Fiction*. New York: St. Martin's, 1990.

Walton, Geoffrey. *Edith Wharton: A Critical Interpretation*. Rutherford, N.J.: Fairleigh Dickinson University Press, 1970.

White, Barbara A. *Edith Wharton: A Study of the Short Fiction*. New York: Twayne, 1991.

INDEX

Brownell, William Crary (*cont.*)
  Criticism, 209; *French Traits*, 205–7, 210–11n.3; *The Genius of Style*, 209; *Victorian Prose Masters*, 205, 207–8, 211n.5
Browning, Robert, 159, 254. Works: "James Lee's Wife," 244n.8; *The Ring and the Book*, 260; *The Soul's Tragedy*, 163n.2
Brunelleschi, Filippo, 113
Buchan, John, 179. Works: *The Massacre of Glencoe*, 179
Burden, Jane (Mrs. William Morris), 139
Burlingame, Edward L., 209, 243n.1, 300
Bussy, Dorothy, 50n.38
Butler, Samuel, 35, 123. Works: *The Way of All Flesh*, 35, 123
Byron, George Gordon, sixth baron, 96

Cadwalader, John, 188n.1
Campanini, Italo, 288
Campbell, Mrs. Patrick (Beatrice Stella Turner), 235n.1
Canby, Henry S., 4, 174n.1
Carlyle, Thomas, 16
Cary, Elisabeth Luther, 46
Casanova, Giacomo, 113, 114n.3
Cather, Willa, 46
Cellini, Benvenuto, 113. Works: *Life of Benvenuto Cellini*, 104
Cervantes Saavedra, Miguel de, 152, 297. Works: *Don Quixote*, 152, 297
Chanler, Margaret Terry, 93n.1
Chapman, John Jay, 44
Chasles, Philarète, 16
Chateaubriand, François-René, 49n.32, 268
Chevrillon, André, 47n.15, 206, 210–11n.3
Choate, Joseph, 231n.1
Clark, Kenneth, 7
Cocteau, Jean, 33
Codman, Ogden, Jr., 7
Coleridge, Samuel Taylor, 16, 131, 139, 211n.6, 254. Works: *The Friend*, 6; "Kubla Khan," 287; "Love," 255n.3; "The Rime of the Ancient Mariner," 11, 35, 97, 103; *Table Talk*, 98n.6, 150n.6
Colette, Sidonie-Gabrielle, 33
Colvin, Sir Sidney, 143, 150n.10
Comte, Auguste, 72
Conrad, Joseph, 50n.38, 143, 164, 165. Works: *Lord Jim*, 34, 151, 164; *Nostromo*, 151

Constant, Benjamin, 265. Works: *Adolphe*, 270n.2, 295, 302, 305
Cooper, Frederic Taber, 289
Cooper, James Fenimore, 208
Correggio (Antonio Allegri), 64
Corti, Luigi, 281
Cosmopolitan, 287n.1
Crawford, F. Marion, 92n.1. Works: *Francesca da Rimini*, 81, 88–92, 92n.1; "The Upper Berth," 273
Croker, John, 179n.3
Cross, Wilbur, 31, 49n.36
Cuffe, Lady Sybil, 231n.1
Cust, Harry, 292
Cutting, Bayard, 188n.1, 231n.1
Cutting, Bayard, Jr., 32, 134n.1, 228–31

D'Annunzio, Gabriele, 92n.1. Works: *Francesca da Rimini*, 81, 84–88, 89, 91
Dante Alighieri, 36, 81, 84, 85, 312, 313. Works: *Inferno*, 92n.1; *Purgatorio*, 313
Da Ponte, Lorenzo, 113, 114n.4
Darwin, Charles, 31, 71, 78n.2
Daudet, Alphonse, 22, 143, 144, 312
David, Jacques-Louis, 312
Davis, Donald and Owen, 42, 263. Works: *Ethan Frome: A Dramatization of Edith Wharton's Novel*, 263–64
Debussy, Claude, 219
de Fitz-James, Rosa, 9–10
Defoe, Daniel, 75. Works: *Robinson Crusoe*, 164
de la Mare, Walter, 274n.5
Derby, Edward George Geoffrey Smith Stanley, fourteenth earl of, 95
de Watteville, Vivienne, 8, 248–49. Works: *Out in the Blue*, 248; *Speak to the Earth*, 248–49
Dickens, Charles, 19, 123, 124, 143, 165, 166, 167, 175. Works: *Pickwick Papers*, 294
Diodorus Siculus, 191
Doctor Faustus (Marlowe), 93n.2, 102, 105n.4
Dolci, Carlo, 280
Domenichino (Domenico Zampieri), 280, 281
Domingo de Guzman, San, 201
Donatello (Donato di Niccolò Bardi), 64
Dostoyevsky, Fyodor, 127, 167, 178, 244, 245. Works: *The Idiot*, 178